Language and the Origins of Psychoanalysis

Language and the Origins of Psychoanalysis

John Forrester

Fellow of King's College, Cambridge

First published 1980 by
THE MACMILLAN PRESS LTD
London and Basingstoke
Companies and representatives
throughout the world

Printed in Great Britain by
Billing and Sons Ltd
Guildford, London, Oxford, Worcester

British Library Cataloguing in Publication Data

Forrester, John
  Language and the origins of psychoanalysis
  1. Psychoanalysis
  2. Psycholinguistics
  I. Title
  616.8'917   RC606

ISBN 0–333–25946–7

What I want back is what I was
Before the bed, before the knife,
Before the brooch-pin and the salve.
Fixed me in this parenthesis;
Horses fluent in the wind,
A place, a time gone out of mind.

Sylvia Plath, *The Eye-mote*

since feeling is first
who pays any attention
to the syntax of things
will never wholly kiss you;

wholly to be a fool
while Spring is in the world

my blood approves,
and kisses are a better fate
than wisdom
lady i swear by all flowers. Don't cry
– the best gesture of my brain is less than
your eyelids' flutter which says

we are for each other: then
laugh, leaning back in my arms
for life's not a paragraph

And death i think is no parenthesis

e. e. cummings

Contents

viii   *Contents*

Preface

There is no doubt that this work refers itself to, and refers to, a number of works in a number of genres of psychoanalytic literature. Three works, each of which has proved of invaluable assistance, represent three of these genres: Jones definitive biography of Freud, Ellenberger's monumental compilation *The Discovery of the Unconscious*, and the exact, methodical and constantly intelligent *The Language of Psychoanalysis* of Laplanche and Pontalis. I have followed the biographical method only in so far as it seemed to me to throw light on the nature or development of the psychoanalytical work that Freud's life represents. The chronological marking and assiduous amassing of historical facts to be found in Ellenberger's work has been of enormous help whenever detailed questions of historical context have seemed to make a significant contribution to the understanding of the conceptual foundations of psychoanalysis: this aspect will be found most prominently displayed in Chapter 1. The working manual that *The Language of Psychoanalysis* embodies has been a continual source of stimulation, as well as putting a brake upon overly speculative interpretations. In so far as the aim of my work is a conceptual reading, rather than a historical account, many of its arguments should be read in parallel with those to be found in Laplanche and Pontalis' book.[1]

There also exists a genre of psychoanalytic writings that is unique in character: analyses either of Freud's own dreams, slips etc., or of those case-histories he wrote, undertaken to vindicate, deepen or criticize the exemplification of psychoanalysis that Freud's work represents. While such 'great-man' history is not an isolated phenomenon, in psychoanalytic terms many of these hagiographical works contain arguments of great theoretical interest and importance. The question of the special relationship that every analyst has with Freud, and that every psychoanalytic text bears to those of Freud's, is beyond the scope of this introduction to this thesis. Suffice it to cite the most illuminating discussion of this topic that I know of, that of Wladimir Granoff in *Filiations*, pp. 7–254, who raises the question whether the relation to Freud is not constitutive of psychoanalysis itself.

There are very few accounts of psychoanalysis which take as their
starting-point the fact that it is a talking-cure, and that one might expect
its theory to deal directly with the importance of language in the course
of the cure. The central problem is, as it was for Freud in 1890, to
explain 'the power of words'. It will be the set of answers to this question
that will interest us; as we shall see, they have implications that
permeate all of psychoanalytic theory. But this thesis cannot claim to be
without forerunners. There are a number of works that have included a
discussion of the exegetical and linguistic character of the science that
Freud developed. For example, Suzanne Langer wrote:

> The great contribution of Freud to the philosophy of mind has been
> the realization that human behavior is not only a food-getting
> strategy, but is also a language; that every *move* is at the same time a
> *gesture*. Symbolization is both an end and an instrument. (Langer,
> 1948, p. 41)

Or we may quote Jürgen Habermas:

> Initially psychoanalysis appears only as a special form of interpret-
> ation. It provides theoretical perspectives and technical rules for the
> interpretation of symbolic structures. Freud always patterned the
> interpretation of dreams after the hermeneutic model of philological
> research. (Habermas, 1968, p. 214)

But this is one of the few works in the English language that takes as
its central concern the relations of speech and language with both
psychoanalytic theory and therapy, from the metapsychology to the
transference.[2] Indeed, I have sometimes made the decision to expose
these linguistic elements in Freud's theory at the expense of other
themes that, on the surface, would seem to be of greater importance. At
times, then, this book will appear obsessively single-minded in the
pursuit of its theme. The extent of this obsession, and the concomitant
omission of other elements of psychoanalytic theory, should not lead
my reader to the mistaken conclusion that I believe or would have
others believe that other themes are of minor importance, that they can
always be reinterpreted in the light of a 'linguistic' framework, or that
any mention of concepts derived from realms other than the 'linguistic'
is of necessity subject to some new linguistic version of a transcendental
critique. But I cannot renounce the conviction, many times tested in the
course of my attempts to find an 'objective' reading of the texts, that
language is the central concern of psychoanalysis.[3]

Amongst the many people who have helped me, often in silence, detach the ideas that this work expresses, I would like to single out the following for especial thanks: Liz Fee, for the initial stimulus; Karl Figlio, for many interchanges concerning the history of medicine; Mike Gordon, for an initiation into the mysteries of linguistics and artificial languages; André Green, for discussion of and comments on an earlier draft of this work, and for his knowledge of issues in contemporary psychoanalytic theory; Dave Holden, to whose fertile mind I am continually indebted, and for the many stimulating discussions we shared on issues in psychological theory and formal models of the brain; Thomas Kuhn, for his outstanding example as a historian of science and for his critical encouragement; Francis Pettitt, for many reminders of that otherness which his work as an anthropologist focused for me; Denise Riley, for discussions on language, dreams, the ideological function of psychoanalysis and for permission to quote one of her poems; Carl Schorske, for introducing me to the cultural history of Vienna; Martin Thom, with whom I have shared many of the intellectual problems arising out of my attempt to understand the relation between psychoanalysis and language; Nick Totton, who has always opened up for me alternative possibilities; Cathy Urwin, for sharing her insights into language development in children; and Bob Young, for advice and comments on the early stages of this work. The manuscript was impeccably and imperturbably typed by Diane Quarrie.

Finally, I owe a great debt to Jim Hopkins, who read the final drafts with more care, critical attention and sympathy than I could conceivably have expected of him. His thoughtful comments and his attempts to encourage me to formulate many passages more clearly have made the text vastly superior to what it would otherwise have been.

March 1979   JOHN FORRESTER

Acknowledgements

This work has had a long and intricate history, and has been subject to many diverse influences. I would like to thank the following institutions which have made my work possible through their financial support: Princeton University (1970–2); The Department of Education and Science for support in Cambridge (1974–6) and in Vienna (1975); King's College, Cambridge (1976–8); the Leverhulme Trust Fund for awarding me a European Studentship that made it possible for me to work in Paris in 1977–8. I would also like to acknowledge the help I have received from libraries and academic institutions while conducting the research: in Britain, the University Library, Cambridge, and the British Museum; in Vienna, Professor Erna Lesky and the Institut für Geschichte der Medizin, the Österreichische Nationalbibliothek, the Bibliothek der Universität, Wien; in Paris, the École Normale Supérieure, the Bibliothèque Nationale, the Bibliothèque de la Musée des Sciences de l'Homme, the Ecole Freudienne, and Professor D. Widlocher and the Bibliothèque de l'Hôpital de la Salpêtrière.

The author and publishers wish to thank the following who have kindly given permission for the use of copyright material: The Hogarth Press Ltd, Sigmund Freud Copyrights Ltd, and the Institute of Psychoanalysis, for quotations from *The Standard Edition of the Complete Psychological Works of Sigmund Freud*, translated and edited by James Strachey; George Allen & Unwin (Publishers) Ltd and Liveright Publishing Corporation, for the extracts from *Introductory Lectures in Psycho-Analysis*, and with Basic Books Ltd, for the extracts from *An Interpretation of Dreams*; Ernest Benn Ltd and W. W. Norton and Company Inc, for the extracts from *The Psychopathology of Everyday Life*; The Hogarth Press Ltd and Alfred A. Knopf Inc, for the extract from *Moses and Monotheism*; The Hogarth Press Ltd and Basic Books Inc, for the extracts from *Studies on Hysteria*, *Project* (in *The Origins of Psycho-Analysis*), *Three Essays on Sexuality*, *Collected Papers of Sigmund Freud* (5 vols), and *A Psycho-analytic Dialogue* (not included in the Standard Edition); The Hogarth Press Ltd and Liveright

Publishing Corporation, for the extracts from *Five Lectures on Psycho-Analysis*, and *Group Psychology*; The Hogarth Press Ltd and W. W. Norton & Company Inc, for the extracts from *Outline of Psycho-Analysis*, *The Ego and the Id*, and *The Question of Lay Analysis*; The Hogarth Press Ltd and Routledge & Kegan Paul, in conjunction with Princeton University Press, for the excerpts from *The Freud/Jung Letters: The Correspondence between Sigmund Freud and C. G. Jung*, edited by William McGuire, translated by Ralph Manheim and R. F. C. Hull (American Bollingen Series XCIV), copyright © 1974 by Sigmund Freud Copyrights Ltd and Erbengemeinschaft Professor Dr C. G. Jung; Routledge & Kegan Paul and W. W. Norton & Company Inc, for the extracts from *Leonardo da Vinci*; the British Psychological Society, for the extracts from the article 'The Theory of Symbolism' by Ernest Jones published in *British Journal of Psychology* (1916); Granada Publishing Ltd and Liveright Publishing Corporation, for the poem 'since feeling is first' by e. e. cummings; The Hogarth Press Ltd, on behalf of Katherine Jones, for the extracts from *Free Associations* by Ernest Jones; Olwyn Hughes on behalf of Ted Hughes, and Alfred A. Knopf Inc, for the extract from 'The Eye-mote' in *The Colossus and Other Poems* by Sylvia Plath; International Universities Press Inc, for the quotations from the Minutes of Vienna Psycho-analytic Society, vols I–IV, translated by N. Nunberg and edited by Herman N. Nunberg and Ernst Federn; and Warner Bros Music Ltd, for the extract from the song 'Gates of Eden' by Bob Dylan.

Notes on Texts and Translations

1. The English text of Freud that I have cited is, of course, the exemplary and extraordinary *Standard Edition of the Complete Psychological Works of Sigmund Freud*, edited by James Strachey in collaboration with Anna Freud, assisted by Alix Strachey and Alan Tyson (1953–74). My debt to the erudition, exactitude and uniform care displayed on every page of its twenty four volumes is as incalculable as every other reader of Freud's now is, whether he is read in English, French or German. In a work of the sort I have written, I can safely say that any fidelity to Freud's thought owes as much to the Editors of the Standard Edition as to my own attempts to maintain standards of rigour and scholarship.

2. Where translations of works cited in this book exist – and I am aware of their existence – I have given references to the translated works, rather than to the original, except where the reference in question explicitly cites the original text. If no translation exists, the translation that I give is my own. I have checked the translations of all passages cited from the *Standard Edition*, using both the *Gesammelte Werke* and the *Studienausgabe* edition, which benefits from the accurate readings of Freud's text established by the *Standard Edition*. Where I have modified the translation, a corresponding note will be found. Perhaps I should make clear that, where I have modified the translation, I do not necessarily believe that my modified text is a more accurate or better translation than that to be found in the *Standard Edition*, although there are instances where I believe this to be so. In many passages my modifications are alternative translations, which are hoped to give at least as faithful or as treacherous a reading in SE, but which attempt to bring out a certain nuance that was not quite captured by the editors. In modifications such as these, I have almost certainly lost another nuance, this latter often being the reason why the SE translation was chosen. My modified translations are thus in the service of a particular reading of Freud to be found in this work. I hope that my

reader will judge that the gain in one dimension of meaning will compensate for the inevitable loss in another. In self-defence, I can only reflect that to be conscious of the choice of readings that translation always involves is perhaps a protection against too high an importance being attached to any given word or words.

List of Abbreviations

SE   *The Standard Edition of the Complete Psychological Works of Sigmund Freud*

Origins   Freud, *The Origins of Psychoanalysis. Letters to Wilhelm Fliess, Drafts and Notes: 1887–1902* (The reference is given to SE only, when the passage in question is reproduced there.)

Minutes   *Minutes of the Vienna Psychoanalytic Society*, vols I–IV, M. Nunberg (trans.), Herman Nunberg and Ernst Federn (eds) (New York: International Universities Press, 1962–76).

Jones   Ernest Jones, *Sigmund Freud Life and Work*, 3 vols (London: The Hogarth Press, 1953–7). (I have employed the second edition of vol. I, published in 1954; references to the second and third volumes are to the first editions).

SP   Abraham, *Selected Papers on Psychoanalysis*.

CP   Abraham, *Clinical Papers and Essays on Psychoanalysis*.

C.   Ferenczi, *First Contributions to Psychoanalysis*.

F.C.   Ferenczi, *Further Contributions to Psychoanalysis*.

Fin.   Ferenczi, *Final Contributions to Psychoanalysis*.

CW   Jung, *The Collected Works of C. G. Jung*.

E   Lacan, *Ecrits* (The first number following E gives page numbers in the French edition, the second in the English translation, *Ecrits: A Selection*.)

1 Aphasia, Hysteria and the Talking Cure

> At dawn my lover
> Comes to me
> And tells me of her dreams
> With no attempts
> To shovel the glimpse
> Into the ditch of what each one means
> At times I think
> There are no words
> But these to tell what's true
> And there are
> No truths outside
> The gates of Eden
>
> Bob Dylan

Psychoanalysis is the theory of a therapy. The therapy, in its purest and most 'original' form, consists of a 'talking cure'.[1] What, we may start by asking, could comprise a therapy in the interchange of words? The cure Freud devised was more than a replacement for the unsatisfactory methods of electrotherapy and hydrotherapy, or the sanatorium cures of turn of the century novels. (Cf. Steiner, 1964.) He unseated physicalism[2] from its pride of place in the treatment of nervous illness and located all therapeutic power in the doctor–patient couple. In order to understand the relation between therapeutic and theoretical discourse, we must find out how it became clear to Freud that the therapeutic situation created the conditions for a cure of a major disease, and hence how Freud located all the necessary conditions for this cure in the necessary conditions of language.

In order to construct the theory, Freud located all his explanatory entities in the psyche; he described a mental apparatus, which we will examine in Chapter 2, for which the 'world' is represented by a series of varying displacements of quantity. Even the transference is the transfer from what is peripheral to what is central in that apparatus.[3] But it would be a mistake to localize the psyche in a body, to materialize it too readily. If we take Freud's favourite science of archaeology as the model through which the psyche can be understood, we see very clearly the way in which a science of the psyche can be practised independently of definite relations to the body. What is required in archaeology is not a theory of the relation of mind to matter – though we would not deny that this would be very useful – but rather a theory of the productions of signs, a theory of representation. It is of great moment both for a philosophy of the human sciences and for a theory of man that the signs of man's death – in particular tumuli and burial mounds – are amongst the first signs to engage the archaeologist. Signs are first and foremost signs of absence and death. If psychoanalysis is an archaeology of the living, it is no less true that its central preoccupation is absence and its signs, now complicated by the dimension of time, so that not only do signs witness absence, but also witness the change of such absence over time – dialectics. The effects of talk – such is the cure – and the theory of talk – such might be expected of the theory of psychoanalysis.

When we speak of language we may be taken in many different senses; here I wish to follow Freud and start with the immediate language of psychoanalysis: the monologue of the patient. The first such monologue was that of Anna O., Josef Breuer's patient of 1881, who insisted on his hearing her out. Breuer, as family physician and personal friend, followed her lead and began to build a set of appropriate structures for understanding her talk. He began collaborating with his young friend Freud and together they came to certain conclusions as to the nature of the cure which Anna O. had created:

> each individual hysterical symptom immediately and permanently disappeared when we had succeeded in bringing clearly to light the memory of the event by which it was provoked and in arousing its accompanying affect, and when the patient had described that event in the greatest possible detail and had put the affect into words. (Breuer and Freud (1893a) SE II 6)

To the two positivistic physicians, well schooled in the fervent reductionism of the Vienna Medical School[4], both master-physiologists and pathologists[5], such a phenomenon as the talking-cure was a great surprise. They met its mystery with the theory-construction of their academic masters: the neurophysiology of the brain was never far from their minds as they contemplated the miracles their patients were performing upon themselves with a minimum of physical therapeutic intervention. Freud redefined the picture of the cure somewhat in a paper of 1894:

> The operation of Breuer's cathartic method lies in leading back the excitation in this way from the somatic to the psychical sphere deliberately, and in then forcibly bringing about a settlement of the contradiction by means of thought-activity and a discharge of the excitation by talking. (Freud (1894a) SE III 50)

Through this conflict and resolution of ideas, words replaced the symptoms of hysteria. Anticipating a later argument, we see the private language of hysteria translated into the public language of the innervation of the pharynx. The translation process becomes audible and visible when the symptom 'joins in the conversation' (*Mitsprechen*).

> While we are working at one of these symptoms we come across the interesting and not undesired phenomenon of 'joining in the conversation'. . . . The intensity of the symptom (let us take for instance a desire to vomit) increases the deeper we penetrate into one of the relevant pathogenic memories; it reaches its climax shortly before the patient gives utterance to that memory; and when he has finished doing so it suddenly diminishes or even vanishes completely for a time. If, owing to resistance, the patient delays his telling for a long time, the tension of the sensation – of the desire to vomit – becomes unbearable, and if we cannot force him to speak he actually begins to vomit. (Breuer and Freud (1895d) SE II 296–7; cf. Freud (1918b) SE XVII 76)

Thus the therapeutic means are verbal. In addition, the theory of the neurotic symptom includes language as an essential component. Each symptom is constructed on the basis of certain ideas, as Freud's first paper on the neuroses demonstrated (Freud, 1893c). The difference between a neurological and a neurotic symptom is that the latter's location in the body is determined by the specific structure of a system of thoughts, whose expression in the body is often bound up with a verbal turn of phrase. The peculiarity of the neurotic symptom is twofold: firstly, the locus of the symptom betrays a false corporeality, in so far as it is not that organ in its bodily solidity that is 'diseased', but the 'idea' of that organ that is the line of crystallization of the neurosis. Secondly, the expression of words in the body amounts to a displacement of the proper locus of words. We will return to the theoretical consequence of this double peculiarity. For now, we should note that the talking-cure has a symmetry[6]:

a. Words replace symptoms in the process of the cure;
b. It is words that give a specific form to the symptoms. We might wish to subsume this under the more general principle that, in order to explain the specific character of each symptom, it is necessary to assume that the symptom is equivalent to a verbal message. (Cf. Szasz, 1962)

Throughout this work I will sometimes be employing the term 'word' where another might think that 'idea' or 'thought' was more appropriate, and sometimes I will appear to make little or no distinction between 'words' and 'ideas'. Obviously, one can distinguish between the concept of a 'word' and the concept of a 'thought'. But, having made this distinction, one might be well justified in treating them as analogous, relying upon certain crucial similarities. Some justification of this practice would seem to be in order. This justification leans mainly upon the usage that Freud made of the terms 'idea', 'presentation', 'word-presentation', 'object-presentation' and their fundamental relation to the key distinction drawn in psychoanalysis between the 'conscious' and the 'unconscious'. (I refer the reader to the entries under these headings in Laplanche and Pontalis (1973).) Let us start with the term 'idea'.

Freud felt free to speak of 'unconscious ideas' and, from this, we may conclude that one aspect of the classical conception of the idea was of secondary importance in his usage of the word, namely, 'the connotation of the act of subjective presentation of an object to consciousness. For Freud, an idea or presentation is to be understood rather as what comes from the object and is registered in the "mnemic systems"' (Laplanche and Pontalis, 1973, p. 200). Thus, in the *Project*, the idea, and the act of thought that denotes the movement of ideas, are essentially a cathexis of memory-traces, which are, as we shall see in Chapter 2, themselves coded into a system akin to that provided by a language. Thus neither ideas nor memory-traces can be thought of as weak 'copies' of the objects they represent; they have their place in 'thought-reality' according to the place that they take up in a system.

But this system is distinct from that which makes up the system of word-presentations; in the *Project* and in later works, Freud spoke of the processes of thought as distinct from the consciousness that attachment to word-presentations lends to them. Indeed, one could say that the aim of psychoanalysis is to go beyond the ideas presented to consciousness in verbal form, in an attempt to reconstruct these unconscious, pre-verbal thought processes. We thus have a model in which there are two separate systems of presentations, which can be used in a topographical fashion, but whose essential properties reside in the distinction between the two systems and in their possible mutual articulation. We then find that another strand in Freud's thought tends to subvert the systemic model. We might call this new strand the instrumentalist or operationalist conception of the unconscious, which Freud expressed succinctly in a letter to Groddeck (*Briefe über das Es*, p. 38): 'Thus the unconscious is only something miraculous, a sign for the lack of better acquaintanceship (knowledge) . . .' Or, more clearly, in *An Outline of Psychoanalysis*:

We have discovered technical methods of filling up the gaps in the phenomena of our consciousness, and we make use of those methods just as a physicist makes use of experiment. In this manner we infer a number of processes which are in themselves 'unknowable' and interpolate them in those that are conscious to us. And if, for instance, we say: 'At this point an unconscious memory intervened', what this means is: 'At this point something occurred of which we are totally unable to form a conception, but which, if it had entered our consciousness, could only have been described in such and such a way.' (Freud (1940a) SE XXIII 196–7)

Now this is a conception of the unconscious that puts to one side the hypothesis of unconscious ideas, and places all the emphasis on what conscious translations it is *necessary* to give of them if some sense is to be given to psychic life – that is, it places all the emphasis on what verbal and conscious insertions must be made. It is a conception for which the forgetting of a word or phrase, its subsequent recovery and the reconstruction of a second, 'intersecting' set of phrases could be paradigmatic. The notion of two systems is set aside in favour of a conception of one system – our conscious, verbal discourse – which has 'unaccountable' holes in it, the filling in of which amounts to the recovery of what was unconscious. The notion that the unconscious is a permanent feature of psychic life could here be expressed by recognizing that as one fills in one 'gap' in consciousness, another gap appears, albeit in a different part of the system. We thus have two different conceptions: one, which is, for the metapsychology, more dominant, and which calls on the notion of a system of unconscious ideas, and on an independent system of word-presentations, whose perception corresponds to thought-consciousness. The second conception emphasized that consciousness is the one 'empirical' point of reference for psychoanalysis, so that all the empirical evidence of psychoanalysis is furnished by the second system, the word-presentations. Any statement about the second system of 'ideas' is purely inferential, a *façon de parler*.

In talking of words as if they were, or as if they were like, unconscious ideas, I will be leaning upon this second conception of the unconscious as a 'sign of a lack of knowledge', although the first view also gives great emphasis to word-presentations, which share with object-presentations a fundamental systematic character. When I talk of the verbal translation of an unconscious idea as being subject to repression, I will be covering two separate notions: the first is the conception that Freud and Breuer introduced when they conceived of repression as the loss of the appropriate *words* for an idea, these words in some way becoming converted into the symptom and actually lending the symptom its specific character. The second notion is actually the more profound, in that on those occasions when it seems more appropriate to speak of the repression of an idea, rather than the words which represent it in consciousness, I can refer my reader to this instrumentalist conception of unconscious ideas, as well as to the notion elaborated by Freud in 1915, that repression consists in depriving ideas of their connection with word-presentations. We should note that, whichever of the two conceptions of the unconscious we work with, the primacy of the words that represent 'ideas' is paramount.

Finally, we might touch upon an issue that is of wider importance than the psychoanalytic theory of language: the ultimate relation of thought to language. This topic arose as a matter for public discussion in the last years of the nineteenth century in a number of fields. e.g. in the Müller-Galton debate around the question, 'Is thought possible without language?'; in the experimental psychologists' debate on the phenomenon of 'imageless thought'; and in the psychological critique of the diagram-makers in aphasia studies, who were accused of not distinguishing language from thought, of not distinguishing disturbances of speech from disturbances of thought. Freud's position in this debate was decidedly unclear. He distinguished thought from its verbal presentation, and discussed the differences that arise when the primary process acts upon word-presentations as well as on thing-presentations. But his discussion of 'trains of thought' always gave the impression that these trains were fully translatable by verbal chains; indeed, one has the impression that he conceived of these trains as having as a full equivalent a verbal chain, speaking often of them as possessing a grammar and certain properties proper to language, e.g. double meaning. The processes he conceived of as specific to the dream-work – condensation, displacement – have close affinities with strictly linguistic devices (metaphor, metonymy, tropes, etc.). Certainly Freud never distinguished sharply between those mechanisms that act *only* upon thought and those that act upon language.

In this sense, he never shared the eagerness of other turn of the century psychologists – Henry Head, Francis Galton, Kulpe – to insist upon a department of psychology independent of the sphere of language and its laws, a department that should become the central concern of psychology. Freud seemed to have assumed that if it were at all possible to talk of the laws of thought, these would be very much like the laws of thought as derived from a study of language. In this sense, he remained very much one of those thinkers who disdained a sharp division between thought and language. Such a position, reinforced by the pre-eminence of the study of language in those sciences dominated by the philological model, entailed that Freud, along with so many others, was a Whorfian without knowing it. We might even say that he was a Whorfian in those days before the distinction between language and thought had made it possible for Whorf to state his extreme hypothesis. And all our commentary leaves aside the question of whether it can possibly make sense to talk of thought as in some manner lying 'behind' words, acting as a 'private' means of representing 'the world' to the 'self'. The fact that there are other languages does not necessarily entail that there is a stable or a privileged set of presentations that all languages re-present in their own way. As Quine puts it 'it is not clear even in principle that it makes sense to think of words and syntax as varying from language to language while the content stays fixed'. (Quine, 1953, p. 61.)

It would also appear that Freud recognized the dangers of infinite regress that beset this topic: if language is the re-presentation of thought, why cannot we say that thought is the re-presentation of something else that lies 'behind', and so on. Arguing along lines parallel to those used by Freud to justify the notion of the unconscious in 1915, we could reply to this by saying: we should let ourselves be content with positing this 'something' that lies 'behind', but we can make very few claims as to its true nature. Certainly whatever we say about it will not have the value of being phenomenally experienced in the way that Freud posited we have awareness of thought expressed in words. But, nonetheless, this 'something' has the status of a valid inference, and one that it is perhaps necessary to draw. But whenever we want to give an account of what this inferred 'thought' is, we have to give a translation in words. Whether this 'something' is on a par with the Kantian noumenon or whether it is really possible to construct its independent existence and its independent properties was a question upon which, as we have already seen, Freud wavered.

In this chapter we will be concerned primarily with the first simple formulation of the theory of psychoanalysis. Two historical themes will be considered in this connection: the theory of the neuroses in the late nineteenth century[7] and the relevance of aphasia theory to the first formulations of psychoanalytic theory. First we shall consider the importance of the talking-cure in the historical context of the theory of the neuroses. After all, Janet was to argue for the whole of his life that the originality of the Breuer–Freud method was minimal, that the Charcot school of the Salpêtrière had come to similar conclusions. What was the position of the cure for hysteria at the time that *Studies on Hysteria* was published?

HYSTERIA

Two features are of primary importance: the notion of functional diseases of the nervous system and the rediscovery of hypnosis, both due to the championship of Charcot.[8] But it would be misleading to think of Freud as advancing along the same road as Charcot, building upon the distinctions and concepts that he had set out. Charcot was primarily interested in hysteria as one part of the vast tableau of nervous diseases to which he had dedicated both his oeuvre and the structure of the Salpêtrière. (Pontalis, 1974)[9] Differential diagnosis was as important to Charcot as to Freud, but for different reasons. Charcot wished to clarify the complete range of nervous diseases and, in this light, hysteria acted as an obstacle to the exact codification of signs and symptoms. Hysteria was a medical work of the devil, a spanner in the works that threatened to disrupt the strict lines of medical reasoning that connected symptom, lesion and nosology. Charcot took a step that turned this devil into an agent of order: he changed hysteria from being the negative of the 'organic' nervous diseases, from being their '*unheimlich Doppelgänger*', to being a positive, if protean, medical entity. From the early work of the 1870s on the differential diagnosis of hysteria and epilepsy, resulting in the constitution of a new entity, hystero-epilepsy

(Bourneville and Regnard (1876–7) I 32ff), Charcot progressed to give an exact description of the stages of hysteria: the four stages of the attack, the spatial localization of the hysterogenic zones, etc. (Charcot (1885b)). Even given its protean unpredictability, under Charcot's nosological guiding hand hysteria could be made to conform to a general spatial and temporal schema, even if it was by noting the absence of a specific sign or symptom in any given case.

With the introduction of hypnosis and the concept of suggestibility[10], a new explanation of the fickleness of hysteria and its deviation from the clinical norm could be given. Thus, with the bizarre play of magnets (*'amants'*) and the concept of *'le transfert'* (of symptoms from one part of the body to another), the proteus of hysteria could be given a new, psychological dimension, without an essential alteration of the clinical schema laid down by Charcot (Barrucand (1967) p. 169; Babinski (1886); Walton (1882/3)). This schema – which made hysteria a positive disease of the nervous system, despite any psychological accretions, such as its determination by ideas, or its panoply of psychically-induced variations – ensured the generality of symptoms, their transcendence of the individual patient and thus their necessary attachment to the concept of disease, in contradistinction to the later Breuer–Freud theory, which found in each symptom an individuality founded in a personal history.

The notion of a traumatic cause for hysteria – crystallized and elaborated in the 1870s and early 1880s[11] – referred explicitly to general theories of the nervous system. Much could be made of the Jacksonian principles of the dissolution of the nervous system, which, applied first and most explicitly to epilepsy, could be brought into service to aid the explanation of traumatic 'shocks'. With his 'discovery' of hypnosis, Charcot could supplement the traumatic cause with an ideational cause, not without recognizing that this was a long familiar idea (Reynolds (1869); see Ellenberger (1970) pp. 90ff and Veith (1965)). But a neurological foundation was still preserved, in the notion of a special state of the nervous system peculiar to both hysteria and hypnosis. The stages of hypnosis (lethargy–catalepsy–somnambulism) replicated and enriched the order of hysteria, and thus reinforced the neurological characterization of hysteria.[12]

Even with a firmly neurological characterization of hysteria and hypnosis, Charcot found an essential place for psychological elements in hysteria. But the 'psychological' element was restricted to what in later Freudian theory would be called predisposing and precipitating causes. With respect to predisposing causes, a concept of hereditary psychic weakness – the incapacity for synthesis of Janet (1889), the degeneration of Magnan (1885) and Séglas (1892, 1894) – opened up a field of psychological elements without specifying the *character* of these elements. The precipitating cause was more specific, but was restricted to those ideas that could generate affective shock, affect being considered as a specific state of excitation of the nervous system. But, even here, the weight of explanation does not fall upon the character of the psychic element: it appears at the horizon of the field of explanation, as the term that *introduces* the specifically hysterical state of the nervous system, but having no bearing upon the further description of that state. The nature of the hysterical symptom remained unspecified in both psychological and linguistic terms.

But there is another feature of Charcot's work that we should consider. His theory of hysteria may have remained indubitably neurological but his therapy was another affair. To consider this, we will look at a lecture he gave in 1885, entitled 'De l'isolement dans le traitement de l'hystérie' (Charcot, 1885a). Charcot argued that the isolation of young people was *the* necessary condition, and often a sufficient condition, for the cure of even the most complex hysterical symptoms. He illustrated its efficacy with a brief history of a case of *anorexia nervosa*. The father of the patient, a 13 year-old girl, wrote from his residence in the provinces to Charcot, who replied:

> A visit is unnecessary, I replied to him; I can, without seeing the patient, give you the appropriate advice: bring the child to Paris, place her in one or other hydropathic clinic, abandon her, or at least let her believe that you have left the capital, inform me and I will do the rest. No reply to my letter was forthcoming. (Ibid., p. 162)

Via the family doctor, Charcot learned that the girl had been placed in a Parisian establishment, as he had recommended, but the parents were resolved not to be parted from her. In consequence, they were afraid to inform Charcot, even though the girl did not have long to live. Charcot became angry: the *sine qua non* of his advice had been ignored. 'Je déclinais toute responsabilité dans cette malheureuse affaire.' Nevertheless, he allowed himself to be persuaded by the family doctor to visit the establishment where the girl was wasting away, saw the poor girl, took the parents aside and informed them how angry he was. The only chance of success lay in their departure back to Angoulême immediately, saying to the girl that Dr Charcot was forcing them to leave. But it was difficult to obtain the parents' consent to this plan;

indeed, it needed all of Charcot's animated conviction and eloquence to persuade first the mother and then the father to leave.

That afternoon, after they had departed, the girl cried for an hour. Then she started to eat. Within fifteen days she was sitting up, and by the end of two months she was almost completely cured. *Then* Charcot interrogated the girl, who entrusted to him the following *confidence*:

As long as papa and mama didn't leave me, in other terms, as long as you hadn't triumphed – because I knew that you wanted to confine me – I believed that my illness wasn't serious, and, as I had a horror of eating, I didn't eat. *When I saw that you were the master, I was afraid*, and, despite my loathing, I tried to eat, and, little by little, it became possible.' I thanked the child for her confession, which, as you see, contains a complete education. (Ibid., p. 163)

Certainly an education for a doctor. But what is the lesson to be drawn from this case? On this, Charcot remained silent, allowing only his '*petite histoire*' speak. We might compare this silence with the lack of consequence that Charcot could draw from the *confidence* he entrusted to the young Freud, that in the neuroses it was always a question of secrets of the bedchamber (Freud (1914d) SE XIV 14). Whether it was a question of such secrets, or of the dialectic of mastery and fear exposed in the therapy of isolation, Charcot would say no more.

Now, this cure by isolation is undoubtedly a psychological cure. It plays upon the fear of the patient, the doctor's 'mastery' and the delicate familial sentiments in play between child and parent. But Charcot drew no theoretical consequence. The theoretical picture of neurosis left a space for the influence of suggestion and then of autosuggestion upon the nervous system.[13] What impressed the girl, what elicited a change in the balance of affects, was the *presence* of the doctor, a presence that was articulated upon the absence of her parents. But the name for the cure – isolation – belied the presence of the doctor, although it implied the 'medicalization' or institutionalization of the patient. What *we* notice, by its absence, is any recognition on Charcot's part that:

i. the cure by suggestion could be accomplished without hypnosis, i.e. without a specific 'hypnotic' state of the nervous system being the object of the masterly control of the doctor.
ii. the power of a discursive relation as well as that of affect is of paramount importance in both the formation of the symptom and its cure.

It is of great interest, then, that we find Freud in 1890 placing *all* the therapeutic emphasis upon words. The experience of hypnosis thus found a different interpretation. To Charcot, it was the hypnotic condition that was of paramount importance, a notion that Breuer was to build into his theory with the concept of the hypnoid state. To Freud, it was the command, and its 'verbal' consequences, that was the key. Rather than the doctor's command being conceptualized as a 'will-power' from outside that, thanks to the hypnotic state, could find a direct and unmediated access to the nervous system, Freud laid all the emphasis on the 'power of words'. As Freud wrote in an article for a medical textbook in 1890:

> Words are the essential tool of mental treatment. A layman will no doubt find it hard to understand how pathological disorders of the body and the mind can be eliminated by 'mere' words. He will feel that he is being asked to believe in magic. And he will not be so very wrong, for the words which we use in our everyday speech are nothing other than watered-down magic. But we shall have to follow a roundabout path in order to explain how science sets about restoring to words a part at least of their former magical power. (Freud (1890a) SE VII 283)

This starting-point marked his theory as different from Charcot's: the starting-point was words, rather than the properties of the nervous system. And the roundabout path Freud was to follow passed via the whole edifice of psychoanalytic theory.

But there are other case-histories from the period which might help put into relief Freud's argument. Take, for example, Schrenck Notzing's cure by hypnosis of a case of sexual inversion in 1889. The young man felt a horror of women and had occasional sexual relations with men. Through repeated hypnotic insistence, this order was inverted, and a clause forbidding masturbation added to the set of commands. After spectacular success for several months, the patient relapsed. He confessed this 'with his usual frankness' and a series of energetic remonstrances under hypnosis brought him to repent it and feel horror at his slip.

> Finally, to put to the test the equilibrium that was being increasingly reestablished, the patient had sexual intercourse with a woman of his own choosing and in the presence of his [male] seducer, with whom he then broke immediately. (Schrenck-Notzing (1889) p. 321)

After strengthening his normal heterosexuality with more hypnosis, the doctor received a card from the young man, announcing his betrothal to a 'childhood sweetheart' (*une amie de jeunesse*). Obviously, the treatment was completely successful, but Schrenck Notzing noted that further relapses were always possible, in which case hypnosis should be used again.

This case appears to be typical of a genre of hypnotic practices of the period. What is striking is the dramatic quality of the measures that are necessary for the cure: the production of guilt and horror, the installation of aversion to his inversion and its final testing in what can only be described as a melodramatic fashion. The test, the proof, sanctioned and almost certainly prescribed by the doctor, amounts to the realization of a fantasy, without the recognition that the fantasy functions in any significant way, either in the aetiology of the sexual condition or in the efficacy of the cure. The relation between doctor and patient remains a theoretical simple, subsumed within the one-dimensional concept of suggestion. What functions as cure, is, again, as with Charcot, a 'psycho-drama' in which the doctor's presence is totally obscured. More to the point, this is not a talking-cure, even though its medium appears to be words. The symptom is not approached to investigate its discursive function; nor is the talk of the patient seen as anything beyond an index of his condition.

But we should not obscure the issue by arguing that no relation is formed between doctor and patient. Quite the opposite: it is the 'human interest' that the doctor displays in his patient that gives the case the impression of being psychological in character. But what is present in Freud's early cases, and absent in these others, is a sense that the neurosis and its cure is determined by the patient's system of ideas, as expressed in words, in which the doctor becomes unavoidably enmeshed. The early concept of transference as being first and foremost a resistance marked Freud's recognition of the importance of the doctor for the patient, but it also points up that it is the *patient*'s responsibility, his activity and mastery, that is the focus of the cure. And this is not a moral responsibility – though the moral dimension of neurosis and its relation to social norms is present very early in Freud's theory, and often found adjacent to the concept of responsibility; rather, it is the patient's responsibility as speaker, as producer of signs, that is in question. The cure depends on his getting his words in the 'right place': into sound, rather than allowing them to become caught up in his body.

It is with the metaphor of the 'right place' that Freud began to depart from Charcot's neurology. As long as the causes of hysteria were thought of in terms of shock, affect or suggestion, a correlation with the nervous system was conceptually feasible, if not exactly rigorous. But as soon as the words of the patient were caught up in his disease, the nervous system became insufficient as a locus for these words. It was at this point, with the question of the relation between the locus of words and the structure of the nervous system, that Freud's work on aphasia assumed its importance. My argument is the following: Freud's work on aphasia – his first book, apart from translations – is the *sine qua non* of the birth of psychoanalytical theory as we can now distinguish it from other contemporary theories of neurosis: a theory of the power of words in the formation of symptoms. To appreciate Freud's work on aphasia, we must turn to the history of that subject in the nineteenth century.

APHASIA

Aphasia has formed the meeting-point of a set of scientific disciplines since the late nineteenth century. Freud's work on aphasia was one of the first essays to appreciate the full scope of the problem of aphasia. Since he wrote that work, in 1891, there have appeared more explicit recognitions of the profound importance of the topic, notably from Bergson (1896), Cassirer (1953–57) and Jakobson (Jakobson 1941, 1956, 1971). Aphasia theory is the point at which four separate disciplines meet: medicine, philosophy, psychology and linguistics. The recognition that this is so, that one must take account of all four, that one must integrate concepts from all four, was only explicitly recognized by Cassirer. Jakobson's essays recognized the necessity for a unity of discourse, drawing upon the epistemological unities of structuralism to unify pathology, psychology and linguistics. Appropriately enough, it was a psychoanalyst, Jacques Lacan, who introduced the explicit extension of Jakobson's concepts into 'psychology' and philosophy (Lacan, 1957). His union of linguistics, pathology, 'psychology' and philosophy mirrors the attempt of the early Freud, from which the conceptual foundations of psychoanalysis were established. To the extent that this conceptual nexus is crucial to the foundation of psychoanalytic theory, Lacan's 'return to Freud' represents something more than just another rhetorical flourish, concealing just another psychoanalytical heresy.

Much of the following discussion will be devoted to discerning the importance of Freud's work on aphasia for the development of psychoanalysis. In order to do this, I wish to sketch a brief history of aphasia, which does not pretend to be comprehensive, but which will pick out the major conceptual shifts of the nineteenth century.[14] Two themes were of dominant importance in the late nineteenth century: the theory of cerebral localization and the doctrine of the association of ideas. In the historical literature there is one date that has assumed overwhelming importance in the rise of aphasia theory to the pre-eminent position it enjoyed: 1861, the date of Paul Broca's paper to the Société d'Anthropologie.[15] Broca demonstrated that a severe loss of speech had a definite correlative lesion in the middle part of the frontal lobe of the left cerebral hemisphere, the third frontal convolution. Although Broca's method – the union of post mortem analysis and a clinical observation – determined the form of aphasia studies for thirty years, it was itself only a part of a wider medical context. Similar attempts to localize the function of speech in a specific part of the brain had been made earlier, notably by the phrenological school founded by Gall (Gall, 1835 V, pp. 7–8; Temkin, 1947; Young, 1970, pp. 11–53, 136–41). These attempts had been ignored or combatted by all those opposed to the biological reductionism of phrenology, such opponents attempting to reduce the debate to a series of local squabbles in the Paris hospitals. The ruling doctrine of scientific medicine of the early period, the doctrine of functional equivalence of Flourens (1824), ruled out of court any attempt to localize functions within the brain. The doctrine, firmly based on experimental physiology as it was, thus became opposed to the biologism of Gall and his followers.

Broca, and the investigators who followed him, circumvented this opposition between biologism and 'physiologism' by avoiding both. Broca's method was a clinical method, joining clinical description to pathological anatomy. Physiology was reduced to a minimum in the accounts of aphasia given in the late nineteenth century.[16] It was only with the work of Jackson and Freud that physiology and the overriding importance of function began to reassert itself. The first generation of aphasia students, from, say, 1860 to 1890, were 'experimental clinicians'. It was the revival of respectable clinical medicine that enabled the issue of aphasia to assume the centre of the neurological stage: a revival that is best represented by the French clinical school of Trousseau and Charcot. The reburgeoning of the clinical tradition also allowed the insertion of psychology into medicine by the second generation of clinicians: Freud, Jackson, Bleuler, Janet. For Freud and Jackson, the point of insertion was aphasia.

A flood of papers immediately followed Broca's, using the methodology so effectively and simply applied to the localization of the speech function. Parallel to this clinical method came the anatomical developments which supplied the language in which to describe localization. The 1860s saw the growth of the observational science of brain anatomy: detailed morphological studies established the architecture of the brain, the pre-requisite for clinical attempts at the localization of 'function'. Hand in hand with the anatomical work, an alternative approach to the problem of brain function was formulated: a chemical approach, perhaps deriving strength from the chemical successes of the Bernard school of physiology. From this perspective, the arterial system of the brain was seen as the centre of function: the process of nutrition was heralded as the banner under which a scientific psychology could progress (Meynert, 1885; Mortimer, 1878–9).

But the attack on the problem of brain function, which found its clearest formulation in the study of aphasia, consisted in the correlation of specific clinical descriptions with the technical linguistic structure mapped out by the anatomists of the brain: the notion of a 1:1 projection of sensory function onto cerebral location was taught by Meynert and Munk. The centre of interest, where the programme of localization of function would stand or fall, remained aphasia theory, right up to the review of the state of psychiatry written by Adolf Meyer (1904).

Wernicke (1874) followed Broca's localization of the function of speech articulation in the second and third temporal convolutions of the left hemisphere, by correlating a distinct clinical entity with a distinctly different cerebral location. He then set out the twin categories of sensory and motor aphasia. With his work, the next logical step in the clinical approach was taken: the diagram. The diagram represented the spatial relation of anatomical centres, with the relations of function superimposed upon it. Naturally this arrangement reversed the true direction of argument within the science: from clinical entity to anatomical location. But once an identity between these two had been established, the direction of argument could be reversed. The identity was located within a *covert* theory of linguistic function, modelled upon the reflex theory of the nervous system, which was itself subtly parasitic upon the doctrine of the association of ideas. The relations of concepts within the science was thus as illustrated in the scheme. The identity established between a clinical entity and an anatomical location was thus founded upon covert assumptions as to the physiology of speech, itself founded upon a psychology of ideas. It was in this manner that a location of a centre for words in the brain failed to trouble a generation

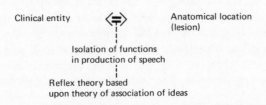

Clinical entity ⟨⇌⟩ Anatomical location (lesion)

Isolation of functions
in production of speech

Reflex theory based
upon theory of association of ideas

unused to the strictures set forth in, say, Ryle's *The Concept of Mind*.

Now we can revise the judgement that aphasia theory was founded upon the separation of physiology from clinical pathology. Rather, physiology functioned covertly as the foundation of the method that created identities between anatomical location and clinical entity. From the 1870s on, there was only one way to think the function of the nervous system: the reflex arc. Argument ceased about the mode of function of the nervous system. With a reflex physiology as the implicit foundation of the discipline, the very terms 'sensory' and 'motor' sanctioned a sliding between two distinct areas: from the physiology of the reflex arc to the clinical entities observed in practice. The loss of ability to 'hear' words corresponded to the 'lesion' of a sensory centre in the brain. Similarly, motor centres of the brain could be identified with 'motor functions' employed in speech. The clear simples of universally accepted physiology thus became the characterizing descriptions of the clinic: inability to speak, correlated with ability to understand, as detected by tests of an informal kind, transformed simply into the notion of a disorder of the motor centre of language. When this simple 'sensory-motor' dualistic account of the speech process proved insufficient, Lichtheim (1885) introduced the notion of a centre for 'ideas'. All aphasias were due to the interruption by a lesion of the linear progression from sensory to motor nerves, via the two centres, the conduction pathways, and the ideas centre.

Other clinicians developed these ideas. Centres proliferated. The clinical signs of speech defects became more finely differentiated; writing defects were either compared or contrasted with speech defects. Philosophical battles came to be fought over the interpretation of clinical descriptions. In France, where the Cartesian tradition, as exhibited early in the century by Flourens, had emphasised the unity of perception, the unity of the *moi* in the perception of matter, these themes of unity and synthesis were resurrected in the debate over aphasia:

> In these facts, as in idiocy, . . . the cerebral lesions isolate, as it were, the different cortical region; and instead of all being in harmony and forming a solidarity, we see the strange spectre of individuals, with special aptitudes perfectly developed but isolated, and contrasting vividly with their sterility as regards other intellectual powers, appropriately deserving the name of wise idiots. (Magnan, 1878–9, p. 119)

The notion of unity and synthesis[17] bound the study of aphasia to the ruling doctrine of the degeneracy of the nervous system, which formed the basis of neurology in France. With the psychological version of this doctrine, developed by Janet in the 1890s and after, the synthetic unity of the *personality* guaranteed the normal functioning of the individual. But in certain psychological versions of aphasia theory developed in the 1890s and 1900s, including Freud's, a crucial rupture occurred: a unity was established, but at the level of language, not of personality. No hint of the unity of the subject was impressed upon the conceptual structure of aphasia theory. Unity was introduced in the associative field of language: the unity of the word, not the *Ich*.[18]

One of the first attacks on the diagram-makers, as Head christened them, came from a union of philosophical and psychological arguments in the work of the English neurologist, John Hughlings Jackson.[19] Jackson was concerned to stop the sliding between psychological and physiological terms that he perceived dogging aphasia theory in particular and neurology in general. His doctrine of concomitances – a hard nosed argument for the strict parallelism and separation of psychic and physical processes – both secured neurology against a creeping psychologism and opened the door to a fully fledged psychology of aphasia. The issue of centres of function seemed to lapse silently within Jackson's overly complicated syntax; but the psychology of aphasia came into its own in the detailed attention he paid to the *individual* utterances of aphasics. He asked a question which betrayed the great gulf that separated him from his contemporaries; why *this* utterance rather than any other? His answer recombined the psychology of the individual and the physiology of the organism. He posited that aphasics suffer a lesion at a particular moment in time: they suffer an attack analogous to epilepsy. The 'nervous arrangements' that had been about to discharge, innervating the series of motor nerves, are caught in the act, as it were, and retain their high level of undischarged energy in a now permanently closed and permanently activated circuit, separated off from the other nervous elements, which, under the impact of the lesion, revert to a lower order of function; the 'arrangements' are fixated upon the moment of the attack. The recurrent utterances of the aphasic thus correspond to what he was about to say at the moment of the attack: 'utterances not "now making", but nearly, if indeed not quite, "ready made up".' (Jackson, 1878–80, p. 169.)

For the aphasic, his recurrent utterance has three characteristics: he has *it*, he has *no other*, and 'he cannot get rid of it.' (Ibid., p. 191.) The lesion led to a dissolution of the nervous system to a lower level of function, that is, to a more highly organized state. For Jackson, higher levels of the nervous system, corresponding to 'propositional consciousness', were characterized by the voluntary, non-automatic nature of their processes. Jackson's theory assumed two axes, one running from organized to unorganized, the other running from conscious to automatic. What is intriguing in this theory is that the dissolution of the nervous system consequent upon a lesion or a functional disturbance entails a regression to a *more* highly organized state: a high level of organization is the mark of a lower level of sophistication of nervous functioning. In this sense, consciousness corresponds to a less structured 'freedom' of the relations between nervous arrangements, whereas automatic functioning involves highly structured and therefore inflexible activity of the nervous system. Hence, when the about-to-be-uttered utterance was caught in the catastrophe consequent upon the disruptive lesion, it remained as a highly organized unit 'trapped' within the now automatic functioning of the system. The notion of organization meshed with the concept of levels of the nervous system: dissolution led the nervous system back to older and more primitive levels of organization, possibly back to the original levels of speech, where language was 'ready made up'.

We can see the shape the psychological critique of the diagram makers was to take: the anatomical identity dropped out, to be replaced by a putative general functional identity of the 'state of the nervous system' and the 'clinical description' of the utterances (or lack of them). Aside from the replacement of anatomy by functional concepts (which would *appear* to be physiological in a general sense), the levels of awareness of the linguistic problems of analysing aphasics began to surface with Jackson. He distinguished the live utterances of the normal, which were voluntary and had meaning, were true propositions, were living structures, from the dead recurrent utterance, the vestigial trace of the higher levels of organization that had been destroyed. In contrast with the diagram makers, who retained a strictly atomistic and nominalistic conception of language, Jackson's notion was far more sophisticated. He argued that the basic units of language were propositions, not words. That is, a structure, a syntax, is necessary to language.

The proposition had meaning insofar as elements in it were subject to substitution, i.e. words only had meaning insofar as they were dispensable, and a structure was only linguistic insofar as it was placed in opposition to the elements that constituted it. This 'structuralist' element in Jackson's thought bore fruit in the work of Pick (1913) on aphasia and the writings of Jakobson in the 1940s and 1950s. What the theory of the proposition entailed was a structural distinction between 'meaningful' and 'meaningless' utterances: aphasic utterances might appear to have meaning, but this meaning had only been inherent in them at the origin, at one particular moment when dynamic proposition formation had suffered its demise in consequence of the lesion. Insofar as the phrase was 'ready made up' it was meaningless, precisely because, being 'ready made up', it was not suited to the other occasions on which it came to be uttered. In other words, failure of the phrase to obey the condition that its elements be subject to substitution entailed that it would be meaningless when it came to be repeated.

It is exactly this distinction that Freud carried over from aphasia theory to hysteria, in the form of the opposition between symptom and speech. The chronic hysterical symptom bore remarkable similarities to the aphasic's recurrent utterance: it was a piece of language that had once had meaning but which, by becoming cut off from the dynamic structure of contingent elements – for different reasons in the two conditions – had lost its meaning, and, for reasons to do with the systemic relations of the nervous system ('conversion' and 'somatic compliance'), was doomed to repetition. Of course, there was a tension between this conception of the symptom as meaningless in contrast to speech, and the conception that these same symptoms have a meaning, insofar as they are equivalent to a verbal phrase or thought. We will consider this at greater length in Chapter 4 'Grammar'. What Freud took from aphasia theory was the notion that a symptom's apparent meaninglessness could be illuminated•by placing it in a very specific, 'traumatic' past context, when it did have meaning. The hysterical symptom, in contrast to the aphasic recurrent utterance, needed an additional operation to restore its meaning – namely translation into the verbal phrase of which it was the recurrent expression – before one could place it in its proper past context.[20] In Freud's psychoanalytic practice, the two procedures – finding the verbal translation and finding the point in time to which this translation belonged – were never separated, being integral parts of one method of investigation. But, in psychoanalysis, as in aphasia studies, patients came to be known by their 'recurrent utterances', for example, Broca's *Tan*, Trousseau's *Sapon*[21] and Freud's *Wolfman*.

Jackson concluded that words only have a meaning when they form part of a symbolic system which represents an ordered and internally dynamic series of inner states. But there were other elements of 'language' that were put into question by the phenomena of aphasia. Was the language lost by the aphasic the memory of the language signs or the capacity to produce signs? Bastian (1887) surmounted this problem on the psychological level: he distinguished between recollection and memory. Again, as so often in the discussion of aphasia, an exact mirroring of brain anatomy and philosophy of language was preserved. The distinction between memory and recollection corresponded to that between neurones and the association fibres connecting them. Losing the power of recollection meant losing the power to connect. But Bastian no longer required that the units – whether they be neurones or words – be localized: they were like Jackson's 'nervous arrangements' in that they existed in an undefined physiological space, independent of the brain. The change in the character of the space in which such units were located was expressed by Freud in 1893 as follows:

> I, on the contrary, assert that the lesion in hysterical paralyses must be completely independent of the anatomy of the nervous system . . . (Freud (1893c) SE I 169)

And he took the argument to its conclusion by asserting that, in hysteria, it is an idea that suffers from a lesion ('*lésion*', '*Verletzung*').

The construction of such a 'physiological' space in which the structures of language were located was to be one of the cornerstones of Freud's theory of the mind. The extent to which that space was physiological can be gauged from the basic categories of the *Project for a Scientific Psychology* he wrote in 1895. There, the unit of the 'mind' is the neurone. The extent to which the anatomy of this space had recaptured its essential metaphorical topography. can be gauged by the virtual identity of neurone and idea in the theoretical structure. And in *The Interpretation of Dreams*, we find that the space of psychic action has become assimilated to the purely ideal geometric space of optics, in which the material support is strictly incidental to considerations of spatial order and function (Freud (1900a) SE V 536–7; see Lacan, 1975a, pp. 89ff and Lacan, 1978, p. 146).

Freud's own increased attentiveness to the contents of the articulated language that formed the object of the study – both in aphasia and hysteria – was part of a growing 'psychologization' of the problems of aphasia in the last decade of the nineteenth century. The newer generation of alienists, psychologists, neurologists, etc., entered the lists in the study of aphasia; their names are familiar from other contexts: Bleuler, Bergson, Liepmann, Goldstein, Abraham, Jones. With the new psychological awareness came a critique of the diagrams of the earlier generation. They did not criticize the notion of the localization of utterances in space; rather, they criticized the identification of centres of verbal activity with locations in the brain. Beyond this, a further critique of psychological and linguistic atomism was mooted. Goldstein, Bergson and Cassirer brought their weight to bear against atomistic associationism, while it was from such an associationism that many important critiques of the brain centre/linguistic unit identity thesis were to emerge. We find an ambiguity between atomistic associationism and formalism in Freud's aphasia theory.

Freud's monograph on aphasia was first and foremost a critique of the diagram-makers. In it he crossed swords with Wernicke's notions of sensory and motor aphasia[22], took much time and trouble demolishing Lichtheim's diagram, and 'even scratched the high and mighty idol Meynert.'[23] Later writers acknowledged their indebtedness to his masterly critique. In Goldstein's eyes, he had opened up the study of aphasia for a psycho-philosophical approach (Goldstein, 1910). But, as Goldstein noted with disapproval, Freud wanted to place a theory of the association of ideas at the centre of aphasia theory, in order to replace the identity of pathological with anatomical units. It was through a subtle confusion of levels that Freud used associationism to demolish the concept of a centre. In laying emphasis on association rather than function, Freud did not at first shift the argument to a purely psychological level. The anatomical (or physiological) correlate of 'association' was 'connection fibre'. Freud used an array of anatomical facts to show that it was such connection fibres that were of primary importance in cerebral functioning. Such an argument also implied the functional 'anonymity' of these fibres. The model thus invoked was a homogeneous field of connection fibres, an abstracted physiology that could *now* be converted into a purely psychological space. Any attempt to segment the field of language was vigorously resisted: at the level of the brain, what one found were connective fibres: at the level of psychological space, one found a hierarchy of interdependent functions of association.

Associationism dominated this schema in a way that dismayed Goldstein. It was true that Freud had demolished the putative spatial unity provided by the brain of the diagram-makers.[24] But he immediately replaced it with an homogeneous associative field of language, which could not aid Goldstein in his broader psychological aims, which were more directed towards the use of categories analogous to the Kantian categories of experience. Goldstein's categories were intended to embody the necessary preconditions for the possibility of ordered perception. To this end he used the perception of space as his model for the construction of meaning in aphasia. This Kantian trend, paralleling the 'synthetic unity' of the French school, received its fullest account in Cassirer's *The Philosophy of Symbolic Forms*. In philosophical terms, it attempted to insert the subject of aphasic discourse at a level above, but necessary to, the laws of the association of ideas. A transcendental unitary subject thus played the same role as the 'brain' of the brain mythologists, the individual categories corresponding to the individual centres, inferred from the location of lesions.

Now it is significant that Meynert had propounded a well known theory that had guaranteed a unitary subject of perception via the notion of the *ego* being a projection of the body onto the brain. By tracing the anatomical connections between the periphery and the cortex, he demonstrated that a 'reality ego' provided a faithful reproduction of the body, which could be immediately apperceived by consciousness (Meynert, 1871, 1885). Freud was most severe on this model in *On Aphasia* for reasons that now appear clear. He was firmly opposed to any hint of a transcendental subject, whether it be the quasi-anatomical lesion/centre of the diagram-makers, or the physiological subject of Meynert's fibre-tract and reflex model. The overriding consideration for Freud was to establish a *self-sufficient* unity at the level of the 'speech apparatus', since any other principle of unity would reopen the possibility of a reduction of the problem of aphasia away from its proper linguistic/psychological level. Language had its own principles of organization and combination which reductionism always obscured. Hence, even the notion of 'cortical synthesis', to be found in twentieth century work on the body-schema (Corraze, 1973; Schilder, 1935), might be misleading, since it might elide the ontological distinction between thing and representation. Freud thus replaced Meynert's 1:1 'projection' of peripheral sense-data onto the cortex with a series of levels of 'representations' (*Vorstellungen*).

Freud's argument against Meynert's projection theory had two functions:

a. By showing that the distinction between a perception and its association was both less marked and more complex than Meynert had thought, he dismissed the 'mirroring' model of representation.

b. If even the 'body-schema' is a combinatory representation, rather than an imagic presentation (a mirroring, a reflection, a veridical projection), then, once we turn to the specific phenomena of aphasia, we must accept that the order of language must have an even greater order of combination and organization.

Freud argued this latter point in a most interesting manner:

> We can only presume that the fibre tracts, which reach the cerebral cortex after their passage through other grey masses, have maintained some relationship to the periphery of the body, but no longer reflect a topographically exact image of it. They contain the body periphery in the same way as – to borrow an example from the subject with which we are concerned here – a poem contains the alphabet, i.e. in a completely different arrangement serving other purposes, in manifold associations of the individual elements, whereby some may be represented several times, others not at all. (Freud, 1891b, p. 19)

What this most sophisticated metaphor supports is an emphasis on the combinatory character of perceptual data: all perception is coded into a system in which the individual elements count for very little, since it is the 'manifold associations' that hold the neural information. Thus, not only is this an associationism that goes beyond atomism towards a formalism or structuralism but it amounts to holding that *all* representations are coded *as if* they were a language. But another passage should give us pause for thought, and help us recognize that the reference to language might not be essential to the argument: we find the same line of thought and conclusion in the *Project* of 1895, where Freud argued in detail how a given quantity Q can come to be represented by a set of facilitations between homogeneous neural elements (Freud (1950a) SE I 314–5). In both the arguments, what is of importance is the coding of 'neural input' into a structure, a system of relations. This associationism is clearly distanced from the classical associationist tradition, in that it immediately reduces the primacy of perceptual elements, placing all the weight upon a structuration of arbitrary elements (arbitrary, not because of any intrinsic lack of differentiation, but because each element only has value as 'information' through being defined by its relations to other elements). The argument also displays the uncompromising dualism that Freud retained throughout his life, including those years from 1900 to the First World War when utopic monism was all the rage (Gasman (1971); Ringer (1969)). As he put it in 1912:

> If the present speaker had to choose among the views of the philosophers, he could characterize himself as a dualist. No monism succeeds in doing away with the distinction between ideas and the objects they represent. (*Minutes* IV (11 Dec 1912) p. 11)[25]

But, as is clear from the history of materialism in the nineteenth century, dualism does not always entail the sort of position that Freud took up. For instance, Huxley's epiphenomenalism granted the autonomy of consciousness while removing all its functions and privileges (Huxley, 1874). Bergson, in his study on aphasia, set out the alternatives in the following manner:

> Materialists and dualists are fundamentally agreed on this point. They consider certain molecular movements of the cerebral matter apart: then, some see in our conscious perception a phosphorescence which follows these movements and illuminates their track; for others, our perceptions succeed each other like an unwinding scroll in a consciousness which expresses continuously, in its own way, the molecular vibrations of the cortical substance: in the one case, as in the other, our perception is supposed to *translate* or to *picture* the states of our nervous system. (Bergson, 1896, p. 11)

Freud chose the dualistic mode, the mode of translation. But, by translating all perceptions into its own 'language', a language that seemed to have very little to do with the nervous system's 'own way', Freud's system discarded any notion of a centre, even at the level of the psychology of language, let alone at the level of anatomy. A free space of language was opened up, which became known as the 'zone of language' in the aphasia literature. The concept of a zone of language came to be regarded as Freud's major contribution to aphasia studies: Ladame (1900), Dejerine (1906), Pick (1894, 1900) and Goldstein (1910) were among those who took Freud's concept as one of the major elements in the 'psychologization' of aphasia studies. And, despite his use of what was to become an increasingly outmoded language of 'images', Freud steered aphasia studies away from the specificity or 'centreing' that the concept of images seemed to imply. As Ombredane has noted with respect to Freud's work:

The essential feature of aphasia will not be so much the loss of this or that order of images so much as the difficulty of evocation of an image of an order determined by other images. (Ombredane, 1951, p. 107)

The reference to a system that determines the elements in question is the death knell of a centre-based *and* contents-based theory of aphasia. Freud had managed to construct a homogeneous zone of language without invoking a transcendental subject.

Freud's work on aphasia included a number of separate critiques. At one level, he surveyed the clinical facts derived from a large number of published cases, and demonstrated their susceptibility to various, equally justifiable, interpretations. Hence one would be justified in choosing one's interpretation on other, non-anatomoclinical, grounds. These grounds were based upon the logical priority now accorded to psychology in the study of the aphasias. As I have argued, Freud made single-minded use of the doctrine of the association of ideas in order to destroy the concept of a centre for psychologically defined entites. Having emphasized that speech is a function, he argued that one can not satisfactorily separate the association of images from their individual revival – the covert distinction upon which the notion of a centre depended. The outcome of this argument is the conclusion that all aphasias are disorders of association. Even in this respect, Freud wished to limit the importance of the lesion in producing the observed defects. The lesion acted by limiting the *general* functioning of the speech apparatus, rather than by eliminating certain separate functions: the unity of the speech apparatus is implicit at all times. Malfunction is simply due to the apparatus being forced to operate at a different, but still unified, functional level.

Freud introduced Jackson's notion of functional regression to explain the failure of speech function in certain forms of aphasia. Different aphasias represent different stages in the process of learning to speak:

Thus the aphasias simply reproduce a state which existed in the course of the normal process of learning to speak. . . . when learning, we are restricted by the hierarchy of the centres which started functioning at different times; the sensory-auditory first, then the motor, later the visual and lastly the graphic. (Freud, 1891b, p. 42)

When one of the functions that was learned later fails, an earlier, more intrenched function comes into play:

It can be assumed that the various speech activities continue to be performed by way of the same associations by which we learned them. Abbreviations and substitutions may be employed, but their nature is not always easy to recognize. Their significance is still further reduced by the consideration that in cases of organic lesion the speech apparatus as a whole probably suffers some damage and is forced into a return towards the primary and secure, though more cumbersome modes of association. (Ibid., pp. 76–7)

A speech function may be said to be overdetermined when there are two pathways or functions that give rise to a given image. This can be illustrated by:

We learn to speak by associating a 'word sound image' with an 'impression of word innervation'. When we have spoken we are in possession of a 'kinaesthetic word image', i.e. of the sensory impressions from the organs of speech. The motor aspect of 'word' is therefore doubly determined. (Ibid., p. 73)

We are safe in assuming that Freud followed Jackson's evolutionary doctrine to the point of believing that the two different determinations of the motor aspect of the 'word' were also learned at different stages of development. Therefore, one of the functions – that is, the 'higher' one that was learned later – can be lost and still leave functional activity intact.

Freud shifted the nosology of aphasia from anatomy to psychology. But it was a traditional psychology he used. Wernicke's schema united anatomy, physiology and psychology, hiding an implicit identity of psyche and physis. Freud shifted the identity, indeed rejected it, by dissociating anatomy from psychology. As he himself recognized, this was a conceptual rather than an empirical shift, stemming from his refusal to separate the association from the perception of presentations. But such a shift had empirical consequences. The perceived afferent and efferent pathways of the speech centre dissolved before the anatomists' eyes into a uniform mass of association-fibres. Having demolished Wernicke's categories, Freud rebuilt the distinctions, starting from the psychology of language: 'The "word" is the functional unit of speech; it is a complex presentation constituted of auditory, visual and kinaes-thetic elements.' (Ibid., p. 73.) His whole discussion led up to the following diagram, which displayed the relationship between the object-presentation and the word-presentation:

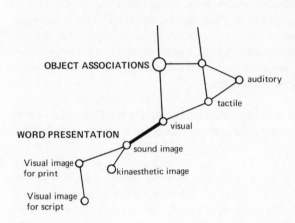

In this psychological schema of the word presentations, the latter appear as a closed complex of images, the object presentation as an open one. The word presentation is linked to the presentation of the object via the sound image alone. Among the object associations, the visual one plays a part similar to that played by the sound image among the word associations.

The word then is a complicated presentation built up from various impressions, i.e., it corresponds to an intricate process of association entered into by elements of visual, acoustic and kinaesthetic origins. (Ibid., p. 73).

In Freud's account, the sound image is the central aspect of the word: the primary meaning of the word is that meaning which was originally attached to it, when words were learnt from hearing them spoken. Similarly, the visual aspect of the object is the most important of the object associations. Using this model, Freud now redefined Wernicke's aphasias. The latter's symmetrical categories of sensory and motor aphasia became the asymmetrical verbal and asymbolic aphasias:

(1) verbal aphasia, in which only the associations between the single elements of the word presentation are disturbed; and
(2) asymbolic aphasia, in which the associations between word presentation and object presentation are disturbed. (Ibid., p. 78.)

Freud then proceeded to correlate his new categories with clinical and pathological cases. The shape of aphasia studies had dramatically changed. In place of a brain anatomy providing the possible categories from which the clinician could choose his combination of lesion sites, we have the psychologist of language positing the objects of concern from which the clinician could draw out his diagnosis. Freud did not deny the relevance of brain anatomy to aphasia studies. On the contrary, most of his arguments were drawn from the detailed examination of lesion sites. Rather, he was pointing out the complexity of localizing defects of a complex mental activity, emphasizing that psychological regulative principles are more important than physiological ones, as soon as one recognizes that the disorders are functional *as well as* organic. He drew on the English functional evolutionism of Jackson and the associationist psychology of J. S. Mill in order to supplant the organic reductionism of the brain pathology of German medicine.

Let us look more closely at the consequences of the word presentation/object association schema. The schema places a word/object dualism at the centre both of aphasia studies and of a theory of the psyche. It is this dualism that necessitates the asymmetry in nosology, since the model is now hierarchical and irreversible, in contrast with the diagram-makers' reflex model.

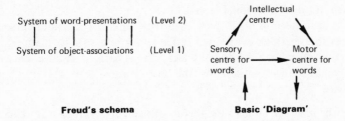

Freud's schema   Basic 'Diagram'

What is noteworthy is that aphasia is now due to disturbances within or between self-sufficient systems of representations. It has been pointed out that the 'speech apparatus' is an earlier version of the 'psychic apparatus' of Chapter VII of *The Interpretation of Dreams*. We see now in what sense this is true: both 'apparatuses' are self-sufficient systems of representation.[26] The system of word-presentations kept its place as a significant sub-system in this later apparatus: it was later called the system of verbal residues – in the *Project, The Interpretation of Dreams, The Ego and the Id, An Outline of Psychoanalysis* – to name only those texts in which the system played an important role in Freud's metapsychological argument. Having noted this theoretical continuity which Freud owed to the model from *On Aphasia*, we should now return to the theme of this chapter: the theory of the talking-cure.

THE THEORY OF THE TALKING-CURE

On Aphasia made available to Freud a psychology of representations independent of the structure of the nervous system, consisting in two systems of representations: word-presentations and object-associations. Both these systems had an order, a code of combination that was independent of a system of relations either of the 'body' or the 'world'. In what did aphasic symptoms consist? Aphasia was the consequence of the altered general functioning of the systems, *occasioned* by a cerebral lesion. In 1893, when he wished to proclaim the independence of the hysterical lesion with respect to the anatomy of the nervous system, Freud had already achieved this independence for the study of aphasia, in which there was a visible and obvious lesion. In showing that, even where there is an organic lesion, the explanation of aphasic phenomena must be understood independently of the location of the lesion, Freud paved the way for the understanding of hysteria as the lesion of an idea. In both hysteria and aphasia it is the two systems of presentations that suffer lesions.

But in hysteria it is a *specific* idea that suffers. The hysterical lesion affects the relations of the two systems, but in a specific manner: it is selective. On what basis does it select? On the basis of an experience that is psychically traumatic. Now, the term 'trauma' carries a number of senses:

    i. the sense given it in the theory of neuroses derived from Charcot and Jackson: an excessive excitation (but, in Freud's theory, now freed from a specific location in the nervous system);

    ii. an experience that is not 'worked over associatively'.[27]

In Freud's earlier theories of hysteria, it is such traumatic incidents that give rise to *thoughts*. The subject turns away from these thoughts (Freud (1894a) SE III 52–3) and they fail to find verbal expression. They then reappear as symptoms. The talking-cure then consists in re-evoking the memory of the trauma and putting the affect associated with the memory into words:

> . . . if he sees things before him with all their original actuality, we shall observe that he is completely dominated by some affect. And if we then compel him to put this affect into words, we shall find that, at the same time as he is producing this violent affect, the phenomenon of his pains emerges very markedly once again and that thenceforward the symptom, in its chronic character, disappears. . . . It could only be supposed that the psychic trauma does in fact continue to operate in the subject and maintains the hysterical phenomenon, and that it comes to an end as soon as the patient has spoken about it. (Freud (1893h) SE III 35)[28]

Sometimes Freud wrote as if the visual memory itself was being dissolved when it was put into words:

> Once a picture has emerged from the patient's memory, we may hear him say that it becomes fragmentary and obscure as he proceeds with his description of it. *The patient is, as it were, getting rid of it by turning it into words.* (Breuer and Freud (1895d) SE II 280)

What is being turned into words is an affect and a memory that had become converted into a symptom. The symptom itself was the expression of these 'lost' words.[29] On the model of the word/object systems, what has happened is that a relation between the *specific* word presentation and the *specific* object association has been refused – a similar mechanism to that which Freud called asymbolic aphasia. As a consequence of this refusal, lower, earlier-learnt functions are brought into play: the words find their material locus in the body, rather than in sound: they become gestures.[30] Jackson had argued that something similar takes place in aphasia: the recurrent utterances of the aphasic are thoughts that are frozen, repeated, ready made up, and hence not true speech. They are insistent and outside of the subject's control, in the same way as hysterical symptoms are. To find out why these utterances and no others are found, one must look to the history of the course of the aphasic syndrome, often finding a specific event or affect as the explanation. Similarly, the talking cure had as its means an historical enquiry, in search of a point in time when the relationship between the two systems had suffered some 'perturbation'. But, with the dimension of time, the theory became more complex.

In studying hysterics, Freud was not led back to *any* memory in the unconscious; these memories themselves possessed an added dimension: their position in time. Symptoms were formed when a precipitating cause – usually a strong affect – resonated with a repressed memory, say, from adolescence, which itself was associated with a similarly repressed memory of an infantile sexual experience. The contemporary idea joined the ideas associated with the repressed memories in the unconscious and so lost touch with the moderating influences of verbal consciousness. Hysteria was due to an inability to transfer these ideas into verbal consciousness. Now this ability was *appropriate* only to that period in a person's life when they could not translate *any* ideas into verbal consciousness: the years up to the age of four. One of Freud's early hypotheses was that sexuality in some way extended the period when such translation was not possible, up to the age of four, which, from the evidence of his cases, seemed to be a crucial age.

The period [up to 4] possesses the character of being untranslated [into verbal images]; so that the awakening of a sexual scene [from this period] leads, not to psychical consequences, but to realizations [i.e., physical consequences] to conversion. The surplus of sexuality prevents translation [into verbal images] . . . In obsessional neurosis the scenes occur during the period [up to 8] and can be translated into words. When they are awakened [either after age 14 or later], psychical obsessional symptoms arise. (Freud (1950a) SE I 175–6)

Hysterical ideas always stemmed from a *sexual* experience of the early period.[31] Incapacity for translating such experience into words was the pre-disposing condition for the hysterical disposition, just as the capacity for translating the memory of the experience into words was the necessary condition for the alleviation of the hysterical condition.

To the extent that he placed such importance on an event that needed to be put into words, Freud was beginning to present problems for his empirical argument. The event was pathogenic because it was impossible to connect it with word presentations at the time of its occurrence. But if it wasn't these words that were forgotten, what exactly was it? The process of construction and remembering in analysis indicates this problem. Patients accept the constructions of the analyst, while exclaiming that they cannot remember them:

Are we to disregard this withholding of recognition on the part of patients, when, now that the work is finished, there is no longer any motive for their doing so? Or are we to suppose that we are really dealing with thoughts which never came about, which merely had a *possibility* of existing, so that the treatment would lie in the accomplishment of a psychical act which did not take place at the time? (Breuer and Freud (1895d) SE II 300)[32]

Hence a gap in the chain of arguments has appeared. On the one hand, the signification of a symptom and the set of memories aligned with it is taken to stem from the signification that was given to an event in childhood. But now we discover that this event did not take place, or, more exactly, the signification attached to this event was never formed, due to the lack at that time of the necessary conditions for such signification. These 'thoughts' only had a possibility of existing: the words had never been formed. But the symptoms themselves seemed to bear witness to some element of verbal transformation, performed on significations that had existed 'before'.

In the language that Freud was beginning to use in this period, some attempt at resolving the paradox might be found in the idea that an infantile memory only undergoes a single registration, in contrast with the multiple registration that is received by 'ordinary' memories. The 'primal' memories, those that occur in early childhood, are those that could not receive the multiple registration that allows conscious memory to take place. They were laid down before the system of speech came into being. Do they exist at all? Or did they only have a possibility of existing?

Freud deflected the emphasis away from the question of the existence of the events to which the memory or construction pointed by stressing two other features: the primacy of memory and the systematic character of experience. A first critical question, casting doubt on the existence of events actually recounted by the patient, might be: 'What proof do you have that these events, to which you accord such enormous importance, took place?' Freud replied that it wasn't the (material) reality of these events that was of importance, but rather the fact that they had a psychic existence.[33] Repression acts on *memories*, not on perceptions, and if a memory of an event has come into existence that is a sufficient cause for repression, whether or not the event had ever actually taken place.[34] Memory was the crucial concept, whether it was a question of the memory of phantasies or of actual events.

The second critical position was implied by the fact that Freud discussed in the quotation given above: patients cannot recollect the event that all the evidence of analysis led him – and them – to posit as having occurred. This event, of course, could be either a 'real' event or a phantasy; but if no recollection could ever be elicited, what status must the analyst accord to this event? Freud surmised that a psychical act hadn't taken place when it should have; the treatment consists in making good this lack. But he had a certain array of reasons, derived from other parts of his theory, which made this lack more comprehensible. That is, he had a set of reasons explaining why certain experiences were 'unthinkable' and thus could not be expected to have left anything but a 'lack' in the texture of experiences systematized into the contents of the psyche.

The first of these reasons was that the psyche lacked the intellectual *materials* with which to think such a thought. Little Hans failed to come to a conclusion as to the nature of sexual intercourse because of the 'intellectual difficulty' of the problem. But, as we will see in our discussion of this case at the end of Chapter 5, at the *end* of the analysis, Hans managed to construct a phantasy that was equivalent to such knowledge (the 'plumber' phantasy, see p. 201).

Secondly, certain subjects proved to be intrinsically recalcitrant for the processes of thought. Sexuality was the most important subject that came into this category. Throughout Freud's writings we find that sexuality evokes a certain sluggishness in the mental apparatus, an absence of thought. (Though we should also be clear that this mysterious recalcitrance was also the occasion for the greatest intellectual efforts of which the psyche was capable; the problems posed *by* the recalcitrance of sexuality are the roots of intellectual activity.)

But the third reason stemmed from the notion that Freud attempted to place at the centre of his early theory of the neuroses: the notion that a certain intellectual *incapacity* (logically prior to the provision of the materials upon which to exercise such a capacity) entailed that the psychical act *could* not take place. And he associated this intellectual incapacity very directly with the pre-verbal period: certain events had not been thought because the verbal residues were not available with which to think them. More generally, he assumed that a failure of transcription into the system of speech residues was what was lacking.

Thus one important theme that is broached here is that analysis allows a person to think the unthinkable: childhood experience. The more extreme version of this thinking the unthinkable comes to mind: the re-experiencing of the act of birth, the attempt to think of death as something beyond mere absence (cf. Jones, 1927 and 1929). Such experiences were unthinkable precisely because they are experienced without language. And, even though Freud modified his early emphasis on the lack of language, by introducing the other reasons accounting for why one could not think such an event, the notion of a failure of the function of language remained an essential feature of his account of neurosis.

Freud finally made explicit in 1915 the notion that it is a lack of translation into words that characterizes a representation as unconscious. Ideas that for one reason or another could not be expressed in words – for instance, the 'mystery connected with the genitals'[35] – were likely to form the core of the repressed unconscious. But this theory had been earlier tied to a chronological determinant of neurosis, the notion that the initial predisposing experience for the disposition to neurosis, the predisposing experience, the first trauma, had to occur before the age at which ideas could be put into words.

Freud discarded the clear-cut relationship between the development of verbal thought and the disposition for neurosis by 1897. But he never stopped looking for a temporal determinant of this 'intellectual' order. We find alternative hypotheses being put forward well into the 1920s. The concept of the developmental stages of the sexual instincts was one of his later answers to this problem. But in 1897, as a result of his self analysis, he proposed another such temporal cause:

Only one idea of general value has occurred to me. I have found love of the mother and jealousy of the father in my own case, and now believe it to be a general phenomenon of early childhood, even if it does not always occur so early as in children who have been made hysterics. (Freud (1950a) SE I 265)

Behind this formulation of the notion of Oedipal desires lay the need to link the development of the instinctual life with the intellectual development of the speech function. Freud was searching for a chronological determinant for the causation of neurosis. And it still lay in a temporally determined lack of synchronization of desire and its integration into 'experience'. Throughout Freud's writings there will remain a conception that there is something about the sexual that is beyond the capacity of the mind to assign. Again, we can refer to the resistance to signification that the loss of the penis awakens in both sexes, a resistance that forms the rock bottom of all neuroses (cf. Freud (1937c) SE XXIII 250–3; also Freud (1909b) SE X 142 and (1905d) SE VII 240–1). After the first enthusiastic hypotheses of the 1890s Freud began to be more circumspect, while still finding the same problematic at the heart of neurosis. Of Little Hans Freud wrote:

It is hard to say what the influence was which . . . led to the sudden change in Hans. . . . Whether the scales were turned by the child's *intellectual* inability to solve the difficult problem of the begetting of children and to cope with the aggressive impulses that were liberated by his approaching the solution, or whether the effect was produced by a *somatic* incapacity . . . (Freud (1909b) SE X 136)

Or the emphasis could be placed on sexual prematurity:

Such cases [of obsessional neurosis], unlike those of hysteria, invariably possess the characteristic of premature sexual activity. (Freud (1909d) SE X 165)

But, whichever option Freud worked with at a given time, what was at issue was the lack of coordination between the sexual and verbal.

We can forge a link between this 'inadequation' and the disturbance of the word and object systems outlined in *On Aphasia*. The intermediate term is the *visual memory trace*. In *On Dreams*, Freud argued that visual memories from childhood form the core around which the elements of the dream crystallize (Freud (1901a) SE V 659; cf Freud (1900a) SE V 546). In other texts, it is precisely such elements that represent 'unreconstructed' elements of the primary process.[36] Visual elements, the elements of the hysterical trauma, sexual experience: all these are 'object associations' that have not been integrated into the system of word-presentations.

We have followed the language of the systems that were first set out in *On Aphasia* in order to indicate the continuity of Freud's arguments with respect to aphasia and hysteria. What is distinctive in the theory of hysteria still remains: the specificity of the words that are both causative and curative of the symptoms. But what is general and common to both aphasia and hysteria is the attempt to find the general conditions involved in the malfunction of the speech apparatus. What Freud recognized as the distinctive feature of hysteria was a *semantic* element, an element of meaning. How this element of meaning came to be found in such an unexpected place as a physical symptom could be discussed using the systems of representation laid out in *On Aphasia*. In essence, Freud laid out a continuum, stretching from aphasia to hysteria by symbolization, in which a common feature united all the elements along the continuum: all involved a disturbance of the relations between object association and word presentation. In order to cure hysteria by symbolization one needs to establish a *symbolic* connection that was never made in childhood.

> . . . we remove the symptom by bringing about, during the reproduction of the traumatic scene, a subsequent correction [*eine nachträgliche Korrektur*] of the psychical events which took place at the time. (Freud (1896c) SE III 193)

The disturbance of the relationship between word and object presentation is corrected subsequently: the talking that fills analysis. In Freud's view in the 1890s, this talking did not even have to take place within the special relationship of doctor and patient. *Any* verbal discharge could correct the disturbance. With regard to Katherina, one of the studies in hysteria, Freud noted:

. . . what we were dealing with was a hysteria which had to a considerable extent been abreacted. And in fact she had reported her discovery to her aunt soon after it happened. (Breuer and Freud (1895d) SE II 132)

Any verbal approach to the object that has become 'lost' to the system of word presentations is likely to be efficacious. Indeed, Freud's remarks on the general functions of speech bear out the impression that any talking, even if it is language at its most unspecific – oaths – will effect the state of psychical health that the hysteric has given up by refusing to speak:

Let us suppose that a man is insulted, is given a blow or something of the kind. This psychical trauma is linked with an increase in the sum of excitation of his nervous system. There then instinctively arises an inclination to diminish this increased excitation immediately. He hits back, and then feels easier; he may perhaps have reacted adequately – that is, he may have got rid of as much as had been introduced into him. . . . The most adequate reaction . . . is always a deed. But, as an English writer has wittily remarked, the man who first flung a word of abuse at his enemy instead of a spear was the founder of civilization. Thus words are substitutes for deeds, and in some circumstances (e.g. in Confession) the only substitutes. . . . An insult that has been repaid, even if only in words, is recollected quite differently from one that has had to be accepted; and linguistic usage characteristically describes an insult that has been suffered in silence as a 'mortification' (*Kränkung*). (Freud (1893h) SE III 36)

What makes the patient ill is silence. But this long passage indicates a subtle fusion of the two elements we have carefully separated so far. 'Talk' is conceived both as lying in the dimension of meaning, of truth, of specificity; and it is also conceived of as a mechanism for the discharge of a tension, an excess of excitation that, at this date (1893), is still conceived of as analogous to the excitation of the nervous system (cf. Andersson, (1962)). We might well call this latter element the cathartic dimension and the former the semantic dimension.[37] What is most interesting is that the aphasia monograph was almost exclusively concerned with the conditions necessary for the understanding of the semantic dimension, even though the distinctive characteristic of the semantic, specificity, was lacking in aphasia. It elaborated a syntax of systems into which the distinctively Freudian concept of hysteria as a 'semantic' disorder could be placed. With the demise of the cathartic method and cure,[38] all the therapeutic weight came to rest on the semantic element.

This is not to deny that the quantitative element was not still bound up in the terminology that Freud developed. But it is important to recognize that these terms – for example, resistance and transference – came to refer primarily to elements of signification: resistance is first and foremost resistance to signification; transference refers primarily to the signification of the analyst in the psychic economy, rather than the displacement of quantity onto this new object.

As a consequence, it is at the level of theory, rather than of therapy, that we find the quantitative mode put most in evidence. It was in the *Project* that Freud attempted to combine the idea of psychic systems developed in *On Aphasia* with a derivation from first principles of the quantitative functioning of these systems. We will not be able to analyse this attempt in detail. What must concern us is the exact position given to the 'speech apparatus' in that abortive work. We will find the elements we have already encountered emerge more clearly, namely, the fundamental importance of the relations between the object associations (traces) and word presentations (verbal residues), and the civilizing function of language, which underpins the therapy of hysteria.

But, before we turn to the *Project* and then to the later theory of language in Freud's work, we should finally try and measure the originality of the talking cure, when contrasted with Charcot's theories of hysteria, hypnosis and aphasia. It has been argued most interestingly by Major (1974, 1977) that the turning point in Freud's therapy was the moment when he attached greater importance to the hysterics' words than to her dramatic gestures. The talking cure turns away from the dramatic relation between doctor and patient to the words of the hysteric, the doctor's gaze is shifted away from the body of the patient, thus creating the presence of a master, filling the field of consciousness of the hysteric and allowing her to become the plaything of the master's desire, i.e. to 'satisfy' her desire. Major links this with a shift of the doctor-patient relationship that Freud brought about by assigning such dominance to the acoustic element of language:

Freud, in 1891, brought to bear a decisive quarter-turn to the radiant occupied by the visual image by placing the acoustic image in a dominant position. The correlative technique is nothing less than the invention of the analytic situation, whose place had thus already been assigned to it by theory. (Major, 1977, p. 22)

This argument, though very attractive in its radical simplicity, does not seem to hold up under further scrutiny. Firstly, the primacy assigned to the acoustic representation of the word cannot be regarded as peculiar to Freud's theory of aphasia. That Charcot's theory of aphasia did not give such pre-eminence to the acoustic element is true (Ross 1887, pp. 87ff; Miraillé, 1896; Ombredane, 1951, pp. 102–6); but neither did his theory *privilege* the visual element of the word (it would be difficult to imagine a theory that did). Secondly, it would seem to ask too much of the historical evidence to relate *so* directly the therapy of the neuroses and the theory of language found in aphasia studies. The chain of argument between Freud's emphasis on the acoustic impression and the therapeutic listening of the doctor is not clear in any of his writings, nor does it seem plausible to reconstruct such a link.[39]

But we are still left with a fertile opposition: that between the dramatic visuality of Charcot's therapy, in which the doctor's presence as master, as we have seen, seems preeminent, and the literary aurality of Freud's talking cure. To link this opposition with Freud's theory of aphasia would seem to be a plausible hypothesis. But beyond its *a priori* plausibility there appears little evidence in favour of it, unless we can bring ourselves to convert into a major theoretical statement such remarks as Charcot's 'Je ne suis qu'un visuel' (Entralgo, 1969, p. 139), a remark that may have definite links with his theory of 'sensory character types' and his theory of aphasia, but does not seem to advance very far into the complex relations of the theory and therapy of the neuroses. What we *can* argue, I believe, is the following: the transition from the cure by dramatic presence to the cure by the magical power of words was *supported* at the theoretical level by the possibilities offered by Freud's theory of language, elaborated with respect to aphasia, as to the psychological mechanisms of the cure through words. In the *Project*, to which we now turn, we find that the speech system receives an inordinate emphasis in its relations with the other systems, and particularly with respect to consciousness. Indeed, the importance of the 'speech apparatus' is such that the same theory, set out first in the *Project*, can be found repeated and remoulded in some of Freud's most important metapsychological writings: Chapter VII of *The Interpretation of Dreams*, 'On the Two Principles of Mental Functioning', *The Ego and the Id*, 'The Unconscious' and *An Outline of Psychoanalysis*.[40]

2 The Metapsychology of Speech

postcard; " I live in silence here
a wet winter   the baby's well
I give her bear's names   Ursula
Mischa   Pola   Living alone makes
anyone crazy,   especially with children"

I live in silence here
x is the condition of my silence
s/he

the tongue as a swan's neck
full and heavy in the mouth

speech as a sexed thing

the speaking limb is stilled

Denise Riley

The *Project for a Scientific Psychology* of 1895 represented an attempt to fuse a sophisticated theory of the psychic apparatus with the concepts needed to explain the structure and aetiology of hysterical symptoms. In the first section of this chapter we will be concerned with the precise function of the 'zone of language' in 'a machine that in a moment would run of itself'. (Freud (1950a) *Origins*, (20 Oct 1895) p. 129). A general account of the *Project*, impenetrable as it will remain, is necessary.[1]

CONSTRUCTING THE MACHINE

The construction of the systems of neurones that make up the psychic apparatus proceeds, as so often with Freud, through binary distinctions.

Firstly, we must distinguish system ϕ and system ψ, respectively corresponding to a system for the reception of external stimuli and a system that records the passage of stimuli. System ψ, on the 'interior' and shielded by ϕ from the 'outside', receives continuous endogenous stimuli from the 'interior'. The natural tendency of neurones to discharge themselves of any accumulated quantity (Q) is offset by the necessity to have Q available in order to control the direction and form of discharge. The nucleus of ψ, which receives its cathexis – or 'charge' of Q^2 – from within, retains a constant level of Q, and thus is able to control overhasty discharge by inhibiting the flow of Q. This nucleus, the ego, performs its inhibitory function by changing the relative value of 'facilitations' (or resistances of the walls of the neurones), thus preventing Q from flowing away to motor neurones, whose activation will signal the initiation of action.

The level of facilitations in ψ corresponds to the memory-system: when Q passes from ϕ to ψ facilitations along its path change their value, thus representing a record of the Q that has passed. If an inner state of need – that is, high cathexis of ψ neurones – arises, a 'specific action' that allows satisfactory motor discharge of this cathexis will create facilitations between the internally cathected neurone and the perceptions that accompanied the 'experience of satisfaction'. Freud took as his example the state of hunger in a newborn infant. The experience of satisfaction consists in sucking milk at the breast: the accompanying perceptions reaching ψ via ϕ – the visual image of the breast and the report of the muscular movements involved in sucking – pass from ϕ to ψ and create facilitations between the 'hunger' neurone cathected from within and the neurones corresponding to these two perceptions. When the need arises again, Q flows this time from the 'hunger' neurone to the image of the breast and the motor image of sucking, and is discharged into ϕ – that is, the baby hallucinates the breast and mimes the movement of sucking.

But this repetition of the experience of satisfaction does not lead to 'real' satisfaction: it does not arrest the build-up of endogenous stimuli from within. The level of unpleasure in the psychic apparatus increases. A second attempt to bring about the experience of satisfaction now follows: the pathway of internal change, by which the 'expression of the emotions' is produced.[3] These seemingly random innervations of the muscular system, which include screaming, are all aimed at discharging the accumulated Q through motor pathways. But again, the experience of satisfaction eludes the subject, unless help is attracted by these motor discharges, particularly by the scream, and the helper then carries out the specific action for the infant. The scream thus lays the foundation for an understanding between the helpless infant and other human beings: the infant's helplessness lays the foundation for all morality.

This accidentally successful achievement of the experience of satisfaction, although it lays the foundation for an understanding with others that will provide the means for attaining satisfaction, does not avoid a large amount of unpleasure. What is needed is both a means of keeping unpleasure to a minimum and a means of controlling the body so as to facilitate the attainment of a situation in which motor innervation – discharge – will achieve its goal in reality, as well as in the perceptual field. The system of the ego attains the first goal by inhibiting all large flow of quantity, and hence of discharge, until 'indications of reality' are received by ψ, informing it that the cathected neurones in ψ – i.e. the image of the object that is wished for – coincide with the perceptions received from the exterior. When a 'perceptual identity' of this sort has been achieved, the ego relaxes the inhibition, and discharge, not only of the 'hunger' neurone, but also to some extent of the ego itself, takes place: the experience of satisfaction is repeated in reality.

The control of the body necessary in order to bring perceptions to identity with the wished-for idea is attained via a process of thought, taking as its object the random movements of the body that were associated in the past with the experience of satisfaction. The ego, while inhibiting the movements of large Q in ψ, allows small Q to retrace the facilitations that are connected with the representation of the wished-for object, the breast, and the representation of the wished-for action, sucking. In this way, the ego finds a set of facilitations that correspond to a set of representations of actions, whose performance will result in perceptual identity being attained. Having successfully conducted this process of thought, which results in thought-identity, the ego releases the pathways that thought has found to lead to the memory of the experience of satisfaction: both a preparatory set of actions and the specific action itself are carried out.

But this account of the process of thought raises a problem. In the process of retracing the facilitations laid down by past experience, a certain cathexis of neurones corresponding to perceptions takes place – indeed, this cathexis, accompanied by an inhibition of discharge and the flow of large Q, *is* the process of thought. How can the ego distinguish between the cathexes resulting from the flow of Q from ϕ to ψ and cathexes owing to its own thought-activity? The first answer Freud gave to this problem depended upon the properties of a third system of neurones that he posited in order to explain the existence of consciousness. The primary attribute of consciousness, according to Freud, is that it possesses *quality*, whereas the systems ϕ and ψ deal only in the passage of Q.

Quality is most manifest in perception; thus the third system, W or ω, is responsive to reception of stimuli by ϕ, but not directly responsive to the processes of marking in ψ. Quality itself is a periodic property of Q received from 'outside', completely independent of the level of Q in both ϕ and ψ. Thus the system ω only registers the quality derived from external stimuli reaching ϕ, and passing through ψ. Registration of quality in ω thus corresponds to *conscious* perception.

Freud then posited that the ω neurones discharge when they are excited by perceptual stimuli, and a report of this discharge is received by ψ. 'It is this report of a discharge coming from ω that constitutues an indication of quality or reality to ψ.'[4] (Freud (1950a) SE I 325.) Perceptions are thus distinguished from the memories cathected during the process of thought (ideas) by the signals supplied by these indications of reality (*Realitätszeichen*).

Little by little, in Freud's account, the emphasis shifts first from the relations between ψ and ϕ to the relations between ψ and ω (the perceptual neurones), and then to the relations between ψ and the indications of discharge (quality – reality) coming from motor neurones attached to the system ω. In order to consolidate the interest that ψ takes in perceptual discharges, owing to the constant recurrence, if not constant presence, of cathected wishful ideas in ψ, Freud postulated a mechanism of attention, in which the ego uses its own Q to cathect those perceptual neurones that have become excited.

But, so far, this mechanism of attention and the attribute of consciousness only apply to perceptions. Thought, the means by which the 'information' derived from perceptions can be converted into the 'planning' of an action designed to relieve ψ (the ego) of the build-up of endogenous stimuli, seems to be losing out. None of these mechanisms facilitate the processes of thought. What Freud then introduced was a 'sub-system' that guaranteed both that attention could be given to thought and that thought could become conscious. This sub-system was the *speech associations*.

The speech associations provide a circumscribed and exclusive system of perceptual (auditory image) and motor (verbal image) neurones. If, during the process of thought, those memories that are cathected because of their proximity to the wished-for idea and to the simultaneously cathected perceptual neurones themselves allow a 'branch-stream' of Q to pass to the speech associations, then the consequent discharges of the speech associations constitute a new order of indications of quality. Thus thought can now have attention directed to it. Just as it is biologically advantageous for ψ to prepare for possible important perceptions by 'pre-cathecting' perceptual neurones, so it is equally advantageous for the ego to pre-cathect the verbal images so as to create 'a mechanism for directing the ψ-cathexis to the memories which emerge during the passage of Q. Here we have conscious, observant thought'. (Freud (1950a) SE I 365)

It is as if, without the sustaining system of speech, thought will come to a standstill for lack of guidance as to what memories to cathect and for lack of Q with which to overcome the large number of resistances (facilitations) involved in long and complex trains of thought. The indications of quality provided by speech allow the ego to send Q to those neurones in ψ which are needed for thought-processes. It is in this sense that Freud states that speech-associations 'make cognition possible'. (Ibid)

But not only does speech make cognition possible, it makes it possible to *record* thought, to treat thought as though it were experience. Thought consists in small flows of Q in ψ, directed by the ego. If this is so, then these passages will create facilitations. How is the ego to distinguish the results of perception from results of thought processes, since both consist in changed facilitations in ψ? The indications of quality from the perceptual neurones inform the ego of what is a memory and what is a perception here and now; but they do not distinguish between memories of perceptions and memories of thought. At this point Freud's argument became confused; I quote:

Now ψ has no means of distinguishing [the results of thought-processes] from the results of perceptual processes. It may be possible to recognize and reproduce perceptual processes through their being associated with discharges of perception; but the facilitations produced by *thought* leave only their result behind them and not a *memory*. A thought-facilitation may have arisen equally well from a single intensive process or from ten less impressive ones. Now the indications of discharge by way of speech help to make good this lack. They put thought-processes on a level with perceptual processes; they lend them reality and *make it possible to remember them*. (Ibid. SE I 365)

Surely, we might ask, a memory *consists* in a facilitation? If this is so, then the result of thought-processes is a facilitation in no way different from a memory. Did not Freud demonstrate, at the beginning of the *Project*, that 'memory is represented by the facilitations existing between the ψ-neurones' (Ibid., SE I 300)? What perhaps led him to a confusion at this point was the introduction of the terminology of 'memory-images' when he came to discuss the experience of pain, thus tempting him to make a distinction between a facilitation and other sorts of memory based upon a notion of a duplication of a perceptual image. But this hypothesis apart, we can see the problem to which Freud addressed himself: how to distinguish between facilitations following upon the flow of Q from ϕ to ψ (i.e. the memory of a perception) and the facilitations following upon the flow of Q within ψ, as regulated by the central inhibitory agency, the ego, and provoked by the difference between the wishful idea, itself activated by the accumulation of endogenous stimuli, and the indications of quality proceeding from ω (i.e. the memory of a thought).[5] When clarified, Freud's argument then amounts to this: a memory of a perception consists not only of the facilitations left behind by the passage of Q from ϕ into ψ and its dissipation, but also of a record of the indications of quality that came from ω when this perception was made. Similarly, the indications of speech give rise to a record of a signal of quality when Q flows in ψ – i.e. when thought takes place. Thus:

Memory of a perception $= \psi$ facilitations + indications of quality from ω

Memory of a thought $\quad = \psi$ facilitations + indications of quality from speech.

A further question might now be asked: how does the ego distinguish between indications of quality from ω and indications of quality from speech?

Freud gave no direct answer to this question, but we may be able to piece one together from the elements of his theory. To do so, we must return to two passages: the first in *On Aphasia*, where he sets out the two systems of word-presentations and object-associations (Chapter 1, p. 28), and the second when he introduced the system of speech-associations in Part III of the *Project*. In both passages he stated that the system of word-presentations is 'closed' (*geschlossen*). In *On Aphasia*, he explicitly contrasted it with the 'open' system of object-associations. In addition, in the *Project*, he stated that:

Speech associations consists in the linking of ψ neurones with neurones which serve sound-presentations and themselves have the closest association with motor speech-images. These associations have an advantage of two characteristics over the others: they are limited [*geschlossen*] (few in number) and exclusive. (Ibid. SE I 365)

What significance could this difference have? The closed system of word-presentations – the limited number of sounds that go to make up the elements of a natural language – becomes instantly recognizable as such, precisely because of the finite – indeed small – number of elementary units that could possibly be included in any given perceptual sequence (or registration of perceptual sequence). It is quite probably this feature of the word-system that allows one both to distinguish quickly between a component of a word and any other noise, and also to screen out other noises, by some process of selective attention.[6] With the 'open' system of object-associations, on the other hand, the continual novelty *and* the necessity for paying attention to such novelties, in order to discover whether they are significant novelties (both in an absolute sense and in a sense relative to the needs of practical thought), entails an ever-growing difference in the order of magnitude of the number of elementary units of object-associations as compared with word-presentations (whether the former be based on a stable species of unit, or, as is more likely, they are continually being recoded). Such a distinction in the behaviour of the two systems, although not an absolute one – since we must not forget that, as Freud's poem/alphabet metaphor suggests, we are dealing with arbitrary representations at both the level of object-associations and the level of word-presentations – could form the foundation for a means for distinguishing the two registers of psychical quality. Hence the thought-processes are now put on a par with perception, through the assistance of the speech associations; but only at the cost of an opacity that Freud passed over: a means for *recording* indications of quality.

But this opacity is partially illuminated by a further argument. What is recorded are the indications of discharge – the kinaesthetic images of *On Aphasia* – that is, reports of the subject's own motor activity. This means of recording also gives speech another important task. Freud outlined the development of the speech function from the path of internal change mentioned above (p. 41), the blind safety-valve that did not lead to the experience of satisfaction, but which now takes on a very great importance.

There are . . . objects (perceptions) which make one *scream* because they cause pain; and it is an immensely significant fact that this association of a sound (which also gives rise to motor images of the subject's own movements) with a perception that is already a complex one emphasizes the *hostile* character of the object and serves to draw attention to the perception. Whereas otherwise, owing to the pain, one would have received no clear indications of quality from the object, the report of one's own scream serves to characterize the object. This association is thus a means of making conscious memories that cause *unpleasure* and of bringing attention to bear upon them: the first class of *conscious memories* has been created. It is a short step from here to the invention of speech. (Ibid. SE I 366–7)

Thus speech – or its genetic precursor, the scream – introduces the possibility of thinking about a pain-causing object without evoking the pain associated with that object. Instead of instituting the primary defence – 'a repulsion, a disinclination to keep the hostile memory-image cathected' (Ibid. SE I 367) – whenever thought comes close to such a memory, inhibition of that ψ-pathway can be maintained while a 'representation' of that memory, a word, can take its place in the thought-process. Thus speech makes possible cognitive or theoretical thinking: thought that can survey *any* pathway in ψ, regardless of the pleasure or unpleasure associated with the cathexis of a memory of a perception that originally caused pain.

The 'opacity' is now clarified by a simple expedient or observation: speech associations themselves give rise to external perceptions. In this way, thought finds what Freud later called a 'special sensory surface': thought finds a way to become perception.

There are objects of a second kind which are themselves constantly giving vent to certain noises – objects, that is, in whose perceptual complex a sound plays a part. In consequence of the impulse to *imitate* which emerges during the process of judging (as to what is similar or different from the subject), it is possible to find a report of a movement (of one's own) attaching to this sound-image. So that this class of memories too can now become conscious. It remains to associate *deliberately produced* sounds with perceptions. When this is done, the memories that arise when one observes indications of discharges by way of sound become conscious like perceptions and can be cathected from ψ . . . . It is well known that what is known as "conscious" thought is accompanied by a slight motor expenditure. (Ibid. SE I 367)

This 'double' account of the beginnings of speech thus highlights two different thought activities:

i. thought concerning a painful memory
ii. memories of thought-processes as distinct from memories of perceptions.

It is clear that in the second case, when one deliberately produces sounds oneself, one is making possible conscious thought about an object that is not present. But it is also true that speech derived from the scream associated with a pain-giving object makes possible conscious thought in the *effective* absence of the representation of that object, since the evocation of the latter, both at the level of consciousness and at the level of normal ψ-processes, is prevented by the action of primary defence, that is, the avoidance of any pathway leading to a cathexis of the pain-giving object's representation. Thus speech pathways act as a 'neutral' alternative set of pathways for thought concerning a painful memory; they provide a second code for the processes of cognitive thought. Thought can now be maintained for an indefinite period of time in the absence of the object; speech seems to be intimately bound up with the absence of the representation of the object.

Speech allows the ψ system to suspend both imperatives of the pleasure principle; it allows thought concerning pain-producing objects to take place as easily as with relatively neutral memories, and it ensures that thought does not get 'stuck' pursuing immediate pleasure. Speech 'ensures the impartiality of the course of association.' (Ibid. SE I 373–4). Only one device can secure thought from either the avoidance of unpleasure or an excessive attention to wishful ideas and purposive association: the indications of quality aroused by speech. Speech residues are not purposive ideas and thus can never hinder association. Speech gains its importance from its uselessness, from the fact that it is *not* a specific action.[7]

But Freud was equivocal about the absolute importance of these speech residues. Practical thought can be conducted without them, although there, as in cognitive thought, 'indications of quality ensure and fix the course of association'. (Ibid. SE I 378) Or, again, Freud asserted that 'the reproducibility of thought-processes extends far beyond their indications of quality; they can be made conscious subsequently . . . ' (Ibid. SE I 380). What these equivocations amount to is this: Freud took it as given that thought could take place *without* the indications of quality derived from speech residues being involved, i.e. he assumed that thought without words was possible. But, aside from the system of word associations, he had no appropriate mechanism either for distinguishing this wordless thought from perception or for assigning to wordless thought the reality and importance it obviously did have over and against perception. Having achieved both of these latter tasks with the system of word associations, these seemed to put the mechanism of thought into a decidedly secondary position. The protest of Freud's own 'common sense' or 'better judgement' against the logic of his own conceptual machinery was to remain in this cautionary and equivocating mode throughout the metapsychological writings of the next forty years.[8]

But let us summarize the three main claims the *Project* made as to the function of speech associations:

i. Speech makes possible a second reality, on a level with the reality accorded to perception; this is thought- or psychic-reality.
ii. speech makes possible conscious memories, by giving the system of memories access to a system whose cathexis and discharge is perceptual in character, without coming from 'outside'.
iii. speech allows both pleasure and unpleasure to be avoided, so that *all* parts of the mental apparatus are accessible to thought-processes at *all* times.

THE MACHINE SPEAKS

But, somehow, this machine refused to run. We do not know exactly why Freud discarded the *Project*: in the letters to Fliess he simply exclaimed: 'I no longer understand the state of mind in which I concocted the psychology . . . it seems to me to have been a kind of aberration.' (Freud (1950a) *Origins* (29 Nov. 1895) p. 134). Five weeks after writing this he was back tinkering with the model, schematically indicating 'a complete revision of all my $\phi\psi\omega$ theories'. (Ibid. (1 Jan. 1896), p. 141). The most substantial change was a more clearcut demarcation between ψ, on the one hand, and ϕ and ω on the other. No Q actually flowed from ϕ and ψ; rather, a record of ϕ's reception of stimuli was achieved as a side-effect, through a sort of induction or excitation of ψ by ω. Thus ω became both more central to the recording of external events in ψ, while ψ became more independent of both ϕ and ω. ψ was now the seat of unconscious processes which could, as before, only 'subsequently acquire a secondary, artificial consciousness by being linked with processes of discharge and perception (with speech-associations)'. (Ibid.) Perceptual processes, on the other hand, automatically involved consciousness.

The new model made clearer the two different 'consciousnesses' of the *Project*. In the latter, consciousness consisted of the excitation of ω by ψ *plus* an indication of quality (either from ϕ via ψ or from ψ via the speech associations). In the new model, perceptual consciousness consisted in the transfer of small Q from ϕ to ω and the transfer of quality from ϕ to ω, whereas 'secondary, artificial consciousness' arose from the 'opposite side' of ω: excitation of ω by ψ plus an indication of quality from speech associations.

But why make this clarification? True, as Freud argued in his letter, it seemed to reduce the arbitrary assumptions of the model.[9] But it seemed to do little for the theory of the neuroses, the search for a solution of which had, after all, both led Freud into his new psychology and remained the main aim of that psychology. In the *Project*, Freud had devoted a relatively small central section to the genesis of hysteria. His argument boiled down to the following: hysteria was characterized by an 'immovable symbolization' (Ibid. SE I 352) due to pathological defence. That is, defence had resulted in the avoidance of an idea for no 'good' reason, because it produces unpleasure; consequently, displacement onto a substitute idea took place. Why couldn't the ego work over the pain associated with this idea? Precisely because, when it occurred, the experience had not been painful, only becoming so because of an internal change in the quantitative cathexis of the idea. Pathological defence – repression – only affected memories, not perceptions, and only memories that aroused pain that had not been elicited at the time of perception.

We invariably find that a memory is repressed which has only become a trauma *after the event*. . . . Attention is focused on perceptions, which are the normal occasions for the release of unpleasure. But here it is not a perception but a memory-trace which unexpectedly releases unpleasure, and the ego discovers this too late. It has permitted a primary process, because it did not expect one. (Ibid. SE I 356–8)

The one class of memories that could act in this way were those of 'presexual' sexual experiences, which had aroused little or no unpleasure or affect at the time at which they had been perceptions, but which, owing to the increase of internal Q supplied to that class of memories at puberty, could release large amounts of unpleasure if aroused after puberty: 'the retardation of puberty makes possible the occurrence of posthumous primary processes'. (Ibid. SE I 359).

This explanation of *why* repression occurs was not very satisfactory and the revisions of the following months did not improve it. We might well ask: why doesn't the process of cognitive thought, made possible by speech, in which attention can be directed to any ψ-pathway, anticipate the change in condition of the memory of the pre-sexual experience consequent upon puberty, and thus anticipate the release of unpleasure from a related post-pubertal experience? Is it that there is something inherently recalcitrant in sexual experience which makes it difficult to think about or to put into words? Such a solution to the problem of repression was to be entertained by Freud in later years, but it obviously left more questions unanswered than it solved. In fact, Freud always found this problem recalcitrant, returning to it frequently. One answer he gave, in the paper on 'Repression', postulated a primary repression which fixed a certain relationship between an idea (memory) and a (sexual) instinct: such an answer still did not approach the question 'why?'. But, from the *Project* on, it would seem that Freud became sensitive to the sort of considerations we have raised concerning the use of speech associations to work over a memory whose condition has changed since its original registration.

In essence Freud's idea was this: repression was due to a lack of synchronization between the inhibitory activity of the ego, further regulated by the speech associations, and the internal excitations due to the sexual processes. The argument in the *Project* had relied solely upon a temporal discontinuity in the level of sexual excitations introduced by the threshold of puberty. Since, as we noted, this explanation seemed to be open to objections arising from the properties of the '$\phi\psi\omega$', why not look to the other side of the process, the mechanisms of inhibition, for the factor predisposing to repression? In other words, why not look to the stages of the development of thought, or, following Ferenczi, the stages in the development of a sense of reality, for the discontinuities that give occasion for the specific vulnerability of the mental apparatus to which repression witnesses?[10] It was true that this angle of approach would not explain why it seemed to be *sexual* experiences and only sexual experiences which were the initial occasion for repression. But Freud recognized that his attempt to find the sufficient condition for repression in the amplifying factor of puberty had not supplied a very satisfactory explanation; and in the years 1895–98 he had little clear idea of additional factors specific to the development of sexual excitations that would provide a sufficient condition for repression. So it was probable that factors on both sides of the equation would prove necessary: one factor, on the side of sexuality, in order to explain why the traumatic experience was always sexual; and another factor, on the side of the development of thought, in order to explain why such a sexual experience could be a trauma.

But, for a time after he had scribbled out the *Project*, and probably as a result of its persistent interest for him, Freud continued to tinker with the 'thought' side of the equation. And, since speech was such an important part of the apparatus for inhibiting unpleasure and producing conscious (as opposed to repressed) ideas, the chronology of the development of language seemed a likely place to look for the conditions under which repression might occur. Thus it was not only the clinical data – the traumas that kept being pushed back earlier and earlier, that were buried deeper and deeper – that led Freud into the prehistoric past; it was also the search for conditions indicating a certain vulnerability of the psychic apparatus that led him to the early years of experience – led him, that is, to a period that would always be as much pre-verbal as it was to be pre-Oedipal.[11]

At the end of 1896, Freud tried out a new schema.

Thus what is essentially new in my theory is the thesis that memory is present not once but several times over, that it is registered in various species of 'signs'. (I postulated a similar rearrangement some time ago, in my study of aphasia, for the paths leading from the periphery. [See Chapter 1, p. 24]) . . . I have illustrated this in the following schematic picture . . .

```
              I              II        III
  Pcpt.     Pcpt.-s        Uc.      Pc.            Consc.
  X  X——X    X————X        X—X  X————————X  X
     X       X   X            X    X              X
                          X
```

Pcpt. are neurones in which perceptions appear and to which consciousness is attached but which in themselves retain no trace of what happens. For *consciousness and memory are mutually exclusive*. *Pcpt.-s.* is the first registration of the perceptions; it is quite incapable of being conscious and is arranged according to associations of simultaneity.

Uc. (unconsciousness) is a second registration, or transcription, ... *Uc.* traces may correspond to conceptual memories; they too are inaccessible to consciousness.

Pc. (preconsciousness) is the third transcription, attached to verbal images and corresponding to the official ego. The cathexes proceeding from this *Pc.* become conscious in accordance with certain rules. This secondary "thought-consciousness" is subsequent in time and probably connected with the hallucinatory activation of verbal images; so that the neurones of consciousness would once again be perceptual neurones and in themselves devoid of memory.

. . . . I must emphasize the fact that the successive transcripts represent the psychical achievement of successive epochs of life. At the frontier between any two such epochs a translation of the psychical material must take place. I explain the peculiarity of the psychoneuroses by supposing that the translation of some of the material has not occurred. . . . A failure of translation is what we know clinically as 'repression'. (Ibid. (2 Nov. 1896) SE I 233–5)

The picture of repression is quite simple: failure of a memory to be translated into words (or into the system *Uc.*) allows the memory to 'proliferate' according to a different set of psychical laws that govern the earlier psychical epoch, thus giving rise to the strange symptomatic formations of neurosis. The process of becoming conscious, 'as regards memories, consists for the most part in the appropriate verbal consciousness – that is, in access to the associated verbal images.' In hysteria 'the [sexual] scenes occur during the first period of childhood (up to 4), in which memory traces cannot be translated into verbal images.' (Ibid. 30 May 1896, SE I 230–2). As a consequence, the symptoms of the neurosis are physical rather than psychical.

Now we see clearly how this mixture of clinical hypotheses and hypothetical models of the psychical apparatus revolved around the concept of a failure of translation, both in terms of the specific symptoms that were analysed in the consulting-room, and in a failure of 'translation' in the theoretical model. The system of verbal images provided the link between the practice of analysis, where the putting into words was both the explanatory and curative procedure, and the theory of the relations between the unconscious and the conscious. Very little of the details found in these hypotheses was to survive into Freud's published work. But they indicate clearly why it was so important to construct theories in which the relations of speech to consciousness were so prominent.

The juggling by which Freud tried to integrate the different organic developments of the sexual and mental apparatuses explains why his theories as to the period at which the speech residues take up their dominant role showed such variable chronologies. In letter 46, the age correlating pre-verbal experience and sexual traumas giving rise to hysteria is age 4; in letter 47, Freud seemed certain of this correlation:

> . . . I have become convinced of something in the last piece of theorizing – hysteria up to the age of four – inability to translate into verbal ideas also belongs only to that period. (Ibid. (4 June 1896) p. 167)

But in the more complex system of transcriptions, *Pcpt./Pcpt.s./ Uc./Pcs./Consc.*, a new chronology, in which verbal trans-lations were effected from age 8–15, made the relations between sexual experience and speech more complex. Then, in letter 55 of January 1897, we find a new chronology: psychosis is determined by traumatic events occurring 'before the psychical apparatus has been completed in its first form (from $1\frac{1}{4}$ to $1\frac{1}{2}$ years of age)'. (Ibid. SE I 240.) And how are we to connect this prehistoric perturbation with the following notion: 'An increase in the uninhibited processes to the point of their being alone in possession of the path to verbal consciousness produces psychosis.' (Ibid. (30 May 1896) SE I 232)? Such a connection was there to be made; Freud was to wait until 1915, as we will see, before publishing it.

The machine for producing consciousness that the *Project* set in motion faded into the background as Freud searched more on the side of sexuality for a genetic account of the aetiology of the neuroses. This account in turn lapsed as his interest was caught by the internal content of the neurotic symptoms – phantasy and its relation to early sexual experiences. Having abandoned much of his theory of the neuroses when the seduction theory proved itself a red herring, Freud turned, almost in consolation, to the one unequivocally secure product of his self-analysis: the interpretation of dreams.

Chapter VII of *The Interpretation of Dreams* was a reworking of the *Project*. Freud returned the systems ϕ, ψ, and ω to their original order, redefining them without recourse to the properties of neurones, and absorbing them all into a new system ψ. We will not give a detailed account of the new model of ψ: we will simply note that the position that consciousness and the speech associations occupied was virtually identical to that in the *Project*. With one difference – a clarification: the system *Pcs.* was clearly separated from the system *Ucs.*, *Pcs.* and *Ucs.* thus corresponding to thought-processes in ψ and processes involving large flows of Q, respectively. Consciousness itself was, as was ω, a system for the registration of psychical qualities; in *The Interpretation of Dreams* Freud called it a 'sense-organ for the apprehension of psychical qualities.' (Freud (1900a) SE V 574)[12] And, as in the *Project*, it was the system of speech residues that made conscious thought possible:

> In order that thought-processes may acquire quality, they are associated in human beings with verbal memories, whose residues of quality are sufficient to draw the attention of consciousness to them and to endow the process of thinking with a new mobile cathexis from consciousness. (Ibid. SE V 617)

Or, as he put it earlier in the book, 'the *Pcs.* system needed to have qualities of its own which could attract consciousness; and it seems highly probable that it obtained them by linking the preconscious processes with the mnemic system of indications of speech, a system which was not without quality.' (Ibid. SE V 574 (translation modified)). With this new system of qualities, a second and finer regulation of the flow of quantity becomes possible. Just as in the *Project*, speech makes possible dispassionate thought-processes, so that ψ is not regulated by the unpleasure or pleasure promised by the balance of cathexes at any one time. And it is this 'dispassionate' and second level of regulation that both gives consciousness its *raison d'être* and gives man his superiority over animals.

Had Freud made any advance towards clarifying the question of what makes repression possible? Certainly he was sure that repression acted first and last upon memories; many was the time, as we shall see in later chapters, in later psychoanalytic discussions, that he was to have forcibly to remind his colleagues of this primary datum. He thus looked to certain characteristics of memory for the causes of repression. Now, the structure of both $\phi\psi\omega$ (*Project*) and ψ (*The Interpretation of Dreams*) was built around the thesis that memory and consciousness were mutually exclusive. Obviously perceptions were not susceptible to repression, since they brought 'with them' the quality that then ensured them the prospect of binding that protected ideas from repression. We begin to see the difficulty that must attach to any claim that something that has once been a perception can become repressed.

But if we look at the question from the side of a memory already stored in the *Ucs.*, we might be tempted to argue that its lack of quality leaves it prey to repression. Freud sketched out this position in *The Interpretation of Dreams*:

> Repression affects memories more easily than perceptions, because memories cannot receive the extra cathexis provided by the excitation of the psychical sense organ. (Ibid. SE V 617)

As we pointed out at some length above, such an argument leaves out of the accounting the excitation that can be aroused by the perception of speech residues linked with these memories. In other words, Freud would have to argue that repression acts upon memories that, for one reason or another, fail to be associated with speech residues. That is, repression acts upon those memories that cannot or have not been put into words. We seem to be coming close to a set of concepts linked by a series of tautologous definitions. Rather than being a criticism of the theory, it might well be a recommendation. What it might indicate to us is this: the true cause of repression will not be found by an examination of the conditions governing the phenomena of memory. Instead, another realm will have to be investigated; it was in the complexities of 'instinctual life' that Freud then searched for the true cause of repression.

A month after completing *The Interpretation of Dreams*, Freud recalled some of the chronological concerns that had preoccupied him in his search for the conditions governing repression:

> What makes a person a hysteric instead of a paranoiac? My first crude answer, at the time when I was still trying to take the citadel by storm, was that I thought it depended on the age at which the sexual traumas occurred – on the time of the experience. I gave that up long ago, and have been without any clue until the last few days, when a connection with sexual theory opened up. (Freud (1950a), 9 Dec. 1899, SE I 279)

He went on to make an attempt to relate the time of traumatic experiences with a sequence of developmental phases of the sexual instincts, particularly with respect to the relation to the object. Sexual development replaced the phases of development of the mental apparatus. Or, rather, Freud was able to recognize that, given the necessity for developmental phases, it was necessary to postulate phases of sexual development, rather than those of a hypothetical mental apparatus. In this new formulation, what became of the factor dependent upon the development of language that he had earlier hypothesized as being of great importance both for the choice of neurosis and for the related and deeper question of the possibility of repression? Certainly the speech factor lost any genetic dimension; but it retained all of its value as the criterion by which to characterize the conscious and the unconscious. The *Three Essays on Sexuality*, written in 1905 after the long silence following *The Interpretation of Dreams* and *The Psychopathology of Everyday Life*, gave repression pride of place within a theory of the sexual instincts. But when Freud returned to his metapsychology in the 1910s, the theory which gave language pride of place was reaffirmed: in 1911 consciousness was defined as consisting in a secondary sensory surface that only verbal residues can activate (Freud (1911b) SE XII 221). And when Freud came to write his definitive essay on the concept of the unconscious, it was to the hypothesis of speech residues that he returned in order to sidestep the conceptual difficulties involved in both the dynamic and topographical conceptions of the unconscious.

It is intriguing that Freud introduced his discussion of the relation between verbal impressions and the nature of the unconscious with a return to the problem of the 'choice of neurosis'. But, having learnt his lesson in the 1890s, he no longer approached the problem from a genetic standpoint: he was to offer no more hypotheses about the relation between pre-verbal childhood and the structure of pathological products. Rather, here, his argument was clinical and logical in character.

> If we ask ourselves what it is that gives the character of strangeness to the substitutive formations and the symptoms of schizophrenia, we eventually come to realize that it is the predominance of what has to do with words over what has to do with things. (Freud (1915e) SE XIV 200)[13]

Instead of lacking words, as other neurotics seem to, the schizophrenic possesses a superfluity of words, a system of language that has been cut loose from any linkage with the unconscious thoughts controlled and directed by the activity of the ego. Schizophrenia is the mirror-image of asymbolic aphasia; where the aphasic loses the whole system of word presentations (or loses a part of that system, in accordance with a hierarchy of non-semantic functions of language, e.g. syntactical complexity), the schizophrenic loses the system of objects to which the word presentations attach. In either case, what appears on the surface of language, on that surface that consciousness perceives, is a salad of sterile fruits, cut off from the tree of thought. We recall Freud's suspicion of the 1890s, that psychosis was an overwhelming of the preconscious by the unconscious, in which the path of language itself has become invaded by the unconscious. But now he could supplement this description: in psychoses the objects are given up and the ego cathexes strive to return back onto them:

> . . . to accomplish this purpose they set off on a path that leads them to the object via the verbal part of it, but then find themselves obliged to be content with words instead of things. (Ibid. SE XIV 204)

The difference between schizophrenia and the psycho-neuroses reduces down to the question: which aspect of thought has been occluded, the thing-presentation or the word-presentation?

> We now seem to know all at once what the difference is between a conscious and an unconscious presentation. . . . the conscious presentation comprises the presentation of the thing plus the presentation of the word belonging to it, while the unconscious presentation is the presentation of the thing alone. . . . We can now state precisely what, in the transference neuroses, repression denies to the rejected presentation; it is the translation into words which should remain [*sollen bleiben*] attached to the object. A presentation which is not put into words, or a psychical act which is not hypercathected, remains thereafter in the *Ucs.* in a state of repression. (Ibid. SE XIV 201–2. Translation modified)

We should perhaps add one note to this: it is more precise, according to the schemes we have examined in this chapter, to say that the conscious presentation consists of the word presentation alone; by definition, the thing presentation cannot become conscious. But for the conscious presentations to avoid becoming pathological, as they do in schizophrenia or in philosophy, these word presentations must [*sollen*] retain an unimpaired relation to the unconscious thing-presentations.

What is perhaps peculiar in this passage, a passage that brought together into one definitive statement the concerns we have mapped out in this chapter, is one phrase: 'all at once'. It was as if Freud had just discovered this precise formulation of the difference between the conscious and the unconscious.[14] But, to us, following the theory of consciousness from 1891 to 1915, the theory seems to have been "already there" from the beginnings of psychoanalysis. It was Jung, as we shall see, who, in 1910, jogged Freud's memory of having once thought about the relations between verbal presentations and the unconscious. But we might offer the following hypothesis as to why it was necessary for Jung to jog Freud's memory, as to why he had forgotten the theory he had laid down in both the *Project* and *The Interpretation of Dreams*. Perhaps it was because he sought the essence of repression in the theory of sexuality – for example, in Fliess' notion that repression was an effect of the conflict between the masculine and feminine components of the bisexual constitution, a notion that Freud was explicitly to repudiate in the 1920s – hoping to find the mechanism of repression as a necessary 'side-effect' of organic processes of sexual development. Be that as it may, there can be no questioning the fact that, during the first decade of the 1900s, the thesis that language gives rise to consciousness was forgotten, was awoken by Jung's stimulus, but had to be rethought by Freud in the 'metapsychological period'; rethought to such an extent that the final formula we have quoted could provide him with a great deal of pleasure and satisfaction when he first communicated it to Abraham in December 1914 (Freud, 1965a p. 206).

We should now retrace our steps in order to gain an understanding of the relationship between the theory of consciousness and the therapy of the neuroses, the talking-cure. But in order to do this, we will find it useful to follow out the uses that Freud made of the theory in his last writings. In *The Ego and the Id* (1923) he repeated, with perhaps greater attention to detail, the ideas set out in 'The Unconscious':

> . . . the real difference between a *Ucs.* and a *Pcs.* idea (thought) consists in this: that the former is carried out on some material which remains unknown, whereas the latter (the *Pcs.*) is in addition brought into connection with word-presentations. This is the first attempt to indicate distinguishing marks for the two systems, the *Pcs.* and the *Ucs.*, other than their relation to consciousness. (Freud (1923b) SE XIX 20)

The material base of word-presentations is constituted by the residues of auditory perceptions, 'so that the system *Pcs.* has, as it were, a special sensory source'.

> . . . only something which has been a *Cs.* perception can become conscious, and that anything arising from within (apart from feelings) that seeks to become conscious must try to transform itself into external perceptions: this becomes possible by means of memory-traces [of words heard]. (Ibid.)

Things arising from within may attempt to become conscious by means other than memories of words; in these circumstances the result is hallucination. We catch a hint of Freud's chronological pre-occupations of the 1890s in a late paper:

> . . . in [hallucinations] something that has been experienced in infancy and then forgotten returns – something that the child has seen or heard at a time when he could still hardly speak and that now forces its way into consciousness . . . (Freud (1937d) SE XXIII 267)

In order to prevent hallucinations – a mistaking of memory for reality – reality-testing is necessary. It is as if the speech residues, by opening up the possibility of things internal becoming conscious, also open up the possibility for 'errors', for hallucinations, to occur – that is, they make possible psychosis.

Conscious processes on the periphery of the ego and everything else in the ego unconscious – such would be the simplest state of affairs that we might picture. And such may in fact be the state that prevails in animals. But in man there is an added complication through which internal processes in the ego may also acquire the quality of consciousness. This is the work of the function of speech, which brings material in the ego into a firm connection with mnemic residues of visual, but more particularly of auditory, perceptions. Thenceforward, the perceptual periphery of the cortical layer can be excited to a much greater extent from inside as well, internal events such as passages of ideas and thought-processes can become conscious, and a special device is called for in order to distinguish between the two possibilities – a device known as *reality-testing*. The equation 'perception = reality (external world)' no longer holds. Errors, which can now easily arise and do so regularly in dreams, are called *hallucinations*. (Freud (1940a) SE XXIII 162; cf. Ibid. SE XXIII 199 and (1939a) SE XXIII 97)

But why this continuous concern with the theory of consciousness? Perhaps it is as well to remind ourselves that psychoanalysis, though first and last the science of the unconscious, can *only* derive its working materials from consciousness.

But none of this implies that the quality of being conscious has lost its importance for us. It remains the one light which illuminates our path and leads us through the darkness of mental life. . . . our scientific work in psychology will consist in translating unconscious processes into conscious ones, and thus filling in the gaps in conscious perception. (Freud (1940b) SE XXIII 286)

In other words, the raw material of psychoanalysis is derived from one single source, consciousness, which itself relies upon two separate sources: perception and the presentations that become conscious through being connected with words. Now, in the actual procedure of analysis, the perceptual possibilities are cut to a minimum: the patient lies on a couch, the analyst takes up a position removed from the visual field of the patient. The analyst hears only words; the patient only has words in his or her consciousness.[15] There is a close fit between what comes to the consciousness of the patient and what comes to the ear of the analyst. The perceptual model of consciousness guaranteed a certain transparency between the unconscious of the patient and the ear of the analyst; the analyst seems to take up the 'inspectionist' function of consciousness. Not that Freud did not have some qualifications to make as to the character of the preconscious thus 'read out aloud' to the analyst.

It would not be correct, however, to think that connection with the mnemic residues of speech is a necessary precondition of the preconscious state. On the contrary, that state is independent of a connection with them, though the presence of that connection makes it safe to infer the preconscious nature of a process. The preconscious state, characterized on the one hand by having access to consciousness and on the other hand by its connection with the speech-residues is nevertheless something peculiar, the nature of which is not exhausted by these two characteristics. (Freud (1940a) SE XXIII 162)

Certainly the preconscious state is not sufficiently defined by connection with speech-residues; but, phenomenologically speaking, this is its most important characteristic. Freud was often to discuss the relations between the *Ucs.* and the *Cs.* as if the intermediary of words sufficed to provide the necessary links between the two, as if words were the alpha and omega of access to consciousness.[16] And we can see the concatenation of themes that made such an equation attractive: the talking cure, the transparency of words on the surface of the patient's consciousness, the privileged access of speech to consciousness and the way in which speech opens up thought-reality that itself both opens the way to 'hominization'[17] and allows the possibility of an error that makes of man an animal uniquely prey to neurosis.

So how can psychoanalysis effect a change in the forces governing repression?

. . . the question how we make something that is repressed (pre)conscious would be answered as follows. It is done by supplying *Pcs.* intermediate links through the work of analysis. Consciousness remains where it is, therefore, but, on the other hand, the *Ucs.* does not rise into the *Cs.* (Freud (1923b) SE XIX 21)

How can we interpret these 'intermediate links' as being anything other than speech residues? An affirmative answer seems over-determined on both theoretical and therapeutic grounds: psycho-analysis, as the talking-cure, requires first and last that the patient should *say* whatever comes into his head, and it is this surface of words that the analyst must study.

> A problem like: Where shall I probe now? should not exist. The patient shows the way, in that by following the basic rule (saying everything that comes into his head) he displays his mental surface from moment to moment. (Freud (1965a), 9 Jan 1908, p. 20)

And, on the theoretical side, the insistent repetition of Freud's theory of 'speech-consciousness' gives a clear and precise concept of the 'process of becoming conscious'.

We can now clarify the therapeutic process. In *The Interpretation of Dreams*, Freud wrote:

> [Psychotherapy's] task is to make it possible for the unconscious processes to be dealt with finally and be forgot-ten. . . . psychotherapy can pursue no other course than to subject the *Ucs.* to the domination of the *Pcs.* (Freud (1900a) SE V 578 (translation modified))

The sign that such a domination is at least possible is the coming to consciousness of unconscious contents via the necessary intermediary of speech. Even if speech in itself does not guarantee the taming of the unconscious, it at least guarantees that, whatever may be the process by which the preconscious allows the forgetting of what was so unforget-table, that process is no longer prevented from acting on memories through their being cut off from the preconscious. It is true that speech is not enough; but it is certainly necessary if conviction or belief, the final touchstones of therapeutic success, are to be attained.[18] Given the plurality of tasks that speech performs for ψ, it should now perhaps be less of a surprise that psychoanalysis starts and ends with a putting into words, according to its single fundamental rule: 'say it aloud'.[19] And this rule is so much more than just a convention that neither patient nor analyst could as much dream of dispensing with it as either could think of giving the other the moon.[20]

3 Symbolism

> Freud mentions various symbols: top hats are regularly phallic symbols, wooden things like tables are women, etc. His historical explanations of these symbols is absurd. We might say it is not needed anyway: it is the most natural thing in the world that a table should be that sort of symbol. (Wittgenstein, 1967, pp. 43–4)

From a cursory reading of *The Interpretation of Dreams* it is clear that there are two different modes of analysis being employed in the interpretation of individual dreams. The variorum edition produced by James Strachey makes it clear that the largest additions to the later editions of the book are to the sections on symbolism. Not only are there these textual additions but their character is markedly different from the sections written for the first edition. The two different interpretative methods seem to correspond to these two different times of writing.[1]

Freud was less theoretically oriented in these newer sections on symbolism: he introduces far more dreams than elsewhere, with less analysis and less detail of the life and loves of the dreamer. We can recognize this as part of a broader discursive movement in the development of psychoanalytic writing, from the short story style most evident in the Katherina feuilleton of *Studies on Hysteria*[2] to the schematism of the case history of the Wolfman, whose autobiography (Gardner (1973)) bears little relation to the anamnesis through which we are conducted in the psychoanalytic work. The movement is even clearer when we go beyond Freud's work to that of Melanie Klein, where the individual details of the patient's life, whose individuality *necessarily* had to be signalled by a blank in the early case-histories of Freud, figure not at all.

This parallel will be shown to be more than just that in this chapter. Simply put, the move is from a personalized interpretation to a stock interpretation, from an interpretation that puts order into a seemingly random set of psychic elements, to an interpretation that orders them through their translation into a more cursory tongue. In terms of the metaphor of translation, which we have already seen to be fruitful in psychoanalysis, but which we now perceive to be self-contradictory in some of its major tenets, the early method of interpretation favoured by Freud led the patient from the text of the dream, via the discursive production of new and disconnected elements, to a new and semantically richer form of discourse, whose principle of rationality springs from within, as it were, guaranteeing its truth in the feeling of certainty that Freud posited as the final arbiter of analytic interpretation.[3] In the later interpretative modes, the analyst searches for the interpretation that makes most sense of a given series of elements through a process of reduction of these elements to a more restricted language of meaningful signs. The concept of symbolism, as conceived of narrowly within the psychoanalytic tradition[4], bears much of the brunt of the work of reductive translation. This chapter will examine the introduction of the concept of symbolism into the armoury of psychoanalytical concepts, indicating the historical conditions that gave it its peculiar character.

Continuing our look through *The Interpretation of Dreams*, we are struck by the incidence of two names who made significant contributions to the later editions of that work: Wilhelm Stekel and Herbert Silberer. Again, we are intrigued to notice that both of their very different contributions were to the field of symbolism. But the substantive intellectual debate that took place within the early psychoanalytical group did not primarily concern the concepts of Stekel and Silberer. More hidden, but now more apparent through the recent publication of their correspondence, is the debate between Freud and Jung over the concept of the symbol. With Jung, the debate was by no means restricted to the subject of dreams. Indeed, it is the sphere of mythology and legend that occupied pride of place both in the collaboration and in the conceptual differences of Freud and Jung.

Freud presided over all the new developments in psychoanalysis, anxiously trying to ensure that his enthusiastic and zealous disciples did not step beyond the bounds of the science, bounds which he felt only he could define, and which would only reveal themselves in the dialectic of passionate and vitriolic debate. Without doubt, the major influences on Freud as a man coincided with the major influences on Freud as a scientist. Between 1890 and the First World War, two men entered his life and work, changing its direction and aiding the development of his theories: Wilhelm Fliess and Carl Gustav Jung. It is to Fliess that we owe the affirmation of biological faith that inheres in the *Three Essays on Sexuality*; it is to Jung that we owe the flowering of psychoanalysis as a science of culture.

When Freud and Jung began their correspondence in 1906, Freud had published a number of papers on the neuroses, *The Interpretation of Dreams*, *The Psychopathology of Everyday Life*, *Jokes and their Relation to the Unconscious* and the *Three Essays on Sexuality*. In the period from 1906 to 1913, when the two men were in constant correspondence, he published some far-ranging works that have become starting points for many sub-disciplines within the psychoanalytic universe: the first foray into child analysis (1907), the essays in non-therapeutic interpretation found in *Jensen's 'Gradiva'* and *Leonardo* (1910), the attempt to take the citadel of psychiatry by storm with a series of hypotheses about the nature of the psychoses and the Schreber case of 1911, and a preliminary dig into the prehistory of neurosis and civilization as found in *Totem and Taboo* (1912–13). Freud, never the most confident of men in his relationship to the public institutions of his world, found support and a champion in Jung, a man who could command respect and attention by dint of his personality and reputation. The intertwining of ideas that effloresced in their correspondence cannot compare with the depth or boldness of the correspondence with Fliess. But in those letters the programme for the psychoanalytic interpretation of culture was set out.

In trying to pick out the main strands of intellectual interaction between Freud and Jung, one becomes aware of nodes where especially important theoretical discussion arose. These issues were to become the foci of their later dissension: the nature of regression, infantile sexuality, the issue of present conflicts versus past events, the theory of the libido and the nature of symbols. Inevitably one of these nodes was the issue of *dementia praecox* and its psychoanalytic interpretation. Freud treasured his friendship with Jung for many reasons, amongst which was the hope that, through him, psychiatry would become annexed onto the psychoanalytic empire. Such a hope was moderated when Jung left his circle in 1913, taking with him many of those who, for a while, had made Freud feel 'a man of property' (Freud, 1963a, p. 23).

The interest in the products of psychosis gave rise, in a way which I will later explicate, to a preoccupation with myth and the primitive mind. This area was to be the area of greatest mutual concern, where hopes of fruitful collaboration were at their highest and where the cultural stakes were greatest. And it was to be in the arena of myth that Freud and Jung came to realize their disagreements. Ostensibly, this arena of research did not deal with the question of symbolism. But Jung certainly made this question the central one, since the founding dualism of his work was the opposition between symbolic and rational thought. From the time of this collaboration on, the articulation of the

psychoanalytic theory of myth and culture was inextricably bound up
with the theory of the symbol. But it is part of my contention that this
was always so: implicitly so, insofar as the methodology that was used
by the early analysts was philological in character; and explicitly so,
insofar as the theory of neurosis and the theory of dreams that were
extended to myth depended upon a concept of the symbol, albeit a
different one in each of these areas. For neurosis, Freud's early
conceptions were explicitly couched, as we have seen, in terms of the
role of 'symbolization'. And in dream theory, his interpretations were
explicitly directed against the 'symbolic' method of interpretation. In
the final analysis, Jung and Freud's differences lay in their perception of
the relationship between language, symbol and reality.

SYMBOLISM IN HYSTERIA

It is certainly premonitory that the first usage of the term 'symbolic' to
be found in the *Standard Edition* of Freud's works explicitly links the
symbolism found in hysteria with the type of thought relations found in
dreams:

> In other cases [of hysteria] the connection [between the precipitating
> event and the symptom] is not so simple. It consists only in what
> might be called a 'symbolic' relation between the precipitating cause
> and the pathological phenomenon – a relation such as healthy people
> form in dreams. (Breuer and Freud (1893a) SE II 5)

Breuer and Freud were here contrasting symbolic connections with
the associative connection by which the simpler forms of hysterical
symptom were formed. Contiguity in time seemed to be sufficient for a
certain pain or state of the body to become fixed in relation to an
insufficiently abreacted affect. The physical state then owed its preservation solely to its accidental temporal contiguity to a trauma. In
contrast, symbolism, or mnemic symbolism (*Erinnerungsymbol*) as it
was called throughout the *Studies*, referred to a more intimate
connection between the symptom and the affect. A verbal phrase, or
train of thought, served as intermediary between the affect and the pain.
The jump from physical pain to psychical pain is effected by such an
intermediary. Thus 'a neuralgia may follow upon mental pain or
vomiting upon a feeling of moral disgust'. (Breuer and Freud (1895d) SE
II 178)

In the majority of cases involving symbolization, Freud thought that the psyche made use of certain organic pains as the *locus* for the attaching of the repressed affect. The linkage was then forged using certain phrases or 'linguistic usages'. For example, the phrase 'a slap in the face' enabled the memory of an argument to become lodged in a trigeminal neuralgia (Ibid.). Freud was at pains to indicate the obscure details of the symbolic construction of the symptom:

> When I began to call up the traumatic scene, the patient saw herself back in a period of great mental irritability towards her husband. She described a conversation which she had had with him and a remark of his which she had felt as a bitter insult. Suddenly she put her hand to her cheek, gave a loud cry of pain and said: 'It was like a slap in the face'. With this her pain and her attack were both at an end.
>
> There is no doubt that what had happened had been a symboliz-ation. She had felt as though she had actually been given a slap in the face. Everybody will immediately ask how it was that the sensation of a 'slap in the face' came to take on the outward forms of a trigeminal neuralgia, why it was restricted to the second and third branches, and why it was made worse by opening the mouth and chewing – though, incidentally, not by talking. (Ibid.)

The mechanism of symbolization involves the enactment of the literal meaning of a verbally figurative expression: the figurative expression 'slap in the face' was expressed as a facial neuralgia. If Frau Cäcilie M. – the patient in question – had not 'retained' her feelings of being insulted and had expressed them in the way appropriate to a civilized woman – i.e. through speech – then she would not have converted her bottled-up feelings into the symptom, via the symbolic expression. As the opening allowed her by the fact that her pains did not hinder her talking implied, in a specific form of speech lay her eventual cure, whereby she could restore her literal expression to its rightful place as a metaphor.

But a tension between the universal and the particular has already been introduced through this characterization of the symbol. The non-symbolic mode of generation of symptoms depends upon 'accidental' contiguities in experience: an emotion of self-reproach became dis-placed onto the contemporaneous tooth-ache (Ibid., SE II 179). The tooth-ache is incidental to the meaning of the symptom: what has to be abreacted is the thought that accompanied that first ache, to which it is connected only by contiguity in time, not by any 'third term'. But the use of figures of speech to displace affect from the psychical to the somatic (even given 'somatic compliance') results in a new state of affairs. When a metaphor is taken literally in this way, is this a purely individualistic use of the language, or does the very existence of such a metaphor point towards a basis for such literality that goes beyond the individual? One might be tempted to accuse the hysteric of wilful – even asocial – abuse of the language in putting it to such symptomatic ends. But Freud chose to go beyond an individualistic, quasi-moralistic view of the matter, pointing to certain characteristics of language for support:

> . . . when a hysteric creates a somatic expression for an emotionally-coloured idea by symbolization, this depends less than one would imagine on personal or voluntary factors. In taking a verbal expression literally and in feeling the 'stab in the heart' or the 'slap in the face' after some slighting remark as a real event, the hysteric is not taking liberties with words, but is simply reviving once more the sensations to which the verbal expression owes its justification. (Ibid., SE II 180–1)

Certainly the hysteric is being highly individual in using language in this way, but he has justification in the history of language and its original relation to the innervation of the muscles. Hence Freud had introduced the theme of a transindividual determination of the character of the symptom as soon as he defined the nature of the symbol. We will find that this tension between the individual meaning and the universality of the symbol will recur again and again in the development of the concept.

Breuer characterized the mechanism of symbolization as being 'often based on the most absurd similarities of sound and verbal associations,' (ibid., SE II 216) or on some 'ridiculous play on words or association by sound.' (Ibid., SE II 209.) Freud specified this further: the difference between normal and hysterical expression is the same as that between figurative and literal uses of language.[5]

A second distinction, which we would seem to be able to subsume under the first, came more to the fore as psychoanalysis developed a theory of sexuality lacking in *Studies on Hysteria*: tendentiously figurative/literal. An assimilation of what was figurative to what was tendentious took place (cf. Freud, (1905c) SE VIII 96ff). As interpretations increasingly came to search out the exact content of the sexual satisfaction that hysterical symptoms represented, there arose a tendency to equate the genital (the absolutely tendentious) with the literal;

that is, when the figure of speech could be shown to be at one end of a series of displacements and substitutions that, at the other end, abutted onto a direct representation of the genital, the interpretation was accepted as complete.[6]

When we speak of the equation 'literal = genital' as the end-point of interpretation, it should be made clear that interpretation was necessary on both sides of the equation before it could be established. The concept of the genital was expanded, so that any bodily sensation could be viewed as a displacement from the genital or – most prominently in Ferenczi's work – as a regression of a genital sensation back onto those parts of the body from which genital sensations had originally been synthesized.[7] On the other side of the equation, the notion of a figure of speech becomes literal – and hence corporeal – interlocked with the newly expanded concept of the genital. As a consequence, a certain typicality of interpretation, based upon the reference to sexuality, entered into the analysis of symptoms. Freud paved the way for these typical interpretations by finding in the acme of sexual satisfaction a loss of consciousness, the *absence*, through which a crossing of the gap between the literal and the figurative became possible (Freud (1909a) SE IX 233–4). This new hypnoid state, firmly attached to the normal processes of sexual satisfaction, thus ensured that the content of the hysterical symptom would be borrowed from the bodily sensations of a polymorphous sexuality. We still retain the verbal intricacies of the earlier conception of the hysterical symptom as abuse of language; but it is now firmly linked to a condition that the end-point of interpretation of these word-plays should refer directly to an inflated genital. When the word becomes flesh it has a singularly simple morphology.

We have established that the theory of symbolization in neurotic symptoms establishes the relation between a bodily state and a figure of speech. Right from the start psychoanalytic theorizing questioned the origin and nature of this process, but explicitly recognized it as a phenomenon that was of great therapeutic and interpretative importance, even without its theoretical explanation. What theory was developed necessarily revolved around the nature and origin of language and the affects. (See Freud (1895d) SE II 180; (1926d) SE XX 133; Green (1973))

What Freud had established in the *Studies*, and which he was to permute in various ways throughout his writings, was that the symptoms of hysteria and the forms of language were related to each other via a third term, a common source. For a variety of reasons, it seemed plausible to specify this common source as a primitive language, a basic language, whose structure is possibly decipherable through the interpretation of symptoms, themselves interpreted through a reduction of the speech of the patient. This theory of symbolism will reappear in the next department of psychoanalysis in which a theory of symbolism was found to be doubly necessary: dream theory.

SYMBOLISM IN *THE INTERPRETATION OF DREAMS* (1900)

It is when we turn to the interpretation of dreams that the concept of symbolism becomes of great importance. Freud changed the text of *The Interpretation of Dreams* in ways that we have already noted: the major structural change in the book from 1900 to 1914 was the addition of a self-sufficient section on symbolism. This change has been marked by many writers (e.g. Laplanche and Pontalis (1973) pp. 443–5). In this section and the one that follows I wish to ascertain the nature of this change, to ascertain what, in 1900, was Freud's conception of in-terpretation and symbolism, and to try and discover the causes and consequences of the conceptual innovation.

Freud was very concerned to distinguish his method from that of previous writers on dreams, and thus involved himself in both a legitimation of his own method and a critique of those of others. At the opening of the main portion of the book, Chapter II, Freud discussed two other methods of dream-interpretation, which shared with his the premise that dreams had a meaning, but diverged in important respects. The first method he called the 'symbolic' method of interpreting dreams, which:

'considers the content of the dream as a whole and seeks to replace it by another content which is intelligible and in certain respects analogous to the original one . . . It is of course impossible to give instructions upon the *method* of arriving at a symbolic interpretation. Success must be a question of hitting on a clever idea, of direct intuition . . .' (Freud (1900a) SE IV 97)

The second method is the 'decoding method, since it treats dreams as a kind of cryptography in which each sign can be translated into another sign having a known meaning, in accordance with a fixed key' (ibid.). The first substantive methodological point that Freud made about his own method was that it should be associated more closely with this latter decoding method than with the former, since they both proceeded by working upon the dream conceived of as a series of elements; they both regard dreams as being of a composite character. The divergence between the methods starts immediately after one has recognized this. Dreams are composed of visual images. The 'decoding' method finds a fixed relation between a given image and a meaning. Freud's method disdains such a simple relation, implying that its very simplicity is a mark against it. Rather, the meaning of the individual element can only be found through a set of intermediary steps, through which the dream-thoughts are constructed. The construction of the dream-thoughts via the method of free association and the discernment of the meaning of the dream-element are two processes that go hand in hand. It is only a matter of the direction of attention whether one finds oneself interpreting the dream-element or finding a background against which the element makes sense. Freud's method of elucidating the dream-element thus consists in placing the element in a series of associations or chains of thought – but not 'just as it is', but, rather, as it can be construed in non-visual terms. The fact that the dream-images are visual in character is an accident of the state of sleep (and accidental at a level beyond that at which one could say that dreams themselves are an 'accident' of the state of sleep). In order to understand the dream-element one has to progress or regress from visual image to 'thought'. The essential means by which this is done we may crudely call verbalization. All images in dreams require translation into another medium – words – before they can recapture their meaning.

There is something inherently unintelligible about images: they do not form the chains of signification that Freud requires for his definition of meaning. A major section of *The Interpretation of Dreams* (1900) is devoted to 'Considerations of Representability': that is, the means by which dream-thoughts are expressed in visual form. It is as if the dream is an inherently inappropriate form of expression. And, indeed, it is, once one accepts Freud's idea that behind the façade of the dream-images lie the non-visual thoughts from which the dream is constructed by the processes of condensation and displacement.

Having distinguished these two methods of decoding and symbolic interpretation, Freud then proceeded to ignore the distinction and to refer to any non-associative or decoding methods of interpretation as 'symbolic'. Throughout the first edition of his dream-book, Freud was determined to show the inadequacy of the 'symbolic' method. The prominence of verbal expression as a means of representing abstract thought highlights the difference between his method and the symbolic method:

I will now record a dream in which a considerable part was played by the turning of abstract thought into pictures. The distinction between dream-interpretation of this kind and interpretation by means of symbolism can still be drawn quite sharply. In the case of dream-interpretation the key to the symbolization is arbitrarily chosen by the interpreter; whereas in our cases of verbal disguise the keys are generally known and laid down by firmly established linguistic usage. If one has the right idea at one's disposal at the right moment, one can solve dreams of this kind wholly or in part even independently of information from the dreamer. (Ibid. SE V 341–2)

Both methods rely upon 'keys to the symbolization' (again, we should be perplexed by the meaning of this term) in their attempt to unravel the meaning of dreams without personal associations of the dreamer. But Freud opposed the non-arbitrariness of linguistic usage to the arbitrariness of 'symbolization'. We have found this tendency in Freud's writings already, in the passages from *Studies on Hysteria* that we have discussed. But the pedagogical function of this argument is different here. In *The Interpretation of Dreams*, Freud wished to assert the correct way to analyse dreams and wished to set this off clearly from alternatives. In the *Studies* there was no such imperative. But Freud did have a definite aversion to specific modes of dream-analysis, which he grouped under the heading of 'symbolic'. The dream that Freud used in the section from which I have just quoted led him to the following conclusion:

[All the material relating to verbal disguise] leads to the same conclusion, namely that there is no necessity to assume that any peculiar symbolizing activity of the mind is operating in the dream-work, but that dreams make use of any symbolizations which are already present in unconscious thinking . . . (Ibid., SE V 349)

Here was one more explicit target against which Freud was arguing: a peculiar symbolizing activity of the mind. In the late nineteenth century context, this activity could be conceived of as a form of degeneracy or a loss of apperceptive ability (a concept which Silberer was later to revive in just this context and with which we shall deal later). Freud wished to assert positively that the keys and solutions to the dream are laid down prior to the peculiar state of mind into which the dream thrusts us. Although the interpreter may take the lead in using them as the clue to the meaning of the dream, it is not an arbitrary, individualistic act, but one sanctioned by the history of culture:

> Wherever neuroses (or dreams) make use of such disguises they are following paths along which all humanity passed in the earliest periods of civilization – paths of whose continued existence today, under the thinnest of veils, evidence is to be found in linguistic usages, superstitions and customs. (Ibid., SE V 347)

We have here two oppositions that are closely linked, but which it is important to separate: the opposition between 'arbitrary' and 'already laid down' (or 'determined'); and the opposition between 'individual' and 'collective'. One of the tensions in Freud's thought was that, on the one hand, he wished that any 'arbitrariness' that entered into analysis should enter from the patient's side, not from the analyst's. But if both patient and analyst can call upon linguistic usage and historically necessary determinations of specific forms of meaning, then the arbitrariness has been foreclosed. Ricoeur confuses these two levels when he characterizes the shift from the *Studies* to the *Traumdeutung* as one in which the mechanisms of displacement and condensation have absolute priority in the *Studies*, to the set of 'cultural stereotypes' of *The Interpretation of Dreams* (Ricoeur, 1970, p. 97, n. 1). The cultural stereotype that we find in the later Freudian symbolism is not individual in any important sense. But the cultural references of linguistic usage are individual *and* collective at the same time. When the patient articulates a figure of speech in the dream or in the neurotic symptom, we perceive a common basis upon which the element draws, but we also note that the figure of speech forms part of a verbal discourse that is completely individual to the patient. In the tension between the cliché and the inappropriate analogy we see the fusion of individual and collective that both allows the analyst to vouchsafe his interpretations and to safeguard against the stereotypical symbolical or decoding methods of interpretation.

Thus I wish to contrast the symbolical method of interpretation with the linguistic method; in the latter the dream-element in question reveals its meaning by the sort of figure of speech that we have already considered in hysterical symbolization. How do such analyses function in practice? The following example illustrated the remarks that I have already quoted:

> Since I had some knowledge of the dreamer's personal relations, I was able to interpret certain of the pieces of it independently of her. . . . I

decided to take the tower in the stalls literally. It then emerged that the man . . . towered above the other members of the orchestra. The tower might be described as a composite picture formed by apposition. The lower part of its structure represented the man's greatness; the railing at the top, behind which he was running round like a prisoner or an animal in a cage – this was an allusion to the unhappy man's name – represented his ultimate fate. The two ideas might have been brought together in the word '*Narrenturm*' (Freud (1900a) SE V 342–3; translation modified)

The same play on words that Breuer deprecated in hysterical symbolization now reappears in the interpretation of dreams. The interpretation characterizes what is essentially a linguistic mechanism built out of the rhetorical device of a misplaced literality and the grammatical device of apposition. The necessity for expressing the dream-thoughts in pictorial form functioned as a constraint upon these thoughts, entailing rhetorical and grammatical elaboration before it was possible for them to enter the dream.[8]

But perhaps the most surprising feature of this dream analysis is the interpretative licence to which Freud feels he is entitled simply on account of the clever verbality of the putative mode of representation. Not only does he feel entitled to interpret the specific figure of speech used in the representation of the tower, but he even suggests a composite word – *Narrenturm* – that synthesized two sets of dream-thoughts. Going even further, in the next paragraph, he interpreted the dream-element 'coal' through a German folk-song in which coal represents secret love. We draw the conclusion that Freud believed that the seeming arbitrariness of this procedure is offset not only by his knowledge of the dreamer's personal relations, but also by his adherence to 'firmly established linguistic usage'. (Ibid., SE V 342)

Now the question presents itself: is the firm establishment of the evidence of linguistic usage of an empirical order, or does it have theoretical and architectonic support? It is this question that is at issue between the symbolism of the image and the symbolism of the word. But, before we answer this question, we must take account of the methodological context. Throughout the early editions of *The Interpretation of Dreams*, Freud continually warned that any interpretation of symbolizations should only be used in conjunction with the methodologically primary technique of interpretation: free association. In a sense, the deciphering of elements by reference to firmly established linguistic usage is the terminal boundary of the field of explanation set up by the method of free association. What is of the first importance is that the interpretations be able to take their place in a series of words and thoughts that have their syntactical structure altered for the purposes of censorship and visual representation. The riches and varieties of linguistic usage are guaranteed to be available both to the interpreter and to the dreamer. But the *essential* position to be avoided is one in which interpretations are available only to the interpreter. As Freud reiterated in 1914, when commenting upon the distinction between the symbolic and decoding methods and his own:

> An insuperable source of arbitrariness and uncertainty arises from the fact that the dream-element may recall *various* things to the interpreter's mind and may recall something different to different interpreters. The technique which I describe . . . differs in one essential respect from the ancient method: it imposes the task of interpretation upon the dreamer himself. It is not concerned with what occurs to the *interpreter* in connection with a particular element of the dream, but with what occurs to the *dreamer*. (Ibid., SE IV 98 n1)

Interpretation by verbal symbolization was a last ditch attempt to ascertain the meaning of elements that, for one reason or another, had not succumbed to the method of free association. Even then, the recourse could only be made to elements that one was certain were available to the dreamer: the *a priori* communality of linguistic usage guaranteed such availability. In 1900 Freud would only allow himself the following guarded statement with respect to a universal symbolism that went beyond this:

> A dream-symbolism of universal validity has only emerged in the case of a few subjects, on the basis of generally familiar allusions and verbal substitutes. (Freud (1900a) SE V 345)[9]

In finding such symbolisms, the dream is, again, not employing some special power of symbolization, but is rather 'following the paths which it finds already laid down in the unconscious' (*die sie im unbewussten Denken bereits gebahnt vorfindet*), (Ibid. SE V 346). For such limited topics, such as the symbolism of the body discovered by Scherner, or the symbolism of seed and plough, 'the way has been well prepared by linguistic usage, itself the precipitate of imaginative similes reaching back to remote antiquity . . .'. (Ibid.)

The final sanction for Freud's method of interpretation was the *accessibility* to the dreamer of the forms of signification that were presented to him. But this was not the only argument against the method of symbolic decoding. His antagonism to the latter no doubt stemmed in part from his conviction of the individuality of structure of each dream, of each neurosis. Such structures were built up out of the same *mechanisms*, but one did not expect these mechanisms to produce the same manifest content or symptom corresponding to a given concealed thought, since the individual's unique experiences were the raw material out of which the structures were built. In his papers on the neuroses in the 1890s, Freud made much of the revolution he was effecting in the nosology of the neuroses: his new classification was based on mechanism, not on symptomatology (e.g. Freud (1895b) SE III 90–1). Similarly, his theory of dreams rested on the delineation of the *mechanisms* of the dream-work, not the superficial themes or common features shared by various dreams.[10] To retreat back to classification by symptom and sign would in effect amount to losing everything that psychology had gained for pathology.

We have seen that the individuality of reference of the content of the dream or the neurosis is guaranteed by the method of free association. Where this source fails, the shared meanings 'stored up' in linguistic usage are available to the interpreter. The articulation of the architectonic within which explanations in terms of linguistic usage are founded still remains undefined, and will remain so until Chapter 5. Now, we should turn to the changes in the editions of *The Interpretation of Dreams* and the impact of the growing psychoanalytical movement upon the method of dream-interpretation for a clarification both of this architectonic support and the concept of the symbol. But, already, in connecting the problem of symbolism and the explanation through linguistic usage we have presaged the form that Freud's later theory of symbolism took.

UNIVERSAL SYMBOLISM: APPROACHES TO THE PROBLEM, 1905–10

In 1926, on the occasion of Freud's seventieth birthday, Ferenczi wrote a paper honouring Freud, in which he defended his manner of conducting intellectual disputation and the manner in which certain analysts had been excluded from the psychoanalytical movement. In particular, he defended the impartiality and scientific fair-mindedness of Freud. At one point he said, 'For a long time Freud overlooked even the scientific gambols of one of his followers, because he recognized his acute sense for sexual symbolism.' (Ferenczi, 1926a, pp. 16–17.) This playful follower was Wilhelm Stekel, who had a whirlwind analysis with Freud in 1902, and became one of the founder members of the Wednesday group that eventually became the Vienna Psychoanalytic Society (Stekel, 1910, 1911–43, 1922, 1923, 1950; Roazen, 1976 pp. 224–34). Stekel quickly established himself as the *enfant terrible* of the group, playing the lead in the two major controversies of the years that preceded the rift with Adler. He disagreed with Freud over two major issues: firstly, the significance of physiological or non-psychological factors in the genesis of neuroses, particularly anxiety states. As a consequence of this debate, Freud made the first revision of the nosology of the neuroses that he had set out in the 1890s: the interposition of a category between the actual- and the psycho-neuroses, namely, anxiety hysteria. The second issue was related to the first: the importance of masturbation. Stekel argued vehemently that masturbation had no ill effects whatsoever. Freud maintained that masturbation could be found to be an aetiological factor in many, if not all, neuroses. Again, Stekel and the debates he aroused in the Wednesday group forced Freud to define his position more carefully: masturbation has no ill effects physiologically – it is a normal auto-erotic method of gaining pleasure with no pathological consequences – until it becomes linked to fantasy-formation. Masturbation plays an aetiological role in neurosis because of its relation to fantasy-formation and the flight from sexual reality that is involved in the 'anti-social' short cut of solitary sexual satisfaction (*Minutes* II, p. 562).

Stekel had the same effect upon Freud in an area that eventually became of greater theoretical importance: the study of dream-symbols. Unwillingly, and with great misgiving, Freud was forced to clarify and change his position upon the nature and the importance of symbols. We have seen the sort of resistance that he presented to what he conceived of as regressive and non-scientific modes of dream-analysis. He retained these misgivings, but under the weight of the 'empirical' evidence that Stekel offered, he seemed forced to concede that a significant amount of the work of dream interpretation could be conducted in a universal and imagistic code of dream-symbols. The slow process through which Freud came to this acceptance is most instructive and can be traced in detail in his publications, correspondence and through the *Minutes of the Vienna Psychoanalytic Society*.

Let us take a passage from the 1905 edition of the *Three Essays on Sexuality*, in which Freud considered symbolism in the perversions:

In other cases the replacement of the object by a fetish is determined by a symbolic connection of thought, of which the person concerned is usually not conscious. It is not always possible to trace the course of these connections with certainty. (The foot, for instance, is an age-old sexual symbol which occurs even in mythology; no doubt the part played by fur as a fetish owes its origin to an association with the hair of the *mons Veneris*.) Nonetheless even symbolism such as this is not always unrelated to sexual experience in childhood. (Freud (1905d) SE VII 155)

Psychoanalytic explanation consists precisely in elucidating the 'course of the connections' between the manifest and latent content of the sexual perversion. That in the case of fetishism this is not possible worried Freud. Thus, he proposed two hypothetical determinations of these connections: one taking its form from a universal association of fur and pubic hair, the other from the connections available in mythological products. In this passage, written before the influence of Stekel was brought to bear upon the problem of the dream, Freud is moving on one step further from a strict limitation to determination by linguistic usage found in *The Interpretation of Dreams*, written five years earlier. Here we already find two of the major themes involved in the exegesis of symbols: the 'silence' of the symbol, its distance from language; and its reluctance to step into line with other elements present to consciousness.

Freud's critical position with respect to a proliferation of arbitrary interpretations remained clear throughout this period, in which the early 'wild' analysts were flexing their new found interpretative muscles. At a meeting of the Vienna Psychoanalytical Society on February 13, 1907, the discussion turned around the recent performance of Wedekind's *Spring Awakening*, and in particular around the figure of the 'headless queen' in that play. After much truly arbitrary interpretation from the discussants, Freud corrected the unilinear, single significations that had been offered (e.g. Reitler had suggested that the figure represented a 'symbol of bisexuality').

The organic source of the fantasy is the anonymity of the fantasied woman; he is still too timid, one might say, to love a specific woman. Women frequently indulge in fantasies about headless men (mask). . . . Lastly, a "headless" individual cannot learn and Moritz is tortured precisely by his incapacity to learn. (*Minutes* I, p. 114)

The very diversity of these modes of elucidation was part of the pedagogical point that Freud was making: symbols are determined precisely insofar as they take up manifold connections with the 'text' that supports them. As Freud put it with respect to one of Stekel's more outlandish interpretations of a symbol at a meeting of the Society in October 1908:

> The interpretation as a sexual landscape may or may not be correct. The only proof in such cases is to be found in whether the interpretation yields a new connection. (*Minutes* II, p. 10)

The emphasis on the 'new connection' points in two directions. Firstly, it emphasizes the sense in which the symbol must take its place in an ever widening context of meaning, in which it becomes a part of the detail that is the only guarantee of the validity of psychoanalytic interpretation in general. In itself, this forms part of the thrust towards an individually unique solution to the 'neurotic equation':

> Each case must be dealt with individually. Our presentation begins to be conclusive only with the intimate detail. (*Minutes* I, p. 172)

We have already noted the importance of this movement towards the individual in the *Studies on Hysteria* and *The Interpretation of Dreams*. But the second feature of the 'new connection' is novel, relating to the place of symbolism in the analytic process, in the dialectic of patient and analyst. In clinical practice, the symbol is characterized and signified by the silence that marks the moment for a new intervention by the analyst:

> Patients are silent in two situations: when they do not accept sexual symbolism, or when the transference situation presents an obstacle. (*Minutes* I, p. 180; cf. Freud (1916–17) SE XV 149–51)

By May 1909, this lack of connectedness of the symbol had become the theoretical starting-point for a book of *sexual* symbols which Freud was going to write. He proposed to the Society that they gather material together for this book, 'with the presupposition that, when nothing else can be uncovered, we have to assume something sexual'. (*Minutes* II, p. 219.) But Freud himself was silent at the meeting of the society in February 1908 when Joachim presented a paper on *The Nature of the Symbol.* An argument between Federn and Joachim served as axis of the discussion. Federn presented a view of the symbol as intimately related to language, a view that could find support in *The Interpretation of Dreams*. He contended that:

> Symbolism comes into being only with language, and it is brought about by the impossibility of adequately reproducing the details of the outside world. Moreover, the multiple meanings of language determines the possibility of symbol formation. (*Minutes* I, p. 319)

Joachim replied:

> Language itself is full of symbolism and could not be formed if the technique of symbolism were not already developed. . . . the problem concerning the relationship between symbol and language depends entirely on what is understood by symbol. (Ibid., p. 322)

Indeed, the problems were often to revolve around a vagueness in the concept of the symbol. But the constellation of language seemed to be the primary reference point for all discussion of symbol, even if it was only to dissociate symbolism from language, as some special and localized means of representation. Such a position might have far reaching consequences. For instance, if Freud were to define the symbol by its lack of connection to the rest of the dreamer's associations and thoughts, by its lack of connection with a universe of verbal discourse, then he would be tempted – perhaps even forced – into finding a dictionary of meanings, a set of standard translations that avoided the question of the precise locus of the symbol in the psychic life of the dreamer. We will encounter a more sophisticated but less overt version of this argument in Jones' classic paper on symbolism.

We can appreciate now that one particular approach to the problem of symbolism arose directly out of the method of dream interpretation. If free association supplies the means with which the elements of a dream can be explained in terms of a coherent and self-consistent structure of thoughts and memories, then the lack of such associations presents an important practical problem. What interpretative strategies are brought to bear upon this problem then have considerable theoretical consequences. The first attempt to circumvent silence, the method of 'linguistic usage', led directly to a preoccupation with the nature and history of language, as we have seen in the *Studies on Hysteria*. The second attempt, in which silence indicates a 'symbol', seems to lead beyond the restricted field of language. A primary theme of this chapter will be that a reference to language, albeit only to its history, was felt to be necessary for psychoanalytic interpretation to retain its character, even when dealing with putatively universal symbols. It was as if the development of knowledge about symbolism put a great strain on the linguistic support of psychoanalytic interpretation; where the history of language had previously appeared to present no problem, the advent of universal symbolism created one.

Let this not obscure the fact that the history of language was always of importance in Freud's work. But the enormous concern with linguistic usage that Freud's first three major works of the new century – *The Interpretation of Dreams* (1900), *The Psychopathology of Everyday Life* (1901) and *Jokes and their Relation to the Unconscious* (1905) – displayed was primarily a concern with the 'morphology' and 'histology' of a set of given texts. To borrow back a metaphor from biology, the period from 1900–1905 was more concerned with the ontogeny of language, whereas the period 1906–1913 dealt with its phylogeny. The concern with mythology and symbolism, with literary texts and with ritual, that characterizes this period appears first and foremost as an extension of the concern with linguistic usage. But, before we turn to this material, we can follow out the vicissitudes that surrounded the symbolic adventures of Stekel.

Stekel was accused by his fellow members of the Wednesday group of manufacturing meanings. His 'Wednesday' case was famous: every meeting he would proclaim that he had had a patient that very morning who had produced material directly relevant to the points under discussion (Jones II, 153). His approach to symbols seemed similar. A dream-element or a specific symptom would be proposed for the group to discuss; his interpretation would follow immediately. Freud was always wary of such direct, non-discursive interpretation, but found that, according to his own criteria, Stekel was usually right (*The Freud/Jung Letters* 253F, p. 418). Jung found the same, taking up a similar position to Freud: Stekel is usually right, is bad for psychoanalysis as a science and is worse for its public (Ibid. 159J, p. 258). In the Vienna Society, Freud would caution against accepting Stekel's dream symbolic mode of interpretation, but he gradually came to accept that the enterprise was now possible, probably on the grounds that Stekel was usually right, and therefore there must be something in it. By November 1909, Freud could write to Jung:

A book on dream symbols doesn't strike me as impossible, but I am sure we shall object to the way Stekel goes about it. He will work haphazardly, taking whatever he can lay hands on without regard for the context, and without taking myth or language or linguistic development into account. (Ibid., 163F, p. 266)

By March 1910 Freud was suggesting group research on symbols to Jung (Ibid., 181J, p. 299). But the emphasis had changed in the year that had elapsed since he had made a similar suggestion to the Vienna Group. Then, he had wanted straightforward 'dictionary' interpretations of dream symbols. By 1910 the theoretically vouchsafed method of the historical investigation of language and myth had suggested itself as the means by which to secure the soundness of the study of symbols. It was this element, the reference to language, as seen in the above quoted letter, that Stekel would surely lack.[11]

In his 1909 lectures at Clark University, Freud found a compromise solution to the problem of symbolism:

> . . . the analysis of dreams has shown us that the unconscious makes use of a particular symbolism, especially for representing sexual complexes. This symbolism varies partly from individual to individual; but partly it is laid down in a typical form and seems to coincide with the symbolism which, as we suspect, underlies our myths and fairy tales. (Freud (1910a) SE XI 36)

Freud now sanctioned the first two of the following three possible conceptions of symbolic expression:

i. An *individual* and *verbal* symbol (a seemingly 'private' symbol): the example of a 'slap in the face' would *appear* to come into this category.

ii. A *universal* and *verbal* symbol. Superficially, the universality would only apply within one language. But etymology extended this into other languages, so that the sphere of application broadened to include all language-speakers. With the concentrated application of the philological method, the two usages i. and ii. could be unified. An example can be found in Silberer's *Problems of Mysticism and its Symbolism* (1914/17 p. 30) the dream-image `Bahnhof` serves as a phallic symbol via the linguistic relation to the English word 'station', thence to the Latin 'to stand, to stare', the genital interpretation of which is supported by jokes about 'stiffs'.

iii. A *universal* and *visual* symbol, seemingly unconnected with language, e.g. a cigar is a phallic symbol.

With his compromise formula, Freud could include both the linguistic definition of symbolization that he had formulated in the 1890s and defended in *The Interpretation of Dreams*, and also, with increasing reliance upon etymology and philology, the new non-linguistic dictionary of meanings elaborated by his disciples. *A priori*, he was decidedly unhappy about the non-linguistic mode, as his opinion of the dream-book Stekel would write demonstrated. But, besides Stekel, another influence was making itself felt: Carl Gustav Jung. 1910 was the year in which both Freud and Jung turned their attention primarily to the problems of symbolism. Eventually it was from Jung that Freud encountered the most important attack upon his theory of symbols.

The first hint of Freud's preoccupation with symbols came just before he left for America in the summer of 1909:

> In the course of an interesting excursion into archaeology, I have conceived some ideas about the nature of symbolism, but they are not yet clear enough. (*The Freud/Jung Letters*, 154F, p. 245)

By October, Jung was well entrenched in the vast new area of study, and found difficulty in finding a description for it: 'Archaeology or rather mythology has got me in its grip, it's a mine of marvellous material.' (Ibid. 157J, pp. 251–2.) Freud replied:

> I am delighted to learn that you are going into mythology. A little less loneliness. . . . I hope you will soon come to agree with me that in all likelihood mythology centres on the same nuclear complex as the neuroses. (Ibid., 160F, p. 260)

By 'nuclear complex' Freud was referring to what later became known as the Oedipus complex. We thus see that the study of mythology, archaeology and religion (these terms seemed to be interchangeable) served two ends: the elucidation of symbolism and an attempt to prove the efficacy of the central concept of his explanation of the neuroses in another field. It would appear that these aims were separate. But the same problems and issues of typicality and universality, of field and possibility of reference, on the one hand, and the discursive structure of the object of psychoanalysis, on the other, arose in the development of the concepts of the Oedipus complex and of symbolism. It will thus be fruitful to turn to the history of the Oedipus complex as part of our account of symbolism.

THE HISTORY OF THE OEDIPUS COMPLEX, 1897–1910

Freud's first published discussion of the play *Oedipus Rex* is to be found in the section on *Typical Dreams* in the 1900 edition of *The Interpretation of Dreams* (Freud (1900a) SE IV 261–4).[12] As we have already noted, this section contained the few examples of symbolism that Freud had 'discovered' at that early date. In 1909 and 1911 the material discovered by Stekel and others found its place in the expanded section on *Typical Dreams*, a separate section for *Symbolism* not being created till 1914 (Ibid. SE IV xii–xiii). In the 1900 edition, then, the first hint of the 'Oedipal impulses' occurred with respect to dreams of the death of relatives. Immediately we should note that the 'Oedipal interpretation' of such dreams disregards one of the fundamental principles that Freud laid down in the rest of the book, namely, the distinction between the manifest and latent content – 'The dream is the disguised fulfilment of a repressed wish' (Ibid. SE IV 160). To dream of the death of the father expresses the dream-wish in an unusually direct, undistorted manner. Freud recognized that his interpretation of such dreams as arising out of death *wishes* indicated that the censorship was not acting in the manner he had demonstrated it usually did in all other dreams. Consequently, he produced a set of arguments to indicate why this was possible (Ibid. SE IV 266–7):

    a. one would never dream of such a wish, so that the very enormity of the thought imbedded in the wish allows it to be expressed directly;
    b. there is a thin disguise of the death-wish behind a day-residue of worry about the person who appears as dead in the dream;
    c. the exception that proves the rule: from this sort of dream, and the similar anxiety dreams, we can show that the purpose of the censorship is to prevent the release of anxiety or other distressing affects: in the Oedipal dreams, this is not achieved.

While being perplexed at this multiplicity, even superfluity, of reasons – a multiplicity that cannot help remind us of one of Freud's favourite anecdotes concerning the neighbour who returned a borrowed kettle with a hole in it together with a series of mutually contradictory reasons which proved that the blemish came from anywhere but the borrower – at this point, we should note simply the place of the introduction of the Oedipal theme: in the section on *Typical Dreams*, from which the material on symbolism was developed.

It should come as a surprise to realize the late arrival of the Oedipus complex as the crucial concept for the explanation of the aetiology of the neuroses. We might well ask what were the relations between Freud's theory of Oedipal impulses in childhood and the aetiology of the neuroses at the time when he wrote the cited passages. We shall refrain from attempting a complete answer to this question, since it will take us far from the issue we are dealing with, but a sketch is necessary.

Some indication of the state of Freud's theory of the neuroses at this period can be had from the case-history of Dora, written in 1901 and published in 1905. Undoubtedly the course of the analysis centred upon 'the family', but this family was certainly not 'nuclear' in either of two senses:

i. the 'family' that constituted the structure in which Dora's desires were articulated, expressed and repressed consisted of a mother, a father, Herr K. and Frau K. Thus at the 'manifest' level her family had four terms, instead of two, and Freud did nothing to remove two of those terms when it came to the latent structure of desire.

ii. we find no trace of a 'nuclear complex' consisting of a relation between Dora, her mother and her father. An instance of the lack of privilege of Oedipal impulses can be seen in the following passage:

> 'Her own love for her father had therefore been recently revived; and, if so, the question arises to what end this had happened. Clearly as a reactive symptom, so as to suppress something else – something, that is, that still exercised power in the unconscious . . . she had succeeded in persuading herself that she had done with Herr K. – that was the advantage she derived from this typical process of repression; and yet she was obliged to summon up her infantile affection for her father and to exaggerate it, in order to protect herself against the feelings of love which were constantly pressing forward into consciousness.' (Freud (1905e) SE VII 58)

We wish to make the following points concerning this passage:

a. The displacement operates here in the interests of the repressed love of Herr K., for which the affectionate impulses towards her father are the conscious representative; one would expect a displacement in the opposite direction, if one were to assume, as is often the case in later psychoanalytic explanation, that adolescence is the occasion for revival of love of the father, for which various other loves represent displacements. Of course, one could argue that a further analysis would uncover a love of the father for which the repressed love for Herr K. is itself a displacement. But Freud seemed to take account of this possibility, which was rendered available to him by his account of the infantile affections that children have for their parents he had given on the previous page, by using the terms 'summoning up' and 'exaggeration' when talking of the infantile 'affection' for her father, terms that call to mind both the description of the *Project*, in which pre-pubertal impulses are magnified on their return to consciousness in adolescence, and a neo-Jungian notion, not altogether foreign to Freud's theories from the 1890s on, concerning the infantile non-sexual affections that are revived in order to provide an escape from present-day problems, such affections receiving a sexual colouration from the specific character of the present-day preoccupations.

b. Such an inversion of the expected order of the appearance of impulses and the expected exigencies of repression parallels the inversion of temporal order in the sequence of memories analysed in Freud (1899a). In that paper, a screen-memory appertaining to an experience at the age of 3 covers a repressed memory dating from puberty. What these two examples – Dora and the screen-memory – would appear to indicate is that, following on the shock that Freud had received with the demise of the seduction theory – and I think we are justified in calling it a shock, since its effect was to prevent Freud from publishing any significant paper on the neuroses from 1897 to 1905 – Freud was much more interested in displaying the structure of psychic products, rather than their final aetiology, so that if it turned out in a specific case that the 'earlier' depended upon the 'later', this would in no way obscure his point. Again, I would argue, the emphasis is on mechanism rather than content.

c. Freud himself recognized certain mistakes or errors of technique in the Dora analysis, which may have a bearing on this passage. In particular, he avowed his failure to single out a homosexual current, which took Frau K. as its object, as the 'strongest unconscious current in her mental life' (Freud (1905e) SE VII 120 n. 1). In ignoring this, he was led to give additional weight, indeed to insist against the evidence, that Dora's primary love-object was Herr K. As Lacan puts it (Lacan, 1975a, p. 207): 'It is absolutely clear that it was Freud's ego that intervened, that is, his own conception of what girls are made for – a girl is made for loving boys. If there is something stuck, something that torments her, that is repressed, it can only be, in the eyes of Freud, this: that she loves Herr K. And she perhaps loves Freud a little in the same manner.' But such a belated recognition, although throwing light upon the prominence of Herr K., does not alter the balance of interpretation in favour of an Oedipus complex, even if inverted. One will have to remain content with the 'incompleteness' of the analysis given in the case-history, if one wishes to view it from a position taken up within the Oedipus complex.

Certainly, at this time, in the early years of the new century, Freud was absolutely certain that neuroses arise out of the failure of a defence against sexual impulses, the latter invariably taking as their model a piece of infantile sexual activity. Involved here was the relation between infantile masturbation and sexual fantasy, again, as we noted above, a topic that was not clarified until Freud was forced to do so under the pressure of Stekel's uncompromising opinions as to the effects of masturbation and the status of the actual neuroses (Freud (1909b) SE X 5–147). Though he discovered, in 1897, without quite knowing what to make of the discovery, that fantasy could have the same aetiological effect as real sexual activity, it was not until the debate concerning masturbation that Freud established the primacy of fantasy in the aetiology of the neuroses (see Glymour (1974) pp. 302–4). Of great interest in delineating this development is the following passage from a discussion at the Vienna Society in February 1907:

Freud remarks, concerning the concept of auto-erotism, that Havelock Ellis uses this term when only *one* person is involved (thus, for instance, also in relation to hysterical symptoms), whereas Freud uses it when there is no object; for example, those who masturbate with images (*Bilderonanisten*) would not be considered autoerotic. (*Minutes* I, p. 118)

In May 1909 Freud used this important distinction (upon which the concept of narcissism was eventually built) to elucidate the aetiology of the psycho-neuroses:

Personally, Freud is more and more inclined toward the view that it is not masturbation that – as the patient asserts – is the source of all these neurotic sufferings; the essential factor is what lies behind masturbation – namely, the primitive masturbation-fantasies . . . Neurotics are persons who in fantasy have not arrived at a detachment from their first objects; and it is from this *content of the primitive fantasies* that all these feelings of repression follow. For persons who can detach these fantasies from father, mother, etc., masturbation has no psychological consequences. (*Minutes* II, p. 229)

This position contrasted strongly with the spirit of Freud's pronouncements upon the aetiology of the neuroses in his paper of June 1905 (Freud, 1906a). The emphasis there had been on the disturbances in the organic sexual processes. By 1909 Freud was emphasizing the means by which such organic disturbances came about, i.e. the defences against various objects or aims that lead to a fixation, or lack of detachment of libido, from various sexual component-instincts. With the works of 1907 and 1908, the new element came to the fore: the consequences of the thought-activity of children for the construction of neurotic symptoms in later life. Two papers were the consequences of this investigation of the 'normal' thought-world of children and young people: 'The Sexual Theories of Children' and 'Family Romances'. Both these papers, written in late 1908[13], concentrated on the relations between the child and its parents, but in a completely different manner from either the seduction theory or the *Three Essays on Sexuality*. The theme of parent and child was located on the level of thought and fantasy: the intellectual attempt to resolve the 'twin' problems of the origin of babies, and the origin of the self (including there, the question as to the origin of the self *qua* sexed being).

With the introduction of the term 'complex' by Jung (derived from the methodology of the association experiment), the issue becomes more complicated. Now 'complexes' referred to circles of ideas possessing a permanent and hidden affective charge. In 1908 we find Freud following Jung, perhaps reluctantly, in using the term complex for a variety of psychical contents: the 'personal' complex, the 'professional' complex – and the 'family complex' (Freud (1901b) SE VI 40; added 1907). We can now see the components that, on top of the concept of infantile sexuality and object choice, went into the construction of the Oedipus complex: the study of the childhood sexual theories, the family romances of adolescence, and the family complex. But as yet we have not unravelled all the threads.

> For a small child his parents are at first the only authority and the source of all belief. The child's most intense and most momentous wish during these early years is to be like his parents (that is, the parent of his own sex) and to be big like his father and mother. (Freud (1909c) SE VII 237)

This statement, taken from 'Family Romances', does not sound at all like a component part of the Oedipus complex. It lacks that essential differentiation between father and mother that characterizes the triadic structure of the Oedipus complex. Indeed, it hinges around a psychological mechanism that comes closer to the non-psychoanalytic concept of 'imitation'. True, it was not until *Beyond the Pleasure Principle* (Freud (1920g) SE XVIII 17) that Freud was to establish an explicit critique of the concept of imitation. But Adler was to make explicit the direction of thought indicated here, when he asserted that the child's wish to be 'on top', to be in a position of power with respect to those toward whom he felt inadequate, was the dominant concern of the neurotic (Adler, 1912–17). So, at this time, Freud and his co-workers were not particularly concerned with the triadic relation of father, mother and child. When Jung wrote a paper on 'the father complex' (as Freud called it in a letter), a paper roughly contemporaneous with Freud's 'Family Romance' and 'Sexual Theories' papers, he was able to assert:

In my experience it is usually the father who is the decisive and dangerous object of the child's fantasy, and if ever it happened to be the mother I was able to discover behind her a grandfather to whom she belonged in her heart. (Jung (1909) CW IV 323).

This and similar passages certainly caused Abraham some disquiet. He wrote to Freud:

Are you, incidentally, also of the opinion that the father is so predominant? It is definitely the mother in some of my analyses; in others, one cannot decide whether it is the father or the mother who plays the more important part. It seems to me to depend very much on the individual circumstances. (Freud (1965a) p. 76)

Freud replied:

My comments on the problem Jung deals with are similar to yours. I have previously believed the parent of the same sex to be more important for the person concerned, but can reconcile myself to greater individual variations. Jung has taken a part out of the whole, but he has done so very effectively. (Ibid. p. 78)

None of the three – Freud, Jung or Abraham – conceived that three terms constituted the complex, the 'whole' that Freud mentions in passing, without, as yet, attaching much importance to its exact constitution. Freud's suggestion that the parent of the same sex was the more important is also seen in the passage quoted above from 'Sexual

Theories'. At this time, Freud's account of the childhood sexual theories revolved around the relation of the child to the *Grossen* – the grown-ups (Freud 1908c) SE IX 214). In that account, the conflict between the authority of the *Grossen* and the 'views for which [the child] feels an instinctual kind of preference' (Ibid.) gives rise to suppressed and unconscious thoughts – the 'nuclear complex' of the neuroses. Hence, in its initial formulation in 1908, the nuclear complex referred to the *thought* relations stimulated by the (imagined) conflict between infantile sexuality and the authority of the parent. We may note the essential continuity between the concept of the nuclear complex and such thoughts *about* the family in another 'aside', from the *Minutes* for January 1908:

> The old "family romance", which is the core of all neuroses, expresses itself also in this case. . . . (*Minutes* I, p. 295)

The family romance and the sexual theories of children went hand in hand in forming the basis of the neurosis. Starting with the gap that exists between the impulses of the child and its knowledge of the means of procreation and sexual activity, the sexual investigation of the child comprises an attempt at sexual knowledge of the parents. The mystery surrounding his own genital sensations bears an unknown relation to the mystery of the parents' sexual relation (Freud (1909b) SE X 134–6). The investigation of this relation is closely connected with the masturbatory gratification of the infantile period: the sexual theories are the first fantasy-structures of the *Bilderonanist*. The family romances of a slightly later age (though we should note that Freud at this stage did not attach much importance to cardinal chronological considerations) are the sexual theories transposed under the pressure of the attempt to liberate the self from the parental authority.

Having arrived 'back' at the centrality of the parents in the life of the child, Freud wrote to Jung in December 1908:

> I am so obsessed by the idea of a nuclear complex in neuroses, such as is at the heart of the case of Little Herbert [Hans] that I cannot make any headway. (*The Freud/Jung Letters*, 118F, p. 186)

Over the next few months the concept was to take the shape that we more immediately recognize as the Oedipus complex, that is, solutions to the problems of the aetiology of the neuroses ceased to have either the structure of '*either* (the mother) *or* (the father)' or 'the-mother-*and*-the-father', and began to take up a form in which opposition *and* identification were both *necessarily* involved. Firstly, Freud brought the sexual curiosity and intellectual activity of the child into close connection with both his tender and hostile impulses:

> The nuclear complex . . . comprises the child's earliest impulses, alike tender and hostile, towards its parents and brothers and sisters, after its curiosity has been awakened – usually by the arrival of a new baby brother or sister. (Freud (1909d) SE X 208n)

But, even at this date, Freud still left a number of features uncoordinated: these features concerned the hostility of the child towards the father. His accounts in early 1909 gave a number of separate reasons for this hostility. Firstly, 'it is entirely characteristic of the nuclear complex of infancy that the child's father should be assigned the part of a sexual opponent and of an interferer with auto-erotic sexual activities' (Ibid.); secondly, much of the hostility of the child is directed towards the father on account of the 'father's concealment of the facts about the sexual processes connected with birth'. (*Minutes* II, p. 72)[14]. Whatever Freud understood by the term 'sexual opponent' (a phrase from the first quote above), it is clear that the father's role as sexual opponent was only *one* of the reasons for the child's hostility to the father. We may assume that, at this time, Freud did not conceive of the child's 'auto-erotic' activities as centred around a phantasy of the mother, to which the father's role as opponent could thus be linked, as it was the case in later writings. Nor, as yet, did Freud seem to ask the question: why is the *father* always assigned the role of withholder of knowledge, rather than the mother? The father *qua* sexual opponent was thus only one of the themes that contributed to the hostile trend that Freud already saw clearly as being essential to the 'nuclear complex'.

We may safely conclude that the essential connection of the father and the mother in the Oedipus complex had not been clarified. Further evidence of this can be found in the first version of the paper on a special type of object-choice made by men, read to the Society in May 1909. Freud summed up the aim of the paper by saying that 'it was meant to provide a stimulus for going beyond the already somewhat dreary formula of the mother, and for not losing sight of the abundance of psychic happenings, which yield the most diverse results'. (*Minutes* II, p. 256) By the time Freud came to rewrite the paper for publication, its character had changed. The father figured as much as the variations upon the 'dreary' maternal aetiology.[15] In the rewriting he coined the term 'Oedipus complex'. The conceptual enrichment that this involved can be seen from the discussion of the theme of 'rescue' that forms part of the 'special type'. Freud argued that the rescue (usually of a woman) was over-determined; the attempt to rescue the mother received additional force from the wish to be one's own father.[16] Perhaps it is at this point that we see coming together all the themes that we have seen connected with the development of the concept of the Oedipus complex: the mystery of birth, the danger of birth, the origin of children, the relation of the father to the mother, both in reproductive and in sexual terms, and the attempt to resolve the conflict of desires and fears that make up what we might call the 'dreary' Oedipus complex.[17] The crystallization of the concept of the Oedipus complex could be said to be complete in this paper; it is one of those occasions, rare in the history of science, when the first usage of a concept and the first usage of the name for that concept coincide. Its crystallization was foreshadowed in the remarks Freud made to the Vienna Society in October 1909:

> In general, neuroses are much more centered than we thought. In this case too [a case-history presented by Wittels] it is the typical problem, the same story as has been disclosed in Oedipus and in little Hans. (*Minutes* II, p. 286)

At this point let us summarize the characteristics of the Oedipus complex as we have presented it. First and foremost, it is a work of thought and fantasy, a coordinated structure of representations, and not a bundle of impulses. Secondly, its importance for Freud was that it formed the core of *all* neuroses: it unified the field of neurosis. But this in itself presented problems: what makes one neurosis different from another? If they have the same structure at bottom, a new set of distinctions must be introduced to allow for the variety of neuroses. In November 1909, Freud proposed the following three-tier structure to the Vienna Society:

> We anticipate that it may turn out by chance that adult neuroses have their prototype in child life. . . . Then we would have a clear understanding of the origin of the neuroses and, between the nuclear complex and the later adult neurosis, we would have to insert the elementary neurosis as an intermediate stage. The pediatrician is in a position to make the distinction definite between the psychologically

conditioned strata of neurosis and a core that falls into the earliest years of life; he can further determine, with regard to this core, what should be shifted over to development and what should be ascribed to heredity. Perhaps it will appear that behind all psychologically conditioned phenomena there lies something else. (*Minutes* II, pp. 322–3)

Formulating this in a schema:

	a. General case	b. Little Hans
	Adult neurosis	–
	Childhood neurosis	Childhood neurosis
	Nuclear complex	Nuclear complex

It was this schema that formed the basis for the polemic *contra* Jung that Freud wrote in 1914, 'From the History of an Infantile Neurosis'(1918b). Freud shut off any attempt, such as those made by Jung throughout the period of collaboration and, more explicitly, after their rift, to deny the importance of infantile experience in the formation of neurosis, by declaring that adult neuroses invariably and only arise on the basis of an infantile neurosis. Consequently, the relation to be investigated is that between the 'latent' Oedipus complex and the 'manifest' (through interpretation) infantile neurosis, not that between the adult and the infantile. The structure of the relation between the two levels is retained, but the relation itself attaches now to two levels that are both one step more 'theorized'. What is more, with this three-tier scheme, Freud could easily outflank a heresy that would be based upon his own concepts of interpretation and *Nachträglichkeit*. We should remind ourselves that the latter concept was originally introduced to explain *away* the possibility of infantile sexual desires, while retaining an aetiology of hysteria that found its original, 'traumatic' event in childhood (cf. Freud (1950a) SE I 347–59). In this new schema, *Nachträglichkeit*, operating between the nuclear complex and the infantile neurosis, operates completely *within* childhood – that is, the two points in time between which *Nachträglichkeit* acted were both located in childhood – thus gainsaying an argument that wished to locate the causes of neurosis in the adult present, and explaining the infantile *content* of the neuroses by a retroactive activation of infantile material. Freud himself now wished to use the concept of *Nachträglichkeit* for a similar purpose: to explain the universal content of the childhood neurosis by 'retroactive' activation of the nuclear complex, rather than the 'amplification of quantity' function the concept had performed in the *Project*.

The polemic against the Jungian position had thus been started long before Jung was to occupy it. Perhaps. But one should not underestimate the explicit recognition of differences and the firm manner in which Freud publicly eschewed some of the 'Zurich tendencies' in the period 1907–12. At the meeting of the Vienna Society in November 1909 at which he set out the three-tier theory we have quoted, he made it quite clear that it was against certain ideas of Jung that he was arguing, specifically Jung's conviction that there were hysterias in which reminiscences played no part, that were simply 'organic' or 'hereditary' in character – exactly the position that Freud's radical attack on the concept of hereditary determination and degeneracy of the 1890s had expelled from consideration in psychoanalysis.

> In an infantile hysteria that appears in the sixth to eighth year, the prehistory must be in no way underestimated, since the decisive impressions are received in the second to fourth years of life. (*Minutes* II, p. 323)

With the introduction of the Oedipus complex *and* its integration into a new schema of the aetiology of the neuroses – a process that one cannot separate from the genesis of the concept and which acts as the gauge of the existence of that concept – Freud gave a new dimension of 'typicality', of 'universality', to psychoanalytic theory. At the base of all neurosis, at the deepest level – and only, to be sure, at the deepest level – was to be found one single structure, transforms of which gave rise to different neuroses. The detail with which a psychoanalytic explanation only makes sense was by implication downgraded: another criterion, conformity to the unitary Oedipal structure, seemed to pull in the opposite explanatory direction. Instead of a finer and finer appreciation of the intimate details of the individual neurosis, an approximation that might have as its ideal conformity with an 'understanding' of that person's life, it becomes more and more tempting to urge analysis towards a single and final end of all interpretation, an apocalyptic twilight of the dialectic of destiny. And what end was this? – The pattern, the image, that had, so surprisingly, appeared to Freud in *The Interpretation of Dreams*, and for which he had virtually created a special category: dreams of the death of relatives and of incest. The disconcerting explicitness of a class of dreams, which, by definition, were at their most implicit when to be explicit would be to disconcert, now came to be the aim and measure of psychoanalysis, whereas then, in 1900, it had been something to be explained away, something to be patched over, the hole in the psychoanalytical kettle.

Symbolism, as the apparatus of explanation that took over the niche created by the makeshift category of typical dreams, functioned in parallel to the Oedipus complex, now grown, as we have seen, out of all proportions to its humble beginnings as a typical dream. Both bypassed detail; both bypassed interpretation; both bypassed the spinning out of words that coagulated meaning through the plurivocality of their reference. The Oedipus complex introduced a transparency between symptom and cause, symptoms now being viewed as one modality among others of a cause already known. One might argue that this transparency occurred only at the level of theory, the level that, as we emphasized above, was strongly emphasized in the new three-tier structure that the Oedipus complex inaugurated; one might argue that, in the realm of practice, just as much detail of the 'inner world', just as many subtle innuendos of symptom and image were examined. But this is precisely what the theory of symbols shows us was not the case. It was a *practical* exigency – the *failure* of detail, the *lack* of a connection, silence – to which the theory of symbols was meant to answer. Its uni-dimensional and irreversible movement along a univocal reference became a formidable part of practice, founding a supporting theory that we are still in the process of examining, matching the movement of simplification – even duplicating and supporting it – that the concept of the Oedipus complex brought to the aetiology of the neuroses. Just as all roads lead (back) to the Oedipus complex, so that the questions of heredity versus accidental, of constitution versus experience, of male and female, have to be asked in terms of 'mummy' and 'daddy', so do the elements of a dream increasingly have to find their final reference in a very limited set of referents: 'the body in all its aspects, the parents, children, brothers, sisters, birth, death, nakedness – and something else besides'. (Freud (1916–17) SE XV 153; translation modified)[18]

We have established that the period 1907–10 saw the formulation of the Oedipus complex.[19] The component parts of the concept were brought together via the concepts of the nuclear complex, the family romance and the sexual theories of childhood. The Oedipus complex acted as a simplifying concept, in the accumulating welter of infantile fantasy and sexual theory. Its *first* simplifying function was to reduce the number of objects of aetiological moment. It was only later that it acquired the function of synthesizing the component instincts, or of mediating between the ego and the social world (as in the genesis of the super-ego).

The simplification worked in two ways: firstly, by exclusion and secondly by subsumption. Certain 'complexes' would necessarily prove of secondary derivation and therefore would function as intermediate steps in the solution of a neurosis. Such would be Jung's 'professional' and 'personal' neuroses. Such, also, might be the religious complex: the reduction of God to the father is bound up with the Oedipus complex.[20] Secondly, certain themes, seemingly of equivalent primordiality to Oedipus, could be subsumed within the Oedipus complex: the themes of birth and rebirth, of the rescue, of the cloacal theory of birth, and so forth. The latent content of the neurosis was affirmed as stable, just at the point where the detailed manifestations of it were proliferating.

Just as symbolism gives direct access to meanings derived from the unconscious, so the Oedipus complex gives direct access to the primary desires. More than that, it gives a justification for a certain irreversibility of interpretation: from the god to the father, and not vice versa. Once one knows what the core of a neurosis is going to be, the process of interpretation becomes more straightforward, less dependent upon the twists and turns of the 'detail' that had been so important. The typicality of Oedipal desires is mirrored in the typicality of their representation.

It is in the domain of mythology and its symbolism that we find the movements towards simplicity of aetiology and towards interpretative verisimilitude most at odds. And it was mythology that came to preoccupy Freud and his co-workers most in the period we are studying.

MYTH AND DREAM, 1910–1911

Freud and Jung both turned to the study of myths and symbols at about the same time: the beginning of 1910. In January 1910, Jung gave a lecture to a student society in Zurich. He wrote to Freud about the richness of the area of study, and how unsatisfactory his first formulation of the problem was. Freud replied:

> Your deepened view of symbolism has all my sympathy. Perhaps you remember how dissatisfied I was when in agreement with Bleuler all you had to say of symbolism was that it was a kind of "unclear thinking". True, what you write about it now is only a hint, but in a direction where I too am searching, namely, *archaic regression*, which I hope to master through mythology and the *development of language*. (*The Freud/Jung Letters* 177F, p. 219)

From this time on, the genetic approach outlined here was to be Freud's argument against the universal symbolizing tendency of Stekel and later of Jung. Through the genetic approach, he could retain his previous theory of symbolism intact. 'The meaning of symbols is to be found in linguistic usage and the historical understanding of language' – this would always be Freud's fundamental attitude to symbolization.

In 1895 he had located this usage in the present *and* the past. In the 1910s he was forced to give up the double determination of the linguistic usage of the present – that is, free association – and resorted to determination of symbolism through the pre-historic origins of language. With Stekel's dream-symbols, language was no longer a direct guide to meaning, leaving the explanatory affection that Freud had for language with the secondary task of explaining *why* the symbols had the meaning they in fact did have. As he phrased his new position in 1914, symbols were 'a relic and a mark of former identity'. (Freud (1900a) SE V 352.)

In his letter to Jung of January 1910, from which I have just quoted, Freud had stated the programme for the investigation of symbolism that he was to follow throughout the rest of his *oeuvre*. First fruit of his investigation of the development of language and archaic regression was a paper written in February 1910: 'The Antithetical Meaning of Primal Words'. Freud made use of a pamphlet, written by a philologist, Karl Abel, on the proto-Egyptian language, showing that in that language there are a number of words with two meanings, one of which is the exact opposite of the other. Freud and Abel constructed an explanation of this phenomenon in terms of the development of language. Freud postulated a stage of language, exactly parallel with the system at work in the dream, in which a word represented a conceptual 'dimension', e.g. 'weak-strong'. A later stage of language differentiated 'weak' from 'strong' by adding to the one word 'weak-strong' two different gestures. Eventually via a 'phonetic reduction (modification) of the original root' (Freud (1910e) SE XI 158), two words separated out on the basis of a coupling of the original conceptual dimension with a gestural sign that fixes the meaning in that dimension. In other words, when the dream-work converts two seemingly separate words first into a relation of antithesis, and then, following further regression, into a relation of identity, the dream is simply reviving the ancient usages of language.

In the correspondence between the peculiarity of the dream-work mentioned at the beginning of the paper and the practice discovered by philology in the oldest languages, we may see a confirmation of the view we have formed about the regressive, archaic character of the expression of thoughts in dreams. And we psychiatrists cannot escape the suspicion that we should be better at understanding and translating the language of dreams if we knew more about the development of language. (Ibid. SE XI 161)

But there is a characteristic of Egyptian that is even stranger: words can reverse their sound as well as their sense. 'Numerous examples of such reversals of sound, which are too frequent to be explained as chance occurrences, can be produced from the aryan and Semitic languages as well.' (Ibid. SE XI 160.) For example,

> *capere* (Latin for 'take') – *packen* (German for 'seize');
> *leaf* (English for 'leaf') – *folium* (Latin for 'leaf');
> *hurry* (English for 'hurry') – *Ruhe* (German for 'rest').

We note that Freud was not discriminating in these examples between synonyms and antonyms; nor did he discriminate the exact genealogy of each language, except by the vague grouping of all these languages as 'Germanic'.

What are we to make of these peculiar etymological connections? Benveniste ridiculed Freud's and Abel's attempt to discover the 'homology between the stages of a dream and the processes of "primitive languages"' (Benveniste, 1971, p. 71). He also isolated the feature that is of most interest to us at the moment: the straightforward, unabashed universalism of the discussion of languages' meaning and sound: 'The distinctions each language brings forth must be explained by the particular logic that supports them and not be submitted straight off to a universal evaluation.' (Ibid.) Freud obviously accepted the premise that there is a universal system of roots common, at least, to the *'arischen und semitischen Sprachen'*, although these may not be visible at the level of speech; rather, they form a stock of 'ideal' roots, transforms upon which are necessary for the production of a given language. The continuity of meaning between languages is similarly guaranteed by a 'Lamarckian' mechanism of survival. The desire for a universalistic and comprehensive explanation was such that Freud was even prepared to venture an interpretation of the classic example of foolish etymology offered by Quintilian: *lucus a non lucendo: lucus* (a grove) is derived from *lucere* (to shine) because light does not shine in a grove. Such a sophistical derivation conformed to the conflation of opposites common to primitive language and dreams, and thus was plausible to Freud, in the same way that the etymology provided by many a joke could never not be significant.

What such studies added to the study of symbolism is not immediately apparent, although we can be sure that the proximity of date between his setting out the programme of research into the archaic regression of language and the writing of the paper signalled the end to which these philological hypotheses were directed. In the paper, Freud only wished to point out that the mechanisms of the dream-work corresponded to the mechanisms of earlier stages in the development of language. Explorations of the roots of languages seemed the most promising – perhaps the only admissible – direction of inquiry into those elements of both dream and myth that seemed most opaque: symbols. Freud was starting the attempt to find a way of underpinning the seemingly non-verbal character of symbols and myths by reference to philological researches. Perhaps the clearest example of this attempt occurs in a letter to Jung of May 1910, which produced an exemplar that Freud was to make much of in later writings on symbolism:

On the scientific side just an oddity. I have two patients with nuclear complexes involving their witnessing acts of infidelity on the part of their mothers (the one historical, the other perhaps a mere phantasy). They both tell me about it in the same day and preface their story with dreams about *wood*. . . . Now I am aware that boards mean a woman, also cupboards, [both these words have sexual connotations in German] but I have never heard of any close connection between wood and the mother complex. It occurs to me though that wood in Spanish is *madera* – matter (hence the Portuguese name of the island of Madeira) and undoubtedly *mater* lies at the root of *materia* (matter). Force and matter would then be father and mother. One more of our dear parents' disguises. (*The Freud/Jung Letters* 190F, pp. 314–5)

Here Freud had found what he was looking for: symbolism sanctioned by contemporary or ancient linguistic usage and origins. With such an explanation he could dismiss the category 'symbolical thought' as being of secondary importance when compared with either word representations or object presentations, which formed the two basic systems of mental functioning. In other words, symbolism did not form the exemplar of non-verbal representation for Freud: symbolism was always secondary, derived from the system of word-presentations, rather than giving direct access to the system of object presentations. Jung, on the other hand, began to ascribe more and more importance to symbolic thought *in opposition to* verbal thought. For a period of time, it seemed to both men that they were working along parallel lines with respect to symbolism: they wrote two important theoretical works at the same time, Freud assuring Jung that he was not plagiarizing, but thinking independently.[21] These two works were the 'Formulations on the Two Principles of Mental Functioning' of Freud, written in November 1910, and Jung's 'Concerning Two Kinds of Thinking', written from January 1910 to December 1910, eventually becoming the major theoretical section of *Wandlungen und Symbole der Libido*.[22]

In his paper, Freud introduced the pleasure principle and the reality principle as the two principles of mental functioning. They were characterized more by aim than by mechanism: the pleasure principle's aim was simply the avoidance of unpleasure, and the release of tension; the reality principle aimed at truth, here interpreted as the best guarantee of future pleasure. Involved in the distinction was the opposition of fantasy and reality, and again, Freud made much of the essential contribution speech and verbal residues made to the functioning of the reality principle, through the conscious perception of inner states that they made possible. He made no mention of symbolism or symbolic thought; indeed, one might ask, why should he, since elsewhere he had reduced the status of symbols to little other than a derivative of language?

Jung started his description of the two kinds of thinking with a characterization of the dream as symbolic. He thus started by shifting the term 'symbolic' to the centre of the problem of interpretation. There was no hint in this work as yet of his contention that this symbolic meaning transcends a verbal hermeneutic, but his focus on the symbolic gave the first hint of how he was to develop the symbolic mode. He continued in the paper with a discussion of our normal mode of thinking, finding, with a whole array of supporting authorities, that it consists in thinking in word forms, which enable thought to take a specific direction. The second mode of thinking is non-verbal, un-directed, subjective 'dream or phantasy thinking' (Jung, 1911/12/15, p. 22). This is the form of thinking that Freud discovered, he maintained, and it is identical with the thought that the ancients expressed in their myths and that we express in our dreams and our psychopathological structures: it is symbolic thought.

These two conceptions of the two forms of thinking did not seem to their proponents to differ very much. As Jung wrote to Freud in March 1910:

The first thing about your conception of the unconscious is that it is in striking agreement with what I said in January on symbolism. I explained there that 'logical' thinking is thinking *in words*, which like discourse is directed outwards. 'Analogical' or fantasy thinking is emotionally toned, pictorial and wordless, not discourse but an inner-directed rumination on materials belonging to the past. Logical thinking is 'verbal thinking'. Analogical thinking is archaic, unconscious, not put into words and hardly formulable in words. (*The Freud/Jung Letters* 181J, pp. 298–9)

Jung began to locate the opposition between the two forms of thought more and more in terms of verbal and non-verbal, as we can see from a comment he made in a letter written in May 1910:

Only Bleuler has taken it into his head to carp at the notion of verbal and non-verbal thinking, without advancing anything positive. (Ibid. 193J, p. 319)

He then took the next step and equated visual 'symbols' with the first, non-verbal thinking. It was here that he began to diverge from Freud's view. As Freud commented upon a draft of Jung's chapter:
The opposites are actually fantastic-real, not symbolic-real. (Ibid. 199aF, p. 333.)
Freud even thought that the 'whole thing should not be titled "Symbolism", but "Symbolism and Mythology", since more light is thrown upon the latter than the former.' (Ibid. p. 335.)
Before we turn to a closer look at the development of Jung's work, let us just note some of the issues raised by bringing together symbolism and myth. Freud conceived of myths as being like dreams. His pupils drew upon the same analogy but with very different methods.[23] For Freud, myths were the dreams of a people and they needed the same detailed analysis as he had outlined in *The Interpretation of Dreams*. Necessarily included in this analysis was a sharp distinction between the latent and the manifest content. Just as symbols had been unwillingly admitted, under firm constraint, into the interpretation of dreams, so they could be allowed to form a minor part of the analysis of myths. The difference between myth analysis and dream analysis consisted in the absence of 'individual associations'. Since this was the methodological point of entry of symbolic decoding of dreams, myth analysis had this in common with interpretation using symbols. Jung certainly equated myths and symbols precisely because of this characteristic: he never paid as much attention to individual associations as Freud did.

But Freud conceived of the myth as a paranoid product of the same order as the secondary revision of the dream. Much of the work of myth-analysis revolved around extricating the 'original' myth from the revisions and distortions that had accumulated in it over long periods of time.[24] This difficulty of ascertaining the original text of a myth had as its consequence that analysis of mythic products would always remain secondary, for Freud, to the analysis of neurotics, with whom a discursive enquiry, such as that conducted with the Ratman in search of the original wording of his obsessional formula, could result in a clear decision as to the *Urtext*.

Another way of putting this point is to assert that Freud was very loathe to give up the contextualist methodology of interpretation. The advantage of the individual dreamer's associations did not derive from their unified source, from their belonging to an individual, although this unity functioned as a precondition for the elimination of certain distortions that were unavoidable in myth analysis. Rather, the individual could supply the detailed context that was necessary for interpretation. For this reason, Freud regarded as doubtful any symbols that did not have support from a number of heterogenous sources: myths, fairy tales, and, of course, linguistic usage. And if dream-symbols needed support from myth before they could be accepted, how could Jung hope to justify the use of dream-symbols in the analysis of myth?

JUNG'S APPROACH TO THE SYMBOL

In 1956, Jung wrote:

> . . . unlike the contents of a neurosis, which can be satisfactorily explained by biographical data, psychotic contents show peculiarities that defy reduction to individual determinants, just as there are dreams where the symbols cannot be properly explained with the aid of personal data. (Jung (1956) CW III 254)

These two themes, the explanation of psychotic contents and the movement towards non-individual explanations of such contents, were among the major preoccupations of Jung's early work on dementia praecox, which first brought him into personal contact with Freud in 1906. The work *Wandlungen und Symbole der Libido* (1912–13) argued for the position that Jung arrived at after years of work with Freud, a position that was in conflict with Freud's. In *Wandlungen*, Jung asserted the essential difference between the neuroses and the psychoses. But in his early work on *The Psychology of Dementia Praecox* (1907), Jung had sided with Freud against the academic psychiatrists, by attributing 'to the individual an almost incalculable significance as regards the origins and specific form of the psychosis. The importance of the individual factor, and of the individual's psychology in general, is undoubtedly underestimated in modern psychiatry, less perhaps for theoretical reasons than because of the helplessness of the practising psychologists.' (Jung (1907) CW III 35.) But Jung could not follow the 'anti-disease' argument to completion; there were significant differences between the clinical pictures of hysteria and dementia praecox that justified a non-individualistic theory of the latter. Jung chose the option of abnormalities of metabolism as the probable non-individual cause of dementia praecox. Toxins lead to the arresting of the complex-formation process, and then one specific (randomly chosen?) complex 'coagulates and determines the content of the symptom'. (Ibid. CW III 37.)

Both Jung and Abraham (1908a) could demonstrate that the psychological mechanisms for the generation of symptoms in dementia praecox were those that Freud had demonstrated at work in the psycho-neuroses. But neither had any idea as to the psychological or sexual aetiology of the psychoses. Jung suggested the toxin theory; Abraham remained silent until he received hints from Freud as to the theoretical possibilities, but, with Ferenczi, made an indirect attack on the toxin theory, by criticizing then prevalent theories of the close kinship of alcoholism and psychosis (Abraham, 1908b). Perhaps, as Jung left the severely anti-alcoholic atmosphere of Swiss psychiatry in the years after 1909, he felt less interest in the toxin theory. Certainly during his association with Freud he found little cause to mention it. But it resurfaced in his papers of the 1930s and 1950s, when orthodox psychiatry was again seeking to assuage its perplexity in the face of psychosis by turning to drugs: insulin in the 1930s and largactol in the '50s. (Cf Jung (1956) CW III 253; Jung (1958) CW III 258ff)[25].

But, however little importance he eventually attached to it, the toxin theory served to emphasize the gulf between dementia and the neuroses. In 1910 and 1911, two points served to stress this gulf: firstly, the 'empirical' point that the fantasies displayed by psychotics were of a typical and mythological character, unlike the individual creations of the neurotic. Secondly, Jung could not accept that the profound disturbances of affective and cognitive relations to the world found in schizophrenia could be due solely to a disturbance in the distribution of sexual libido. In other words, he rejected the sexual aetiology of the psychoses.

Jung's primary concern with psychosis was thus, from the very first, allied to his conviction, at first vague, that a non-individual solution to the problem of psychosis separated it off from neurosis. We find a series of oppositions and identifications in Jung's thought: psychosis/neurosis; mythology/individual fantasy; symbolic thinking/verbal thinking; universal/individual. What Jung lacked, as we shall see, is the third term that Freud felt was necessary between these oppositions: history and language. In the Wolfman's case-history, Freud presented the argument for history: neurosis (and, implicitly, psychosis) cannot be understood solely in terms of the fantasy content of the present, but must be referred to definite past events, when certain permanent fantasy-structures and libidinal investments were founded. In the lecture on Symbolism which formed part of the *Introductory Lectures* (1915–17), he set out the theory of the historical development of symbolism out of language that ensured both that a trans-individual non-verbal unconscious could never be a viable concept and that symbolism was not the privileged means of access either to mythology or to the unconscious.

But the dispute between Freud and Jung did not take place either on the terrain of psychosis or explicitly with respect to symbolism. Rather, the problem of incest, itself the focus of Freud's interest as he began to elaborate the overarching importance of the Oedipus complex, occupied the central place in the explicit disagreement that terminated their intellectual collaboration. (*The Freud/Jung Letters*, pp. 501ff). Why incest? True to his first overtures to the Freudian system, Jung perceived immediately that the problem of incest lay at the heart of all his mythological material. But he saw the problem of incest as much deeper than 'just' infantile sexuality, which, at that period in the development of psychoanalysis, was preeminently identified with 'perverse' sexuality. Jung wrote to Freud in 1909:

. . . without doubt there's a lot of infantile sexuality in it but that is not all. Rather it seems to me that antiquity was ravaged by the struggle with *incest*, with which sexual *repression* begins (or is it the other way round?). (Ibid. 170J, p. 279)

Jung's problem was clear: both the contents of psychosis and mythology, when duly interpreted, revealed the problem of incest. What then distinguished him from Freud was a fundamental ahistoricity in his argument. At the level of interpretation, he made no distinction between the original and the derived versions of myths. Hence all myths resolved themselves into a uniform field of symbolic presentation. At the level of explanation, Jung refused the concept of an origin as cause, even in its sophisticated Freudian guise of *Nachträglichkeit* (deferred action). So Jung's method of analysis was essentially timeless. And this aspect tied up neatly with his contention that the contents of psychosis were essentially non-individual in character. Surely, he argued, what we are faced with in psychosis is the raw unconscious, without any intervention of consciousness: we are confronted with the symbols that furnish out the Freudian unconscious. And, since Freud had established the timeless character of the unconscious, Jung's arguments concerning psychosis and mythology seemed to be the way of the future for psychoanalysis: direct confrontation with the unconscious.

A condition of this argument was the elision of the distinction between the manifest and the latent contents of a myth or a dream, a distinction that had been undermined by Abraham with respect to myth, and Stekel with respect to dreams, with their focussing on the dictionary of symbols. But Freud wished to retain this firm distinction as a bulwark against any attempt to read the contents of the unconscious directly. Apart from such a project being a contradiction in terms, the unconscious was only ever available through the systems of the *Pcs.* What was Freud to make of the strange character of psychotic products and of mythology? His argument, as ever, was to concentrate on mechanism (displacement, condensation etc.) rather than on contents. A first essay can be found in the Schreber case, where he noted that the contents of Schreber's paranoiac universe were the result of the transformation of the legal universe constructed by sublimation (Freud (1911c) SE XII 73). Thus the paranoia takes on the formal structure of a rigorously civilized and verbal structure of thought. The argument is made more specific and applicable to the more recalcitrant schizophrenic in Freud's paper on 'The Unconscious' (see Chapter 2). There, what distinguishes psychosis is that unconscious mechanisms have come to act upon the system of word-presentations, rather than on the object-presentations (as found in the repressed contents of neurosis). Psychotic contents, rather than being the naked revelation of object-presentations, as Jung might wish them, are a derivative of verbal thinking. Psychosis was, then, in a twisted sense, one step *further* away from the unconscious than neurosis: a privileged access such as Jung wished for in the analysis of schizophrenia was thus cut off.

Jung was concerned to discover from the unconscious a universal myth: he found such a myth in the detachment of the libido from the mother, involving rebirth and sacrifice. Thus, appropriately, he divided the last section of *Wandlungen und Symbole* into chapters with the following titles: 'The Unconscious Origin of the Hero', 'Symbolism of the Mother and of Rebirth', 'The Battle for Deliverance from the Mother', 'The Dual Mother Role', 'The Sacrifice'. Strangely enough, the major feature of his paper of 1909 was absent: there was no reference to the father. His account of the genesis of myths is one that deals only with the relation to the mother and with the themes of escape from the all enfolding mother into reality.

Jung felt no necessity for making his enquiry an historical one. Each myth was a valid story, a fantasy constructed by a people in their search for the liberation of their libido from its past attachments, in the face of an especially difficult but unknown adaptation that was presented to them with the force of necessity (Jung, 1911/12/15, pp. 464–5). It is as if Jung were asserting the primacy of the symbol and thus cutting off any possibility of grounding the symbol in 'another' realm. The Freudians were only later to realize, after Jung's defection, that a grounding of the symbol directly in the body would short-circuit any such theory of the symbol.

The same themes found in the *Studies on Hysteria* re-emerge. Jung was opposing biology and psychology, while conceiving of biology as, on the one hand, a species-preserving function, and, on the other, a consummation of sexual desire. Having conceived of biology as adaptive, he could then reject its relevance for the incest question, which was 'patently' not concerned with desire, thus leaving him with a homogeneous, undifferentiated field of psychic events, in which a reference to a 'real' mother provides at most an occasion for, and certainly not the cause of, the importance of the series of mother-symbols. Freud certainly never conceived of the incest taboo as the pure reflection, on the psychic level, of a biologically species-preserving instinct. But, on the other hand, he did oppose to 'psychology' a conception of the incest taboo as grounded outside the field of representation. Just as the physiological theory of the affects was insufficient, needing an 'historical' moment to bridge the gap between physiology and representation (Freud (1926d) SE XX 133), so a biological theory of the sexual impulse – even that venture into biology found in the *Three Essays on Sexuality* – was insufficient to ground the continual reproduction of the incest taboo: a 'historical' factor was necessary.[26] This factor was the story of the murder of the primal father.

Elsewhere, we have noted that the term 'primal' signifies an elision of the distinction between psychical and material reality, of the distinction between what is real and what is thought (to be real). A primal event thus has a double character: it is the starting-point, the 'first cause', of both systems of reality: it is both psychic and material. Through the concept of the primal, one can link the two systems in a manner which evades the dualistic postulate which initially characterizes them. The primal is the pineal gland of the Freudian system. But, true to his times, Freud's concept of the primal is perhaps first and foremost a concept that gives the *temporal* order its character. As the first event, it both partakes of the same character as those events that follow (it is a part of a sequence) and it partakes of a transcendental, 'timeless' character, its 'firstness' cutting it off from the temporal sequence, casting everything that follows into its shadow. Everything that is not primal has some qualities that belong to it by virtue of its being in the sequence initiated by the primal, and some qualities that are first and foremost the negative of what is primal, the absence of what is primal: the never-to-be-forgotten marks everything that comes after.

The peculiar character of the primal 'historical event', then – whether primal murder or primal scene – is that its historicity grants it the status of being accidental, of being just the first of that series of events that fill up time. And yet the very existence of the series points to the first event as being of overwhelming importance, as being 'necessary' in a sense that none of the events that follow are. It is the play between the contingent (accidental) and the necessary character of the primal that gives the debates concerning the primal their elusive, inconsequential and exasperating quality (cf. Kant (1781–87), A444/B472ff). On the one hand, its contingent character seems to make the ascertaining of its existence a question of the empirical order, open to evidence which speaks to one side or the other. On the other hand, its necessary character seems to undermine the use of evidence either for or against its existence, since the evidence itself seems to depend on the existence of the primal. The primal event's existence seems to be subject to an overwhelming necessity, so overwhelming that, in discussion of whether or not a particular primal event has taken place or not, the discussion will come to a point where a shrug of the shoulders indicates the misplaced criterion upon which one disputes the reality of past events.

There is no primal father in *Wandlungen und Symbole der Libido*. Nor should we mistake the all-enfolding mother, the principal theme, the archetype, the noumenous object of that work, for a primal point of reference, placed outside the field of symbols. The mother, having been removed from all contact with the biological, indeed, with the bodily, the 'real' mother – even with the prehistoric mother of the 'cultureless' matriarchy – is *just* a symbol. For whom? As soon as we ask this question, the difference between Jung and Freud becomes stark. Jung's starting-point, that the individual productions of the psychotic and the collective symbolic representations of the *Volk* are of the same order, eliminated the individual subject. And, if he were reluctantly to admit that neurotics displayed a highly individual set of symbols, he found a number of ways to minimize this individuality. Firstly, he wished to find hysterics in whose symptoms individual memories played little part (cf. above p. 94). With Freud, any such movement towards typicality and universality was reluctant. An exchange between the two, from October 1911, captures the difference of attitude well. The subject under discussion was the symbolism of twins, particularly in mythology (e.g. Romulus and Remus), for the elucidation of which Freud considered, amongst other things, the 'after-life' born with the baby. But the topic gave him cause to remark:

> If there is such a thing as a phylogenetic memory in the individual, which unfortunately will soon be undeniable, this is also the source of the *uncanny* aspect of the *doppelgänger.* (*The Freud/Jung Letters* 274 F, p. 449)

Jung replied, enthusiastically taking up Freud's remark:

> . . . it fits in very well with certain other observations which have forced me to conclude that the so-called 'early memories of child-hood' are not individual memories at all but phylogenetic ones. (Ibid. 275J, p. 450)

One can already read here, between the lines, the future divergence, in which Jung would reject the importance of memories of infantile sexuality, since they were neither sexual nor memories, and Freud would emphasize their importance, despite the fact that they were not memories of reality, and despite the fact that they were not sexual in any conventional sense.

But their divergence was one of fundamentals: Freud wished to allow anonymous collectivity only as the last resort, the *limit* of the psychoanalytical field. He equated ancestral experience with hereditary factors, and, insofar as the motor of his early theories of neuroses had been a radical attempt to expunge heredity from the aetiology of the neuroses, he fought shy of reinstating it, arguing that even if phylogenetic memories existed, individual experience was still necessary to 'activate' them. The enthusiasm with which Jung extended the scope of Freud's remarks in the direction of expunging the primacy of infantile memories was symptomatic of the wish for collectivity that his theory of psychoses and myth implied.

Secondly, Jung would later make of the 'individualistic' portion of analysis a preliminary and superficial stage, a slightly distasteful confrontation of the analysand with the false gods of his family and his past, beyond which the real work of analysis, contemplation of the collective unconscious, could start. It was only insofar as symbols *lost* their individual associations that analysis made any progress.

Conversely with Freud. Where he and Jung seemed to meet – the question of phylogenetic memories – was also the point of departure. Freud's phylogenetic memory – and we can take as our exemplar the primal coital scene of the Wolfman – was only the barest outline, a sketch of a figure, upon which the real work of analysis was brought to bear: the filling in of details so individual as to leave finally the question of non-individual origin as little more than a debating-point. We will see this more clearly when we come to discuss the Grusha episode in the Wolfman's case-history.

Hence, for Jung, *true* symbols were lacking in individuality. A symbol was a symbol for all or for none: it was not for someone. Freud, in reluctantly recognizing, as we have seen, that symbols were transindividual in character, only terminated the analysis when it had been determined whose phallus this sword was a symbol of, even if the bearer of this phallus turned out to be a father finally become mythical.

Jung's approach managed to maintain a fine contradiction: each symbol was unique and indivisible in its expressivity, and yet each was equally anonymous in being a representative of homogeneous libido.

> . . . symbols are not to be understood 'anatomically' but psychologically as libido symbols; . . . One loses one's way in one 'cul de sac' after another by saying that this is the symbol substituted for the mother and that for the penis. In this realm there is no fixed significance of things. The only reality here is the libido, for which "all that is perishable is merely a symbol." It is not the physical actual mother, but the libido of the son, the object of which was once the mother. (Jung (1911/12/15) p. 249)

Freud achieved the same interpretative results as Jung, while avoiding this axiom of the homogeneity of the libido as the one fixed point of reference. Of course, the principle of over-determination and that of psychic determinism were completely at odds with Jung's reflections on the fluidity of representation in the unconscious. But it was more a question of levels than of a dispute over the importance of the libido:

> . . . this primal identity [of the instincts] may well have as little to do with our analytic interests as the primal kinship of all the races of mankind has to do with the proof of kinship in order to establish a legal right to inheritance. (Freud (1914c) SE XIV 79)

The homogeneity of the libido (Jung's reference point for the grounding of symbols) is besides the point: what is of importance is the detailed structure of the symbolic net (as in 'kinship structure'). Jung's single libido loses altogether the concern with structure that Freud's concern with the 'linguistic structure' of myths and neurosis guaranteed. And it was this grammar of symbols that, aligned with an etymological foundation for these images, secured psychoanalysis against the noumenous and anonymous flux of symbols.

> The collective unconscious, moreover, seems to be not a person, but something like an unceasing stream or perhaps ocean of images and figures which drift into consciousness in our dreams or in abnormal states of mind. (Jung (1931) CW VIII 349–50)

The stream is libido; what it bears are the images and figures that recur in dreams, myth and psychosis, each image remaining equally unimportant or important until it seizes upon a piece of neurotic preoccupation and finds expression. The chief mark of the neurotic is his indolence in turning to outmoded symbolic expressions for comfort when he should be confronting the present-day problems that confront him. To Jung, the neurotic was questionable from a moral point of view, while his symbol was efficacious from a spiritual point of view. Its spiritual efficacy, its prospective function, marked another clear difference between Jung and Freud. Insofar as the mother-symbols were not the mother, the neurotic succeeded in finding an alternative to the incest complex. The symbol had a positive function in that it pointed 'beyond' the mother, beyond the symptom to a spiritual resolution. Where Freud emphasized the derivative nature of the symbol, Jung emphasized its creative and forward-looking function. For Freud symbols were repressed or regressed concepts; for Jung they were transcendent concepts.

What the conflict amounted to was a fundamental difference of attitude towards the ineffable. Freud, in absorbing the ineffable into the inexpressible, and in his verbal rationalism, distrusted the symbol insofar as it became pure Image, and was detached from the Word. Jung wished to find in the symbol a transcendence of verbal rationality: the opposites for him really were 'Symbolic-Real'. Symbolism opened up onto the secrets of myth as an allegorical quest. The myths and traditions of other societies could not only be understood, but they could be recuperated, be brought back to life, through the interpretation of symbols. Not only did Jung and Silberer embark upon a psychological interpretation of alchemy – perhaps the only way in which twentieth century thinkers could come to terms with that episode in the history of thought – but they hoped to show that such an allegorical search could be useful in the parallel adventures of a modern Robert Fludd. The silence of the symbol was to be welcomed as an opening onto the ineffable. Freud took the silence of the symbol, just as he took the silence of the transference, as creating a practical exigency: the necessity of connection. But the symbol and the transference phenomenon – the two occasions for silence – lay at the opposite ends of a spectrum: to find the *symbolic* connection a detour via the most alien – alien to the patient – associations, and very often, as we shall see, via the most obscure linguistic forms, was found to be necessary. Whereas, with the transference, what was required lay close at hand, too close at hand, a silence signifying the danger of proximity, of 'overconnection'. At the other end of the spectrum, cloaked by the silence of a long dead language, a putative ignorance made it imperative to try and catch the echo of a reader whispering to himself in the Library of Alexandria.

FREUD'S THEORY OF SYMBOLISM

If Jung's work on mythology had led him to a Platonic theory in which the symbol represents the derivative, the earthly representative, of the Noumenon, Freud's theory now needed to be articulated fully. In 1915–17, in the *Introductory Lectures*, he accomplished this by integrating symbolism with a theory of language. This lecture on symbolism and Jones' paper on symbolism effectively ended the psychoanalytic debate on the nature of symbols and the nature of language. We find very little theoretical discussion, either in correspondence or in publications, after this date.[27]

In his lecture, Freud gave a long list of symbols and the objects (usually sexual) that they represent in dreams. He then raised the question as to the origin of these symbols, a question which, he noted, ranges much further than either dreams or sexuality. But there did seem to be an intimate relation between sexuality and symbolism. The whole train of thought culminated in the exposition of a philological hypothesis of Hans Sperber's, which argued that sexual needs have played the biggest part in the origin and development of speech. Yet again, Freud resorted to hypotheses about the origin of language in order to explain the always perplexing phenomena of symbolism:

> According to him, the original sounds of speech served for communication and summoned the speaker's sexual partner; the further development of linguistic roots accompanied the working activities of primal man. These activities, he goes on, were performed in common and were accompanied by rhythmically repeated utterances. In this way a sexual interest became attached to work. . . . As time went on, the words became detached from the sexual meaning and fixed to the work. . . . In this way a number of verbal roots would have been formed, all of which were sexual in origin and had subsequently lost their sexual meaning. . . . The symbolic relation would be the residue of an ancient verbal identity; things which were once called by the same name as the genitals would now serve as symbols for them in dreams. (Freud (1916–17) SE XV 167)

How strange to find such a full-blown hypothesis about the origin of language in a lecture on symbolism. Only strange if we forget the intimate connection in Freud's mind between the theory of language and the nature of symbols. The theory fits psychoanalysis like a glove, the origin of language grows out of sexual need and bears an intimate relation to reality – 'work'. Symbolism drops out of the theory as a secondary relic, the mark of a former *verbal* identity (Freud now stating explicitly what he had only implied in his programmatic letters to Jung of 1910), a vestigial representative of origins. Freud had made the same conceptual manoeuvre in 1895 when he pondered the question of symbolization in hysteria (see p. 93ff.) The 'common source' of both language and hysteria that he had posited in 1895[28] was the primal language of sexuality that he finally found in the hypothesis of the origin of language that he used in 1916. Behind his eagerness to use this hypothesis was his old desire to indicate the source of language in copro-erotic terms (see Chapter 5). The movement here is parallel to the move in the overall direction of psychoanalysis from the 1890s to the twentieth century. Freud looked to his friend Wilhelm Fliess to supply the organic level – the 'bottom storey' (Freud (1950a), *Origins*, p. 300) – for his psychological theories of the aetiology of neuroses. The fruit of his pious hope was the *Three Essays on Sexuality* and the grounding of the aetiology of human action in general in sexuality. From that point on, Freud clung to sexuality as the stem by which to root psychoanalysis in a universe of discourse other than its own. Whether couched in the Malthusian mode[29], the problematic distinction between psycho-analysis and biology[30], the relation of natural and social law[31], the problematic of the biological or cultural origin of history[32], or the final opposition between material and historical reality, whereby a pre-verbal event determines the turning-away of language from reality that characterizes psychosis – all these alternative formulations serve only to tie down the theory to the 'bottom storey'. As Freud wrote to Jung:

> I am rather annoyed with Bleuler for his willingness to accept a psychology without sexuality, which leaves everything hanging in mid-air. In the sexual processes we have the indispensable "organic foundation" without which a medical man can only feel ill at ease in the life of the psyche. (*The Freud/Jung Letters* 84F, pp. 140–1)

In 1916 Freud had found a theory that grounded even language in sexual need and allowed symbolism of all kinds – including the symbolization found in neurosis – to be seen as a sexual precipitate of language, which itself had turned to face reality. Symbolism would always be derivative of verbality.

We can even turn back to Freud's reply to Jung's subjectivization of the incest problem to see the form of his historical theory of sexuality and language:

> A father is one who possesses a mother sexually (and the children as property). The fact of having been engendered by a father has, after all, no psychological significance for a child. (*The Freud/Jung Letters*, 314F, p. 504)

What is at issue here is the definition of a 'father'. A father is one who 'possesses' a mother sexually: the word 'possess' thus amounts to a synonym for the sexual act (as in the Biblical 'to know'). Hence the sexual relation between the 'father' and the childrens' mother determines the relation between the 'father' and the children: they become derivatives of his sexual possession, they become property. But, at some point in time, the word 'possess' or 'property' 'loses' its sexual connotation: it becomes a 'word'. But the sexual meaning remains 'in' the symbol, so that 'children' splits off, and comes to represent the genital organ of either sex (Cf. Freud (1900a) SE V 357, 362–4; (1916–17) SE XV 157). The concept of the 'child of a father' or 'father's son' is thus parasitic upon the representatives of the sexual act; conversely, in its representation in consciousness, the sexual act is parasitic upon 'the child'. That Freud could liken the object of psychoanalysis to a kinship structure should come as no surprise (see above, p. 110).

As the meaning of words change – both in the ontogeny of the individual and the phylogeny of the race – so symbols accumulate in the unconscious of the individual and the race. Symbols are vestigial residues. Freud had returned to the promise he had made to Jung of mastering archaic regression through the development of language. Symbols are the vestiges of a time when sexuality and language were identical. In the analysis of the individual he presumed the same order; thus in his analysis of little Hans he found evidence that the little boy's faculty for symbolic representation was intimately bound up with his learning to speak (Freud (1905d) SE VII 193–4). Again, in 1908, when Freud elaborated the relationship between the character traits of obstinacy, parsimoniousness and orderliness, and anal erotism, he spoke of the symbolic relationship between money and dirt, and the ancient Babylonian identification of gold as the faeces of hell:

> everyone is familiar with the figure of the *Dukatenscheisser* (shitter of ducats, spendthrift). Indeed, even according to ancient Babylonian doctrine gold is the 'faeces of Hell' (Mammon = *ilu manman*). Thus in following the usage of language, neurosis, here as elsewhere, is taking words in their original, significant sense, and where it appears to be using a word figuratively it is usually simply restoring its old meaning. (Freud (1908b) SE IX 174)

The symbolism of gold as excrement reduces to the expression both of a contemporary linguistic usage, and of an ancient and primitive linguistic identity. Freud intimated that all symbols are reducible to linguistic usage, either past or present. I believe that Freud thought he had found 'case-historical' foundations for all the symbols he cites, though he often omitted to give the original network of linguistic usages and etymologies that had been thrown up in practice. I will give two examples from published histories, the first being the 'jewel-case' cited in the *Introductory Lectures*:

> Another symbol of the female genitals which deserves mention is jewel-case. Jewel and treasure are used in dreams as well as in waking life to describe someone who is loved. (Freud (1916–17) SE XV 156)

In Dora's case-history, written in 1901, Freud went into the symbolism of the jewel-case in some detail, since it occurred in one of the two dreams, the analysis of which comprised most of the paper. In accordance with the rules of dream-interpretation, Freud split the word into two halves: jewel and case. Jewel (*Schmuck*) is found to be very rich in associations in both Dora's 'own' language and that of accepted usage: *Schmuck* meant clean, dirty (by opposition) from which it came to represent semen and sexual wetness in general. A second verbal bridge allowed it to represent the sexual intercourse of Dora's parents. Finally, it came to represent Dora's own genitals through the set of fears constellated around semen and her worrying vaginal discharge (catarrh in Freud's terminology, which allowed him to make a bridge to the other mucous membranes, which formed the organic foundation of the concept of erogenous zone). Freud had introduced his discussion of the jewel-case with Dora by pointing out that *Schmuckkästchen* was a 'favourite expression' for the female genitals. At the end of the paper he noted:

> The element of 'jewel-case' was more than any other a product of condensation and displacement, and a compromise between contrary mental currents. (Freud (1905e) SE VII 92)

For Dora's jewel-case, Freud also had a 'lateral' determination of its symbolic meaning as female genital. A few days before, he had analysed a piece of her symptomatic behaviour concerning a reticule she was wearing. Freud suspected that Dora had masturbated as a child and wished to do so again. The playing with her reticule and the dream of the jewel-case seemed to support one another in confirming his suspicions. He noted with respect to such seemingly indirect evidence:

> There is a great deal of symbolism of this kind in life, but as a rule we pass it by without heeding it. When I set myself the task of bringing to light what human beings keep hidden within them, not by the

compelling power of hypnosis, but by observing what they say and what they show, I thought the task was a harder one than it really is. He that has eyes to see and ears to hear may convince himself that no mortal can keep a secret. If his lips are silent, he chatters with his finger-tips; betrayal oozes out of him at every pore. (Ibid. SE VII 77–8)

Hence, in the context of Dora's use of the 'symbol' jewel-case, Freud had lateral evidence concerning its symbolic referent, he had linguistic usage as a guide and he had the whole intimate fibre of Dora's admittedly non-committal revelations concerning those significations she had hidden. From this case, and perhaps from similar concordances arising out of analysis, Freud assigned jewel-case to the generic class of symbols representing the female genitals.

A few lines after he had mentioned the jewel-case in the *Introductory Lectures*, Freud noted: '*Sweets* frequently represent sexual enjoyment.' (Freud (1916–17) SE XV 156). This remark is expanded upon in the case-history of the Wolf-man, probably written a year earlier:

Permanent marks have been left by this oral phase of sexuality upon the usages of language. People commonly speak, for instance, of an 'appetizing' love-object, and describe persons they are fond of as 'sweet'. It will be remembered, too, that our little patient would only eat sweet things. In dreams sweet things and sweetmeats stand regularly for caresses or sexual gratifications. (Freud (1918b) SE XVII 107)

Here we find the reference to pre-historic periods of development combined with a call upon the good offices of 'linguistic usage'. With such analyses Freud could reassure himself that the symbols he and his followers were using had a firm basis in the past usage that had accumulated in the unconscious of present-day patients. There now seems little reason for avoiding the term 'collective linguistic unconscious' for such architectonic supports of the interpretative practice at issue.

Clearly, on the basis of the theory of the primitive sexual language, symbols are determined by a 'foreign' language of which the dreamer has no knowledge. And it was not only in 1916 that Freud had entertained such a possibility. In the first edition of *The Interpretation of Dreams* the following dream involved the analysis of the word '*geseres*' that Freud, on waking, had found incomprehensible:

. . . The boy refused to kiss her, but, holding out his hand in farewell, said 'AUF GESERES' to her, and then 'AUF UNGESERES' to the two of us (or to one of us). (Freud (1900a) SE V 441-2)

The elements 'auf geseres' and 'auf ungeseres' received two separate determinations:

i. Freud made inquiries of the philologists (*Schriftgelehrten*) who told him that:

. . . 'Geseres' is a genuine Hebrew word derived from a verb 'goiser', and is best translated by 'imposed sufferings' or 'doom'. The use of the word in slang would incline one to suppose that it meant 'weeping and wailing'. (Ibid.)

ii. Following another train of thought, Freud was led to recollect an incident (we are left in the dark as to whether he had been present, had had it reported to him, or had used his imagination in filling in the details) in which a doctor had lost his temper with the worried mother of a sick child, exclaiming: 'Was machen Sie für Geseres?'

Are these two separate determinations of the meaning of the dream-element or does i. only serve as a prologue to the lifting of a repression whose next most accessible representative is the phrase 'Was machen Sie für Geseres?'? The text does not clarify this question, but we are left with a strong impression that one of the methods available to the dream-interpreter is a philological inquiry into foreign languages. But does the recovery of an incident which provided a spoken context, an experiential point of reference, for the word 'geseres' entail that the philological inquiry did not have an independent value in elucidating its meaning?

Assuming that the Hebrew philologists did have something more to offer than just the occasion for jogging Freud's memory, we can see that, even in 1900, Freud was prepared to venture outside of the languages that he knew – or thought he knew[33] – for the elucidation of dream-elements. At this juncture, we can detach two separate points: firstly, the relation of foreign languages to the dream-elements; secondly, the relation of the individual dreamer's experiences and associations to these elements. Of course, a foreign language that was part of the individual's conscious linguistic equipment, and hence part of his dream-vocabulary, would be perfectly acceptable, even if Freud restricted possible interpretation to elements that the dreamer supplied. But what we find in the 'ungeseres' dream and, at the theoretical level in the 1916 lecture on symbolism, is the idea that a foreign language *unknown to the dreamer in waking life* can supply elements that take a place in the latent elements that determine the content of the dream. As a consequence of this assumption, Freud could continue to preserve the close relation between linguistic expression and the dream, without such an assertion conforming to the methodological individualism that the 1900 edition of *The Interpretation of Dreams* had so strongly advocated, while, at the same time, excluding the arbitrary interpretation that Freud continued to associate with imagistic symbolism. Universalism without arbitrariness: such was the aim of Freud as he shifted away from the narrower position of 1900. Philological analysis could point towards universalism and still give support to the individuality and uniqueness of each interpretative determination. Philological analysis seemed to bypass the individual associations without giving rise to monotonous and dreary translations.

In Jung's later work the concept of 'collective unconscious' came to play an important part in explaining the origin of the archetypal symbols that emerged in every analysis. Freud's psychoanalysis revealed the same phenomenon: symbols were generated in analysis and by children that seemed to cross the lines drawn up by different languages and by each individual. They seemed to represent the one certain proof of a phylogenetically inherited archaic heritage. Yet Freud attempted to minimize the importance of any such conclusions by recourse to hypotheses about language. As he wrote with regard to the phylogenetic inheritance of symbols in *Moses and Monotheism* (1938):

> Here, then, we seem to have an assured instance of an archaic heritage dating from the period at which language developed. But another explanation might still be attempted. It might be said that we are dealing with thought-connections between ideas – connections which had been established during the historical development of speech and which have to be repeated now every time the development of speech has to be gone through in an individual. It would thus be a case of the inheritance of an intellectual disposition similar to the ordinary inheritance of an instinctual disposition . . . (Freud (1939a) SE XXIII 99)

That Jung's concept of the collective unconscious might seem remarkably like such an archaic heritage might well have been a reason for airing the hypothesis of a recapitulation of the development of symbols in every generation's acquisition of language. But, in *Moses and*

Monotheism, he finally had to admit that psychoanalysis seemed to give unequivocal proof of an inherited store of symbols. But, before admitting it, he tried, once again, to put some distance between himself and Jung:

> It is not easy for us to carry over the concepts of individual psychology into group psychology; and I do not think we gain anything by introducing the concept of a 'collective' unconscious. The content of the unconscious, indeed, is in any case a collective, universal property of mankind. (Ibid. SE XXIII 132)

What exactly Freud thought he was 'saving' from Jung by this assertion would repay some thought. But certainly it then gave him the licence to assert the universal character of symbolism:

> We must finally make up our minds to adopt the hypothesis that the psychical precipitates of the primaeval period became inherited property which, in each fresh generation, called not for acquisition but only for awakening. In this we have in mind the example of what is certainly the 'innate' symbolism which derives from the period of the development of speech, which is familiar to all children without their being instructed, and which is the same among all peoples despite their different languages. (Ibid.)[34]

Such a passage, which had capitulated to all the pressures of Jung and Stekel – as well as perhaps even of the facts – still leaves us wondering about the different languages and the period of the development of speech. Is its implication that there was one primaeval speech that gave rise to a universal symbolism, and then was dissolved, by unimaginable catastrophes, into the diversity of tongues that exist today or of which we have record? Yet again, the relation of plurality/diversity to individuality and generality is evoked. The unitary past has a certain indeterminate but necessary relation to the plural present. Yet, now, the plural present does not express its diversity in the way it did in *The Interpretation of Dreams*: the stock of symbols, the relic of a spark of linguistic creativity that lies outside of history, now provides an alternative to the diversity of association, the *bricolage* of the dreamer, and the explanation that roots both these modes of dream-interpretation in one primal root, the explanation through the development of language, is now a pale shadow of a justification. It seems to do little work in the practice of analysis.

What Freud had feared in 1900 came true: symbolic methods of interpretation came to dominate analysis. During the period of debate (1907–16), one can still catch Freud castigating his followers for their wayward symbolic interpretations. For instance, in October 1912, Freud presented a case to the Vienna Society entitled: 'Communication about a Case, combined with some Polemical Observations'. One part of the polemic consisted in the following detail:

> After four months of treatment, she brought a dream that explained the essentials of her childhood history and of her neurosis – provided one did not try to interpret it merely symbolically, but drew upon the patient's associations. (*Minutes* IV, p. 108)

When we turn to the case-history of the Wolf-man, written for the most part in 1914 but not published until the end of the First World War, we find a similarly polemical remark, set in a work that is first and foremost a polemic against Jung. Freud discussed the Wolf-man's screen memory of a 'beautiful big butterfly with yellow stripes and large wings which ended in pointed projections'. The elucidation of this memory gave Freud occasion to indicate two of the possible 'pitfalls' in analysis, both stemming from the analyst attempting to impose upon the patient's material, without taking due account of the complex and highly individual structure of associations at issue.

> One day he told me that in his language a butterfly was called '*babushka*', 'granny'. He added that in general butterflies had seemed to him like women and girls. . . . I will not hide the fact that at that time I put forward the possibility that the yellow stripes on the butterfly had reminded him of similar stripes on a piece of clothing worn by some woman. I only mention this as an illustration to show how inadequate the physician's constructive efforts usually are for clearing up questions that arise. . . . After this the little problem was once more left untouched for a long time; but I may mention the facile suspicion that the points or stick-like projections of the butterfly's wings might have had the meaning of genital symbols. (Freud (1918b) SE XVII 89–92)[35]

The facile suspicion turned out to be wrong. One feels how pleased Freud was that the second anonymous and dreary suggestion proved so inadequate to the 'reality' of the 'memory'. Rather, the Wolf-man's infantile thought processes revelled in the sort of word-play that Freud always found the more convincing manner of explanation.

One day there emerged, timidly and indistinctly, a kind of recollection that at a very early age, even before the time of the nurse, he must have had a nursery-maid who was very fond of him. Her name had been the same as his mother's. . . . Then on another occasion he emended this recollection. She could not have had the same name as his mother. . . . Her real name, he went on, had occurred to him in a roundabout way. He had suddenly thought of a store-room, on the first estate, in which fruit was kept after it had been picked, and of a particular sort of pear with a most delicious taste – a big pear with yellow stripes on its skin. The word for 'pear' in his language was '*grusha*', and that had also been the name of the nursery-maid.

It thus became clear that behind the screen-memory of the hunted butterfly the memory of the nursery-maid lay concealed. But the yellow stripes were not on her dress, but on the pear whose name was the same as hers. (Ibid. SE XVII 90–1)

Yet, even now, with the elucidation of the magical significance of the butterfly-pear, the playing with words was not finished.

He confirmed the connection between the Grusha scene and the threat of castration by a particular ingenious dream, which he himself succeeded in deciphering. 'I had a dream,' he said, 'of a man tearing off the wings of an *Espe*.' '*Espe*?' I asked; 'what do you mean by that?' 'You know; that insect with yellow stripes on its body, that stings.' I could now put him right: 'So what you mean is a *Wespe* (wasp).' 'Is it called a *Wespe*? I really thought it was called an *Espe*.' (Like so many other people, he used his difficulties with a foreign language as a screen for symptomatic acts.) 'But *Espe*, why, that's myself: S. P.' (which were his initials). The *Espe* was of course a mutilated *Wespe*. The dream said clearly that he was avenging himself on Grusha for her threat of castration. (Ibid. SE XVII 94)

Freud was always happier if he could find the justification for the use of some image in a dream or in a symptom in the sphere, however defined, of 'linguistic usage'. Yet, by 1916, Freud was forced to admit that 'linguistic usage covers only a small part of [these symbols]'. (Freud (1916–17) SE XV 166) Even so, as we have seen, Freud wished to find a language that secured these symbols in a past linguistic matrix, in lieu of the present foundations of individual and folkloric language: 'And here I recall the phantasy of an interesting psychotic patient, who imagined a "basic language" of which all these symbolic relations would be residues.' (Ibid.)

Throughout his works, then, Freud found the origins and the nature of language as the alternative to a conception of the symbol as the overarching root of all unconscious products. Here, as elsewhere, Freud found the resolution of problems in historical hypotheses. As we have seen, the debate in his mind shifted from regarding symbols as an indirect representation of contemporary linguistic meanings, to finding the linguistic roots of a given symbolic reference in the past. Symbolism forced him to turn from the contemporary social system of meanings to the archaic and the pre-historical, both in the theory of hysterical symptoms and in the theory of dream symbols.

THE DEBATE CLOSES: JONES' THEORY OF SYMBOLISM

As we have argued in this chapter, it was the notion of symbolism that determined the parting of the ways of the Zurich and Vienna schools of psychoanalysis.[36] It is therefore appropriate that the definitive psychoanalytic study on symbolism was written as a polemic against the Jungians. But Jones also took as his target the work of Silberer. The argument against Jung and Silberer was often a joint one, but Silberer's work was of a quite different kind from Jung's and requires a separate discussion.

Silberer's contributions to the study of symbolism fall into two categories: (i) the experiments he conducted upon himself, observing the production of images in states of drowsiness and fatigue; (ii) the revival of the anagogic and 'symbolic' method of dream-interpretation that he built upon these. The so-called functional phenomena that he discovered in his self-observation consisted in the turning of mental *processes* into images, rather than the representation of mental contents with which Freud had concerned himself in his dream-book. Freud recognized this phenomenon as a 'second contribution on the part of waking thought to the construction of dreams' (Freud (1900a) SE V 505); that is, the self-observing critical agency directs a certain attention to the processes of dream, so that these can, in turn, become the objects of the dream-work. Having admitted that such an interpretation of specific dream images was possible and useful, Freud then diverged from the main line of Silberer's argument. As Dalbiez put it, Silberer confused the topic of symbolism by taking the functional phenomena as the most important example of symbolic representation in general (Dalbiez (1936) I p. 107). In a paper written in 1912, he described the law of symbols as follows:

. . . a tendency to replace the abstract by the concrete, and by the choice of representations which have, so to speak, a vital connection with what is to be represented. (Silberer, 1912, p. 208)

A consequence of this definition was that metaphor was a sub-class of symbols; Silberer could then define symbols as 'the form of appearance of the underlying idea'. (Ibid. p. 211) Having defined symbolism so as to include all images that were not abstract ideas, Silberer went on to argue that not all symbols represented sexual matters, the empirical crux of the argument being his own observations of the functional symbolism (or 'auto-symbolism', as he called it at times). At this point, he introduced the teleological conception of the symbol that also marks Jung's theory: symbols 'appear when man's mind reaches out for something which he cannot as yet grasp'. (Ibid. p. 217) The conditions favourable for symbol-formation are found when there is either a movement 'towards' or 'away' from an idea.

Symbol-formation appears as a falling-short-of-the-idea, as a regression to a *previous* and inadequate mental level. (Ibid.)

Silberer found the cause of symbol-formation in the Wundtian concept of 'apperceptive weakness' or 'insufficiency of apperception.' Waking life, with its apperceptive predominance, was contrasted with dream-life, in which there is a regression to lower levels of the mental apparatus. Symbols represent a movement away from the intellect towards the senses, from the idea to the image.

What was involved in Silberer's concept of anagogic interpretation was two different arguments: firstly, that symbols are attempts to represent a level of thought that is, for the moment, beyond the mental capacity of the dreamer or teller of myths; secondly, that this sphere of more abstract thought was one stage further removed from the impulsive and egocentric than the symbol. Freud agreed that certain dreams and myths included allegorical modes of representation, but denied that this represented a progress towards higher forms of thought. Rather, these indicated the difficulty of representing a thought which was both abstract and liable to arouse unpleasure in the dreamer. Freud, in other words, did not see degree of abstraction as necessarily related to the movement away from the infantile and the sexual. Once again, we encounter a theme that was often misunderstood by his followers, namely, that thought is as much in the service of desire and sexuality as perception, indeed, in certain accounts, more so: our discussion of the elaboration of family romances and the sexual theories of children, with their production of the Oedipus complex as a work of thought, demonstrates this. If we were to represent the relations of thought and symbol in Silberer's and Freud's theories, it might look like this:

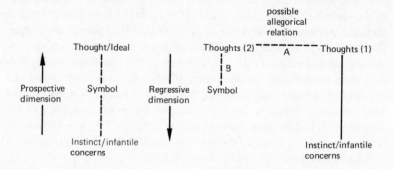

Silberer's theory

Interpretation may move either in the regressive ('Freudian') dimension or in the prospective ('Jungian') dimension.

Freud's theory

Processes A & B represent problems of the means of representation. *True* interpretation requires movement via Thoughts (2) and (1) to the infantile concerns; no direct access from the symbol to the instinctual level is encouraged. I have placed the symbol to one side to indicate that interpretation via symbolism is a minor part of Freudian interpretation. In most cases Thoughts (1) will be arrived at via free association.

Yet again, we encounter the crucial difference between Freud and his colleagues that we have met so many times in this chapter: the symbol was never at the heart of the method of dream-interpretation he advocated, so that he was determined to demonstrate that, when symbols are encountered, they are derivatives of thought which have to be constructed before the 'real' business of interpretation can start. Even then, the end result of interpretation will concern thoughts that occurred (or should have occurred) in infancy; the Freudian account always remained within that band of thought bounded by impulse and transcendental images. Whereas Jung and Silberer located symbols at the cross-roads of two different movements of interpretation – the regressive (the Freudian) and the prospective (the path of individuation and transcendent knowledge) – Freud saw symbols as only part of the more general problem of the means of representation of thoughts in the essentially alien form of visual images, forced upon the dream by the independently determined mode of regression of the mental apparatus.

In his paper, 'The Theory of Symbolism', Ernest Jones felt his first task was to distinguish symbolism from linguistic metaphor: the easiest way to find the true meaning of symbolism was by clarifying the linguistic representations of metaphor. Jones defined the metaphor by reference to the figurative/literal opposition with which we are familiar (Jones, 1916, p. 133). He then proceeded, almost without reference to the discussion of metaphor, to give the primary characteristics of the symbol, as outlined by Rank and Sachs (1913): representation of unconscious material, constancy of meaning, independence of individual conditioning factors, its evolutionary basis, its linguistic connections and its phylogenetic parallels. But it is the very monotony of the ideas represented by symbols that is so striking a characteristic, and Jones explained this feature as follows:

> All symbols represent ideas of the self and the immediate blood relatives, or of the phenomena of birth, love and death. In other words they represent the most primitive ideas and interests imaginable. The actual number of ideas is rather greater, however, than might be supposed from the briefness of this summary – they amount, perhaps, to about a hundred. . . . (Jones, 1916, p. 145)

Jones' argument then took on two different characters; a biological and a philological one. Firstly, let us look at the biological basis of the theory of symbols, which took its character from a special privilege accorded to the genetic origin of the instincts: their first objects and aims (the concrete and immediate bodily concerns, on the one hand, and the 'blood' relatives, on the other) constitute a privileged primitivity that closes off the arena of continual displacement and movement that characterized human sexuality in the *Three Essays*. Symbolism reaches back to a time – indeed, fixes it – when the contingency of instinctual aim and libidinal object is yet to be revealed. We can note this ambiguity in Freud's essay 'Instincts and their Vicissitudes' (1915) in which the 'source' of the instinct does indeed reach down into the organic, and, perhaps, defines the possible objects and aims: the mucous membrane of the anus seems to define the aim of expulsion and retention before the psychic takes its hand in determining the 'splitting off' of sexuality from the self-preservative instincts. Jones' argument, then, seems to take us back to the very source of the instinct, skipping over the level at which one might say there were only 'first' objects and aims. It is this biological level that assures him of the permanence, universality and reassuring monotony of those things symbolized.

But we are more interested in the philological arguments, and, as in Freud's lecture on symbolism, Jones makes a theory of the symbol depend upon a putative primitive language. What seemed to be empirical questions as to the meaning of this or that symbol could then be answered with evidence founded on the notion of a primitive language, thus supporting a particular directness of interpretation. The 'constant meaning' of symbols, which Jones assumed, had been the object of direct attack by Freud in the first edition of *The Interpretation of Dreams*, since it opened the door to arbitrary interpretation. But, if the symbol is referred to 'the uniformity of the fundamental and perennial interests of mankind' (Jones 1916, p. 140), the problem of arbitrary interpretation is undercut.

Jones asserted that the individual 'cannot give a regular symbol a different meaning from any one else'. (Ibid.). What is the nature of this constraint? On the one hand, we have the assertions concerning the perennial interests of mankind, the preoccupation with the body and the first objects, with its covert biological reference. But, on the other hand, we can look to another feature of symbols that guarantee their fixity of reference: their determination by the history of language.

> Now, the study of etymology, and especially of semantics, reveals the interesting fact that although the word denoting the symbol may have no connotation of the idea symbolized, yet its history always shews some connection with the latter . . . (Ibid., p. 141)

But the exact relation of the symbol to its 'determining word' is not always the same. 'It may appear in an older and now obsolete use of the same word, in the root from which the word was derived, or from other words cognate with it.'(Ibid.) Even then we may not have found the association that brings the symbol into connection with language, and thus fixes its reference. The sphere of linguistic usage in which one might have to cast one's net in search of the word grows wider and wider: jokes, folklore, etc. Or, sometimes, the relations between phrases in foreign languages and the word that stands for the symbol must be pursued, a path mapped out most bizarrely by Freud's use of Abel's work on the antithetical meaning of primal words. Jones does not look quite as far as ancient Egyptian:

> Even with symbol words where it is hard to trace any association between them and the words denoting the ideas symbolised, such an association is often apparent in the case of synonyms or foreign equivalents. A good example is our word 'room' – a room is a regular unconscious symbol for woman – where one has to go to very remote Aryan sources – e.g. Old Irish to find any trace of a feminine connotation; one has only to turn, however, to the German equivalent, *Zimmer*, to find that the compound *Frauenzimmer* is a common colloquialism for woman. (Ibid., p. 143)

We have the strange spectre of a quasi-universal language (perhaps not even restricted to the Aryan tongues) in which, unknowingly, the dreamer will dream his symbols. He has the freedom to choose another means of representation other than the universal symbolism thus guaranteed, but he does not have the freedom to use these symbols for other meanings than those laid down in language. We must conclude that the dreamer 'knows' the linguistic connections that underlie these symbols, even though he may be uncultured and unilingual in everyday life. The unconscious seems to have become a receptacle for all the languages and usages of a historically determined group of tongues. The next step is to posit a primary or primal language that supports this polyglottism of the unconscious.

And yet Jones' argument against Silberer ignored this linguistic dimension entirely, and emphasized instead the fundamental importance of unconscious affects in determining symbols. Silberer believed that symbols that had been originally used in a material sense, to represent contents of the mind, were then used to represent mental *tendencies*. Hence the specific content of the symbol – the phallus, the desire to eat the mother – would be attenuated; until the symbol would be simply representative of 'love', 'hate' or other mental tendencies. As Jones pointed out, this was simply the consequence of regarding symbols as a concrete image for an abstract idea, occasioned by the apperceptive insufficiency of the mental apparatus, an insufficiency that in Silberer's account could be explained secondarily by the interference of affects, but which rendered the symbol's exact relation to the affect of indirect and secondary significance. As Silberer said:

... the more established and pronounced typical figures become, the more do they recede from the original ephemeral signification, the more do they become the symbolic representation of a whole group of similar experiences, ... until finally one may regard them as simply the representatives of a mental tendency. (Silberer, 1914–17, p. 153, German edn.)

Jones rebutted:

if there is any truth at all in psychoanalysis, or, indeed, in any genetic psychology, then the primordial complexes displayed in symbolism must be the permanent sources of mental life and the very reverse of mere figures of speech. (Jones, 1916, p. 167)[37]

The primordial complexes remain primordial because of the affective significance that remains theirs, thus conferring a permanent literality upon the symbols forever tied to them. The important things in life do not change; there is no progress that can be gauged by the movement of symbols towards the abstract (Silberer) or towards the noumenal (Jung). Symbols represent both what is past and what is primary, often equated by Jones through a slide in the meaning of regression.

Metaphor and figures of speech escape from this model of the unconscious determination of symbolic meaning. Metaphor is only preconscious: any metaphorical relation of symbols is secondary to the primary reference, referring 'across' to collateral meanings, rather than directly to the unconscious source. Silberer's confusion, Jones argued, amounts to a confusion of symbol and metaphor, so that the functional phenomena that he took as the model for symbolism in general amount to simple metaphors.

... what Silberer, however, calls the passing of material symbolism over into functional I should prefer to describe as the replacement of symbolism by metaphor – i.e. by an associative connective between collaterals – and the difference is a great deal more than one of words. (Jones, 1916, p. 169)

Herein lay Jones' primary attack upon the Jung–Silberer interpretations: they took metaphor to be the primary form of symbolism, whereas Jones saw metaphor as not symbolical at all, since it does not involve unconscious affective forces. Around this thesis were arraigned three arguments that Jones shared, however uncomfortably, with his opponents. Firstly, symbols are concrete since that mode of representation is both easier and more primitive. But whereas Silberer in particular saw their concreteness as a primary characteristic of symbols, Jones saw it as as a by-product of the strength of the unconscious affects, which firmly attach symbols to the primary processes of thought, through which identify is asserted, in contrast to the 'similarity and difference' of metaphor.

Secondly, we find that Jones granted to symbolism the privilege that Freud wished to refuse it: direct access to the unconscious. Thus Jones came very close to Jung's position at this point: what distinguished his line of argument was the assertion that the primary affects are sexual in character. Thirdly, how does this mesh with his argument about the linguistic determination of symbolism? Strangely enough, the methodology of symbol interpretation through etymology and semantics was common to all the psychoanalysts and the post-psychoanalytical school (as Jones called Jung, Maeder and Silberer): the study of the Aryan languages, the rummaging around in the cultural baggage of the Aryan peoples in search of meanings, and the preoccupation with cross-cultural and universal connections was common to all. But it was only Freud and Jones who endeavoured to use this material as the evidence for a primal language which coincided with the primordial and biologically determined complexes of mankind. An empirical demonstration of the convergence of all these facts upon such primary meanings, a conceptual dissection of the inadequacy of a conception that tried to orient symbols towards a less sordid and less bodily future was not enough: the psychoanalysts seemed to need a foundation of symbolism both in language and in biology. The oddest part of that foundation was that it detoured via the whole system of meanings found in the Aryan languages.

Symbols are privileged since they refer us back to a time when the name and the thing matched each other perfectly. Strange spectre! The unconscious, the source of all ambiguity and incomprehensibility in its recurrent surfacings, is the locus of a language that is unambiguously univocal in its reference. In order to gain a foothold on the universal, a nominalism has been sneaked in round the back door, into the language of the unconscious, from which all other languages derive. This nominalism opposes the Platonic idealism that Jung cultivated in the concept of the archetype:

Were I a philosopher, I should continue in this Platonic strain and say: Somewhere, in a "place beyond the skies", there is a prototype or primordial image of the mother that is pre-existent and supraordinate to all phenomena in which the "maternal", in the broadest sense of the term, is manifest. (Jung (1938–54) CW IX Part I 75)

For all its emphasis on language as an independent system, psychoanalysis is continually threatened by a nominalistic theory of language, which it strives to support through a recourse to regulative principles stemming from outside its domain: the reference to biological facticity limits the free play of the system.[38] In Freud's writings, such a reference, indicating the insertion from 'outside', is signalled by the use of the prefix '*Ur-*', translated in English as primal. Whether it is the primal father, the primal horde, primal words, primal repression, the primal language, the primal scene, *Urgeschichte* – whichever it is, we are aware that a stop has been put to the sliding of meaning that continually threatens to erupt from the unconscious. The uninhibited sliding is celebrated in schizophrenia, a condition whose name has an etymology which tells us exactly the opposite of what it is: a collapse of the separate levels of meaning and reality that constitute the essence of sanity. In Lacan's revision of psychoanalysis, we find the same theoretical locus, the '*Ur-*', occupied by a metaphor, by 'the upholstery button through which the signifier stops the otherwise indefinite sliding of meaning'. (Lacan E 805/303.) Meaning has to be tied down to reality at *some* point. It is the position of such a determination that in turn determines the configuration of meaning for the subject. At some point, an identification of thing and word must be achieved, a mutual devouring of subject and object must take place, a mysterious crossing of the gap between the sound 'tree' and the concept 'tree' must be braved. Perhaps it is appropriate to let Jung have the last word upon this grand piece of mythologizing:

The alchemist saw the union of opposites under the symbol of the tree, and it is therefore not surprising that the unconscious of present-day man, who no longer feels at home in his world and can base his experience neither on the past that is no more nor on the future that is yet to be, should hark back to the symbol of the cosmic tree rooted in this world and growing up to heaven – the tree that is also man. In the history of symbols this tree is described as the way of life itself, a growing into that which eternally is and does not change; which springs from the union of opposites and, by its eternal presence, also makes that union possible. (Jung (1938/54) CW IX Part I 109–110)

4 Grammar

I fear that we do not get rid of God because we still believe in grammar.

Friedrich Nietzsche[1]

Old rule of grammar: what does not lend itself to declension, attribute to – transference.

Sigmund Freud[2]

The idea of passive includes in it the case, in which the action that I suffer is performed by myself.

A Greek Grammar, 1824[3]

SYMPTOM AS TALK: TALK AS SYMPTOM::SYMPTOM AS SYMPTOM: TALK AS TALK

In this chapter we will be concerned with the structure and location of the language that forms both the means and the object of psychoanalysis.[4] Firstly, we are obliged to take note of a fundamental ambiguity introduced into Freud's theory from the start, when he recognized both that symptoms are structured like a language – in the sense that they are *only* comprehensible when 'read' as a concealed and distorted expression of thought, whose translation into words allows them to take a place in the chain of events that constitute the experience of the subject – and that the means by which this 'place' is discovered, and by which the symptom is cured, consists in finding this translation, but this time in *spoken* language. Surely we cannot treat these two languages – the language of the symptom and the language of the cure – as the same? Surely it is precisely because the symptom is *not* spoken language that psychoanalysis becomes necessary? Having made the discovery that a symptom is the *equivalent* of a spoken message, a discovery that constitutes the very possibility of the talking cure, we are obliged to make a fundamental distinction between the language of neurosis – the incomprehensible ritual of the bed-chamber, the chronic and perpetually elusive ache or pain – and the talk with which the subject will conduct a boot-strap pulling operation, straining to bring into a coherent spoken account the little incomprehensibilities that open up to him the possibility of secreting his meaning inside a 'symptom'.

It would seem clear that, to a first approximation, the distinction between the language of the symptom and speech can be expressed as follows. The symptom is marked by its permanent character, its 'chronicity' (even if it is a question of repeated 'acute', rather than 'chronic' symptoms).[5] The language of the symptom is characterized by its relative imperviousness to discursive change, a permanence seemingly independent of all 'external' factors. In the *Project*, Freud called it an 'immovable symbolization' (*die* Symbolbildung *so fester Art*).[6]

On the other hand, the speech of the analysand is characterized by its evanescence, its dialectical character[7] through which its meaning is intrinsically bound up not only with past experience, but also with the other to whom the words are addressed, who will eventually participate fully in a dialogue.[8] Such 'speech' is here essentially opposed to the act. It is hoped that the analysand will remember rather than act out, will put things into words rather than into actions. Ideally, the speech of analysis is held to escape from the irreversible effects that speech and action inevitably produce outside analysis. The analyst presents to the analysand a screen whose properties of infinite absorption it is hoped will remove the pole by which the standing waves that constitute the analysand's unconscious are supported.

In what follows we will be touching upon the oppositions built into three closely related psychoanalytic concepts: forgetting, remembering and permanence. There is one sense of forgetting that is equivalent to repression; a memory, rather than being forgotten, is remembered too well, so well that it is a permanent feature of the psychic life of the subject, but without him knowing it. There is one sense of remembering that is captured in the formula: 'hysterics suffer from reminiscences' (Breuer and Freud (1893a) SE II 7), and their suffering, permanent, 'chronic' as it is, is due to their not being able to forget. There is one sense of 'permanent' best evoked by the term 'indestructible': 'it is a permanent feature of unconscious processes that they are indestructible. In the unconscious nothing can be brought to an end, nothing is past or forgotten'. (Freud (1900a) SE V 577)

And then, we can turn each of these three concepts around, and look at them from their other side. The other sense of forgetting is what is aimed at in analysis: one wishes to allow the normal processes of wearing away to take place: 'The task of [psychotherapy] is to make it possible for the unconscious processes to be dealt with finally and be forgotten.' (Ibid. SE V 578.) The other sense of remembering we might perhaps call recollecting, when the resistances surrounding what is remembered too well in the form of a symptom dissolve and the recollection of what had previously been forgotten dispels the permanent mark of the symptom. The other sense of permanent will refer to the ideal possibility, one of the aims of analysis, of making the past always available to the subject, so that he will be able to recall what had previously been forgotten: a permanent capacity to recollect at will.

We thus have three pairs of concepts, linked closely in their mode of operation, and ranged in opposition to each other:

Repression – Forgetting – Forgetting – Wearing away
Suffering from memory – Remembering – Remembering – Recollecting
Indestructible – Permanent – Permanent – Available to recall

Some further comments on the play of opposition associated with these pairs of concepts, although seemingly at a tangent to our main theme, may help clarify the privilege of the words spoken in analysis. In making these comments we will be bringing out certain tendencies in Freud's thought that remained, for one reason or another, in the background in his writings.

Firstly, we should note the close relation between these paired concepts and the opposition 'memory-consciousness' to be found in Freud's metapsychology. This latter opposition was sometimes couched as follows: 'consciousness and memory are mutually exclusive'[9]. The ephemerality we have noted as attaching to the speech of analysis is the counterpart of the 'inexplicable phenomenon of consciousness [that] arises in the perceptual system *instead* of [an Stelle] the permanent traces' (Freud (1925a) SE XX 228.)[10] In the *Project* of 1895 and its reworking of 1920, *Beyond the Pleasure Principle*, the mutual exclusivity of consciousness and memory was the result of an argument pertaining to the fundamental character of consciousness: the most fundamental characteristic of memory is a permanent trace or mark, left in a system by the passage of excitation; what characterizes consciousness is its responsiveness to new stimuli, a responsiveness that would be soon deadened, clogged up, if the *Cs* were subject to 'marking'. Thus the system *Cs.* shows no resistance to passage from one element to another. (Freud (1920g) SE XVIII 26–27.)[11]

Now we should note that this argument that memory and consciousness are mutually exclusive, based upon the necessary properties of the simplest possible systems of memory and consciousness, does not yet yield the conclusion that consciousness arises *instead of* (literally, in *place* of) memory traces. (Even the most sophisticated presentation of these issues, that found in 'A Note on the Mystic Writing Pad', does not go beyond the 'logical' interrelation of two systems whose necessary properties are infinite *depth* of registration and perpetual and perfect *exteriority*. See Derrida, 1966.) What introduces this relation of *replacement*, a notion that implies a temporal irreversibility and necessary connection? As we might have guessed, the notion is connected with the special character of infantile experience, or, to put it more generally, the special character of those past events to which little or no attribution of consciousness can be made. The issue is presented in an inverted manner in the following passage from *The Interpretation of Dreams*:

> . . . the impressions which have had the greatest effect on us – those of our earliest youth – are precisely the ones which scarcely ever become conscious. But if memories become conscious once more, they exhibit no sensory quality or a very slight one in comparison with perceptions. A most promising light would be thrown on the conditions governing the excitation of the neurones if it could be confirmed that in the ψ-systems memory and the quality that characterizes consciousness are mutually exclusive. (Freud (1900a) SE V 540)

Now, we not only have the opposition 'memory-consciousness', but also: 'memory-perception'. Let us align this new opposition with another hypothesis, derived from Freud's ruminations on the problem of memory, and noted in the margin of the 1904 edition of *The Psychopathology of Everyday Life*:

> Normal forgetting takes place by way of condensation. In this way it becomes the basis for the formation of concepts. What is isolated is perceived clearly. (Freud (1901b) SE VI 134 n2)

Perhaps concepts arise instead of memory traces of perceptions, just as Freud was later to rework the opposition of memory and consciousness into a formula whereby consciousness *replaces* memory. There would thus seem to be an alignment of 'concepts' with 'consciousness', both products of the effacement of the trace that constitutes memory. We might even venture a hypothesis that infantile amnesia is in large part due to the fact that the speech residues are built out of sensory experience of that epoch. Just as learning in general – concept-formation – takes place through forgetting, so a very special sort of learning, that of speech, goes hand in hand with a very special sort of forgetting. We could view such a hypothesis as an alternative formulation of Freud's argument in the *Project*, whereby the scream characterizes a pain-giving object that otherwise could not become a subject of thought: what it is not possible to recollect, what is vigorously defended against, causes the first conscious, verbal thought. (Cf. Bion, 1967, pp. 110–19).

Be that as it may, it would seem to be on this level, meshed with 'concepts' and 'consciousness', that we should situate the speech of analysis. As are they, so is it opposed to the permanent mark of unconscious memory. Indeed, one might say that not only the traumatic *force* of memory, represented in the insistent and repetitive marking of that memory, but a kind of memory *itself* disappears in the speech of analysis.

Such a paradoxical statement would appear to contradict one of Freud's criteria for the successful end of an analysis: the 'filling in' of all the gaps in the patient's memory. But, as we shall see later in this chapter, this criterion refers to amnesias conceived as duplicating, as it were negatively, the symptoms of the patient. At no point did Freud conceive of the *experience* of recalling a memory as being the same as bringing a memory *qua* trace into consciousness. We have already touched on this in clarifying the two notions of 'remembering' with which Freud worked. His radical critique of a conception of recollection as a subjective mirroring of objectively recorded traces of 'events' is perhaps most clearly seen in the last paragraph of his paper on 'Screen-memories'.

> It may indeed be questioned whether we have any memories at all *from* our childhood: memories *relating* to our childhood may be all that we possess. . . . In the periods of arousal [of memories] the childhood memories did not, as people are accustomed to say, *emerge*; they were *formed* at that time. (Freud (1899a) SE III 322)

Memories are constructed, not recorded. Again, at a meeting of the Vienna Psychoanalytic Society in February 1909, he affirmed his radical position on memory:

> . . . all childhood recollections are created at a later period, the genuine ones as well as the others. (*Minutes* II p. 159)

In consequence, then, the criteria for the genuineness of a memory must be sought elsewhere than in the fidelity with which a recollection reproduces the trace.

We may conclude, then, that the speech uttered in analysis must be efficacious in so far as it partakes of the character of consciousness, with its lack of permanence and its ephemerality, over and 'against' the permanence of memory, which is here the correlate of symptom.

Freud's labours, if nothing else, were a perpetual witness to the force of memory; but, if psychoanalysis aimed at bringing this force into ever increasing evidence, it also aimed at going beyond memory, at finding the royal road to forgetting.

[Unconscious wishes] share this character of indestructibility with all other mental acts which are truly unconscious. . . . These are paths which have been laid down once and for all, which never fall into disuse and, which, whenever an unconscious excitation re-cathects them, are always ready to conduct the excitatory process to discharge. . . . Processes which are dependent on the preconscious system are destructible in quite another sense. The psychotherapy of the neuroses is based on this distinction. (Freud (1900a) SE V 553 n1)

But earlier, on page 132, I mentioned another characteristic of the speech of analysis, namely that it is efficacious only in so far as it is not an act. Just as the good man dreams what the evil man will do, so the analysand brings into his discourse what the neurotic lets fall into the silence of the symptom (cf. Ibid. SE V 620). But, we may well ask, what is wrong with the silence of the symptom? In the first place it isn't really silent: the repressed may be, but its return is noisy enough.[12] The effects of its return are not only 'noisy' – pain, obsessive thoughts, delusional formations – they also represent the consequences of the 'first lie' that forms the kernel of the neurosis.[13] Symptoms represent the consequence of lies. What the speech of analysis will allow that an 'act' does not is the possibility of lying without having to accept the normal consequences of a lie. The symptom oppresses the subject insofar as he is, in consequence of it, 'living a lie'. After all, lying is a dimension of truth, not of reality. And, when the analytical rule asks of the patient to say whatever comes into his head, the expectation, at any rate after the seduction theory had been exploded, was that these first things would be 'lies'. It is only through such lies, those transitional objects through which one is obliged to pass *en route*, that any 'truth' becomes possible.[14] It is only through the medium of speech that a lie can open out onto the truth. *Veritas non in re, sed in dicto consistit.*[15] And only insofar as this series of lies do not become lived, do not become acts, can the speech of analysis attain its goal.[16]

Our discussion has led us, via the concept of memory, to consider speech as essentially opposed to the permanent mark or trace that constitutes the basis of memory, even if the psychoanalytic concept of memory is to be clearly distinguished from this mark. In some manner that is still unclear, speech is the agent by which permanent marks that lead to the suffering of the symptom are dissolved, forgotten. If the aim of analysis is a recollecting which leads to forgetting, through a bringing-into-consciousness, it is language that is the agent of consciousness, the agent by which consciousness effects this aim. A curious reversal of commonplaces associated with the properties of language is the consequence of this argument. Instead of language being the support of all symbolic permanence, the means by which human beings preserve the past – indeed, create the 'past' – and thus derive their humanity from the capacity of language to make this 'thing', through the mark it bears, have an existence before, speech is now the means by which the mark which language introduces can be dissolved, transformed – and forgotten. If language is the means by which permanence and memory *qua* insistent reminiscence come to be found at the heart of the symptom, it is via the ephemerality of speech-consciousness that a symptom can be dissolved, worn away – and forgotten. It is as if the possibility of a symptom is also based on that feature that makes language possible: iterability.[17] And yet it is the function of speech in analysis to try and unmake this very possibility that makes possible its own existence, insofar as speech is the means by which the effects of language can be undone. Such a seemingly paradoxical formulation may not satisfy; but perhaps its paradoxical character simply reflects all those other paradoxes in psychoanalysis: the concept of the unconscious itself, and the tensions we have noted between 'forgetting' (repression) and 'forgetting' (wearing away), between 'remembering' (insistent reminiscences) and 'remembering' (the dissipation of the symptom by discharging it in verbal recollection).

Having made somewhat clearer the difference between the speech of analysis and the symptom, we should now move on to consider the fact, and a notorious fact it is, that the patient's speech *itself* is a symptom. There are a number of different ways in which this is true; it becomes important to distinguish them. Firstly, a whole series of verbal 'acts' are constructed like symptoms: slips of the tongue, dreams, jokes. In other words, they 'say' what could be said, but in 'in other words'. The relation between such symptomatic 'speech-acts' and the talk that functions as cure is not different from that between the ostensibly more remarkable symptoms of conversion, lodged in the body, and the early conception of the talking-cure. But what these symptoms of talk indicate is how the talk of the patient is itself an *index* of the progress of analysis. All symptoms appear eventually in the talk of analysis, even if only negatively, even if only in the *absence* of talk. In conversion hysteria, what takes up a place in the body is lacking from the discourse of the patient. Hence, theoretically speaking, one would be able to infer the symptoms from the 'absences' in the discourse. It is these absences that certainly mark the self-description of hysterics:

> I cannot help wondering how it is that the authorities can produce such smooth and precise histories in cases of hysteria. As a matter of fact the patients are incapable of giving such reports about themselves. . . . The connections – even the ostensible ones – are for the most part incoherent, and the sequence of different events is uncertain. . . . The patients' inability to give an ordered history of their illness is not merely characteristic of the neurosis. It also possesses a great theoretical significance. (Freud (1905e) SE VII 16)

Freud moved easily from this observation to the idea that these gaps and incoherences in the patients' self-descriptions were the counterpart of the memories that had been lost to consciousness through being used to construct neurotic symptoms. From whence the idea of a double criterion for their cure: either the removal of the symptoms or the restoration of these memories to the consciousness of the patient (and we can here note the tension between this criterion and the psycho-analytic conception of memory, as discussed above).

> Whereas the practical aim of the treatment is to remove all possible symptoms and to replace them by conscious thoughts, we may regard it as a second and theoretical aim to repair all the damages to the patient's memory. These two aims are coincident. When one is reached, so is the other; and the same path leads to them both. (Ibid. SE VII 18)

The talking cure is thus not only a cure for the symptoms: it is a cure of the patient's talk, according to a criterion which, at its simplest, requires that the patient's account of himself 'makes sense'. The consistency and coherence of a life story can thus serve as a means of differential diagnosis:

> In my first hour with the patient I got her to tell me her history herself. When the story came out perfectly clearly, in spite of the remarkable events it dealt with, I told myself that the case could not be one of hysteria, and immediately instituted a careful physical examination. This led to the diagnosis of a not very advanced stage of tabes . . . (Ibid. SE VII 16 n2)

A curious inversion is taking place here: instead of examining the 'symptoms' of the patient, using the traditional methods of the neurologist, Freud began to concentrate more and more on the story the patient had to tell. The symptom seems to slide into the background, only appearing negatively in the examination of discourse. From a concern with a symptom and its determinants, Freud turned more and more to the *structure* of the story the patients had to tell. This development was later given an important place in the history of psychoanalysis: the change from the cathartic cure, with its emphasis on the abreaction of the psychic elements associated directly with the symptom, to the method of analysis of resistances. Freud explained the method to Pfister in a letter of 1910:

> You have seen correctly that the association technique [of Jung] is suitable for a first orientation but not for carrying out the treatment, for with each new stimulus word you put to the patient you interrupt him and cut off the flow. The spontaneous production of word series you use in analysis is certainly incomparably better, but it does not give a good picture or clear insights, and it seems to me to save no time. Where the patient is able to produce such a series, he would certainly have been capable of producing whole speeches. This would have been slower only in appearance, and would have produced a clear picture of the resistances into the bargain. The production of word series is only a way of circumventing the resistance, and for that I have no use whatever; I neglect the complexes for the resistances and try to approach the latter direct. (Freud (1963a), 5 May 1910, p. 39)[18]

The resistances are thus made manifest through the structure of the patient's talk, and it is this structure that becomes the object of the analyst's attention. Of course, it is only 'when the patient descends to minute details from the abstractions which are their surrogate' (Ibid. p. 38), that the analysis really gets going; but it is his attention to the structure of talk that allows the analyst to aid this process.

Such minute observation of the patient's talk goes back to the first psychoanalytic works. In *Studies on Hysteria*, Freud gave the following account of his first interview with Frau Emmy von N. in 1889:

> What she told me was perfectly coherent and revealed an unusual degree of education and intelligence. This made it seem all the more strange when every two or three minutes she suddenly broke off, contorted her face into an expression of horror and disgust, stretched out her hands towards me, spreading and crooking her fingers, and exclaimed, in a changed voice, charged with anxiety: 'Keep still! – Don't say anything! – Don't touch me!' She was probably under the influence of some recurrent hallucination of a horrifying kind and was keeping the intruding material at bay with this formula. (Breuer and Freud (1895d) SE II 49)

This 'symptom' displays many of the features we wish to focus upon: its repetitive character, its lack of connectedness to any parts of her conversation that came before or after, its figurative and stereotypical qualities. Or, again, from the analysis of Frau Emmy von N.: in one session, Freud asked her to 'work on' this protective formula under hypnosis. Four events, widely separated in time, came to her consciousness as a consequence. Freud commented:

> Though these four instances were so widely separated in time, she told me them in a single sentence and in such rapid succession that they might have been a single episode in four acts. Incidentally, all the accounts she gave of traumas arranged like these in groups began with a 'how', the component traumas being separated by an 'and'. (Ibid. SE II 57)

Obsessional neurosis provided the training ground for much of the intricate verbal juggling that Freud found to be necessary in the analysis of symptoms. From very early on in his theorizing, 'self-reproach' was a primary element of the aetiology and content of obsessional symptoms. (Freud (1950a) *Origins* p. 136; (1950a) SE I 223ff; (1896b) SE III 184). Starting from a primary self-reproach, distortions and transformations, acting upon the words that constituted the self-reproach, gave rise to the symptoms. In 1896 he argued:

The obsessional ideas, when their intimate meaning has been recognized by analysis, when they have been reduced, as it were, to their simplest expression, are nothing other then *reproaches* addressed to the subject by himself on account of this anticipated sexual enjoyment, but reproaches distorted by an unconscious psychical work of transformation and substitution. (Freud (1896a) SE III 155)[19]

The 'simplest expression' forms the kernel of the neurosis, finding itself repeated in the derivative or compromise symptoms, or again at the next stage of secondary defensive symptoms. These reproaches must be brought into the speech of the patient. When they have been spoken, the work of dissolving them into the discourse of analysis can start. Whether it is a question of a bodily symptom or a symptom displayed in the talk of the patient, it is this rigid linguistic structure, continually repeated, that forms the focus of analysis. And this structure is either a linguistic phrase *or* must be paraphrased by such a phrase. The infinitude of possible combinations that is the privilege of human language has been sacrificed by the neurotic, sacrificed and replaced by a monotonous insistence.

The permanence and repetitiveness of the symptomatic formations will now be the object of our study. Psychoanalytic theory developed two alternative modes of conceptualizing these structures: that which I will follow in this chapter, which turns around the grammatical variants of certain key phrases or sentences – what Freud had called 'their simplest expression'; and another, which highlighted the seminal importance of a phantasy that forms the template for later experiences and upon which symptomatic products are constructed, as a building is built upon its foundations. (Cf. Klein 1975, *passim*. and Laplanche and Pontalis, 1968)

THE PROPOSITIONAL STRUCTURE OF NEUROSIS

What will now concern us is a certain mode of analysis, which I will call propositional or grammatical analysis, that Freud and other early psychoanalysts[20] found useful in the explication of the permanence that characterizes neurosis. That this mode of analysis was never rigorously defined will be apparent from our discussion; that it owed its attraction to a 'primitive' concept of grammar may also be apparent. But that it offered a means of linking the concept of instinct, lying as it seemed to on the borderline of biology, with the preoccupations with language that had marked psychoanalysis at a theoretical and practical level from the beginning, will also perhaps explain its perennial allure. That it could be abandoned as circumstances warranted might also sanction a low estimation of its importance; but that it served as the mainstay for some fundamental hypotheses of psychoanalysis also witnesses to its fertility.

It will come as no surprise to find that the terms 'subject' and 'object' were a fundamental part of the conceptual armoury which Freud supplied to psychoanalysis. But it may be more surprising to sketch out to what extent these terms had a grammatical, rather than a logical or epistemological, reference. Obviously, as concepts, these terms had a relative independence of any given proposition. But, as working concepts, they more often than not found their most satisfactory reference in the parts of given sentences to which they, *qua* grammatical terms, could apply. More intriguingly, we find that the 'verb' that links the subject and the object was treated as being equivalent to what in psychoanalytic theory is called 'an instinct'. Having said this, we find that a neurosis will be the 'psychic structure' equivalent to a proposition or a set of propositions and their transformed derivatives.

Now this is an altogether more ambitious claim than that put forward in *Studies on Hysteria*, where specific symptoms were taken to be the equivalents of certain phrases, or figures of speech. We find ourselves at an altogether more sophisticated theoretical level: instead of the symptom, the visible and surface manifestation of a hidden 'disease' or 'cause'; and instead of a peculiar phrase or figure, a simple proposition. The movement of theory is parallel to that mapped out in Chapter 3: an increasing complexity of interpretation coupled with an increasing simplification at the level of 'first causes'. We move from a haphazard and heterogenous collection of phrases, in which the more complex the neurosis the greater number of such phrases will have to be uncovered, to one or a few propositions, which we might call 'primal sentences'.

The thesis in question, then, is that a neurosis is formed around a 'core proposition', whose structure is grammatically simple, consisting in a subject, a verb and an object. The relation between subject and object is defined by the verb. The verb itself corresponds to the instinct, or, more strictly, each component-instinct corresponds to a class of verbs. For example, the 'oral instinct' corresponds to a class of verbs including 'suck', 'bite' and, at a more sophisticated level of analysis, 'whistle', 'froth'. The class to which a given verb belongs characterizes the sexual aim of the component instinct (or, as Freud defined it in 1905, 'the act towards which the instinct tends' (Freud (1905d) SE VII 135–6). Let us look at one example of how modifications or 'vicissitudes' of the subject–verb–object system gives rise to important 'psychical' consequences.

(a) Sadism consists in the exercise of violence or power upon some other person as object.
(b) This object is given up and replaced by the subject's self. With the turning round upon the self the change from an active to a passive instinctual aim is also effected.
(c) An extraneous person is once more sought as object; this person, in consequence of the alteration which has taken place in the instinctual aim, has to take over the role of the subject. (Freud (1915c) SE XIV 127)

The relation between subject and object revolves around the active character of the verb. The 'instinct' behaves here as all verbs do in language: a verb is active unless qualified in mood by modal auxiliary verbs. The subject takes on a quality when the verb takes on a mood or a time. Defensive transformation such as 'turning round upon the subject's self' are effected by specific transformations of the indicative form of the verb. The above schema receives its instantiation in the following set of transformations performed upon a simple sentence:

1. I am beating him   Active voice
2. I am beating myself   Middle voice[21]
3. He is beating me   Passive voice

Each of the sentences 1, 2 and 3 is correlated with a certain instinctual position, upon which a neurosis or a perversion could be built. But further transforms can be derived from these sentences. Obviously, the following sentence is derived in some way from the primitive sado-masochistic positions of 1, 2 and 3:

4. My father is beating (the child), (whom I hate).

It was around this latter proposition that Freud centred his analysis of a phantasy expressed by a number of patients as: 'a child is being beaten'. That paper was an important step in the formulation of a new theory of masochism which could supplement, or perhaps supplant, the account derived from the passage from 'Instincts and their Vicissitudes' quoted above. (See Freud (1924c)). Since both papers made use of the method of propositions, it will be of interest to see how – or whether – one can link up the set of propositions elaborated in 'Instincts' with the more clinical material discussed in ' "A child is being beaten" '.

Let us first set out what Freud called the three 'phases' of the beating phantasy that he believed to have uncovered:

4. My father is beating (the child), (whom I hate)
5. My father is beating me
6. A child is being beaten

How could we envisage proceeding from the propositions 1, 2 and 3 to No. 4, or, going further, to the proposition, actually spoken in analysis, 'a child is being beaten'? Obviously, there are a number of different transformations, each of them grammatically simple and perhaps analytically plausible, which could serve as means by which to generate these propositions. For instance, a replacement of the subject of 1. – an 'identification' – by "my father" would result in the following:

4a. My father is beating (him)

or, alternatively, the extraneous person (*fremd Person*) could be identified as 'my father' (in 3.), giving:

5a. My father is beating me.

Following upon such an identification, a displacement of the object from the self to a similar gives:

6a. My father is beating the child

Such might have been the procedure to be followed if the method of 'Instincts and their Vicissitudes' were being followed. But Freud wrote ' "A Child Is Being Beaten" ' partially in order to demonstrate that the derivation of beating phantasies was more complicated than the discussion of sado-masochism of 'Instincts . . .' might have led one to believe. The propositions 4a and 6a lack an essential element of the beating phantasy; they lack the element 'love/hate'. Freud made the following comment as to the revelation of this element:

> The first phase of the beating-phantasy is therefore completely represented by the phrase: '*My father is beating the child*'. I am betraying a great deal of what is to be brought forward later when instead of this I say: '*My father is beating the child, whom I hate*.' (Freud (1919e) SE XVII 185)

We are not dealing here with the pure sadistic component-instinct, as Freud intimated one could in 'Instincts and their Vicissitudes'. Rather, the beating-phantasy involves love and hate, signs under which the Oedipus complex comes to dominate the instinctual vicissitudes, a domination at which we might have guessed as soon as 'the father' took a part in the phantasy, whether by identification (as in 4a) – the standard defensive transformation adopted in the resolution of the Oedipus complex (Freud (1924d)) – or by other means. The introduction of the Oedipus complex entails a proliferation of complications for the method of propositional analysis. What the Oedipus complex amounts to is a recognition that all instinctual propositions are *conditional*. Simply put, the propositions 'I love my mother' and 'I hate/fear my father' are dependent upon another: they cannot be treated as independent propositions. It is this element of interdependence that makes the first phase, 'My father is beating the child, *whom I hate*', of crucial importance, thus inducing Freud to write the paper on beating-phantasies, in order to clarify the nature of masochism via its interpretation in the light of the ever-increasing importance of the Oedipus complex. The proposition's conditional character entails that it cannot be broken down into two simples – 'My father is beating the child' and 'I hate the child' – without losing an essential element of their interdependence. Thus what is important in the beating element of 4. is that it is in the service of a more important instinctual current: love of the father. Indeed, Freud gave the following proposition as being equivalent to, as being a simpler, perhaps less distorted, version of, proposition 4:

7. My father does not love this other child, *he loves only me*. (Freud (1919e) SE XVII 187)

But clearly this is not the full translation of 4., since it gives no weight to the 'beating' component. Alternatively, we can say that 'beating' does not here have an erotic or specifically sadistic connotation: it serves only to exclude others from the field of the father's possible objects. One might even doubt 'whether the phantasy ought to be described as purely "sexual", nor can one venture to call it "sadistic" '(Ibid.).

What introduces an erotic component into the beating phantasy is the revival of a precocious sadistic constitution, when the wave of guilt that is both heir to the Oedipus complex and the means for its repression transforms the love that the subject has for its father into denial of this love. Being beaten by the father thus represents the fusion of the trend representing guilt and the trend representing the erotic – and now sado-masochistic – pleasure derived from the relationship with the father. That is:

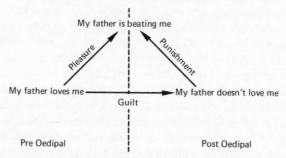

As Freud noted, on the face of things, one would appear to be able to move from 'phase 1' (our proposition 4) – 'My father is beating the child, whom I hate' – to phase 3 (our proposition 6) – 'A child is being beaten' – by placing all the emphasis on the main clause and omitting the dependent clause. Such a procedure would give no explanation of the decidedly erotic element that accompanies the evocation of the phantasy (phase 3). How can one take account of this 'affect' in the formulation of the proposition?

To do just that we must make the detour that we have outlined above: demonstrate that the passage from propositions 4 to 6 passes by the unconscious masochistic phantasy of being beaten by the father, a phantasy which represents both the repression of the Oedipal love and its 'return', its satisfaction on the level of the anal-sadistic organization.[22] In contrast, then, with the schema set out in 'Instincts and their Vicissitudes', the sequence of transformation that occupies the centre of the stage is that associated with love/hate, beating only entering in as representing egotistical interests, or as a means, revived 'after the event', of endowing this guilt-sponsored proposition with a pleasurable component. Masochism is a spin-off of the vicissitudes of the Oedipus complex; its propositional analysis is entirely dependent upon the vicissitudes of propositions representing Oedipal love.

Freud had foreshadowed the dominance of the Oedipus complex in his paper of 1915, when he had discussed the restriction of the term 'love' to a 'mature', perhaps even 'genital', relation of the ego to the object, concluding that:

> The fact that we are not in the habit of saying of a single sexual instinct that it loves its object, but regard the relation of the ego to its sexual object as the most appropriate case in which to employ the

word 'love' – this fact teaches us that the word can only begin to be applied in this relation after there has been a synthesis of all the component instincts of sexuality under the primacy of the genitals and in the service of the reproductive function. (Freud (1915c) SE XIV 137–8)

With love restricted to the arena of the genital and that of the 'whole-ego', the dominance of the Oedipus complex, as an extension of the 'interests' of the ego, entails a lesser emphasis on the vicissitudes of the component instincts. Hence the shift of emphasis we have found, from 'Instincts . . .' to " 'A child is being beaten' ". In the former, a simple proposition, representing a component-instinct, sadism, suffers a series of grammatical transformations (1–3), thus giving rise to masochism. In the paper on beating phantasies, all such component-instincts must be subordinated to the Oedipus complex, with its dominant 'instinct', love. Let us now lay out, in a schema, the whole of the set of propositions that are necessary in order to give rise to 'a child is being beaten'.

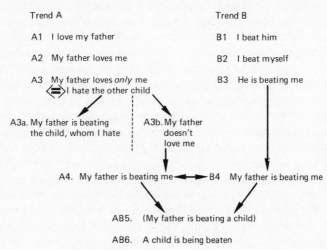

Trend A

A1   I love my father

A2   My father loves me

A3   My father loves *only* me
⟺ I hate the other child

A3a. My father is beating the child, whom I hate

A3b. My father doesn't love me

A4.   My father is beating me ⟷ B4   My father is beating me

Trend B

B1   I beat him

B2   I beat myself

B3   He is beating me

AB5.   (My father is beating a child)

AB6.   A child is being beaten

Trend A = An egotistical, oedipal and genital trend

Trend B = A sadistic and erotic trend

Note Freud's basic schema was:

1. My father is beating the child (whom I hate) = A3a
2. My father is beating me   = A4 plus B4
3. A child is beating beaten   = AB6

The sequence B can *only* give rise to masochism when combined with sequence A. The vicissitudes of 'love' take on the supreme position: all other instinctual propositions have to be read as clauses conditional upon the love and the hate that the subject brings to his first true objects, mother and father.

We can now return to the sequence that Freud took as his starting point: A3a via A4/B4 to AB6. Our diagram indicates that this sequence is not the result of a straightforward linear series of transformations. Freud's text had shown that further propositions (e.g. A3) have to be introduced in order to make sense of the sequence. Freud was obviously attracted to the notion of a simple linear sequence of transformations, such a sequence being both clinically plausible and grammatically appealing. His own demonstration, while making use of further propositions to demonstrate the 'logic' of the clinically derived sequence (though how clinically based this sequence was we shall examine in some detail shortly), thus undermined the idea that these sequences had come about by simple linear transformation. We thus perceive a struggle between the desire for a grammatically simple and a clinically verifiable sequence. The idea set out in 'Instincts and their Vicissitudes', set out there with grammar in mind, proved to be inadequate to the complications introduced by the Oedipus complex. Or, rather, we could say that the notion of grammatically simple sequencing could be made to 'fit' the data, but only at the cost of the over-formal clarification we have given. Freud, perhaps wisely, eschewed the formalism that the idea of grammatical transformation leads to, being able to order his clinical material and his instinctual hypotheses without its aid at all stages of the argument. But there is no doubt that he started the paper by giving the impression that the conscious beating phantasy was the end product of a simple sequence of transformations. When he came to examine this sequence, he found it to be inadequate. Not only was there a clause missing – ' . . . whom I hate' – that betrayed a confluence of Oedipal and sadistic currents, but the important phase 2 – that is, A4 'My father is beating me' – does not arise directly from the first phase. As we see from the schema, they both arise from a more primary proposition: 'My father loves *only* me'.

Having given this reconstruction of the method of propositional analysis employed by Freud, we should take account of the change that this brings to the practice of analysis. In Chapter 3, we saw that the introduction of the Oedipus complex as the central *explanatory* concept of psychoanalysis put somewhat at a distance the detail that makes analysis 'convincing' or 'intelligible', putting a premium on the simplification – perhaps even the reductionism – that the monotonous story of mama and papa attains. It is on this level, the level of simplification and explanation, rather than the level of detail and interpretation, that the propositional analysis is found. To say that the Oedipus complex came to take a central place in all psychoanalytical work is to fail to highlight the subtle change in psychoanalysis: 'clinical' papers came to take on a more and more abstract quality, in which the method of propositional analysis was a wooden horse by which the Oedipus complex was introduced into the citadel of the neurosis, while giving the impression that one remained close to the clinical material. But, as we have seen, in so far as the Oedipus complex entailed that all propositions include a conditional clause, it introduced complications for a propositional analysis, complications such that the method became too clumsy to handle. In consequence, we might hypothesize that the initial explicit use of the method was never turned to great account in the mid 1920s and later precisely because it would have proved too unwieldy. In addition, we should note that the method gives rise to a series of questions which prove difficult to answer: for example, what is the 'material' out of which these propositions are constructed, such that one can treat them as linguistic propositions? In languages which display a very different syntactical structure, how is one to make the rules of transformation apply? Are we to expect that the 'mechanisms of defence' will be different in different languages?

What we have called propositional analysis bears an interesting relation to what Freud, in a late paper, called the 'method of constructions'.

> If, in accounts of analytic technique, so little is said about 'constructions' that is because 'interpretations' and their effects are spoken of instead. But I think that 'construction' is by far the more appropriate description. 'Interpretation' applies to something that one does to some single element of the material, such as an association or a parapraxis. But it is a 'construction' when one lays bare before the subject of the analysis a piece of his early history that he has forgotten . . . (Freud (1937d) SE XXIII 261)

We might express the relation between the two methods as follows: propositional analysis is to the method of constructions what the method of constructions is to interpretation. Just as a construction is meant to unify into one account, into one narrative, a number of incidents, which each represent 'instinctual positions', and each of which has been arrived at by one or more interpretations, so does propositional analysis attempt to synthesize a number of constructions into one sequence. The hypothesized propositions will hopefully cover a class of analytic 'types' – for instance, masochists – being intended as a generalized account of the transforms needed to pass from an earlier position to a later. Both constructions and propositional analysis put themselves at a distance from empirical detail, in the interests of generalization. With this distance from 'the facts' came a difference in the conditions which the proposed explanation was required to meet. Quoting again from ' "A child is being beaten" ':

> This second phase 'I am being beaten by my father' is the most important and the most momentous of all. But we may say of it in a certain sense that it has never had a real existence. It is never remembered, it has never succeeded in becoming conscious. It is a construction of analysis, but it is no less a necessity on that account. (Freud (1919e) SE XVII 185)

Just as the Oedipus complex began to take on an importance, regardless of its immediate applicability to the individual case (or, in later disputes, to an individual culture), so the propositions posited as giving rise to or representing clinical material seem to lack empirical confirmation, but nonetheless are 'necessary'. A similar sort of necessity belongs to the psychoanalytic theory of the phases of the development of the libido:

> It was only with the help of the psychoanalytic investigation of the neuroses that it became possible to discern the still earlier [pregenital] phases of the development of the libido. These are nothing but constructions, to be sure, but if you carry out psychoanalysis in practice, you will find that they are necessary and useful constructions. (Freud (1916–17) SE XVI 326)

In the light of our equation between the simple proposition's verb and an instinct, to which will correspond a phase of libidinal development, we see the 'closeness of fit' between the necessity for postulating a certain phase in ' "A child is being beaten" ' and the necessity for postulating these stages of the development of the libido.

But what sort of necessity is this? Let us briefly examine the different modes of explanatory necessity that Freud employed. In his papers of the 1890s, he invoked a form of necessity pertaining to an economy of explanation of the manifest signs or symptoms of a neurosis, particularly when he spoke of the fact that symptoms have a meaning. He stated in 1896:

> ... the aetiological pretensions of the infantile scenes rest not only on the regularity of their appearance in the anamneses of hysterics, but, above all, on the evidence of there being associative and logical ties between those scenes and the hysterical symptoms. (Freud (1896c) SE III 210)

In order to explain why the symptoms take the form they do, it is necessary to embark upon a prolonged inquiry into the *meaning* of the symptom. From this, arises what we might call 'hermeneutic necessity': the long and arduous search for the meaning of a symptom will ensue in a necessity being attributed to the elements that together go to make up the story or incidents that the symptom recounts. 'Hermeneutic necessity' bears much upon the details of a case.

The second type of necessity also appears to arise out of close work with detail, with the products of interpretation. This second form arose naturally out of the first, although they are logically quite distinct. This second form pertains to a temporal order: certain prehistoric events not only appear to be inextricably bound up with the character of symptoms, but also appear to function as 'necessary conditions' for their coming into being. These events appear not only to be hermeneutic factors, but also aetiological factors. But the relationship between these events and the symptoms is not a simple causal one, as the concept of *Nachträglichkeit* indicates. But this form of necessity does seem to be of a temporal order, even if we would not wish to speak of it as causal necessity. An example of this form of necessity would be the manner in which Freud suggested to the Ratman that he had indulged in masturbation in his infancy, a suggestion that was meant to explain a peculiar midnight ritual and which then elicited a memory of his infancy in which he had flown into a rage with his father, the putative prohibitor of the masturbation and thus a suitable object for rage. (Freud (1909d) SE X 204–5.)

Such necessity belongs to the order of construction. Construction and interpretation both share those forms of necessity pertaining to the manner in which an array of evidence is meshed with certain explanatory entities – whether the latter be 'meanings' in general (Dora's jewel-case and reticule are explained in a loose manner by being referred to thought-activity concerning her genitals) or past incidents (the Wolf Man's dreams refer to a set of events, none of which can be brought (back) to consciousness, these dreams acting as the witnesses for positing that these events 'took place', even to the point where the conviction of the patient will be the phenomenological correlate of this explanatory necessity).

But we are concerned more with yet another form of necessity, for which 'empirical considerations' are of secondary importance. This necessity arises from the need to find a simple sequence of the basic propositions of the neurosis. An incomplete sequence of propositions would be of little value. Hence it becomes necessary to postulate the existence of intermediary and, perhaps more importantly, 'junction' propositions. Freud's problem in the paper on beating phantasies was simple: how can one demonstrate the sequence by which beating, at first only egotistical in character, could become an erotic event. His answer was to postulate the existence of an intermediary proposition that could also function as the junction between two different instinctual trends. In this way, 'My father is beating me' came to function as a 'switch-proposition': but not in the patient's associations this time, rather in the analyst's theoretical schema. Without the constructed proposition, one cannot inject the necessary erotic component into the idea of beating; without the constructed propositions one cannot pass in an unbroken sequence from one proposition to another. We might call this type of necessity, 'architectonic' or 'structural' necessity.

It is clear that 'architectonic necessity' can be of importance when an analyst offers his patient a construction. Freud intimated as much when he spoke of the 'false combinations (*irrige Kombinationen*)' that the analyst is quite likely to offer. When an analyst conjectures that the birth of a sibling occasioned the transfer of affections from the mother to the father, he is obviously postulating an event in accordance with certain constraints arising from the propositions or early instinctual positions that have already been established, together with constraints stemming from a theory concerning what sort of early events might conceivably be an intermediary stage between those phases already known to be of importance in any given case. With propositional analysis, the influence of theoretical constraints is that much more marked. It is the proximity of the basic propositions to the level of instincts that both acts as an incentive to the development of propositional analysis, and acts as a constraint upon the sort of propositions and sort of transformations that might be acceptable in its employment. We will return to this topic at the end of the chapter, in order to clarify what might be the criteria for accepting a proposition as 'primal'.

Let us here return to the manner in which these three varieties of necessity bear upon the concrete example of the beating-phantasies. It is clear that Freud took very little account of the manifest symptomatology of the cases he used to construct the propositional sequence engendering the 'neutral' phantasy actually found in analysis. He gives little or no empirical justification in and of itself for postulating phase 2 (proposition 5). In other words, neither 'temporal' nor 'hermeneutic' necessity plays a significant role in the analysis of the phantasy structure. As Freud observed,

> The analytic physician is obliged to admit to himself that to a great extent these phantasies subsist apart from the rest of the content of the neurosis, and find no proper place in its structure. (Freud (1919e) SE XVII 183)

We can conclude that the form of necessity pertaining to the mode of explanation found in *Studies on Hysteria* and the earlier works on the neuroses, namely the postulation of certain unconscious elements in order to unify diverse manifest signs of a neurosis, plays little part in the analysis of the beating-phantasies. What is of importance is the necessity imposed, on the one hand, by the theory of the instincts and their different developmental phases, and, on the other hand, by a principle of architectonic simplicity, whose concomitant is a concern with the order of grammatical transformations performed upon the 'primal' instinctual representatives.

These different forms of 'necessity' correspond to different forms of explanation found in psychoanalytic work. Thus, when we talk of different forms of 'necessity' being used, we are referring to the mixture of modes of explanation that might make up any given piece of psychoanalytic work. That different types of explanation may be combined when at work on a specific piece of material should come as no surprise. What our investigation here shows is that one type of 'necessity', pertaining to an internal logic of an explanation which is concerned with the relations between constructed propositions, was the dominant mode in '"A child is being beaten"' and perhaps in other papers where the propositional logic of the neurosis was at the forefront. The internal logic refers to the sequence of transformations performed upon a given instinctual position.

Such transformations correspond to the mechanisms of defence. One often infers their existence upon most indirect evidence, in accordance with criteria of simplicity and uniformity. The procedure is parallel to that adopted in explaining the genesis of certain manifest forms of spoken language: a grammar is posited that governs the possible transformations of a given sentence. More pointedly, given the concept of 'construction' in psychoanalysis, the grammarian infers an intermediate form, or set of such forms, between a 'primitive' sentence and a manifest one. And such intermediate forms would never be attributed to the consciousness of native speakers. Note that any subsequent temporal articulation of these distinct forms upon a chronological dimension is predicated upon their first having been ordered according to the admissible laws of transformation.

The parallelism of method between the grammarian and the psychoanalyst is not the most interesting feature of our discussion. Rather, the fact that the analyst's objects are sentences – either ones that have been spoken in analysis, or ones that represent the ideal types of numerous similar sentences – justifies our treating the activity of construction and interpretation as – to coin a term – a 'metagrammatical' one.

But metagrammatical analysis is not primarily focused on the patient's utterances – indeed, one hardly needs to refer to the patient's utterances. The examples we have analysed are schemata corresponding, perhaps, to 'instinctual representatives', rather than being pivotal moments in the discourse of analysis. Certainly the analyst would like the patient to be able to incorporate the propositions into his own speech, to recognize them as the clearest possible statement of what he had repressed, and to be able to accept them as such, in order to judge them and hence forget them, instead of repressing them anew and thus 'remembering' them. Such a passage from saying to judging would then mark a psychic full-stop to that episode of rhetorical persuasion on behalf of the analysand. A further example of the method of propositional analysis, or metagrammatical construction, will indicate both the fertility of the method and its distance from any analysis of the speech of the patient.

The starting-point of the analysis of beating-phantasies was a sentence spoken in analysis: 'a child is being beaten'. From there, the analytic argument leaves all reference to the speech of the patient to one side, following out the implications of a propositional analysis. In the case-history of President Schreber, there is not even this spoken (or written) starting-point. Propositional analysis acts strictly at the level of a deductive structure of the paranoia, with only the most general reference to the clinical detail. Freud's propositional model was intended to contribute to a general theory of the paranoiac psychoses. All of these, he thought, arise from the repression of a primary 'idea', a 'primal sentence', expressive of homosexual love. The idea that suffers repression and subsequent transformation can best be expressed in the form of a simple sentence: 'I love him'. The return of the repressed necessarily takes the form of a compromise between the force attached to this idea and the force of the censoring ego; the means by which this compromise is effected are the grammatical transformation of the primal sentence. Each of the three elements of the sentence might be the point of application of this grammatical operation. But each of these three operations must give rise to a proposition that is in conformity with a principle peculiar to paranoia, namely, that the repressed should return from 'without'.

One way to formulate this principle is to say that the mechanism of 'projection' is the defence mechanism proper to paranoia. But, as we shall see, the mechanism of projection is not a necessary condition for this group of transformations. Rather, one might wish to couch the principle as follows: *admissible transformations of the primal sentence must not include the subject as first person of the statement.*[23] The most common means by which this principle asserts itself in 'practice' is through the replacement of the first person pronominal subject ('I') by the third person pronominal subject ('he', 'she' or 'it'). It is this procedure that Freud followed in his discussion of the Schreber case.

(a) Firstly, the verb can be transformed, and, as is so often the case with Freud's more formal considerations of defence mechanisms, the fundamental transformation is 'turning into its opposite'. Thus the verb 'love' becomes 'hate':

1. I love him

    1–2 = Defence: Turning into its opposite

2. I hate him[24]

    2–3 = 'Projection', or Principle of the exclusion of the first person subject

3. He hates me . . . therefore I hate him[25]

The consequence of this double transformation is the classic clinical form of paranoia: delusions of persecution.

(b) Secondly, the *object* can be transformed:

1. I love him

    1–2 = Defence: Turning into its opposite

2. I love *her*

    2–3 = Principle of the exclusion of the first person subject

3. She loves me. . . therefore I love her

The clinical picture arising from this transformation of the object of the sentence is *erotomania*: compulsive falling in love with objects of the opposite sex. The clinical picture corresponds to 2. But each of these compulsive affairs, Freud noted, starts not with an interior perception of loving, but with an external perception of being loved. Thus the fully 'projected' sentence, no. 3, chronologically precedes the full clinical picture. The accent falls on the activity of the subject ('*I* love *her*'), in a way that is not the case in paranoia, where persecution is more prominent than the subject's hatred of the persecutors. Freud explained this by pointing out that 'the intermediate proposition "I love *her*" can also become conscious, because the contradiction between it and the original proposition is not a diametrical one, not so irreconcilable as that between love and hate: it is, after all, possible to love *her* as well as *him*.' (Freud (1911c) SE XII 63.) In other words, when it is a question of transformation of objects, the principle of the exclusion of the first person subject is not rigorously binding.

(c) Thirdly, the subject of the sentence can be transformed:

1. I love him	1–2 = Defence: Turning into its opposite
2. *She* loves him	2–3 = Projection, or Principle of the exclusion of the first person subject
(3. *She* loves him)	

Since this proposition already includes the third person as subject – i.e. it is couched in the form of an external perception – it requires no further transformation beyond stage 2. That is, this is the form of 'paranoia' that does not involve projection, although it still conforms to the principle of the exclusion of the first person subject. The symptoms produced by this transformation are those of pathological jealousy.

(d) Fourthly, the whole sentence can be transformed, thus highlighting the distinction between the subject of the enunciation and the subject of the statement that is implicit in the principle of exclusion of the first person subject:

Now, it might be supposed that a proposition consisting of three terms such as '*I love him*', could only be contradicted in three different ways. Delusions of jealousy contradict the subject, delusions of persecution contradict the verb, and erotomania contradicts the object. But in fact a fourth kind of contradiction is possible, – namely, one which rejects the proposition as a whole: '*I do not love at all – I do not love any one*'. And since, after all one's libido must go somewhere, this proposition seems to be the psychological equivalent of the proposition: 'I love only myself'. (Ibid., SE XII 64–5)

It is interesting to try and reformulate the rather crude principle that Freud made use of here: 'one's libido must go somewhere'. In terms of the distinction we have made between the subject of the statement and the subject of the enunciation, 'rejection of the proposition as a whole' is equivalent to the refusal of the subject of the enunciation to 'enounce'. This refusal can take two forms, corresponding to two different 'readings' of the proposition, 'I love only myself'. The first reading conforms to the principle of the exclusion of the first person subject, being equivalent to a radical rupture of the relation between the subject of the enunciation and the subject of the statement ('the ego' in this example): 'He (my ego) loves only himself'. This would correspond to what Freud called 'sexual overvaluation of the ego', and would be the 'noisy' version of megalomania – it is as if the libido of the subject is trapped within the ego, completely lacking a relation to the subject of the enunciation. Such a reading of 'extrovert' megalomania would emphasize the manner in which the frenzied proclamation of selfhood, of the 'I', forecloses the subject from any place in the order of language.

The second reading would correspond to a refusal to recognize the possibility of there being any *distinction* between the subject of the statement and the subject of the enunciation; this time it is the subject of the statement that suffers foreclosure. Such a situation is altogether more difficult to represent in a proposition: the following version may give some hint of this confused, unordered situation: 'I (that is, me) love only myself (that is, me)'. The introverted side of megalomania – catatonic silence – corresponds to this refusal to come out of an order that has collapsed the essential dualism of language into a homogeneous reality, where *only* self-referring ontological units are permissible, and which thus refuses the absence around which language is built. Such a position might correspond to the 'ejaculatory speech' that Jackson contrasted with 'propositionizing'.

With this example drawn from the Schreber case, it is quite clear that the method of propositional analysis can be employed completely independently of the direct speech of the analysand. The system of propositions and their grammatical transformations correspond to the nucleus of the neurosis and govern its rigid and repetitive structure. But the grammar of the neurosis and the speech of the patient *can* be brought close to one another: the phrase 'a child is being beaten' was the spoken starting-point for analysis. If we now turn to an example that was never analysed as formally as those we have been discussing up to now, we will see more clearly the manner in which transformations of a 'primal sentence' can both pervade the structure of behaviour and be analysed by its appearance in spoken analysis.

It is a question of a sentence that formed a nodal point in Freud's self-analysis. Three of the most important dreams in *The Interpretation of Dreams* were dreams of self-justification: the 'dream of Irma's injection', the 'dream of the botanical monograph', and the '*Non Vixit*' dream. The need for self-justification stemmed often from disputes with colleagues, from feelings of guilt about professional judgements, from mortifying comparisons with admired friends and colleagues – men who often had not lived to fulfil the promise that Freud had seen for them and which he had inherited from them.[26] The infantile experience that formed the back-drop for all these later dreams involved a dispute with his nephew John, a year older than himself, when he was four. The curiously roundabout character of the account Freud gave of the incident, having already broken up the analysis of the '*Non Vixit*' dream into two portions, separated by sixty pages of text, indicates a degree of distortion, indeed of grammatical transformation, active even as he wrote the account. Bearing in mind the argument of this chapter, the switch in the narrative from the third to the first person is especially of note: it perhaps corresponds to a 'victory' over the Principle of Exclusion of the First Person Subject, to a mastery of the tendency to justify oneself by a 'projection' of the subject of the deeds in question, to a reversal of the vilification of others by which self-justification achieves its ends.

> For the purpose of dream-interpretation let us assume that a childhood memory arose, or was constructed in phantasy, with some such content as the following. The two children had a dispute about some object. (What the object was may be left an open question, though the memory or the pseudo-memory had a quite specific one in view.) Each of them claimed to have *got there* before the other and therefore to have a better right to it. They came to blows and might prevailed over right. On the evidence of the dream, I may myself have been aware that I was in the wrong. However, this time I was stronger and remained in possession of the field. The vanquished party hurried to his grandfather – my father – and complained about me, and I defended myself in the words which I know from my father's account: 'I hit him 'cos he hit me'. (Freud (1900a) SE V 483)

The sentence, 'I hit him 'cos he hit me' – '*Ich habe ihn gelagt, weil er mich gelagt hat'* – is the 'intermediate element in the dream-thoughts, which gathered up the emotions raging in them as a well collects the water that flows into it'. (Ibid., 484.) Its very baldness, its very inability to be misconstrued, necessitated the distortions that made up the dream, represented in condensed form by the replacement of the living letter '*v*' by the dead letter '*x*' in the inscription, *Non Vivit*. The distortions of later years, found in the analyses of the dreams, are again transformations of the grammatical simplicity of the original sentence. Thus they move from the compensatory equality of the original, with its symmetry and its punitive causality (introduced by '*weil*'), to the egotistic finality of 'It serves you right if you have to make way for me. Why did you try and push *me* out of the way? I don't need you, I can easily find someone else to play with.' And from there to the next level of distortion, a colloquialism from a foreign language, thus two removes from the clarity of the childish claim for talion justice: '*Ote-toi que je m'y mette.*' The final transformation of this sentence is a pure example of sublimation, that attempt to freeze desire into cultural form: 'As he was ambitious, I slew him.' (Ibid., pp. 423–5.)

The discomfort we feel when confronted by the belligerent child is replaced, at fourth remove, by the exquisitely judged conceit of a man whose right to decide life and death, if tortured, at least cannot be denied. We can hypothesize that, when the 14-year-old Sigismund came to play Brutus to the 'vanquished party's' Caesar, the 'cadence' (*Klang*) of the speech he uttered led him back to that other sentence, uttered when he was three years old, and, at that very moment, a movement of distortion, of disguise, operated, and continued to operate, so that those words of Brutus' would become a permanent and obscurely evocative memorial to an event whose meaning now lay hidden. Freud's consequent identification with the slayer of Caesar, represented by the intense aesthetic value attached to the words from Shakespeare, would be the conscious *and* symptomatic evidence of both the prehistoric event and its repression. Yet how are we to trace this distortion, if not by the subtle shifts of grammatical structure – which sometime go under the name of style – the thread that runs from the bald simplicity of the nursery rhyme to the metaphysical gossamer web that the poet spins. Or, alternatively, to the disarming dishonesty of the witticism:

I was delighted to survive, and I gave expression to my delight with all the naive egoism shown in the anecdote of the married couple one of whom said to the other: 'If one of us dies, I shall move to Paris.' (Ibid., p. 485)

Each of these 'allusions' that make up the series of associations is structured on the model of the infantile sentence 'I hit him 'cos he hit me'. What unites them is a single 'deep' grammatical structure – what Freud called their '*Satzbau*' – through which a retributive egotism can be expressed. A conditional clause provides reasons for the act whose 'true' reason always lies elsewhere, indeed whose 'true' reason seems to be overshadowed by the absolute quality of its assertion. The *mode of construction*[27] is the connecting link between all these different associations; the form of thought, also the same in these examples, is inseparably linked to the grammatical structure, such that we may regard the series of associations as transforms performed upon this one structure.

But how 'primal' is this sentence, 'I hit him 'cos he hit me'? Freud certainly gave the impression in *The Interpretation of Dreams* that this proposition forms the core of the dream-thoughts, the infantile residue that allows the dream to take place. And the theme of the dream, male friendship, is well covered by the sentence. But what of little Pauline, the third member of the triangle, who might well be covered by the term 'object', if not on that specific occasion, certainly on many others?[28] Perhaps there are deeper layers waiting for interpretation, as indicated when Freud came to repeat the allusion to *Julius Caesar* in a note added to the case-history of the Ratman: '. . . these words [Brutus' speech] strike us as rather strange, and for the very reason that we had imagined Brutus's feeling for Caesar as something deeper.' (Freud (1909d) SE X 180.)[29] Are we to conclude, then, that the primal sentence is not primal, because there are hints of 'something deeper' that underlies the attenuated form found in Shakespeare, and, also, by implication, in its original nursery form?

So what is a primal sentence, or, more precisely, what weight does the term 'primal' have? In the discussion of the four examples we have used in this chapter, the primal sentence was taken to be the first sentence in a sequence of transformations. This seems to have been Freud's practice when he discussed the transformation of sadism into masochism, and of voyeurism into exhibitionism in 'Instincts and their Vicissitudes'. It is certainly true that transformations always have a temporal dimension; transformation from p to q can quite generally be used to explain why q followed p. This temporal dimension, however, is not always the dimension of theoretical importance, along which a transformation operates. What is sometimes of more interest – for instance in the Schreber case – is the dimension from 'deep' unconscious to conscious. Indeed, in his discussion of the transformations in the Schreber case,

Freud gave no temporal marking at all, indicating no temporal location for the sequence by which Schreber's paranoia was produced. We thus have two dimensions of theoretical interest upon which transformational sequencing takes place: unconscious to conscious, and early to late in the subject's development. In 'Instincts', both of these dimensions were left unspecified, so that we are presented solely with the transformational apparatus itself. In the Schreber case, the focus is entirely on the dimension of 'depth', from unconscious to conscious. In '"A child is being beaten"', the transformational sequence receives specification along both the temporal and the depth dimensions. And in the example drawn from the *Non Vixit* dream, both dimensions are again involved in a complex way. The obvious temporal ordering of 'I hit him 'cos he hit me' as earlier than 'As he was ambitious, I slew him' serves as a ground for taking the thoughts concerned with the 'I hit him . . .' as deeper in the processes underlying the formation of the dream.

For transformations from depth to surface, it would seem that what is primal is what is 'deep'. And for transformations from early to late, it would seem that what is 'first' is primal. We can now see that the method of transformational sequencing involves an abstraction – or, as in 'Instincts', an under-specification – leaving to one side these two dimensions of 'depth' and 'time'. With this abstract and formal notion of transformational sequence go two formal or abstract criteria for what is primal in a sequence of transformations: 'closeness to instinct' and 'grammatical simplicity'. Because of the proximity of the notion of instinct as 'deep' and instinct as 'early', 'closeness to instinct' gives a criterion of primality which maps on to the dimension of depth and on to that of temporality. Grammatical simplicity is itself a purely formal characteristic applicable to the base of any transformational system. But the 'closeness of fit' between a simple grammatical sentence and a basic instinctual position as defined by Freud in 'Instincts' again provides a criterion of the primal which coincides very closely with that derived from the criterion of 'closeness to instinct'. Primal sentences would seem to correspond closely to the definition that Freud gave of instinct when we conceive of this definition in 'grammatical' terms: pressure (essential characteristic of the verb), object, source and aim (the latter two specifying the 'content' of the verb). We would certainly not now accept as primal any sentence that was couched in anything other than the indicative, a criterion that approaches close to the seemingly independent notion that the 'primal system', that under the sway of the primary process, knows no distinction between past, present and future, between wish and reality, between optative and indicative (Freud (1900a) SE V 534–5, cf. (1909d) SE X 178–9).[30] The grammar of the unconscious has neither modes nor tenses. And the idea of the primal sentence including a conditional clause, although, as we have seen, necessitated by or equivalent to the Oedipus complex (provided that one of the clauses contains a direct derivative of the instinctually ambiguous verbs, 'love' or 'hate'), would seem to lie on the borderline of the primal. After all, we cannot expect the unconscious to 'if' or 'but', we cannot expect it to countenance an ontic heterogeneity in its reality.[31]

From our discussion of the derivatives of a primal sentence, still unknown, found in the *Non Vixit* dream, we observe that these transformations emerge in the guise of rationalizations, self-justifications, the flow of fine poetry and the underhand subtlety of the *bon mot*. Primal sentences become transformed into the later derivatives that appear in consciousness through a process of distortion and the introduction of syntactical complexity. The simple and childlike battle of wills becomes in later life a play in which the knife in the back takes place off stage, becomes a displaced shadowy web of half-expressed animosities.

But our analysis of 'As he was ambitious, I slew him' involved great attention to the 'spoken' set of associations derived from the given dream-elements. The propositions were not 'constructions' of analysis. What bound these elements together was their common grammatical structure, a structure that thus corresponds to the core (or one of the cores) of Freud's 'neurosis'. But now this core has become manifest in the 'talk' of analysis (or, in Freud's case, in his publications): it now permeates that very element that is supposed to free the subject of his neurosis. Between the dialectical freedom of speech and the analytical fixity of neurosis, a third and intermediate sort of language emerges: a speech that is structured in the same manner as the neurosis. By noting this fact, that sometimes the propositions formulated by theory coincide with the sentences spoken in the session, we make clear the true innovation of the *I* and the *it*, found in the 1923 structural reformulation of the metapsychology. The first person subject of a sentence, the '*I*', does not cover our true nature; rather, *das Es*, the grammatical term which Nietzsche 'habitually used . . . for whatever in our nature is impersonal and, so to speak, subject to natural law' (Freud (1923b) SE XIX 23 n. 3), must be taken as the 'true' subject, a subject which will occur unexpectedly in the utterances spoken in analysis: a fairy story suffused by the mysterious phrase, 'It came about that . . .', or the emergence in language of a realm always beyond the 'I', when one says, '*Es träumt mir . . .*'.[32] The *I* and the *it* form the bridge between the language of neurosis and the speech of analysis.

But the most important theoretical bridge between the unspoken neurosis and the free speech of the patient does not lie in the overlapping of 'theoretical' and 'observational' languages. Rather, it lies in the transference. It is in the transference that the propositional structure of the neurosis is translated into spoken words and thus forms the intermediate stage between the neurosis and the cure.

One way in which Freud conceived of the transference runs as follows. The transference represented a new edition of an old text (Freud (1905e) SE VII 116). The new edition is often a 'euphemistic transformation' or 'sublimation' (as Freud called it in his 'Dora' case history). In so far as transferences are new editions of the *Urtext* of the neurosis, they are the most suitable material for the construction and reconstruction of the primal sentences that determine the structure of the neurosis. Transferences owe their great importance to a number of features; here, I wish to select one: their recent origin. They are the activation of the 'permanent text' of the neurosis in a 'novel' form. Certainly their *persuasive* function in analysis is paramount (Freud (1912b) SE XII 108). But, according to Freud, they should be restricted as far as possible to the sphere of language rather than that of action. Recollection (in words) must predominate over acting out. And this is precisely because of two features of acting out: firstly, it is not reflected upon, whereas the canons of reflexivity are built into spoken language. Secondly, any acting out that does take place must be translated back into trains of verbal thought. We might take as our exemplar of this procedure the analysis of bungled actions set out in *The Psychopathology of Everyday Life*. One such example involved Freud picking up a tuning fork from his desk, instead of the hammer he intended to take hold of. The interpretation ran:

> The error of picking up the tuning fork instead of the hammer could thus be translated into words as follows: 'You idiot! You ass! Pull yourself together this time, and see that you don't diagnose hysteria again where there's an incurable illness, as you did, years ago with the poor man from the same place!'. . . . It will be observed that this time it was the voice of self-criticism which was making itself heard in the bungled action. (Freud (1901b) SE VI 166)

The action is only understood when a verbal translation of its meaning has been given. In addition, the action only becomes a 'significant action', of the sort psychoanalysis deals in, owing to a verbal chain that can find suitable expression in the bungled action. Otherwise, we are dealing with a mistake, and there is no more to be said. This phenomenon involves what Freud called 'linguistic compliance', assuming great importance in another passage in *The Psychopathology*:

> Every time we make a slip in talking or writing we may infer that there has been a disturbance due to mental processes lying outside our intention, but it must be admitted that slips of the tongue and of the pen often obey the laws of resemblances, of indolence or of the tendency to haste, without the disturbing element succeeding in imposing any part of its own character on the resulting mistake in speech or writing. It is the compliance of the linguistic material which alone makes the determining of the mistakes possible and at the same time sets the limits up to which the determining can go. (Ibid., pp. 221–2.)[33]

Here Freud indicates that the limits of the field of analysis are set by the field of language: what is not within that field does not admit of a *significant* connection between cause and effect, only its 'necessary conditions' being specificable. Acting out must be brought within the field of language; as much as possible of the transference must be said, not acted. In other words, emphasis upon the transference corresponds to a fixing of the limits of the field of analysis as those of language. What was previously the silent object of analysis – the symptom, putatively structured by transformations of primal sentences – is replaced by the transference neurosis (Freud (1914g) SE XII 154). But this new neurosis must be made to 'talk' if its creation is to be marked as a gain. The advantage of the transference neurosis is that the phantasy-structure generated by the deformations of the primal sentences coalesces around the object that is present, to which the seducing words are impotently offered. A dialogue can ensure that these words do not once again become frozen into symptoms, so that the ephemeral character of words is restored to them, so that they will no longer be emblematically fixed – no matter with what serious loving intent – to imaginary objects.[34]

Perhaps we can now reformulate the divergence with which we opened this chapter by drawing upon the grammatical mode of analysis we have discussed. The language of the symptom could be conceived of as a set of marks that are structured by derivatives of primal sentences – the core of the neurosis. The language that is spoken, when it is not itself symptomatic – when it is not the cliché, the repetition of words heard and tendentiously forgotten, when it is not complacently and fearfully rigid, in other words, when it does not retain the structure of the primal sentence – rejoices in its ephemerality, which it is hoped will allow it some escape from the blind insistence that characterizes the transformed derivatives of the unconscious primal sentences. What is said in and by this spirit, this spirit embodied in *Geistigkeit*[35], always has the character of a movement, impelled by powerful and invisible forces: the change that 'saying it aloud'[36] engenders bears witness to the inexplicable efficacy of speech in subverting a permanence that, before it is dissolved, appears to be constitutive of the subject. Or, to return to the simple beginnings, to the *Studies on Hysteria*, 'it is only with the last words of the analysis that the whole clinical picture vanishes'. (Breuer and Freud (1895d) SE II 299.)

5 Philology

I am not yet so lost in lexicography, as to forget that words are the daughters of earth and things are the sons of heaven.

Dr Johnson[1]

How can man be the subject of a language that for thousands of years has been formed without him, a language whose organization escapes him, whose meaning sleeps an almost invincible sleep in the words he momentarily activates by means of discourse, and within which he is obliged, from the very outset, to lodge his speech and thought, as though they were doing no more than animate, for a brief period, one segment of that web of innumerable possibilities?

Michel Foucault (1966/70) p. 323

By now, our discussion has given rise to a backlog of only partially answered questions. Let us try to make some of them explicit. If psychoanalysis was at its inception so much concerned with language, what were its relations with those sciences whose explicit aim was the study of language? A reading of any psychoanalytic work of Freud's – a dream-analysis, a case-history – would convince us of the great seriousness and importance attached to a playing with words, to plays on words, to the veering off of meaning that every analysis reveals. Was this preoccupation something to do with Freud's own individual make-up, his own mental bent? Was it something peculiar to him that allowed all these clevernesses? One answer would perhaps be that all 'that' is a necessary consequence of the nature of the unconscious, so that we can attribute the uncomfortable preponderance of what has to do with words over what has to do with things to the hegemony of the unconscious that the first psychoanalyst was the first to discover. Or are we to look elsewhere for the capacity to perceive as significant such irresponsible playing with words?

It is a commonplace of the history of the human sciences in the nineteenth century that biological or organic terms came to dominate many of the theories of society, of language, of psychology – either as guiding metaphors or as working models.[2] It is less widely recognized that the sciences of language – philology, exegetical sciences, comparative linguistics, historical linguistics, call them what we will – played a parallel and sometimes opposed role in the development of the human sciences.[3] John Burrow, in an article entitled 'The uses of philology in Victorian England' (Burrow, 1967), argues that the philological sciences and the biological sciences were in a state of competition as to which was to become the dominant model for the human sciences. Analogies from biology gave rise to a social evolutionist positivism, whereas a non-materialist, non-progressionist trend of social thought gained its support from philology and its sister disciplines. Philology was the one discipline that could provide an alternative to the organic evolutionism of the later nineteenth century, or to the functionalist natural history of the earlier half.

An altogether more ambitious historical hypothesis is to be found in Michel Foucault's *Les mots et les choses*. Foucault argues that, with the creation of the concept of 'man' at the beginning of the nineteenth century, replacing the central 'category' of 'representation' through which eighteenth century sciences gained their unity, three sciences – biology, economics and philology – were constituted that could each provide possible models for the study of the new object, man. Thus psychology was constituted on the basis of the pair of concepts 'function/norm', derived from biology; sociology was grounded on the pair 'conflict/rule', derived from economics; and the sciences of literature were founded upon the pair 'signification/system', derived from philology. Foucault also argues that borrowings from the other two models could enrich the conceptual apparatus of a given human science, and it is the possibility of these borrowings that permits the debates between human scientists as to the proper foundations of a given human science.

Foucault gives a time-scale for the period of dominance of each of these three models: the organic model was obviously dominant in the first half of the century, as all the histories of sociology have argued. With Marx, the economic model is seen to become dominant. And, so Foucault argues, 'Freud more than anyone else brought the knowledge of man closest to its philological and linguistic model.' (Foucault, 1966/70, p. 361.) The exact time-scale of these 'take-overs' is of relatively minor importance. What is clear is that a science of man could take its concepts from one or more of these three disciplines. What of psychoanalysis?

It was the field of the philological sciences that acted as a source and inspiration for Freud's and psychoanalysis' preoccupation with language. This is not to deny the fact that Freud made nearly all his discoveries with the material supplied to him by his neurotic patients. But in this chapter we will find that the quality that Freud claimed was the foundation of his discoveries – a certain courage, a certain bravery – seemed to need a certain mobilization, and that it was the philological sciences that served for this purpose: they offered him a support in external reality to which he could turn when plagued with doubt as to the value of the discoveries he was making in mental reality. We will discuss one example of the loss of nerve that was connected with one episode in his use of philological evidence, and we will see in another example that the audacity to follow out the logic of psychoanalytic discoveries was intimately tied to the possibility of philological support for this logic. Freud's courage undoubtedly went much deeper than a faith that 'someone has already *said* all this'. But the exercise of his courage was often inextricably bound up with a philology that attempted to retrieve the hidden meanings of all that had ever been said.

Having demonstrated in the previous four chapters the preoccupation of psychoanalysis with language, we shall now shift our focus away from psychoanalysis for a while, to look at these philological sciences and the models they engendered, returning to psychoanalysis at times to see the manner in which certain strands or theses found in psychoanalytic work gained their validity from their affinity with the philological background. To say that psychoanalysis was preoccupied with language is, as we have seen, to say many things at once. Similarly, to employ the phrase 'philological sciences' is to cover a multitude of forms of knowledge with a category that only reveals its validity through an argument of justification.[4]

PHILOLOGY IN THE NINETEENTH CENTURY

The end of the eighteenth century and the beginning of the nineteenth century marked a revolutionary phase in thought about language and in the study of languages. At the empirical level, one trend was of fundamental importance: an enormously increased concern with non-Classical languages. This trend gained force from an intellectual movement very directly associated with that mélange of romanticism and historicism centred in Germany; its direct antecedent and consequence was the concern of scholars with the relations between languages. The delicate balance that was to be found in historicism, between the uniqueness that is characteristic of a specific historical formation, and the set of laws that, once discovered, characterizes that formation through the series of temporal transformations that they describe, is found most clearly represented in the study of language. With Humboldt[5], Herder (1772) and Hegel (1910) we find an emphasis on the inner creative force that is peculiar to language and peculiar to each language; with Bopp, Rask and Grimm (and, earlier, the work of Sir William Jones), we find an attempt to demonstrate the laws by which one language becomes another, in the course of a time now undefined by an external chronology, a time in accord with the sequences laid down by the inner logic of language's development, rather than as marked by those 'external' events whose very externality was brought into question by the new science of language.[6] It was Grimm's Law, regulating the transformations of consonants from Sanskrit, through Greek and Latin, to German, English and French, that was to capture the imperialistic imaginings of the sciences of man, just as Cuvier's law of the correlation of parts and the law of supply and demand could sustain other and parallel hopes as to the rule of law over man.

The ideal of laws that act forever below the surface of what is spoken, determining what can be spoken without recourse to what can be represented, was the goal of the new philologists. When language's relation to the world became something that could be investigated as problematic, rather than assumed, language itself took on a new weight, a new density and opacity, a certain strangeness. Comparative linguists turned to a formalistic account of language that sheered the system of sounds off from any system of the world. In this sense, the Saussurian account of the arbitrariness and self-sufficiency of the signifier with respect to the signified was the achievement of a century of striving to map out the independent laws of sound-transformation.[7] The overall effect of the preoccupation of philologists with the internal laws of language was to detach language off from other histories, to turn it in upon itself, to make it the object of a science that no longer confused itself with a science of thought, or the science of representation.

In consequence, language found its own history. Each language, the product of a unique and specific creative force, possessed an individual chronology, its own cycle of birth and death, of youth and old age, or, later in the century, was subject to an efflorescence and a demise according to its success in the struggle for linguistic survival.[8] And each family of languages, and thus, conceivably, all languages, received its own internal chronology, as defined by the sequences of transformations that bound them together as a family, but which seemed to define them as a family first and foremost through their common historical derivation. It was at this point that the Humboldtian strain could fuse with the more formal studies, giving rise to the notion of a unified field of expression, uniquely determined by the morphological laws that determined the structure of a language, that was specific to a race, a culture, a people – indeed, that was, in the last analysis, the distinctive defining feature of that culture. With the Grimms, with the Schlegels, with Herder, the study of linguistic transformations was continuous with the collation and organization of a cultural 'heritage'[9]: the fairy tales, the mythologies, the 'folklore' of a 'nation' that was defined by a limited and homogeneous field of expression made distinguishable by the laws of phonetic transformation.

The study of languages in the 19th century demonstrated the same fusion of the unique and the comparative that students of historicism[10] have made familiar: each language revealed a uniqueness and specificity that guaranteed its separateness, while the comparative method acted as the means by which the complete field of languages could be covered.[11] This common double characteristic may explain the adjacency often credited in this period to history and philology. Adding a third element, religion, a conceptual grouping characteristic of the great 'humanistic' projects of the century emerged:

> All history of the religious consciousness must repose upon language, not only because it is the historical record, but also because it is the primordial work of the human intellect.[12]

The study of language took on a great importance in the quest for what was primordial: firstly, because the production of language was the oldest trace of the primitive origins of man's intellect; secondly, because language was the human artifact that lay closest to the pure forms of thought:

> The structure of thought revealed by its deposits in language precedes all other coinage of human intelligence.[13]

The thin red line that distinguished thought from its products could be reduced to a minimum by studying the product that lay closest to thought, that always seemed to lie closer to thought than any metaphors of mirroring or moulding could capture. All the metaphors that are normally employed to characterize the relation of language to thought failed to capture the inexorable necessity felt by many linguists in the nineteenth century for assuming that thought could be adequately seized by language.

We thus find in historical linguistics a curious mixture of a cultural relativism and a rigorous idealism. First, one detached a language from the category, common to all languages, of 'representation-of-the-world', in order to demonstrate its peculiar uniqueness. Then one could demonstrate how this language expressed a thought that, through its strangeness, might reveal the strangeness of thought itself.[14] But the laws of comparative linguistics indicated how these unique systems of thought could be bound together into one or a few systems of transformation of form, so that thought itself would find its own unity in what gave languages their own unity. One detached language from the history of man, only to return it, once bound by its own laws, to found a new history, in which not only its age, but also its adjacency to the cognitive categories, guaranteed it pride of place.

Two categories of experience served as the principal objects of philological analysis: myth and religion. The school of Higher Criticism, represented by Strauss and Renan, undertook the examination of the various texts of the Judaic and Christian religions. Their aim was twofold: to employ philological methods to establish what was 'mythical' in the histories there set out; and then, having eliminated what was mythical, to establish a 'historical' life of Jesus. One sees here the double movement of philology: establish the separate history appropriate to words, through whose aid, both positive and negative, a history of one man or of men in general could be rewritten. The chronology accorded to words precedes and determines the chronology of life.

Such a method was applicable to 'myth' as well; indeed, myth and religion dissolved into one another insofar as philological analysis undermined the sacred innocence of the word. If the final arbitration of language by 'history' was continually postponed, as it tended to be in the analyses of those texts taken to be purely mythical, a natural 'first cause' or an event that formed the rock-bottom of the analysis of the mythic distortion of reality failed to emerge as the new repository of religion; *ideally*, philology could always postpone the excavation of the historical exemplars that might serve again as the foundation of religion. When analysing a Babylonian creation myth it might not be of value to attempt to discover the event or person represented in a distorted fashion by the myth, although nearly every philologist might have recourse to such an explanation if need be. It was quite good practice to remain content with the linguistic reduction of miracle to illusion, of myth to metaphor.

But this original event was often to return, as if the comparative philologists could never be content to leave the synonyms and reductive chains of signification hanging in thin air. We do not have far to go, from the reconstruction of the life of the historical Jesus, to the reconstruction of the death of the primal father. And, if such a continuum seems questionable, we may possibly give it more body by looking at the intermediate terms, such as Prometheus, or Moses.

It was not only from the side of Christianity that the coupling of myth and religion was encouraged. Humboldtian ethnology and work such as Rask's on the Old Norse languages highlighted both the importance of the non-European languages and the necessity to study previously ignored languages, both living and dead, in order to establish the full field of which comparative linguistics was the science, even if the final interest of the researcher would still remain the Germanic tongues. Not only were Greek and Latin demoted in favour of Sanskrit, but also Old Irish, Norse, Old Danish, etc., took up a place equal in scientific value to the languages of Cicero and Homer. And, if Cicero and Homer might still supply the texts for the study of the morphology and phonology of their respective languages, where were the texts for Old Irish and Danish to come from, if not from the sagas and myths, the 'histories' of those languages? The methodological necessities prescribed that the linguists extend their interests far beyond those of the form of words. How does one establish a homology between the form of two words unless one has a parameter that acts as a mediating third term? The achievement of Champollion is the paradigm of this process of decoding: in order to begin work on the syntax, morphology and phonology of a language, one must have a base line, and this base line is supplied by an identity of *meaning*. The inquiry into meaning cannot be separated from the inquiry into form. Hence, in order to establish the unity of law-like transformations between a set of languages, the linguists were required to undertake an ever more detailed inquiry into the nuances of meaning of the basic texts. In other words, they undertook to establish the web of identities and differences that made up the mythological systems that these texts represented. It became as imperative to establish the exact signification of the heroic exploits recounted in Sanskrit as it was to trace the possible fate of the fishermen from Galilee.

Even if the philologists finally came to the end of their analyses and established an end that was also the definitive beginning, this might not be a historically proven event. It might have an altogether different character, while still being the end and achievement of the analysis. Thus the chain of transformations by which the Assyrian '*Yoni*' became the English '*Mary*', when retraced by Thomas Inman[15], indicated the primal feminine significance of the number '*one*'. And this number, when coupled with the number '*three*', representing the masculine, could be shown to underly all mythology and religion, Christianity included. Both Bopp and Schleicher were concerned to demonstrate that the reconstructed language proto-Indo-European resided upon a pure triadic base-structure of vowels: '*a*', '*i*', '*u*'.[16] Obviously this end-point was not one of pure signification; rather, it was the opposite: an end-point that could be guaranteed by reference to the physiology of the organs by which sounds were produced.[17] Or, again, we may take another example from the work of Franz Bopp, who could demonstrate that the primitive verb-form of the Indo-European languages was a suffix, '-*s*', signifying the primal verb 'to be'. (Bopp (1816); Pedersen, 1931, p. 257).

Now these are extreme examples, in which a universal origin or a point of absolute linguistic plenitude (cf Lovejoy, 1936) was the immanent principle by which a unification of the manifold forms of a 'word' could be attained. On a smaller scale, a reference to a stable point of reference, the signification of a word-form, was always necessary, if the changes from one language-system to another were to be shown to be lawlike. An identity of sound (or of consonantal form in more obscure areas, particularly with Hebrew) might serve as evidence for the development of neighbouring forms from one another. But the coincidence of forms was not usually enough – and could never be enough if it were a question of series of such identities – to guarantee the law. A semantic element was necessary to establish that this identity was more than a 'coincidence'. So the more obscure and fragmented the evidence with which linguists had to work, the further into the semantic complexities of myth and custom were they led. Thus Max Müller's translation of the Rig-Vedas, his exposition of the Hindu cosmology and mythology, and his research into the structure of Sanskrit were all part of one essentially linguistic project (Chaudhuri, 1974; Müller, 1864, 1875, 1902).

Hence we can see clearly the manner in which the two main characteristics of nineteenth century linguistics were interdependent. The first characteristic was the search for the laws which governed the transformation of phonetic, morphological and syntactical forms from one language to another. The second characteristic was the search for etymological trees, for the genealogy of signification, a genealogy that found its evidential specification in the 'irrational' dimension of myth, religion and folklore, and which could be generalized, under the pen of the renegade philologist Nietzsche, into a 'genealogy of morals'. Etymology employed differences of form only to subsume these under an identity of signification. Or, to put it another way, differences of form enabled one to recognize difference of signification. As the distinction between semantics and syntax became firmer, their mutual interdependence became more pronounced. If a continuous series of transformations of a phonetic or morphological character could be demonstrated, the resulting chain of terms promised to bear a rich fruit when an inquiry into the meanings thus interlinked was undertaken. The larger the system of words brought into the system of lawlike transformations, the more it was likely to be able to find a 'significant' set of displacements of meaning thus sanctioned. A new ambitious project became feasible: the mapping out of the key significations for a given group of languages, corresponding to the primary forms of thought expressed in that language. And, as often as not, these original forms of thought were the expression of a fundamental intuition of God's existence, so that the regressive analysis conducted via phonology and etymology led to the foundations of religion.

> The power of the mind which enables us to see the genus in the individual, the whole in the many and to form a word by connecting a subject and a predicate, is essentially the same which leads men to find God in the Universe and the Universe in God. Language and religion are the two poles of our consciousness mutually presupposing each other.[18]

Or, as Müller confessed in his *Autobiography* (1887), his life work followed 'the thread that connects the origin of thought and languages with the origin of mythology and religion.' (Müller, 1901, p. 3).[19] For Müller, and for many other linguists, the thread of language led to a system of roots, what he called basic 'phonetic types produced by a power inherent in the human spirit, . . . roots created by nature, . . . and we hasten to add that by nature we understand the hand of God'. (Müller, 1864, p. 486). Curtius defined the root as the significative residue that remains once one had cut away from the word all that has been added to the primitive sound (Curtius, 1886 I p. 47). Thus the chain of transformations of form and of meaning met in the root. Not only was the root the metaphysical pre-requisite for the theory that conferred a transcendental unity upon a group of languages, it was also the prerequisite for establishing the point at which man's consciousness opened up on to 'infiltration' from another realm, whether that realm be that of religion, of thought, or of 'meaning'.

The root promised access to the primary units of thought. Let us return to the question we asked in Chapter 3 *vis-à-vis* the symbol: for whom? One answer, that of Müller and Bunsen, was: a divine subject, installed within man at the beginning of things, and conferring upon language the characteristic of being a barrier to the naturalism of Darwinian evolutionary theory, a barrier separating the natural from the divine, separating nature and man.[20] But another answer, less marked by the coarse oppositions between science and religion of mid nineteenth century Britain, was offered by those linguists who founded *Völkerpsychologie:* Lazarus, Steinthal and their followers.[21]

Völkerpsychologie was an attempt to extend Herbartian dynamic psychology from the individual to the collective. Such a project had been foreshadowed by Herbart himself, who had claimed that the statics and dynamics of the collective mind (the State) would prove to obey the same laws as the individual mind, upon which his system had concentrated. Lazarus and Steinthal set out to indicate the ways in which the categories of individual psychology reappeared at the level of the collective: the category of image reappeared as art, emotion as religion, judgement as codes of conduct. But their Herbartian project only became possible as a consequence of the binding concept of language, the third term that mediated between each of the individual categories and its collective correlate. It was through the mediation of language that collectivity was possible. At one level, then, language was a contentless form upon which collective contents could be grounded – 'a contentless connection of consciousnesses' (Steinthal, 1855, p. 333). But language was itself grounded in a further category that both specified the character of a language and, in the final analysis, owed its own characterization to the laws of that language: the *Volksgeist.* Such a concept, borrowing much from the dialectic of the *Geist* and of language in Hegel's *Phänomenologie des Geistes,* was the lynch-pin of collective psychology. Lazarus and Steinthal characterized it as the subject of the collective products studied by *Völkerpsychologie,* in which it corresponded to Müller's divine subject. It is the *Volksgeist* that is the subject of language. With this dictum, with this weaving of *Sprache* and *Volksgeist* together, the analysis of *Völkerpsychologie* through the diverse products of folklore, art, religion and myth was assured of a collective character independent of the individual.

The concept of the *Volksgeist* was to be transformed into others, more particularly the concept of *race* that came to dominate a large part of ethnological and linguistic science in the latter half of the century. But at the start, and in many of its later forms (e.g. Boas; cf. Stocking, 1968), it could be actively opposed to a naturalism that tried to unify biological 'givens' with philological findings (see Prichard, 1833). Such an opposition was often accomplished by specifying the 'contents' of the *Volksgeist* as being essentially linguistic in character. It was first and foremost etymological studies of mythological and religious texts that established these contents, as we might have guessed from the title of the journal that Lazarus and Steinthal established: *Zeitschrift für Völkerpsychologie und Sprachwissenschaft* (1861–90). In this journal and in monographs, we find attempts to solve the key religious and historical problems through a strictly linguistic analysis. For example, much energy was devoted to a debate as to the relationship between the Indogermanic and the Semitic groups of languages and the peoples whose spirits were expressed in these languages. One much debated hypothesis was that the Indogermanic peoples/languages were inherently polytheistic, whereas the Semitic languages/peoples were inherently monotheistic. Oswald, in his *Das grammatische Geschlect und seine sprachliche Bedeutung* (1866), attempted to resolve the question as to the essential nature of Christianity, whose linguistic 'roots' lay equally in both Indogermanic and Semitic tongues, by an examination of grammatical gender. His monograph elicited the following cautions response from Steinthal:

> Language is formed from the *Geist*, not the *Geist* from language. We must crystallize the *Geist* out from language, but also from many other sources. (Steinthal, 1868, p. 103)

Despite such a qualification, which belied its own stated aim by restating clearly the basic working hypothesis of the philologists, the primacy of evidence drawn from studies of language was clear in Steinthal's own work. Abraham cited such an example, approvingly, in his *Traum und Mythos* (1909): in his paper, '*Die Sage von Simson*' (1862), Steinthal argued that the expression '*gleichwie*' (*as if*) has wrought the most profound change in the intellectual development of mankind, proving his contention with philological evidence (Steinthal, 1862b pp. 170ff.; Abraham (1909) p. 184). On the other hand, Lazarus and Steinthal's stated aim was to draw from linguistic science a collective psychology, to go beyond what philologists normally attempted. Their programme, stated in 1861, was 'to study languages not as philology or empirical linguistics does, but to discover, with the aid of physiology, the psychological laws of language'. (Lazarus and Steinthal, 1861, pp. 4ff). But the psychological laws of language – i.e. the categories of thought, the 'as ifs' of the collective mind – were often found to be as much tied to language as they were the resultant of the parallelogram of psychical forces, or the side-effects of physiology. They recognized that the development of consciousness is only possible with the development of language, and employed the latter as their index of the former. The project of *Völkerpsychologie* was to go beyond the work of other philologists and linguists insofar as it attempted to establish the laws of *semantics* as well as the laws of phonetics. Such a project was to remain an ideal for many philologists throughout the century.[22] It reappears in many works, for example, in Gomme's *Folk-lore as an Historical Science* (1908), christened by a friend the 'grammar of folk-lore', in which it was claimed that folk-lore may be accounted for 'by some law analogous to Grimm's law in the study of language' (Gomme, 1908, p. 159).[23] The chains of etymological substitution, the evidence of the connectedness of superficially unconnected words, kept this hope alive: they were the empirical evidence that might one day prove susceptible of a higher-level theoretical organization.

Some such organization was essayed in Max Müller's work, despite his abrogation of the ideal of semantic laws. Müller wished to exercise a two-fold reduction upon the languages making up the Indo-Germanic tongues. Firstly, in company with many other comparative linguistics, he wished to show the fundamental unity of these tongues, combining the phonetic laws and the evidence of semantic continuity to prove this. Secondly, in consequence of the first reduction, he could proceed to show that *all* the words of these languages could be traced back to 800 roots, in turn expressive of 120 concepts. 'These one hundred and twenty concepts are really the rivers that feed the whole ocean of thought and speech.' (Müller, 1888b, p. 32.)

We have already encountered a psychoanalytic argument that employed philological means in order to gain a similar end: Ernest Jones' conception of symbolism, which employed philology to indicate that the ideas capable of being represented in symbolic form were limited to those concerned with death, birth, sexual activities, relatives, etc. (See above, Chapter 3, pages 125–9). As we noted there, Jones hoped to be able to give an exclusively philological proof of such a limitation, although he also had a quasi-biological conception through which such a prior limitation of the possible objects of representations might be enforced. When the psychoanalysts ventured into the field of mythology and religion – the field that, as we have seen, presented them with the problem of symbolism to which their theory of *dream*-symbols was a solution – they entered a field already occupied by philologists such as Müller, Frazer, Kuhn, Bastian, Winckler, Stucken *et al.*[24] In their struggle to secure the specifically psychoanalytic theory of myth, they sought both to present themselves as living under the same roof as the philologists, while at the same time providing the latter with a key that could stop all the wrangles between partisans of differing mythological systems, the functionalists versus the naturalists, the advocates of creation myths against those who looked to heaven for the final point of reference of all mythology. (See Rank, 1909/1964).

But, before we turn to a closer look at the relationships of psychoanalysis to philology, we must complete our account of the conceptual furniture with which the philologists furnished out the house that was often claimed to be the Temple of the Sciences of Man. We have noted the connection that was established between the Hegelian *Geist* and the philologists' *Sprache*. One consequence of this accommodation was the reinforcement of the Humboldtian theme of the immanent character of the creative activity of language. For Humboldt, language obeyed an *inner* law of development and decay. The history of a language was made up of two periods:

> One in which the sound-creating force of the language is still in growth and living activity; the other in which an apparent standstill takes place after complete formation of at least the external form of the language and then a visible decline of that creative, sensual force follows. (Humboldt, 1836, p. 63)

An ideal language would act with a necessity imposed on it by its own form:

> [In perfect languages] the formation of words and constructions undergoes no other limitations than are necessary to combine regularity with freedom, that is, to assure for freedom its own existence through limitation. (Ibid., p. 64)

Such a theme meshed well with the notion of a *Volksgeist*, giving an absolute activity to language, placing each speaker in a passive relation to language; it neutralized the arbitrariness of the individual speaker. Such a theme is of course also to be found in other linguistics: one might even say it is the abiding theme of theorists of language since Humboldt, from the formalistic determinations of the structuralists to the immense apparatus of transformational rules that the Chomskyans impute to the 2 year old.[25] But, before the concept of 'system' came to dominate linguistics, this hegemony of language over the subject was conceived of in terms of an inner creative force.[26] In this way, just as the concept of 'nature' became for many Darwinians the representation of an active force, for some blind, for some endowed with powers of choice and selection (Young, 1971), so each 'language' became the embodiment of social 'activity', endowed with an independence which its speakers did not share.

It has been argued by some historians of psychoanalysis that the 'dynamic' aspect of the play of ideas from the unconscious to the conscious, for the understanding of which repression is the key concept, is historically derived from the important place that Herbart's mathematical metaphors gave to the dynamic play of ideas above and below the threshold of consciousness.[27] This argument has borne little weight, perhaps because it takes no account of the strange displacements of meaning that are almost always the correlate of the dynamic psychic forces that Freud invoked.[28] Or, to put this point more exactly, in Herbartian psychology there is no hint of the fact that it is 'unexpected' and 'bizarre' ideational products, seemingly derived from another psychical epoch, that are brought to consciousness by the play of mental forces. Now, if we place together, as the *Völkerpsychologischen* did, the inner creative force of language emphasized by Humboldt, the notion of a Herbartian statics and dynamics of the collective psyche ruling the play of forces acting 'below' consciousness[29] and the methodological privilege they accorded to deriving the manifest and irrational forms of myth and language from ancient chains of linguistic signification along which these psychic forces play, we derive a model that is much more akin to the Freudian unconscious. Herbartian mental dynamics included a concept of unconscious ideas and forces, but no hint of the strangeness, the 'different psychical locality' that distinguishes the unconscious from the preconscious (Freud, 1950a, *Origins*, p. 244; 1900a SE IV 48, SE V 536). But the investigation of language led one group of Herbartians to a parallel recognition of the strangeness of what lies below the surface, this strangeness being related to the layering of languages and their different meanings, each receiving an ascription to an undated prehistorical epoch in which meanings were made as well as accepted.

The activity of the unconscious would seem to have been borrowed as much from the creative and archaic activity of language as from a conception of biological forces overflowing into the psychic. A tension between the individual and the collective – a tension hidden but not dissipated in the notion of a biological base for the psyche – always, as we have seen in previous chapters, characterized psychoanalytical concepts. One more way of representing this now occurs to us, starting from the notion of a creative force of language. Did Freud have the audacity to ascribe a creative function of language to the individual neurotic, a creative function that, with Breuer, he could at times recognize only as an 'arbitrary', 'crazy' play with words? Or would he have the audacity – and again the word is his – to ascribe to some hypothetical and hidden relation between men, a new version of the *Volksgeist*, the burden of explanation for the displacements of signification that psychoanalysis always revealed? Theorists of language always tempted him towards the second choice. And it seemed as if drawing upon the history of language could always supply psycho-analysis with the evidence it needed, when even the psychoanalyst could not bring himself to trust the lies of the neurotic. He turned to philology when he had lost his nerve, when he could no longer carry on alone without evidential support from elsewhere. The way seems to have been prepared for psychoanalysis by a Herbartian philology that had elaborated a set of concepts belonging to the same family as those of psychoanalysis, even if they did not belong to the same generation. But to specify further the relations of psychoanalysis and philology we must now turn to some psychoanalytic texts.

A QUESTION OF NERVE: LEONARDO, MOSES AND THE PROBLEM OF TRADITION

Freud gave a first account of his 'psycho-biography' of Leonardo da Vinci in a paper presented to the Vienna Psychoanalytic Society on 1 December 1909. The element in his argument that I wish to discuss here is best introduced by Leonardo's earliest recollection: 'it seems to me as though a vulture had flown down to me, opened my mouth with his tail, and several times beaten it to and fro between my lips'. (*Minutes* II p. 340.)[30] Freud first noted that dreams of flying 'originally have invariably the meaning: "I can mate [*Ich kann vögeln*], I am a bird, I am sexually mature."' (Ibid. p. 341) He continued:

> Now, there is another strange path that leads a little step further into the story. In hieroglyphic writing, the vulture stands for something quite definite – i.e. the mother – and indeed the pronunciation of that character is *"mut"*. If we attempt to insert this into the fantasy, then it would mean that his mother bent over him, put her penis into his

mouth and there moved it to and fro several times . . . . the Egyptians had a deity that was called *Mut* and was represented as having a vulture's head. Now, there is no other Egyptian deity that has been so frequently represented as an androgyne (that is, with a penis). The primitive idea of the child, which ascribes a penis to the mother (infantile sexual theory), has also remained alive in folk experience. (Ibid., p. 341)

The essence of Freud's argument consisted in establishing a connection between the vulture of the phantasy recollection and the penis of the mother. What sort of evidence did he use? The Egyptian material furnished a number of lines of argument. Firstly, the vulture-headed goddess represents the mother, as the sound of the name 'proves'. Secondly, this goddess is often androgynous: its 'tail' is a penis – a fact that is supported (independently?) by the infantile sexual theory in which all beings, and especially the mother, are assigned penises. Hence the Egyptian evidence, of hieroglyph and statue, furnished sufficient evidence for the equation: 'vulture's tail = mother's penis'.

We can regard this equation as being made up itself of two subsidiary equations: firstly, 'tail = penis', which we can establish by translating from the phantasy's 'own special language into words that are generally understood'. (Freud (1910c) SE XI 85.)

A tail, '*coda*', is one of the most familiar symbols and substitutive expressions for the male organ, in Italian no less than in other languages. . . . (Ibid.)

Let us start our interrogation of the text at this point. Freud had here cited linguistic and (seemingly) non-linguistic evidence: he spoke of 'substitutive expressions' and also of the tail being a 'familiar symbol'. What he did *not* say was that the tail was an obvious 'natural' symbol for the male organ, an argument that might seem 'obvious'. Rather, he referred to linguistic evidence, and, bearing in mind what we learnt in Chapter 3 Symbolism, even the symbolic equation 'tail-penis' was, for him, based on 'linguistic evidence'.

The argument for the second subsidiary equation, 'mother = vulture', was introduced in the published essay in the following manner:

At this point a thought comes to mind from such a remote quarter that it would be tempting to set it aside. In the hieroglyphics of the ancient Egyptians the mother is represented by a picture of a vulture. . . . (Ibid., SE XI 88)

And, as he had remarked before to the Society, the goddess called *Mut* was a mother.

There is, then, some real[?] connection between vulture and mother – but what help is that to us? For have we any right to expect Leonardo to know of it, seeing that the first man who succeeded in reading hieroglyphics was François Champollion? (Ibid.)

Thus, having established the 'real connection' between the mother and the vulture, Freud perceived a problem in the movement of meaning from the Ancient Egyptian language to Renaissance Italian, even though he could ask, rhetorically, 'Can the similarity to the sound of our word *Mutter* be merely a coincidence?' (Ibid.) The lack of a pathway from Egyptian to Italian could be partially circumvented by a tracing of Greek and Roman textual influences upon Leonardo, through which Freud felt able to conclude that Leonardo became aware that the Ancients regarded the vulture as a bird that could give birth without intercourse with a male. Leaning upon his reconstruction of the details of Leonardo's early life, Freud felt able to conclude that Leonardo had made the connection (when? how?): 'vulture = mother'.[31]

Let us clarify the structure of the argument that Freud used:

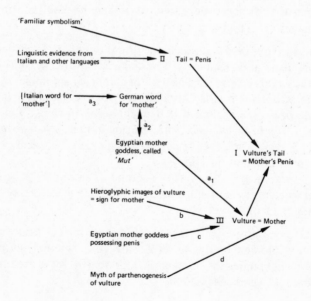

If we consider the more complicated equation III first, we note that Freud conceived of four independent arguments to support it. But, having set them out, he recognized that the sources of information which Leonardo had at his disposal might have been limited. Having investigated the Renaissance availability of sources concerning the Egyptians, he concluded that Leonardo was almost certainly aware through his reading of Horapollo that the vulture was an Egyptian symbol.[32] But Horapollo's text only yields sufficient information to warrant two of the four arguments that Freud presents: b., that the hieroglyphic image for mother is a vulture, and d., that the Egyptians believed that there are only female vultures, procreation taking place through fertilization by the wind. The arguments a_1 and c receive no further discussion as to their availability to Leonardo. Indeed, Freud's final conjectural historical sequence was as follows: Leonardo read of the virgin vulture's procreative capacity in one of the Church Fathers, and, *solely* from this piece of evidence (roughly equivalent to d. in the diagram), equated the vulture and the mother.

It would seem that, judged simply from a historical point of view, the arguments about hieroglyphics, the sound of the Egyptian goddess' name, and the representations of the androgynous goddess[33] are strictly irrelevant to the point at issue: Leonardo's conception of the vulture.[34]

Of course, as we have seen, Freud introduced a further, seemingly non-philological element, derived from his paper on the sexual theories of children, the theory that the nipple and the penis are equated in phantasy, and that the endowment of the mother with a penis is a common infantile theory. The former throws light upon equation I, 'tail = penis', and the latter throws light on both the peculiar androgyny of the Egyptian goddess *and* upon the combination of the two equations, 'tail = penis', 'mother = vulture', into the final equation, 'mother's penis = vulture's tail' (Freud (1910c) SE XI 97). But, since the phallic appurtenances of the Egyptian vulture goddess were 'unknown' to Leonardo, this argument only has force for the step in the argument from 'tail = penis' to 'tail = *mother*'s penis'. Indeed, we can now recognize that the whole argument concerning the Egyptian vulture-headed goddess is irrelevant – a fact arrived at by an alternative route by Maclagen (1923), Schapiro (1956), Strachey (SE XI 60–2) and Spector (1972).

As the Editors of the *Standard Edition* note, once one recognizes that the bird named in Leonardo's recollection is a kite and not a vulture, one has to recognize the consequent irrelevance of the Egyptian material – 'though this nevertheless retains much of its independent value' (SE XI 62). But, through our clarification of the form of Freud's argument, we have come to see that nearly all of the Egyptian material is irrelevant, *whatever* the correct translation of '*nibio*'. Only the step from the virgin vulture to the mother was recognized by Freud as 'known' by Leonardo; the rest of the Egyptian material only serves to assert a *general* connection between the vulture, *Mut*, hieroglyphics, and androgynous mother-goddesses. As we disentangle these arguments, we find that the brunt now falls upon the infantile sexual theory of the phallic mother.[35] The admittedly fascinating Egyptian material seems to have no part to play – at least in Leonardo's case.[36]

So what purpose does the Egyptian material serve, given that even Freud recognized, admittedly in passing, and without undue emphasis, that it does not contribute significantly to the argument concerning Leonardo's phantasy-recollection? With Spector, we could argue that it served a self-analytic function for Freud, expressive, in some manner, of his personal complexes; we might even say that, having pared away what is superfluous to the solution of Leonardo's personal equation, the residue represents what belongs to Freud's personal equation. But I prefer to see its function as that of a significant survival, a pointer, towards an argument that Freud *wished* to make. We could hypothesize further that Freud believed that he should substantiate his conclusion as to the phallic significance of the tail and the maternal significance of the vulture via a philological inquiry that he recapitulated in the lecture, and, with slightly more rigour, in the published paper. That his questioning as to the existence of the *links* between the Egyptian and the Renaissance texts was subsequent to his certainty of the correctness of his philological conclusions would also seem likely. But, as a result of his self-questioning, *après coup*, he found himself forced to rely upon another argument, less philological, referring only to the thought-connections of infancy, rather than to the thought-connections laid down by 'folk experience'. Instead of the continuum of symbolic forms extending from the Egyptians to Leonardo's phantasy – vulture hiero-glyphic, *Mut-Mutter*, phallic goddess representations, vulture's tail – Freud was forced, by the uncomfortable gaps in the historical record, to explain both the Egyptian and 'Italian' symbolic forms by reference to a 'common source' – the sexual theories of childhood. From the manner in which Freud presented his argument, one can surmise that he would have preferred to have established a straightforwardly philologically-grounded reconstruction of Leonardo's 'Egyptian' phantasy, so that the argument would not have to depend upon the prior validity of the infantile theory of the maternal phallus. (Perhaps even it was mythological evidence, such as that offered by the Egyptian symbols, that formed the evidence for that theory.) Freud would have preferred to argue from the sustained vitality of 'folk experience', rather than having to invoke theories about childhood. As it is, the evidence drawn from 'folk experience' was purely circumstantial and evocative – though one has to read very carefully to realize that such is the case – rather than furnishing the essential links (associations) in a train starting with the vulture and ending with the phallic mother. Certainly the purely circumstantial character of this evidence is masked by the form of argument Freud employed.

But why have we invoked this particular episode in our discussion of philology? Freud's first argument, derived from the Egyptian material – an argument that I wish to call the philological one – broke down in the face of a confused but honest attention to the problem of tradition. Freud recognized that there was a break in the continuity of the tradition from the Egyptians to the Renaissance – a break in the sequence of markers of meaning. If he had been able to establish the continuity of the tradition, he would not have had to rely upon the infantile theories of sexuality. It would appear plausible that Freud assumed that such a continuity existed: exactly the assumption that the concept of the *Volksgeist* embodied. His critical attention to the actual evidence for this continuity arrived too late to save his account from the inconsistencies that we have been able to point up. It is as if the breaks in the continuity of tradition, having been papered over, reappeared as breaks in the continuity of Freud's argument. To save his argument, he introduced an ahistorical cause that produced, independently, and at different points in history, the repetition of the markers of signification that could retrospectively justify his discussion of Egyptian hieroglyphics and symbolism.

With the concept of infantile sexuality and the related concept of phantasy, Freud was supplying what the philologists had themselves always been searching for: a means for tying the dispersed elements of myth, art and religion together. He was supplying the psychological theory that Steinthal and Lazarus had aimed for, and which, as we can see from the paper on Leonardo, filled in the evidential gaps when etymological chains or 'external' evidences of the transfer of significations were lacking. In this way, the theory of infantile sexuality supplied a 'primitive language' that corresponded to other languages proposed by philologists in order to codify and comprehend mythical discourse: Müller's 200 roots, or the basic elements of the celestial universe that astral mythologists appealed to. And this primitive language, by definition, did not have to take account of the gaps in the historical record. The fact that, even though supplied with such a trans-historical explanatory recourse, Freud wished to draw so much from the dispersed significations of Egyptian, German and Italian only proves to us how much more he would have preferred to give a complete philological proof *as well as* those derived from the theory of infantile sexuality, rather than being forced to rely almost completely upon the phantasies of children.

But there was something unsatisfactory to Freud about this solution to the problem of tradition. This unease was one of the reasons why he became more and more interested in a 'Lamarckian' solution to the problem. That it was indeed a problem, and recognized as such in terms familiar first and foremost to philologists, can be gauged from the long discussions upon the subject, to be found in *Moses and Monotheism* (1934–8). In his preliminary discussion in that work, Freud argued for the parallel efficacy and occasional primacy of oral as compared with written tradition. The analogy of the efficacy of the 'memories' of Minoan civilization amongst the Hellenic peoples, where very little written record of the former civilization was to be found, was brought forward to support this argument (Freud (1939a) SE XXIII 70–1). But the problem ran deeper than the power and permanence of oral tradition.

Oral tradition did not seem to be able to account for the enormous 'after-effect' of events that had taken place long before, and which had almost certainly passed out of 'folk-memory'. In casting about for solutions to this problem of the preservation of traces, Freud first considered the universal symbolism he had uncovered in language (Ibid., SE XXIII 98). He then turned to the 'archaic heritage' of neurotics and children, uncovered in cases such as that of the Wolfman (Ibid., SE XXIII 99; Freud (1918b) SE XVII 119–21). Freud then addressed the problem in its most general form, rather than considering the question with respect to this or that inherited contents.

On further reflection I must admit that I have behaved for a long time as though the inheritance of memory-traces of the experience of our ancestors, independently of direct communication and of the in-fluence of education by the setting of an example, were established beyond question. When I spoke of the survival of a tradition among a people or of the formation of a people's character, I had mostly in mind an inherited tradition of this kind and not one transmitted by communication. Or at least I made no distinction between the two and was not clearly aware of my audacity in neglecting to do so. (Freud (1939a) SE XXIII 99–100)

One feels that the surprise at his own audacity concealed the fact that the question had been at issue for a long time. After all, it was precisely lack of audacity that made Freud step back from asserting the continuity of signification between the Egyptian goddess's phallus and Leonardo's vulture's tail. Now, late in his life, he took the step of guaranteeing the continuity of symbolic forms, without relying either upon the evidence of written traditions or upon the imputations of 'invisible' oral tradition, and could immediately assert that, in consequence, 'we have bridged the gulf between individual and group psychology'. (Ibid., SE XXIII 100.) And, as if to underline the importance of bridging this gap, he then argued that, since group psychology must be amenable to *some* sort of analysis, 'the audacity cannot be avoided' (Ibid.).

The curious feature about this argument concerning the inheritance of mental characteristics, which has come to be associated, in the twentieth century, with the biological debate between 'Lamarckian' and 'Darwinian' theories, is that it was mobilized in order to solve a historical or psychological problem: tradition and the continuity of the contents of the mental register. Freud never associated the argument with the name of Lamarck, whose theories were put to another, though related, use for a brief period in the First World War. Freud, in fact, knew his Lamarck better than those who described the theory of the inheritance of acquired characteristics as 'Lamarckian' – when such a theory was held equally by Darwin and most other biologists in the period 1865–1930. Remembering this, we will not be led astray into thinking that the 'inheritance' of acquired characteristics pertains to the biological foundations of psychoanalysis.[37] Rather, it arose out of Freud's relation to the accepted conceptual armoury of philological research in the nineteenth century, which would often pay scant attention to the vicissitudes of time and space in the linking of word-forms. In the essay on Leonardo, Freud backed away from such audacity, only to find out later that he had to restore at least *one* form of such an argument, since psychoanalysis, as much as philology, had need of the temporal and spatial continuity that the concept of tradition secured. Just as the *Volksgeist*, relying on its primary manifestation, language, transcended the individual (whether it be individual society or individual speaker), licencing the linking of diverse word-forms from one epoch to another, so did Freud feel obliged to introduce a parallel concept of the continuity of tradition, the continuity of 'folk-memory', at exactly those points where philological and linguistic research focused most sharply: the continuity and singularity of reference of *names*.

One might argue that Freud's psychoanalysis replaced the concept of tradition[38] by giving each individual a set of psychic schemas by which he could produce from 'within', as it were, the phenomena analogous to those discovered by philological analysis to have occurred at different times and places. Certainly the infantile theory of the phallic mother served this function in the explication of Leonardo's phantasy, once Freud had cut the link that connected Egypt and the Renaissance. But Freud was aware that the individualistic, *sui generis* solution to all problems of inter-psychic relations might not be sufficient. He had explicitly addressed this point in *Moses and Monotheism*; and his *practice* in the analysis of Leonardo's childhood recollection, whatever the final recourse to infantile sexual theories might suggest, indicated that he thought it would be preferable to employ a philological argument, if one existed, relying as such arguments did on evidence that cancelled out, almost *a priori*, the accidental discontinuities that were the special insignia of an individual subject. It is thus strange to see the path by which one theme in the development of psychoanalysis, that which followed out the logic of a philological methodology in order to secure a broader evidential base upon which to secure the 'intimate detail' with which psychoanalysis must work, found itself exactly in contradiction with another theme, namely that which looks to the accidental discontinuities of the subject's relation to his symbolic universe for the clue to the symptomatology he offers.

THE SPECIMEN THEME OF PSYCHOANALYSIS

It is in this context that we can again recall Freud's insistence that dream-symbols be based upon 'linguistic usage'. Linguistic usage represented, in a sense, the accumulated and collective syntheses of free associations. What free association provided for the analysis of the individual, linguistic usages provided for the analysis of the collective. But, as has often been noted with surprise, an individual's free associations may provide the clue to the meaning of a collective phenomena. And, inversely, when the topic of dream-symbolism became an important issue, linguistic usage could stand in the place of free association as evidence for the meaning of the symbol.

We do not have space to give a detailed example of the manner in which free association and philological evidence could freely stand in for one another in a detailed psychoanalytical argument. Suffice it to point to one extremely interesting example in which this could be shown to be the case: the theme of the relation of one man to three women, first adumbrated in the 'specimen dream of psychoanalysis'[39], the dream of Irma's injection, and 'reworked', to different self-analytic ends, in the 1913 paper, '*Das Motiv der Kätschenwahl*'.[40] In the first 'version', in the dream, the evidence is drawn entirely from Freud's free associations, and, despite this, the theme is never overtly approached. But we have the evidence of a letter Freud wrote to Abraham in 1908 as to what he regarded at that time as the central theme of the dream:

> Sexual megalomania is hidden behind it, the three women, Mathilde, Sophie and Anna are my daughter's god-mothers, and I have them all! There would be one simple therapy for widowhood, of course. (Freud, 1965a, 9 Jan 1908, p. 20)

A sexual relation with three women. Indeed, the number '3' figures largely in the dream, both in the manifest content and in the associations Freud gave to the latter, but nowhere more 'symbolically' than in the chemical formula which Freud saw 'printed in heavy type' – the formula for trimethylamin[41]:

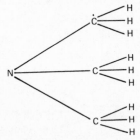

The dream-analysis that we find in *The Interpretation of Dreams* (Freud (1900a) SE IV 106–20) centred around a wish for self-vindication, a wish that entailed the vilification of others. We have already encountered this theme and one version of its elaboration in the '*Non Vixit*' dream (Chapter 4, p. 158ff above). All the dreams of self-justification received unconscious support from the infantile memory that we discussed there: Sigismund's attempt at self-justification in the face of parental justice, following the battle of wills with his playmate, John, over an unspecified object that, we surmise, in some way represented

Pauline, the third member of the playgroup. The recurrent 'symbolic structure' that represented this insistent pattern of wish-fulfilling thoughts consisted in four terms: Freud (self), a rival or fellow-conspirator, a judicial representative of the older, parental order, and the object, a woman or her representative.

According to the account Freud gave in his letter, then, we find this 'object', explicitly sexual now, replicated three times in the dream. In fact, it is not only the object that is 'triplicated'; we find that each of the other terms of the 'self-justificatory' infantile scene figures in the dream-analysis under three different guises:

(i) as authorities, Dr M. (Breuer), whose judgement is shown to be absurd and shortsighted, as well as being in conflict with the dreamer's; Fleischl, the friend who had poisoned himself with cocaine (*sich mit Kokain vergiftet hat*), and concerning whose death Freud was often to feel a need for self-justification, as if he had been responsible for this death of an ideal; and Freud's 'elder brother' (*mein im Auslande lebender älterer Bruder*), who, for the purposes of the dream's aim, had been assimilated to Dr M. as being too 'stupid' to accept Freud's suggestions or theories.

(ii) filling the posts of conspirator and competitor, we find Otto (Oskar Rie), who was compared unfavourably to Leopold (Ludwig Rosenstein), another medical colleague; and, finally, we find Fliess, who had supplied Freud with the formula that we can now use to re-represent, in a cursory form, as did Freud in his dream[42], the 'meaning' of the dream:[43]

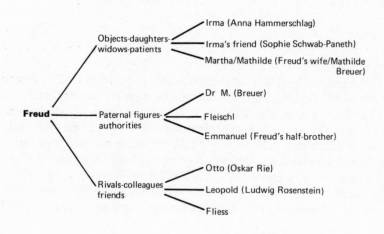

We thus find the theme of the relation to the three women embedded in the symbolic structure of the dream, modelled upon an infantile scene, and represented in a 'pure' symbolic form: a chemical formula. One could even, as did Lacan and Anzieu, discover the sexual theme of the three women without knowing of Freud's letter to Abraham, since it is the underlying triadic structure which organizes all of Freud's associations. But, we will now leave aside the themes of the rival and the authority in order to follow Freud as he pursued the theme of the three women-daughters-widows-patients in 'The Motives for the Choice of a Casket' (1913).[44]

In this second version, Freud started by examining the choice to which Bassanio must submit in order to gain Portia's hand in *The Merchant of Venice*: a choice between three caskets. Freud argued that this choice is homologous to Lear's 'choice' between his three daughters. In this well known paper[45], Freud argued, via a range of mythological sources[46], that Lear's refusal to choose his third and youngest daughter, the daughter who represents death, is equivalent to an intellectual triumph over death, a triumph that ends in tragedy, since

> it is in vain that an old man yearns for the love of woman as he had it first from his mother; the third of the Fates alone, the silent Goddess of Death, will take him into her arms. (Freud (1913f) SE XII 301)

We may surmise that the theme of the three women found in both the dream of Irma's injection and in the theme of the choice of a casket was central to Freud's self-analysis. But one of the versions employs material derived from free association as its evidential base, while the other employs an altogether different sort of material, but one entirely familiar to philologists: the close-reading of two Renaissance plays, East European and Graeco-Roman myths, and Germanic folklore. Insofar as they referred to the same theme, these two modes of argument seemed to be interchangeable. Indeed, in the text of 'The Motive for the Choice of a Casket', there were only three points at which Freud called upon specifically psychoanalytic arguments: to take the step from the theme of the choice between caskets to that of a choice between *women*, via the symbolic equation, well known to be a significant feature of Freud's own symbolic map, 'casket = woman'[47]; secondly, to demonstrate the equation 'dumbness = death', for which demonstration dream-interpretation proved in fact to be insufficient, necessitating recourse to the category of linguistic usage, mythology and folklore (in this case, two of the Grimms' *Märchen*); thirdly, to resolve two contradictions, the first of which arises when one notes that the woman who represents death has all the characteristics of a beautiful and loved one[48], the second of which arises from the fact that both the plays and the myths replace the *inevitability* of death by the *choice* of a woman.

Wahl steht an der Stelle von Notwendigkeit, von Verhängnis. So überwindet der Mensch den Tod, den er in seinem Denken anerkannt hat. Es ist kein stärkerer Triumph der Wunscherfüllung denkbar. [Choice stands in the place of necessity, of destiny. In this way man overcomes death, which he had come to recognize through *thought*. No greater triumph of wish fulfilment is *thinkable*.] (Freud (1913f) SE XII 299; translation modified; my emphasis).

Such psychoanalytic arguments were not even far removed from modes of reasoning employed by philologists: replacing the caskets by women was the sort of symbolic substitution with which the work of Steinthal, Kuhn and Stucken was rife and, as we shall see, it was their work that often sanctioned such substitutions. Even the concept of ambivalence embodied in the woman who is both loved and represents death could find no better representation than those of Kali, the creator and destroyer.

We have the feeling, in analysing these two episodes in the history of psychoanalysis, that there is a strict parallelism between what the patient utters and what can be found to be of significance in the field of cultural representations. In other words, the method of free association, seemingly specific to psychoanalysis, is parallel to and interchangeable with a philological collation of collective 'associations'. So that if we return to the question: what is specifically psychoanalytic about the argument in 'The Motive for the Choice of a Casket', we find it difficult to find an answer. Certainly it was not the theme actually worked through in the paper, which Freud called, perhaps over-harshly, 'superficial and allegorical'[49], nor the evidence brought to bear at each stage of the argument, nor even those crucial stages in the argument where philologists would not have been able to tread the path that Freud trod. One theme only was specifically drawn from psychoanalysis: the notion that representing death as a choice instead of the ineluctable destiny it actually is is the most complete wish-fulfilment possible, the acme of mythopeic thought. But the connection with the dream of Irma's injection indicates that another specific feature of psychoanalysis is less unassailably peculiar: free association. If we regard Freud's sexual megalomania and Lear's refusal of death as developments of the one theme, we could well imagine a reversal of the evidential forms employed in unfolding its development. When Freud sanctioned the possibility of substituting 'linguistic usage' for free association, his choice could not but rebound back onto the evidential status of free association. And such an effect might not have been wholly out of keeping with a conception of free association as a specialized, microcosmic variant of the collection of philological data. At the moment, it is not possible to go beyond such a formulation of the interrelatedness of free association and philological evidence. But the would seem to make plausible the suggestion that free association was in some way intimately tied to the philological methods generated in the nineteenth century for the investigation of the hidden centre, the hidden meaning of language.

WHO WERE THE PHILOLOGISTS?

We are now in a position to throw light upon an enigmatic feature of the history of psychoanalysis that we noted in passing, when we considered the development of the theory of symbolism in Chapter 3. We noted there that Freud's followers – in particular Rank, Abraham and Jung – were championing Freud's theory of dream-symbolism long before it was published. What was their source of knowledge of this theory? Why did they make so much of a theory that was, at best, incidental to, at worst, in conflict with Freud's own theory of dreams, as set out in *The Interpretation of Dreams*? We can allow Jung to clarify this problem for us, quoting from a 1908 paper:

> The public can forgive Freud least of all for his sexual symbolism. In my view he is really easiest to follow here, because this is just where mythology, expressing the fantasy-thinking of all races, has prepared the ground in the most instructive way. I would only mention the writings of Steinthal in the 1860s, which prove the existence of a widespread sexual symbolism in the mythological records and the history of language. . . . The Freudian symbol and its interpretation is therefore nothing unheard of, it is merely unusual for us psychiatrists. (Jung (1908) CW IV 23–4)

What we can surmise is the following: the psychoanalytic theory of the symbol was created as much by Freud's followers as by Freud, and for a very good reason: it was one department of the inner life of mankind's history that had already received much exposure from the researches of philologists and mythologists. For any 'psychiatrist' conversant with the philological sciences, sexual symbolism was a source of respectable support for Freud's interpretative methods, which, much to Jung's indignation, had come in for many 'cheap philological criticisms' (Ibid. CW IV 17).[50] The sexual symbolism that was one of the major findings of philology and mythology became grafted onto Freud's method. And the apparent affinity of Freud's method with those employed by philologists perhaps accounts for the fact that those philologically-minded psychoanalysts – Rank, Jung, Abraham, Ferenczi, Stekel, Jones, to mention only the best-known, a list to which we will return in a moment – could confuse findings which were almost exclusively philological in character with those that were more properly psychoanalytical.

But who were these philologically minded psychoanalysts? At the head of the list, we must place Freud. We have already seen, in Chapter 3, 'Symbolism', the uses to which Freud could put philology and some of the modes of philological reasoning he employed. Here we will simply note a few more aspects of his philological bent. He drew a large number of comparisons between the dream-work and linguistic mechanisms, thus, by implication, pointing towards linguistic mechanisms as the appropriate area in which to find the specific characteristics of the action of the unconscious, though the linguistic mechanisms in question might either be present-day ones, or ones appropriate to the development of language or those belonging to a hypothesized primitive language.[51] For example, he called upon philological evidence to support his account of the transformation of the first *gift*, a child's faeces, into those highly valued faecal substitutes, *gold* and *money*, on the one hand, and *baby* and *penis* on the other (Freud (1933a) SE XXII 100). When Freud wished to indicate profitable areas of application for psychoanalysis, he turned first to philology (Freud (1913j) SE XIII 165–90; (1924f) SE XIX 205ff). But the relation was more one of disciplinary contiguity than of a possible assimilation of philology to psychoanalysis; as we noted above (p. 98), Freud went out of his way to indicate to the other analysts that they had much to learn from a study of philology. And it was to the philological sciences that he looked to provide a more adequate training for the psychoanalyst than could medicine when he wrote, in *The Question of Lay Analysis*:

. . . analytic instruction [in a college of psychoanalysis] would include branches of knowledge which are remote from medicine and which the doctor does not come across in his practice: the history of civilization, mythology, the psychology of religion and the science of literature. Unless he is well at home in these subjects, an analyst can make nothing of a large amount of his material. By way of compensation, the great mass of what is taught in medical schools is of no use to him for his purposes. (Freud (1926e) SE XX 246)

Freud by no means regarded himself as an expert in philological matters. His period of collaboration with Jung was rich in philological researches, but it was clear that Jung's erudition in that sphere was vastly superior to Freud's, and Jung was to keep the relation of depth psychology to philology a close one, when the psychoanalysts had turned away, after the First World War, from philological researches towards sociology and ego-psychology. But in the period of 'splended isolation' before the formation of other analysts had begun, it appears that Fliess, along with his many other talents, along with the many other functions he fulfilled for Freud, was *'mein sprachgelehrter Freund'* of *The Interpretation of Dreams* (Freud (1900a) SE V 466). Fliess thus combined in himself two intellectual traditions, that of romantic biology and that of 'romantic' philology, preoccupations that fused, perhaps for both Fliess and Freud, in the fervour with which they searched for the meeting-point of the arbitrariness of chance, of numbers, with the determinism derived from a hidden temporal order.

But, along with Fliess, Freud also had his favourite philological authors, foremost amongst whom we must place Rudolf Kleinpaul, who, with Rank, appears to have been 'house-philologist' for the early psychoanalysts.[52] In a letter to Fliess, dated 12 December 1897, Freud recommended he read Kleinpaul's *Die Lebendigen und die Toten* (1898).[53] It seems likely that the following paragraph from the same letter owed something to Kleinpaul's stimulus:

Can you imagine what "endopsychic myths" are? They are the latest product of my mental labour. The dim inner perception of one's own psychical apparatus stimulates illusions, which are naturally projected outwards, and characteristically into the future and a world beyond. Immortality, retribution, the world after death, are all reflections of our inner psyche . . . psychomythology. (Freud (1950a) *Origins*, 12 Dec 1897, p. 237)

Was it again only a coincidence that the next letter to Fliess, written ten days later, ventured into the area that supplied the stock-in-trade of Kleinpaul and the other philologists: the double meaning of words?

> . . . in the case of obsessional ideas the most disparate things tend to be brought together under a word with more than one meaning. . . . A girl attending a sewing class which was soon coming to an end was troubled by the obsession: "No, you mustn't go yet, you haven't finished, you must do [*machen*] some more, you must learn all that it is possible to learn." Behind this was the memory of childhood scenes; when she was put on the pot, she did not want to stay on it and was subjected to the same compulsion: "You mustn't go yet, you haven't finished, you must do some more." The word "do" permits identification of the later with the infantile situation. (Ibid., (22 Dec. 1897) SE I 272–3)

It might be said that this concern with double meanings is not connected with the double meanings of the philologists, which, as we saw in the first section of this chapter, were the empirical *sine qua non* of the construction of etymological genealogies, the other half of the working principle of etymology being the comparison of two words with different forms, via the intermediary of a single meaning. (As Bain had written in 1870, to be cited by Abel and then by Freud in 1910: 'either every name must have a double meaning, or else for every meaning there must be two names'. (Freud (1910e) SE XI 159)) But it seems that Freud was half-afraid – again, he lacked the audacity . . . – that this 'childish play with words' (Freud (1905c) SE VIII 170) was too 'crazy (*ganz toll*)' (Freud (1950a) SE I 273) to be valuable as a scientific finding: it evoked the fear, perhaps, of being accused of putting words into other people's mouths – or worse places.[54] So the support of a philologically-based theory was very welcome; so welcome, indeed, that it might even have been the *possibility* of such a theory that allowed Freud to understand, even to discover, the play with words that his patients practised.

All this is not entirely arbitrary. The word *machen* has itself undergone a similar transformation of meaning. An old phantasy of mine, which I should like to recommend to your linguistic perception, deals with the derivation of our verbs from such originally copro-erotic terms. (Freud (1950a) SE I 273)

Certainly a philological project on the grand scale, and one which never came close to fruition. The deference to Fliess' linguistic talents[55] strikes one as out of place, perhaps a part of those other deferences, numerological, nasal and otherwise, that comprised what has come to be known as Freud's transference to Fliess. It occurs to us that these references to grandiose philological schemes are of the same ilk as all the other grandiose schemes Freud proposed to Fliess: the *Project for a Scientific Psychology*, the projected book entitled *Bisexuality in Man*[56], to mention only the most striking. These grandiose schemes might have been the necessary correlate both of Freud's self-analysis and of the slow crystallization of psychoanalysis out from the slurry formed by all those other sciences in epistemological adjacency to it; in other words, they may have been necessary to the construction of the epistemological space of psychoanalysis. If the detaching of psycho-analysis from neurology happened silently, its witness, after the event, being Chapter VII of *The Interpretation of Dreams*, the hopeful fascination evoked by the prospect of support from philology waxed as well as waned: a cycle one can observe in those eminently philological works of the turn of the century, *The Psychopathology of Everyday Life* and *Jokes and their Relation to the Unconscious*, as well as in the sporadic but regular references to philology across the entire corpus of Freud's psychoanalytical work until his death.

Wladimir Granoff has captured well the tone of Freud's hopeful relation to philology:

. . . [in Freud's relation to science], something functioned for him along the lines of 'Perhaps one day this issue will resolve itself, or be resolved [*décidé*]'. And, along this path, he invoked two sciences – although it is beholden upon us to stress the fact that he didn't invoke them in the same manner. Two sciences, one of which was chemistry, the other linguistics. Of chemistry, he invoked it in saying, 'Perhaps one day. . . .' To this hope, chemistry has replied with silence. As to linguistics, one could say that it is Lacan who has made it answer. (Granoff, 1975, p. 418)

What we can add to this remark of Granoff's is the different *tense* of Freud's fantasy of scientific support to be derived from these other disciplines: chemistry was always invoked in the future tense, whereas Freud believed, without really knowing the exact details, the exact sources, that linguistics – philology – had *already laid down* the scien-tific base, the manifestations of which Freud was (re)discovering in another form; that all these audacious, 'arbitrary', 'crazy' confusions of words were *already there*. (In the unconscious? In a dusty and already old volume of the *Zeitschrift für Völkerpsychologie und Sprachwissenschaft*? In the 'history of the development of language'? In 'linguistic usage'? Or, even, in the domain of knowledge possessed by those transferential objects that Freud was more and more successfully teaching himself to do without, even if such a withdrawal did involve the retrospective phantasy of a splendid isolation?)

We can read the following passage from a lecture that Ferenczi gave to the Free School of the Social Sciences in Budapest in 1911:

[The psychoanalyst] takes on the part of the successful caricature, Professor Tomb who, instead of letting poetical works in their original form influence his students, takes them to pieces and murders their beauties by his philological and aesthetic analysis.

Like every caricature, that of Professor Tomb has a core of seriousness. What this tedious philologist does in all simplicity namely, making what is beautiful dull by his analysis and thereby producing a comic effect upon everyone, Professor Freud does quite deliberately and uses it to obtain astonishing psychological information. . . . The very method by which he set out to analyse wit was an ingenious idea that, on the basis above mentioned, we might call 'the method of the tedious philologist'. (Ferenczi (1911b) pp. 332–3)

This characterization of Professor Freud – and, by implication, psychoanalysis in general – certainly had a greater accuracy than the occasional reference to the Talmudic or Kabbalistic character of psychoanalytic interpretation, a characterization fully argued for, if not convincingly, by Bakan (Bakan, 1958, esp. pp. 220–70). And there is plenty of evidence to indicate that the role of the tedious philologist could be comfortably shared by other psychoanalysts. Abraham, whose first love had been languages, and who was always glad of the opportunity that psychoanalysis gave him to return to this first love[57], had been the first of Freud's group to enter the field first mapped out for Freud by the stimulation he received from Kleinpaul, in his work entitled *Traum und Mythos* (1909). Abraham found that Freud's method of free association could not be employed for the interpretation of myths; he thus came to rely heavily on sexual symbolism, derived from the researches of the *Völkerpschologischen* and mythologists, and upon his own reworking of the philological evidence that they put into his hands. For example: one of the myths with which Abraham dealt was the sun-god cycle found in both Semitic and Aryan accounts, the best known representatives being Samson and Prometheus. Abraham's sources were Cohen (1865/69), Kuhn (1859/86) and Steinthal (1862a, 1862b). He focused his account on the word *Prometheus*, showing how it was derived from the Sanskrit *Pramantha*, itself derived from a term describing an implement, a 'borer'. This borer was a stick that was inserted into a bowl and rotated, generating fire. It was at the next level of theorizing that controversies between mythologists were rife: why was a myth elaborated around this technological device? Certain mythologists (sometimes Frazer, certainly Tylor) argued that myths such as these are a form of science distorted through ignorance, or through employing false premises. Abraham, in company with other psychoanalysts, found this rationalistic explanation unsatisfactory, turning more towards a form of explanation to be found in Müller's work: mythology arises from a distortion of language, mythology is an abuse of language.

Müller and Kleinpaul both argued that mythology arose from an earlier stage in the development of language, when language was more 'alive'. Although Müller argued that neither language nor thought could exist without the other, he admitted that 'language necessarily reacts upon thought, and we see in this reaction, in this refraction of the rays of language, the real solution of the old riddle of mythology.' (Müller, 1871, p. 593; cf. Kleinpaul, 1893, pp. 299ff). In the 'mythopeic period', when language was still young, objects were named by their characteristic attributes, thus giving rise to a complex system of homonyms and synonyms, a system which could already open out onto a play within language, a metaphor. 'Words were heavy and unwieldy. They said more than they ought to say. . . . ' (Müller, 1881, p. 369; quoted in Henson, 1971, p. 14). Myths were then generated, from these first words which described objects in terms connoting human activity, e.g. the sun is the 'shiner', the river the 'runner' (cf. 'riverrun, past Eve and Adam's, from swerve of shore to bend of bay, brings us by a commodius vicus of recirculation back . . . '). And such etymologies, as James Joyce also knew, could be proved from an examination of Sanskrit. Such a primal language having come into existence, the precondition for the generation of myth was that the 'true' reference for these words be lost – a sliding of meaning must take place – a process that Müller described as the 'death' of language, when it had lost its 'etymological conscience'.

It is the essential character of a true myth that it should no longer be intelligible by a reference to the spoken language. (Ibid., p. 376)

Müller's famous dictum, that mythology is a disease of language, arose from his conception that the 'true' meaning of words had been 'forgotten'. Abraham could thus easily graft the psychoanalytical theory of repression onto this account of the genesis of myth: mythology develops through repression acting within a language. And he could find a further etymology to add to the *Prometheus–Pramantha–borer* series: the 'borer' is also a synonym for 'penis'. Abraham undertook a brief comparative survey of languages in order to indicate the generality of this equation, as well as relying on the fact that the Sanskrit root *-mantha* has this double meaning, this origin.[58]

In this way Abraham could argue that the myth was a distorted representation of a sexual phantasy, a phantasy whereby the representations of the making of fire were sexualized. Implicit in this account was a notion that the sexual meanings of words are not only the cause of repression and subsequent mythic production, but also the primary units of language. Abraham could amalgamate Freudian psychoanalysis with Müller's and Kleinpaul's conception of myth as a 'disease of language', since, in assuming that the first words designated things sexual, he had also laid down the reasons why language should become diseased.

We even find an echo of this mythological etymology in a case-history that Freud wrote in 1908, just after he had received the galley-proofs of Abraham's essay (Freud, 1965a, p. 47). The key phantasy in this case-history, that of little Hans, concerned a plumber's borer:

I was in the bath, and then the plumber came and unscrewed it. Then he took a big borer and stuck it into my stomach. (Freud (1909b) SE X 65)

Here, as in the case of Leonardo's vulture-phantasy, an interpretation based on the directly represented content of the phantasy strikes a 'post-Freudian' eye as obvious: a big borer representing a penis is stuck into little Hans' stomach – a seemingly obvious representation of sexual intercourse. Such an interpretation could have been very easily integrated with those themes of pregnancy, castration and the anal theory of childbirth with which the case-history is concerned. But, strikingly, this interpretation was not made: Hans' father translated it as follows:

I was in bed with Mummy. Then Daddy came and drove me away. With his big penis he pushed me out of my place by Mummy. (Ibid.)

Freud expressed reservations about this interpretation. But these reservations were not due to his having considered the 'obvious' interpretation we have just mentioned, as what follows clearly indicates. Hans solved the problem for him by producing more material, which allowed Freud to correct Hans' father's interpretation with evidence from language, the evidence that Freud regarded as both preferred and clinching.

At the end of the analysis the plumber reappeared in a phantasy that represented Hans' final victory over his phobia:

The plumber came; and first he took away my behind with a pair of pincers, and then gave me another, and then the same with my widdler. (Ibid., SE X 98)

Hans' father commented:

In the light of this, we may review the interpretation of Hans' earlier phantasy. . . . The big bath meant a "behind", the borer or screw-driver was a widdler. The two phantasies are identical. (Ibid.)

But, following him, Freud had this to say:

Yes, the Doctor (the plumber) *did* come, he *did* take away his penis – but only to give a bigger one in exchange for it. (Ibid., SE X 100)

Still, this phantasy of castration feared and then overcome seemed to contain more than the 'borer-penis' equation might lead one to believe. True to Freudian psychoanalysis, let us ask the question: 'Whose penis?' Once one asks such a question one sees that the phantasies can give two different readings, with two very different effects upon the resulting interpretation.

In the first phantasy, it would seem not to be a question of Hans' penis. It is the 'plumber's' – his father's (according to his father). And it would seem that Hans is suffering an act of aggression from this penis, an act of aggression perhaps similar to those aggressive 'breaking throughs' to which his own primitive genital sensations seemed to lead. There does not seem to be a question of castration here. But the next moment of the analysis resulted in the discovery that one of Hans' phobic symptoms – his fear of heavily loaded carts – corresponded to 'the fear of a heavily loaded stomach'. (Ibid., SE X 66.) And yet neither Freud nor Hans' father made the connection *yet* between the borer that the plumber stuck into his stomach and this piece of knowledge that Hans now revealed: his fear of a stomach heavily loaded down . . . with a baby.

In the second phantasy, Hans' bottom and his widdler were first *taken away* and *then* he received another pair, bigger and better, 'like Daddy's'. In this triumphant phantasy, it appears that Hans accepted the reality of castration, which he had previously feared and rejected, but was able to triumph over this fact by receiving from his castrator a new penis, like Daddy's – or, to put it in terms familiar to us from Freud's papers of the 1920s (Freud, 1924d), he overcame his castration fears by an identification with the father.

But there is more to this second phantasy than meets the eye. 'It was not until later that it was possible to guess that this was a remoulding of a *phantasy* of *procreation*, distorted by anxiety.' (Freud (1909b) SE X 128.) Freud introduced this theme of procreation in the following note to the text:

Perhaps, too, the word 'borer' [*Bohrer*] was not chosen without regard for its connection with 'born' [*geboren*] and birth [*Geburt*]. If so, the child could have made no distinction between 'bored' [*gebohrt*] and 'born' [*geboren*]. I accept this suggestion, made by an experienced fellow-worker, but I am not in a position to say whether we have before us here a deep and universal connection between the two ideas or merely the employment of a verbal coincidence peculiar to German. Prometheus (Pramantha), the creator of man, is also etymologically 'the borer'. (Cf. Abraham, *Traum und Mythus*, 1909) (Ibid., SE X 98 n1).

And, despite the 'perhaps' with which he had introduced this interpretation, Freud concluded that the phantasy had the following meaning:

The big bath of water, in which Hans imagined himself, was his mother's womb; the 'borer', which his father had from the first recognized as a penis, *owed its mention* to its connection with 'being born'. The interpretation that we are obliged to give to the phantasy will of course sound very curious: 'With your big penis you "bored" me' (i.e. 'gave birth to me') 'and put me in my mother's womb.' (Ibid., SE X 128; my emphasis)

Let us take stock. The first feature we notice is the omission of a certain interpretative theme that was to figure largely in the case-history of the Wolfman and that would seem to be of importance here: the phantasy of sexual intercourse with the father, and the wish for the father's baby (= penis), a wish that entails the loss of his own penis (castration) (Freud (1918b) SE XVII 47, 63–4, 100). Such an interpretation would mesh well with the seemingly obvious interpretation of the first plumber phantasy (borer in stomach) as denoting sexual intercourse. In the light of such an interpretation, one would translate the equation of 'borer' and 'born' – if one would ever arrive at such an equation – as being equivalent to '(your) penis = (my) baby'. Such an interpretation would thus involve a certain licence with the actual wording of the phantasy. But, whatever the reasons, Freud did not wish to introduce an interpretation of this kind, which would have involved positing a strong passive-feminine component in little Hans' constitution, even though it would have made sense of the element in the first phantasy, in which a borer is stuck into little Hans' stomach. He left completely to one side this interpretation, in favour of one that followed more closely the linguistic evidence, a line of evidence that might have seemed implausible to many another.

Freud ignored the passive homosexual theme of the analysis, in favour of the interpretation that little Hans had phantasized his *own* procreation.[59] It was the bridge from 'borer' to 'being born' that attracted his attention, since it involved the form of argument that we have come to recognize as akin to the arguments of the philologists. The similarity in sound of '*gebohrt*' and '*geboren*' was the path by which Freud (and *not* Hans' father) imputed to little Hans the means with which to forge a link between the theme of the penis and the theme of procreation: the crucial link in the analysis. The sentence, 'With your big penis you 'bored' me . . . ' doesn't mean 'With your big penis you 'fucked' me . . . '; it means 'With your big penis you 'gave birth' to me . . . '. In all probability, it was Otto Rank, who was at that time, as he was to be later, preoccupied with the theme of birth, who was the 'experienced fellow-worker' who had drawn Freud's attention to the link between the words. And we can be almost certain that he derived the connection from his philological researches into the mythology of birth. Alongside of this philological source, Freud could call on Abraham's work in order to forge the link between the 'borer' and the theme of procreation.[60] So that the etymologies derived from the Indo-European languages seemed to 'lead', to go on before, the material elaborated in the case-history in the crucial passage from the theme of the penis to the theme of birth. It was as if the facilitations laid down between '*Geburt*' and '*Bohrer*', between '*penis*', '*borer*', '*Pramantha*' and '*Prometheus*', were already in place, as a consequence of the existence of these words. Apart from the issue of the grammatical discernments that the little boy possessed, – an issue that has recently perplexed transformational grammarians, enticing them to postulate an innate set of grammatical categories – we are at least forced to ponder the question of a possible 'deep and universal connection between the two ideas', a question raised by the homophony of the words representing these ideas. An alternative solution to that which would postulate an inner connection between a group of ideas and their phonetic representations would be to hypothesize a set of pathways, 'already there', as a by-product of the history of language.

   What we hope to have indicated through this account of little Hans's 'plumber' phantasy is that the crucial theme of birth entered in by the path of a homophony sanctioned by philological evidence. We have here a parallel to Leonardo's vulture-phantasy: where a 'post-Freudian' analyst might have assumed without further ado that the vulture was a mother-substitute, or that the borer pushed into Hans' stomach was a representative of sexual intercourse, we find that Freud only produced such interpretations when philological evidence – Egyptian mythology, a possible 'deep' linguistic connection between '*gebohrt*' and '*geboren*' – could vouchsafe such a step. And in the latter case, the interpretation Freud gave was *crucially* determined as different from that which another analyst might have offered, precisely by the linguistic evidence that he employed: 'being born' rather than 'sexual intercourse'. Freud's translation of the plumber phantasy remains very close to a homophony where meets the babble of a little boy and the mythological research of Rank and Abraham; it does not extend beyond what the evidence of language will allow. Indeed, it follows the evidence of language to the extent where a conclusion is reached that would almost certainly not have been reached via the straightforward equation upon which Freud was working at that time: 'penis = faeces = baby'. As if the past history of language could not but have its effect on the 4-year-old boy's attempt to elaborate the myth of his own creation.

   The historical realism of the comparative linguists (Ardener, 1971) seemed to necessitate something more than the simple statement, 'These words were once spoken'. It seemed as if, once spoken, one could never escape from their echo. Or, by believing one could, one was then presented with a neurotic, a primitive man or a child who spoke a word without a history. And such a word could have no meaning.

It always seems to us as if meaning – compared with life – were the younger event, because we assume, with some justification, that we assign it of ourselves, and because we believe, equally rightly no doubt, that the great world can get along without being interpreted. But how do we assign meaning? From what source, in the last analysis, do we derive meaning? The forms we use for assigning meaning are historical categories that reach back into the mists of time – a fact we do not take sufficiently into account. Interpretations make use of certain linguistic matrices that are themselves derived from primordial images. From whatever side we approach this question, everywhere we find ourselves confronted with the history of language, with images and motifs that lead straight back to the primitive wonder-world. (Jung (1934/54) CW IX Part I 32–3)

Such a recognition, here made explicit by Jung in 1934, was common ground to both psychoanalysts and philologists. What was of import-ance in the history of language was two contradictory elements: the movement of history itself, by which one could hope to find an anchor for meaning in a history finally became perspicuous; and the starting-point, the moment when a meaning and a word were created. Although there seems no good reason for assigning this moment to any other point in time than 'now' – however that may be defined – the psycho-analysts seem to struggle with a great fear, or perhaps a great suspicion, of the seeming arbitrariness that such a turning-away from past determinations might entail. In 1897 Freud had said 'All this is not entirely arbitrary,' with Kleinpaul's book at his elbow. In 1908 Abraham wrote:

The objection that symbolism and the importance ascribed to it exists only in the imagination of a few biased theorists is untenable. Kleinpaul expresses his opinion on this point emphatically and incisively: symbols are not made, they just exist; they are not invented, but merely recognized. (Abraham, 1909, p. 169)

How not to obey the pressure to push back, to the beginnings, when sexuality was represented directly and without ambiguity, when language was as yet undistorted and not yet mythical, when one could find a pre-mythical and pre-metaphorical state of language, when the 'original predicates', the 'kinship relations' (Kleinpaul, 1916, p. 8) of the first speech, were not yet covered over, when one could find a state of language that included as part of its *raison d'être* the incomprehensible identities that analysis and philology relied upon for their continual progress? And with this drive back into the history of language, the problem of the preservation of linguistic traces could not be avoided. We have already hinted that there could be two solutions to this problem. Let us now address them.

When we studied Freud's paper on Leonardo, we found that the problem of the permanent preservation of signification – i.e. the problem of tradition – lay behind the contorted form of his argument. The point of attack in Leonardo was the problem of the preservation of a word from one epoch to the next. Similarly, when he came to write his essay on Moses, a similar opening seemed possible: why not solve the seemingly intractable problem of the relation between the Egyptians and the Jews by reference to one word that can cross the barrier? But perhaps his not altogether happy experience with Leonardo had forewarned him against such a simple solution.

> The Jewish confession of faith, as is well known, runs: '*Schema Jisroel Adonai Elohenu Adonai Echod.*' If it is not merely by chance that the name of the Egyptian *Aten* (or *Atum*) sounds like the Hebrew word *Adonai* and the name of the Syrian deity *Adonis*, but if it is due to a primaeval kinship of speech and meaning, then the Jewish formula might be translated thus: 'Hear, o Israel, our god Aten (Adonai) is a sole god.' . . . But in all probability this is making things too easy for us. (Freud (1939a) SE XXIII 25)[61]

Such a solution, then, relying upon 'a primaeval kinship of speech and meaning', is too easy. But what other option is there? It was at this point that Freud turned to the more difficult path, which, as we have seen, entailed a means for the preservation of tradition; a solution which could only push further back the moment when a less than arbitrary relation between speech and meaning, when a 'kinship' could be found.[62] So we can recognize that it was the problem of the double meaning of words, analysed and comprehended through the agency of etymology or of free association, that drove philology and, following it, psychoanalysis, to a cornering of meaning in a past moment that is made present by a principle of subsistence that finds no better explanation than a reference to a concept such as the *Volksgeist*, or to tradition, or to a 'polyglot unconscious'.[63]

To round off our account of the relations between philology and psychoanalysis, we can return once again to the group of early analysts, this time to the work of Ernest Jones. Jones may have been the outsider, the *shabbeth goy* with the inexhaustible pen, but the path via which he came to psychoanalysis was much like that of his codisciples: a training as a neurologist, a distinct but unchanneled interest in the medicine of childhood and the peculiar combination of interests that I have tried to highlight in this book: a twin interest in aphasia and philology.[64] In his autobiography, he described the course of his intellectual development as follows:

> I was then [c. 1900] under the illusion that [man's biological nature] could best be studied in neurology, where it would seem that human impulses and the control of them could well be examined. . . . Not that I was in any way unaware of the philosophical problems involved. On the contrary, I even conceived the idea that a profound study of speech and language – the only mental function where some counterpart can be localized in the cortex of the brain – with their disorders would be the most promising path to investigating the relationship between mind and brain; with this end in view I did an immense amount of work in that field, which remained for some years one of my side interests. Incidentally, it has a certain irony that the only position I have ever held in the University of London is that of membership of the Board of Studies for Comparative Philology. (Jones, 1959, pp. 18–19. Cf. Jones, 1907, 1908, 1909)

In this strange shift in Jones' account, from the neurology of speech and language to the study of comparative philology, we find re-capitulated the movement we have been studying in this work: from neurology to philology. And how else can we fill in this seeming gap in Jones' train of thought other than by pointing to psychoanalysis, which occupied most of Jones' life, and which bridges the gap between neurology and philology with its central concern, language?[65] And, in addition, the fact that Jones held this particular academic position on the Board of Studies for Comparative Philology indicates to us that he was no mere amateur when it came to the study of languages.

As Jones' intellectual biographer, Claude Girard, has noted, Jones' psychoanalytic method consisted in 'relating the analysis of the characteristics of his theme, its psychological meanings and their symbolic relations to the different forms of infantile sexuality, complet-ing these givens with those of etymology' (Girard, 1972, p. 210). Etymology could either be the means of discovery of hidden significations, or a means of providing evidential support for these significations, come upon elsewhere. His etymological researches made up the bulk of his work before his analysis with Ferenczi in 1913, and made up a significant portion throughout his career. They show what Girard calls a 'certain predilection' (Ibid., p. 247) for the use of phonetic associations combined with etymological arguments. It is as clear in Jones' work as it is in Freud's that etymological analysis functions as a form of free association, in which the change of phonetic form and meaning are linked, although their transformations may not be parallel at all times. And, again, as with Freud, psychoanalysis can either draw upon etymology for its proofs, or contribute to etymology through discovering in neurosis a series of etymological connections previously undiscovered by philologists. For example, Jones attempted to throw light upon the meaning of the Sanskrit root *MR*, claiming in particular that its *R* represented oral sadism (citing as evidence the fact that French gentlewomen of the sixteenth century were not supposed to roll their 'r's). From there he wished to trace out an etymology for the word *MR*, usually taken to mean 'horse', by which it came to represent the masturbation terror of the 'night*mare*'. (Jones (1913)).

Another paper of Jones' indicates clearly how the study of the history of languages and the psychoanalytic theory of the defence mechanisms could be drawn together. This paper, written in 1920, was called 'A linguistic factor in English characterology'. Jones' starting-point was the question: why are the English so prudish? His answer depended on the structure of the English language, a structure that facilitates repression. English contains three separate languages laid over one another: at the base, Anglo-Saxon, upon which Norman French has been imposed, followed by a coating of Latin. As a result of this heterogeneity, the language has an unequalled range of synonyms and endows the English with an unparalleled freedom to indulge in fastidiousness, through 'translation' from one stratum to another. The stages of this process, exactly that of repression, can be traced in a large number of examples, e.g. the Anglo-Saxon '*gut*' was replaced by the French '*bowel*', which, in Jones' day, had succumbed to the Latin '*intestine*' (Jones, 1920).

Both Jones and, as we saw, Abraham had managed to fuse Freud's early theory of repression as a 'failure of translation' with the etymological method, so that what was translated were the distinct languages, found discovered in the collective unconscious or group mind (*Volksgeist*). The 'radiation of meaning' (Jones, 1923, p. 354) that formed the bread and butter of the psychoanalyst was to be found in the history of language and in childhood, so that Jones could rely on philology to make intelligible and respectable 'the far-fetched associations we are accustomed to meet in the unconscious'. (Ibid.) The philologist was the pioneer when it came to the implausible radiation of meaning that psychoanalysis came to rely on in the progressive unveiling of what was said but not known (cf. Descombes, 1977).

Neither Jones nor Freud ever fully confronted the problem that the philological method and the psychoanalytic investigation of the neuroses raised, and which we have seen in this chapter come more and more to the fore, namely, the problem of the preservation of traces that 'still' signify. To refer the problem to a collective system of representation, as did the *Völkerpsychologischen* with the concept of the *Volksgeist*, or as did some psychoanalysts with the concept of the collective unconscious, was only to crystallize the problem, to name it rather than to solve it. Again, we have noted how Freud explicitly recognized the necessity for assuming a means for the 'survival of a tradition' only late in his work, in *Moses and Monotheism*, although he had implicitly assumed such a means throughout his work: psychoanalysis, no more than philology, could not function without such a means. Jones, for one, quarrelled with Freud over the mechanism for such a survival, reading Freud's theory as a version of a biological theory known as Lamarckianism, and, in the excessively 'Darwinian' atmosphere of Britain, finding such a theory unacceptable. But he himself, in his more philological works, assumed that such a means for the transference of word-forms and significations existed; and it was in this domain, rather than in the area of the preservation of 'instinctual' impulses, that Freud and psychoanalysis required a means for preserving the effects of the past.

It was this unaccountable preservation of psychic traces that finally put a wedge between psychoanalysis and archaeology, the analogy between these sciences having been of some importance and significance to Freud (Freud (1896c) SE III 196; Bernfeld, Suzanne, 1951). In contrast with the objects of archaeological research, 'it may, as we know, be doubted whether any psychical structure can really be the victim of total destruction.' (Freud (1937d) SE XXIII 260). It is things of the mind that have an almost limitless power of preservation (Freud (1930a) SE XXI 71). And this doctrine, this finding, represents a curious reversal of commonplace opinions concerning the character of the different sciences, namely, that subjectivity is peculiarly untrustworthy, and that permanence is to be found better represented by the material than by the psychic. We find a parallel notion in the discussion of chance in *The Psychopathology of Everyday Life*, where Freud avowed that the distinction between the superstitious man and the psychoanalyst resides in the different sense they give to 'determinism'. For the superstitious person, chance exists in the mind but not in the material world; whereas, for the psychoanalyst, chance exists in the material world, but not in the mind.[66] Obviously this was a crucial doctrine for Freud, but also a sensitive one, and Fliess chose to take it as the target of attack when he broke with Freud, when he accused Freud of being a 'thought-reader'; it was also this aspect of the development of Freud's thought that Ernest Jones found so disturbing: the question of telepathy. And it is towards the limit question of telepathy that our whole argument points, a question which we could reformulate as follows: if the contents of the unconscious are supra-individual in character, under what conditions is the simultaneous realization of such contents in different consciousness possible? To Freud, the fact that this question brings one close to the occult was a reason for treating it with circumspection, but not for refusing to ask it.[67] And perhaps we should see the question of telepathy, like the question of Moses, returning Freud to the problem of the preservation of significative traces across those times and spaces not yet proven to have been implicated in their transmission.

Conclusion

> I used to have a morbid idea
> *that my parents knew my thoughts;*
> *I explained this to myself*
> *by supposing that I had spoken*
> *them out loud, without having heard*
> *myself do it.* I look on this
> as the beginning of my illness.[1]

It will not have passed unnoticed that it will not be easy to find this work a disciplinary niche. Is it a historical work, attempting to get straight the historical record, attempting to find a certain 'reading' that could be reiterated endlessly, and still remain a definitive reading, as if, once read, Freud would not have to be reread? Or is this work an attempt to reformulate, via a historico-conceptual argument, the foundations of psychoanalysis, so that, where we once saw biology we now see philology, where we once saw symbolic decoding, we now see phonetic switching, where we once saw the discharge of fixated energy we now see the rule-like transformations of a personal script?

I can deny neither of these ways of reading this work. But there is no doubt that a third way of reading it is possible. We might call this its Lacanian dimension. What may strike many readers is the absence of the name 'Lacan' in a work that is devoted to the topic of language and psychoanalysis. Such an absence could not but be a deliberate act, an omission that owes its *raison d'être* to a series of decisions. What results from these decisions can now be seen in one of two ways: firstly, it is possible to demonstrate the fundamental nature of the theory and practice of language and speech in psychoanalysis without partaking of the heady prose, or the ineffable ambiguities, of Lacanian analysis. Secondly, we can read this work as the prolegomena to a more direct approach to the Lacanian school of analysis, which, in the 1950s, explicitly referred itself to a reading of Freud that runs parallel to this thesis in its emphasis on the function of language in analysis, in the talking-cure. To put it another way, if we read Freud *this* way, it may help us to understand how it is possible for Lacan to construct his theory under the banner of a return to Freud.

To conclude on such a note may appear strange. After all, this work makes historical claims. But it is as well to record the fact that these historical claims were first and foremost hypotheses arising out of a close reading of Freud's texts, rather than being the slowly accumulated suspicions arising out of a general survey of late nineteenth century culture. If one can try to demonstrate a unity that encompasses neurology and philology, it would certainly be a difficult task if psychoanalysis had never existed. I may have had to become acquainted with that background, that context, that culture, in order to carry out this study. But such an acquaintanceship was in the service of a desire to throw light upon certain obscurities in the psychoanalytic texts: jumps in the argument, assumptions that seemed to be less demonstrable than demonstrative, the specific form of a debate.[2] The issues that such topics raised for me required the long detours that, when reorganized, made linear, make up this work. Put simply, a 'slip' of Freud's pen was the occasion for an inquiry into the constitution of the sciences of language and mind in the nineteenth century. And we should not be surprised that such strange detours were necessary in order to try and discover what Freud could possibly have meant when he talked in 1890 of the 'magical power of words'.

So this work as history revolves around a corpus of writings that – need it be said? – remain the primary focus of psychoanalysis. And the fact that our history looks 'forward' to Lacan, just as it looks 'backwards' to Jackson and Kleinpaul, does not, I trust, make it a historical monster, out of step either with the past or with the present. I make no pretensions to writing the history of the past as if it were a self-sufficient system of permanent traces that could be closed off by a remark such as that of Ernest Jones', when he was assessing the significance of Freud's self-analysis: 'Once done, it is done for ever.'[3] In this work I have tried to do nothing other than write the history of the present. In history, as in psychoanalysis, one understands what comes before through what came after.

Notes

1. Two other books on Freud have provided continual stimulation: Richard Wollheim's *Freud*, and Philip Rieff's *Freud: The Mind of the Moralist*.
2. Very similar ground to that covered in the latter part of Chapter 2 is covered in Laffal (1964) and Marshall (1974). There are a large number of commentaries that discuss the last section in Freud's paper on 'The Unconscious' (1915e) where he linked consciousness to word-presentations and unconsciousness to thing-presentations. Some of these are cited in the bibliography. A number of papers by Otto Marx have proved invaluable, especially his paper on aphasia and linguistic theory in the nineteenth century, discussed in Chapter 5. Litowitz and Litowitz (1977) attempt to relate Freudian theory to contemporary (Chomskyean) linguistics; they also include a very useful review of the historical relations between psychoanalysis and linguistics, although their interests do not overlap very much with my own.
3. The most significant contributions to the history of psychoanalysis in recent years have come from the pen of Michel Foucault, despite the fact that, as he admits, he has never directly addressed the question of its history, all the illuminating remarks he has made appearing as asides within works that have other concerns. But it is clear that, from his earliest writings on – in particular the 'Introduction' to the French translation of Ludwig Binswanger's *Le rêve et l'existence* (1954) esp. pp. 20–7, 75–80 – he has been concerned with the 'historico-conceptual' place of psychoanalysis. Despite this concern, he has never dealt with psychoanalysis face on. But, in a series of works, *L'Histoire de la Folie*, *Les Mots et les Choses*, and the more recent *La volonté de savoir*, his 'contributions' to the history of psychoanalysis have nothing less than revolutionary implications. These implications are of wider significance than can be dealt with here, and I refer the reader to my article, 'Michel Foucault and the History of Psychoanalysis', forthcoming in *History of Science*. But let us just note briefly two implications of Foucault's work: firstly, that the possibility of psychoanalysis was intimately related to the employment of the model derived from the philological sciences in the nineteenth century. We will discuss and expand upon this notion at some length in Chapter 5. Secondly, Foucault points out that the 'discourse on sexuality' is not peculiar to psychoanalysis. Rather, it should be seen as part of a more broad-ranging compulsion to confess the secret of secrets, a compulsion that has its roots in the religious tradition of spiritual regulation and the bourgeois system of social control via the construction of fields of technical expertise, fields of esoteric knowl-

edge. What these two different arguments lead one to ponder are the following:

(i)   The techniques of interpretation and of hermeneutic analysis are not
      original or specific to psychoanalysis, whose main claim to 'originality'
      might reside in a purification of these philological techniques and their
      generalization to new areas, in particular to the areas previously under
      the domination of a medico-biological model of disease; in other words
      the originality of psychoanalysis must be seen in its application to the
      expressive, significative or semantic modes of the body.

(ii) If the idea that sexuality is somehow hidden, unspoken, crying out to be
      spoken, if this idea is found to have a history that stretches back to the
      mid eighteenth century, then the key feature of the interpretative
      machine that psychoanalysis sets in motion, namely, the discovery of
      the meaningful that is also sexual, and in some sense primary, this
      feature is revealed to be simply a crystallization of tendencies that
      doctors, teachers and moral leaders of one sort or another had been
      working towards for the century that precedes the moment when Freud
      found himself confronted by the sexual pantomime-show for which
      Charcot was the impresario.

To put the arguments somewhat differently, Foucault's first argument,
from *The Order of Things*, will make of *The Interpretation of Dreams* an
original synthesis of the categories of possible knowledge available to the
human sciences in the nineteenth and early twentieth centuries, without
finding there anything more than an inversion of concepts that had served
to furnish out the sciences of ethnology, philology and mythology
throughout the nineteenth century. Foucault's second argument, from *La
volonté de savoir*, will make of the *Three Essays on Sexuality* nothing more
than a codification – and perhaps a neutralization – of the discourses on
perverse and abnormal sexuality that the institutions of organized and
scientific sexual confession had progressively revealed and created from the
eighteenth century on. The cogency and validity of these historical theses is
still in question and require much further debate and research. But it is clear
that these are the most challenging historical hypotheses on the history of
psychoanalysis since Freud wrote 'On the history of the psychoanalytical
movement'. (See also the debate between members of the *École Freudienne*
and Foucault, which took place shortly after the publication of *La volonté
de savoir* in *Ornicar?*, *10*, 1977, esp. pp. 76ff.)

CHAPTER 1

1. One of the names that Anna O., Breuer's first patient, gave to the method
    she had created (Breuer and Freud (1895d) SE II 30). She employed the
    English words, since, at that point in the course of her neurosis, she could
    not speak German.

2. From the beginning of his psychoanalytic work, Freud detached himself
    from two doctrines, obviously related to each other, that we can call

'physicalism' and 'organicism'. The first had a more philosophical sense, namely, the prescription that all possible medically explanatory entities had a physical reference, a scientific examination of the other side of the implicit dualism being either fruitless, impossible or, allowing of a complete translation into scientific languages which included no reference to 'mind'. In 1890, Freud had noted the finding that 'in some at least of these (nervous) patients the signs of their illness originate from nothing other than *a change in the action of their minds upon their bodies* and that the immediate cause of their disorder is to be looked for in their minds. What may be the remoter causes of the disturbance which affects their minds is another question, with which we need not now concern ourselves'. ((1890a) SE VII 286), and the continual postponement of any approach to a physicalist reduction of 'the action of the mind' throughout psychoanalytic writings is a witness to the *irrelevance* of recourse to physical explanations. Apart from a short flirtation with psychophysical parallelism, Freud was an unrepentant and rather old-fashioned dualist in his theory and in his practice, if not on every occasion when pressed to give an opinion concerning the final causes of the phenomena that psychoanalysis discovered.

As to organicism, this doctrine had a more specifically medical flavour, being the general term to cover those theories of 'disease' that presumed to find the explanatory entities in the bodily organs. There was thus an emphasis on the spatial locality of the causes. We might, indeed, contrast physicalism and organicism on this point: physicalist theories were not necessarily concerned with the actual locus of a disease. For many physicalists, to speak of 'nervous fibres' or even Jackson's 'nervous arrangements' would qualify a theory as physicalist. But an organicist would search for specific loci: the search for the specific cerebral artery whose anaemia or hyperaemia had caused a certain disturbance of the mental faculties would be a typically organicist project. In this sense, Freud had renounced organicism in psychology by the time he published *On Aphasia* but was still prepared to embark upon a physicalist programme in the *Project*, even if the units of 'matter in motion' soon got squeezed out of what became an essentially non-reductionist account.

3. See, for instance, Freud (1900a) SE IV 181n; SE V 553, 562–4, 594–6, 604–5. Cf. Steinbach (1953).

4. The best general account of the history of physiology touching on the reductionism of the late nineteenth century is Rothschuh (1953, 1973), although the classic Lange, vol. III (1865, 1925) and the unsurpassed Merz (1904–12) are more thought-provoking. More specifically, the works of Amacher, Bernfeld, Cranefield, Gode-von-Aesch, Riese, Stengel, Young give the background to what Bernfeld called the 'school of Helmholtz', which Cranefield renamed 'the biophysics movement'. Jones, vol. I is accurate, although limited by the form of the biography. On Vienna in particular, see Lesky (1965), and Hoff and Seitelberger (1952). For the place of medicine in Austrian culture the best source is Johnston (all cited in full in bibliography).

5. For Breuer's early work, see Cranefield (1958, 1972). For Freud's early work as a pathologist, Amacher (1965), Andersson (1962), Brautigam (1960) Brun (1936), Dorer (1932), Ellenberger (1970), Galdston (1956),

Jones (1953), König (1962), Lebzeltern (1973), Levin (1974), Rosen (1972), Spehlman (1953), Stewart (1969).

6. For instance, the 'cure' achieved by Zoë in Jensen's *Gradiva* consisted in her helping Hanold to recognize that he had displaced his love from Zoë Bertgang to the Pompeian Gradiva. '[The analyst] brings about something like what Norbert Hanold grasped at the end of the story when he translated back the name *"Gradiva"* into *"Bertgang"* [both mean 'who steps along brilliantly']. The disorder vanishes while being traced back to its origin; analysis, too, brings simultaneous cure.' (Freud (1907a) SE IX 89).

7. There is no comprehensive account of theories of nervous diseases in the nineteenth century. My work is drawn from those partial accounts that do exist, mainly focused on theories of hysteria, such as Abricossoff (1897–8), Ellenberger (1970, p. 240ff), Temkin (1971), Veith (1965); good contemporary surveys are to be found in Jolly (1878) and Gowers (1903).

8. Charcot, Jean-Martin, (1886–90). The *Oeuvres Complètes* is by no means complete, lacking several important papers and books. Secondary sources devoted to Charcot divide into two classes, both hagiographical in tendency: the first focuses primarily on the advances in neurology (Guillain (1959), Janet (1895), Meige (1925), Owen (1971)) and those which are primarily interested in Charcot because of his relations with Freud. A peculiar characteristic of the writings of Charcot, a peculiarity pointed out to me in a private communication from M. Foucault, is the apparent disparity between the 'flatness' of his published work, the lack of fundamentally novel ideas or practices, and the enormous esteem in which he was held by those who had been his pupils, who created his reputation. As the example we will examine in this chapter indicates, Charcot's lectures and his case-histories could be fascinating; but these gems are few and far between in the corpus of his work. Even the method of isolation he employed in the case we will study was an accepted and important part of the therapeutic practices employed by alienists from the mid eighteenth century on, as Castel (1976), Foucault (1963/1973), Foucault (1976) have pointed out.

9. I have not been able to find evidence of this architectural modification in the archives of the Salpêtrière; Pontalis' source was a statement of Charcot's.

10. The concepts of suggestability and suggestion were to remain vague throughout the heyday of the interest in hypnosis, signifying a 'psychological influence' of some sort, sometimes said to act directly on the 'nervous system'. Freud's criticism of both Charcot and Bernheim singled out this vagueness as being a serious defect. But it was obviously the 'point of entry' for psychological concepts into the study of the nervous diseases.

11. 'Traumatic Neuroses' were common in the nineteenth century: amnesias, anaesthesias, hyperaesthesias, paralyses, disturbances of the senses (blindness, deafness, buzzing in the ears, etc.), whose appearance was directly dependent upon an accident or a shock, paradigms of which were railway accidents, accidents at work, falling off horses etc. Charcot demonstrated that the clinical picture in these neuroses was similar to that found in hysteria, thus creating the class of 'traumatic hysterias'.

12. See Charcot (1885b). This lecture was one of those translated by Freud in

Neue Vorlesungen über die Krankheiten des Nervensystems insbesondere über Hysterie (1886f).

13. The concept of suggestion covered the direct effects of commands and entreaties uttered by the doctor on the patient's nervous system. In order to give the concept some specificity, Freud 'put forward the view that what distinguishes a suggestion from other kind of psychical influence, such as a command or the giving of a piece of information or instruction, is that in the case of a suggestion an idea is aroused in another person's brain which is not examined in regard to its origin but is accepted just as though it had arisen spontaneously in that brain.' (Freud (1888–89) SE I 82). When a certain element of independence of the physician is observed in the phenomena produced by suggestion, it is said that the suggestion has led to autosuggestion: these are indirect suggestions 'in which a series of intermediate links arising from the subject's own activity are inserted between the external stimulus and the result' (*Ibid.* SE I 83). It can thus be seen that the relation of suggestion to auto-suggestion is the same as that between a direct reference and an allusion. 'It is autosuggestions . . . that lead to the production of spontaneous hysterical paralyses and it is an inclination to such autosuggestions, rather than suggestibility towards the physician, that characterizes hysteria' (ibid., SE I 83). We should bear in mind that the concept of suggestion was not always used with any precision, either by Charcot or Bernheim, or by Freud and the other younger neurologists.

14. Of the historical studies written of aphasia, the following can be regarded as of primary importance: Cassirer (1953–7), Head (1926), Moutier (1908), Ombredane (1951). Both Schoenwald (1954) and Stengel (1954) attempted characterizations of the significance of Freud's work on aphasia with respect to the development of psychoanalysis, but neither related Freud's work to the tradition of aphasia studies (with the exception of the obvious importance of Jackson's work for Freud). Schoenwald's argument characterizes *On Aphasia* as the first occasion on which Freud wrestled with the problem of the relation of physiology to psychology. Stengel points up a number of similarities between the work of Jackson and that of Freud (see also Stengel (1963)), and characterizes the speech apparatus of *On Aphasia* as the 'elder brother' of the psychic apparatus of *The Interpretation of Dreams*, finding that both of these terms have their origin in Meynert's writings, concluding that 'they demonstrate Freud's lasting attachment to physiological concepts'. (Stengel (1954) p. 86). But the fact that the prototype of the speech and psychic apparatuses can be found in Meynert's work does not licence the conclusion that Freud was lastingly attached to physiological concepts; one of the abiding themes of aphasia theory – and brain anatomy in general – was the general confusion between physiological and psychological concepts, such that important advances in the subject, such as Freud's, could be made simply by a clarification of what was psychological and what was physiological. It was probably Jackson's determination to separate the two that made his work of fundamental importance, both for the history of the discipline and for the development of Freud's thought. Another topic has led to some debate in the secondary literature, namely the contemporary recognition of Freud's work on aphasia (see Ellenberger, 1970, p. 476, and Bloom, 1975). I have no space to

enter into the details of the historical evidence, but it should be clear from my account that Freud's work was sufficiently recognized to be cited regularly in both French and German literature as being of some importance, and, in the early years of the century, was taken as a pioneering example of the 'psychological' approach to aphasia.

15. It is interesting to note that a crucial test-case (Adèle Anselin) seemed to disprove definitively Broca's theory as early as 1864, when the *post-mortem* conducted by Broca and Charcot showed no lesion of the third left frontal convolution (see Trousseau, 1868, p. 235, and Bouchard, 1865, p. 489); but instead of the programme for the correlation of symptom and brain pathology being abandoned, a proliferation of theoretical complications, of which the most significant was Wernicke's, ensued. Trousseau quoted Broca as having admitted, after he had assisted Charcot at the *post-mortem*, that 'the case invalidated the anatomical law which he had laid down'. (Trousseau, 1868, p. 247).

16. Wernicke championed physiology against the dominance of anatomy, by referring to fundamental physiological units: the 'sensory nerve' and the 'motor nerve' became the basic units manipulated in the schemas found in aphasia theory. As we will see, it is the slippage made possible by these terms that allowed Wernicke to claim his theory as a psychological one. It is the notion that a sensory nerve is a physiological unit that lies at the heart of the mind-body problem in the late nineteenth century.

17. Similar notions of unity and synthesis, perhaps with more of an awareness of 'splitting' and 'fragmentation', can be found in mid-twentieth century aphasia literature, but with one crucial difference: instead of the cortex being split, a phenomenological 'bracketing' disqualifies any certain reference for this split. See, for example, Alajouanine (1968), p. 290.

18. This rupture was conceptualized by Freud when he referred to word presentations as forming a closed system, and to object associations – the system commonly referred to in the late nineteenth century as the *ego*, e.g. in Meynert (1885), pp. 171ff – as being open. We will return to this crucial distinction.

19. See Jackson (1925, 1931). John Hughlings Jackson (1835–1911) was a neurologist who worked in London from 1863 to his retirement in 1906. His most famous work was on epilepsy. Although he remained a neurologist all his life, keeping to strictly neurological problems, the fertility of his ideas can be well judged from his wide-ranging, though incoherent, papers on aphasia, essays on the nature of the joke and the dream, and his philosophically acute papers on dualism. See secondary works by Engelhardt (1975), Greenblatt (1965, 1970) Riese (1947, 1954), Riese and Gooddy (1955), Walshe (1961) and Young (1970).

20. One could possibly illuminate these two different conceptions by distinguishing between the meaning and the reference of the recurrent utterance or hysterical symptom.

21. Broca's *Tan* was reported in the paper cited above; Trousseau's *Sapon* was reported in a long footnote to the lectures cited above, and then used extensively by Jackson (1878–80).

22. Cf. the following remark that Freud made *a propos* of Wernicke's confusion of anatomy and psychology, at a meeting of the Vienna Psychoanalytic

Society, 20 March 1907, *Minutes* vol. I pp. 49–50:

> [Obsessional deliria] are conscious systems of thought by which the patients try to justify it and to understand it. These deliria represent merely projections. . . . An example of such a system in science is Wernicke's delirious psychology, as one might say. He transferred his brain anatomy directly into the realm of psychology.

23. Freud (1950a) *Origins*, 2 May 1891, p. 61. The critique of Meynert appears to be beside the point, since the major target of the monograph was the concept of the centre, and the attempts to identify anatomical space with that centre. But, besides taking a personal pleasure in attacking a teacher who had at one time thought of Freud as his 'favourite', and who had then created great difficulties for him when he turned his interest away from brain anatomy, Freud was clear that a critique of the projection theory of the nervous system was, as we shall see, a crucial element in the critique of the centre.

24. We should note the difference between the unity achieved by the diagram-makers and Flourens' argument against the possibility of any spatial localization of function. What the diagram-makers did was to install the unity at the level of the diagram – the unity of positivistic science – and *then* argue that this diagram was an exact replica of cerebral reality, using names instead of things. It is this elision between the order of names and the order of things against which Flourens stood firm, placing himself in a Cartesian dualist position, in which the mind, by definition, could have no extension, and thus forestalling any possibility of localization or atomization of function.

25. It is probable that Freud was thinking of the sort of argument employed by Jackson, i.e. a version of psychophysical parallelism, to which Freud had subscribed in the early '90s, whereby the neurologist should be absolutely clear about keeping separate his 'languages' of nerves and his 'languages' of ideas. By 1912, when he made this remark, and, more explicitly, when he wrote 'The Unconscious' (1915e), he had come to see that the doctrine of psychophysical parallelism 'plunges us into insoluble difficulties' (SE XIV 168), and that it was necessary to abandon such a doctrine in order to preserve the fundamental principle of the continuity of psychic processes. Such a decision was equivalent to taking up an uncompromisingly dualistic position.

26. The term 'apparatus' is misleading. Its character is specified by the microscope-optical model in *The Interpretation of Dreams* (see page 21) and by the poem-alphabet model in *On Aphasia* that we have quoted in the text. No mechanical or material substrate is necessary for the constitution of the system, although, of course, it has one.

27. Freud (1893h) SE III 37. The phrase in German reads, ' . . . *die assoziative Verarbeitung, die Erledigung durch kontrastierende Vorstellungen*'.

28. The German phrase is '*wenn man ihn dann nötigt, diesem Affekte Worte zu leihen . . .* ' – that is, literally, 'if one then compels him to lend words to this affect . . .'. Freud used a similar word, *verleihen*, to describe how the indications of discharge from speech put thought-processes on a level with

perceptual processes: 'they lend them reality and make it possible to remember them.' (See Chapter 2, p. 44)

29. Of course, not all symptoms will express the words that have been lost quite as directly as the patient whose trigeminal neuralgia replaced the 'slap in the face' that she felt she had received (see Chapter 3, p. 67). For example, the Ratman's delighted horror over the rat-torture enabled him to defend himself against the unconscious thoughts to which the word *Ratten* was a verbal bridge: *Raten* (debt, instalment), *Spielratte* (gambler), *Hieraten* (to marry). See Freud (1909d) SE X 213ff. A number of translations may be necessary before one arrives at the lost words. Even when the words are 'staring' one in the face, one may have to pass via a long archaeological investigation to find them, as was the case for Norbert Hanold, for whom the translation of '*Gradiva*' into its synonym '*Bertgang*' might have saved him digging in the stones of Pompeii.

30. It was along these lines that Ferenczi developed a theory of hysterical symptom-formation in correlation with the stages in the development of a sense of reality. See Ferenczi (1919) and our comments on this paper in notes 6 and 7 of Chapter 3.

31. Why this experience was necessarily sexual is a question which lies beyond the scope of the present discussion; suffice it to be said that this question engaged Freud in a discussion of temporal causality, from which emerged the concept of delayed action (*Nachträglichkeit*). See Chapter 2.

32. The sentences that follow the passage quoted in my text are also instructive:

> It is clearly impossible to say anything about this – that is, about the state which the pathogenic material was in before the analysis – until we have arrived at a thorough clarification of our basic psychological views, especially on the nature of consciousness. It remains, I think, a fact deserving serious consideration that in our analyses we can follow a train of thought from the conscious into the unconscious (i.e. into something that is absolutely not recognized as a memory), that we can trace it from there for some distance through consciousness once more and that we can see it terminate in the unconscious again, without this alternation of 'psychial illumination' making any change in the train of thought itself, in its logical consistency and in the interconnection between its various parts. Once this train of thought was before me as a whole I should not be able to guess which part of it was recognized by the patient as a memory and which was not. I only, as it were, see the peaks of the train of thought dipping down in the unconscious – the reverse of what has been asserted of our normal psychical processes.

We wish to make two points:

(i) it was often when Freud came to a problem belonging to the theory of consciousness that he broke off his discussion. The most notable example of this was the missing chapter(s) of the proposed book on metapsychology (see Editor's Introduction to the Papers on Metapsychology, SE XIV 105–7).

(ii) The idea that an unconscious train of thought cannot be distinguished from a conscious train of thought by its 'logical consistency' or by the 'interconnection between its various parts' would appear to be in flat contradiction with some of Freud's later ideas as to the distinctive character of thought processes under the sway of the primary process. But we should bear in mind that this contradiction, or perhaps tension, existed throughout his writings, it being possible to find passages similar in implication to the one just quoted throughout Freud's writings, especially in those texts where the assignation of meaning to the superficially meaningless is at issue, e.g. Freud (1900a) SE IV 96, or where Freud was concerned to emphasize both the ultimate inaccessibility of the unconscious and the possibility of finding suitable translations for products derived from it, e.g. (1940a) SE XXIII 197, quoted on page 5 above.

33. The discussion of the 'reality' of the primal scene in the Wolfman's case-history is obviously of relevance here. See Freud (1918b) SE XVII 49–60, 57–9, 95–7. As is clear from the discussion there, the *existence* of the 'primal' event is intimately bound up with the question of its efficacy as 'cause'. And, to clarify this latter question, Freud had another set of concepts already elaborated, the most interesting of which is, perhaps, the concept of deferred action: What only had a possibility of existing 'at the time' is effectively brought into existence at a later date, and the effect of its existence is such that it is as if it had existed at the earlier time: 'what emerges from the unconscious is to be understood in the light not of what goes before but of what comes after.' (Freud (1909b) SE X 66.)

34. Cf. Freud (1963a), January 10, 1910, p. 31: 'All repressions are of *memories*, not of experiences; at most the latter are repressed in retrospect.'

35. Freud (1919e) SE XVII 188: ' . . . *und solcher Inhalt eher in Wortvorstellungen erfasst werden kann als das Dunkle, das mit dem Genitalen zusammenhängt.*'

36. Note the relation between the concept of hallucination and that of the seduction scene that Ricoeur (1970), pp. 95–6, points out:

> It is not difficult to recognize in the background of this quasi-hallucinatory theory of dreams, just as in the *Project* of 1895, the belief in the reality of the childhood scenes of seduction. The perceptual traces corresponding to that scene are eager for revival and exercise an attraction on the repressed thoughts, themselves struggling to find expression. . . . According to the pattern of the infantile scene, which Freud regards as a model, the residual core of dreams would consist in a complete hallucinatory cathexis of the perceptual systems. What we have described, in our analysis of the dream-work, as 'regard for representability' might be brought into connection with the *selective attraction* exercised by the visually recollected scenes touched upon by the dream-thoughts. (SE V 548).

These texts clearly show that Freud regarded the predominance of pictorial representation in the dream-work as the hallucinatory revival of a primitive scene that had actually been perceived. See also Ricoeur, (1970), pp. 106–7, esp. note 42 on p. 107. He concludes that the seduction theory 'prevents the topography of *The Interpretation of Dreams* from completely freeing itself from natural spatiality and from drawing all the consequences implied in the idea of a "psychical locality".' (p. 107).

37. Ricoeur built much of his account of Freud's work around these two notions of 'quantity' and 'meaning'. Cf. the attack on Ricoeur by Lacan (1973), and by Tort (1966); the latter sees the denial of the quantitative dimension by Ricoeur in favour of the hermeneutic tendency as reinstating the motive-cause opposition, which, he argues, has been relegated by historical studies to the 'museum of ideology', where psychoanalysis should leave it. Despite Tort's fervent rhetoric, the question of the relation of psychoanalysis to the hermeneutic tradition, highlighted by Ricoeur, remains of great significance, as Foucault implies in the last two chapters of *The Order of Things*. Some of our discussion in Chapter 5 will bear on this issue.

38. It is remarkable how few of the many accounts that Freud gave of the development of psychoanalysis included any substantial discussion of the *difference* between the cathartic cure and the psychoanalytic method. Most of these accounts were content to state that it was with the abandonment of hypnotism and its replacement by the method of free association that the move to psychoanalysis proper took place (e.g. (1923a) SE XVIII 237–8; (1924f) SE XIX 195–8). The implications of this methodological shift – that the emphasis had shifted from the expression of 'strangulated effect' to the observation of thought-processes ('skimming off the surface of consciousness') – was not made explicit until 1925, in (1925d) SE XX 30: 'The theory of repression became the corner-stone of our understanding of the neuroses. A different view had now to be taken of the task of therapy. Its aim was no longer to 'abreact' an affect which had got on to the wrong lines but to uncover repressions and replace them by acts of judgement which might result either in the accepting or in the condemning of what had formerly been repudiated. I showed my recognition of the new situation by no longer calling my method of investigation and treatment *catharsis* but *psychoanalysis*.' We may hazard that it was the debate with Rank (and to a lesser extent with Ferenczi, over his use of 'active' methods) that prompted a sharpening of the distinction between the cathartic method and psycho-analysis. The sharpest criticism of the cathartic method that Freud wrote is to be found in (1926d) SE XX 151, where, it should be noted, he did not seem clear whether the argument against the notion of abreaction was of a conceptual or an empirical order:

> Rank's formula – that those people become neurotic in whom the trauma of birth was so strong that they have never been able completely to abreact it – is highly disputable from a theoretical point of view. We do not rightly know what is meant by abreacting the trauma. Taken literally, it implies that the more frequently and the more intensely a neurotic person reproduces the affect of anxiety the more closely will he approach to mental health – an untenable conclusion. It was because it did not tally with the facts that I gave up the theory of abreaction which had played such a large part in the cathartic method.

39. Of course, this is entirely separate from the question whether or not Freud
    had a distinctively aural bias: all the evidence would seem to indicate that he
    did. (Although Granoff (1975) and Leclaire (1967), in their discussions of
    the notion '*überdeutlich*', try to show how this aural bias overlaid a strong
    visuality that left traces in the form of Freud's 'key-signifiers'.) But to try
    and explain the specific character of a scientific theory from the personal
    idiosyncrasy of one man would seem both to be a methodologically
    implausible hypothesis and to weigh down the already straining 'body' of
    historical causes with yet another organ that has changed the 'face' of
    history: alongside Cleopatra's nose we would have to place Freud's ear.
40. Not only did the theory of the 'speech residues' found in the *Project* remain
    essentially unchanged throughout the period from 1895 to the last works of
    1938, as we shall see in the following chapter, but the 'project for a scientific
    psychology' that was Freud's life work retained a consistent structure of
    argument from 1895 on. The clearest and most remarkable demonstration
    of this fact, which will often licence us drawing upon a variety of texts
    written at different times, as if they were the work of one writing subject, is
    the identity of structure of the *Project* and Freud's last and finest expository
    work, *An Outline of Psychoanalysis*. Let us compare these:

Project	*Outline*
I General Scheme	I The Mind and its Working
II Psychopathology (Hysteria, Affect)	II The Practical Task
III Normal Processes	III The Theoretical Yield

The parallel is even more striking if we compare the contents of Section I in
the two works:

Project		*Outline*
1.–3.	General theorems concerning the activity of neurones	1. The psychical apparatus
4.–5.	The biological standpoint and the problem of quantity	2. The theory of the instincts
6.	Pain	3. The development of the sexual function
7.–18.	Quality, consciousness, ego, thought.	4. Psychical qualities
19–21.	Dream analysis and dream consciousness	5. Dream-interpretation as an illustration

The one major difference between these two accounts is the complete absence
of the topic of sexuality from Section 1 of the *Project* (although the
importance of sexuality for the aetiology of the neuroses was discussed in
Section II Psychopathology). What we find instead of sexuality is '*pain*'. We
are entitled to make the following two comments. Firstly, we have found yet
another support for Freud's conviction that it was the introduction of a *theory*
of sexuality into the model of the psyche elaborated in the period 1895–1900
that gave psychoanalysis its distinctive cast. Secondly, this homologous
relation of sexuality and pain might give us pause for thought as to the general
psychoanalytical conception of the erotic, despite the ever increasing
insistence with which Freud, as he grew older, pleaded the cause of Eros.

CHAPTER 2

1. In the account of the *Project* I will not give detailed references to the text, except where my reading depends upon specific passages, or where I quote directly. On the *Project*, the following works are of value: Amacher (1965, 1972), Andersson (1962), Hettleman (1974), Pribram (1962), Pribram (1969), Pribram and Gill (1976), Safouan (1968), Solomon (1974), Wollheim (1971).

2. The term 'cathexis', coined by Strachey, vexed Freud as much as it has vexed some of his commentators and later psychoanalytic theoreticians. The German words, '*besetzt*', '*besetzung*', do not have the technical flavour that the Greek-based 'cathexis' has, and do not unduly encourage the overly mechanistic readings that cathexis has seemed to. It is much too late to suggest an alternative translation, even if one were to find one that was satisfactory. The natural translation, 'occupied', 'occupation', although having some interesting connotations and potential allusive qualities, such as in 'pre-occupation', is perhaps less flexible than 'cathexis'.

As to the much debated question of the ontological status of 'Q', a reading of Strachey's note following the *Project*, SE I 392–7, establishes its claim as the main precursor of the 'economic mode' of psychoanalytic metapsychology. As to its reference, as to its relation to the various realities depicted by anatomy, physiology, neurology, etc., there is a vast literature on this topic, much of it marked by fundamental confusion. Here, I wish only to note that I see no difficulty in dissociating Q entirely from any anatomical references, nor any difficulty in refusing to equate it with a neurophysiological concept whose empirical correlate must be a certain quantitative characteristic of nerve-cells. I believe that Solomon is quite right when he distinguishes between neuroanatomy and neurophysiology, wrong when he claims that 'the essence of Freud's theory . . . is not dualistic' (Solomon, 1974, p. 26) and on extremely weak ground when he writes that ' "Q" is essentially a borrowed notion, and to divorce the Freudian notion of "Q", and, later, "psychic energy", from its physicalistic origins is to rob the concept of its substantial meaning. . . . if the model of the "psychic apparatus" is divorced from the neurophysiological model, the central notion of "energy" becomes little more than a metaphor.' (Ibid. p. 32). Apart from the curious fetishism of 'substance' seen in this passage, found in many of the discussions of the material base of theories of the psyche, and brilliantly analysed by Bachelard in *The Philosophy of No*, we have only to remind ourselves that Freud's last 'appendix' to the *Project* concerned a device that had as much materiality as a brain, provided as rigorous a model as could be wished for, and yet could under no conceivable circumstances provide occasion for identifying Q with any other sort of energy than the 'psychic'. I am thinking of the Mystic Writing Pad. This is also obviously not the occasion on which to preoccupy ourselves with the variety of philosophical reasoning that uses the word 'metaphor' as a means for the assignation of conceptual vacuity.

3. We are tempted to equate this mechanism of muscular innervation with that of hysterical conversion, as Freud was to do in discussions with Ferenczi during World War I, when he equated this pathway of internal change with

Lamarck's notion of 'Necessity'. Freud wished 'to show that the "necessity" that according to Lamarck creates and transforms organs is nothing but the power of unconscious ideas over one's own body, of which we see remnants in hysteria, in short the "omnipotence of thoughts". This would actually supply a psychoanalytic explanation of adaptation (or fitness (*Zweckmässigkeit*)); it would put the coping stone on psychoanalysis. There would be two linked principles of progressive change, adaptation of one's own body and subsequent transformation of the external world (autoplasticity and heteroplasticity), etc.' (Freud (1965a), pp. 261–2. See also Jones, vol. III, pp. 334–5.) Cf. Ferenczi (1913), pp. 223–226, for the relation between hysterical conversion and the omnipotence of thoughts. Cf. Freud (1916–17), SE XVI 366; (1910c), SE XI 125; (1912–13), SE XIII 93; (1924c), SE XIX 168 and n. 4.

4. It is worth noting that the German term '*Zeichen*' is translated uniformly throughout the *Project* as 'indications', hence concealing to a small extent the general 'semiological' context of Freud's discussion of quality.

5. Freud himself recognized the paradoxical nature of his argument later in the *Project*, without providing a satisfactory solution of the problem (SE I 378–9).

6. In this sense, to call the speech-associations 'exclusive', as Freud did, is not quite correct. They can be excluded from the rest of one's perceptual input owing to their limited and closed character. But, often as not, Freud appeared to assume that the speech-associations were exclusive in a more primary sense, thus allowing him to accent the privileged character of aural perception. Such a privileged position of the speech residues is displayed in many of his works, amongst them a passage from Freud (1923b) SE XIX 21.

7. We could profitably relate this idea of the impartiality of speech to its function in analysis, where it is placed in opposition to action. See Chapter 4.

8. The ambiguous character of Freud's position with respect to wordless thought is clear in the following passage, in which he discussed '*reproductive thought*' (ibid., SE I 379–80):

> [Reproductive thought] follows back a given thought-process in a reversed direction, as far back, perhaps, as a perception – once again, in contrast to practical thought, without an aim – and, in doing so, makes use to a large extent of indications of quality. In thus following a backward direction, the process comes upon intermediate links which have hitherto been unconscious, which have left no indications of quality behind them but whose indications of quality appear subsequently. This implies that the passage of thought in itself, without any indications of quality, has left traces behind it. In some instances, indeed, it looks here as though we should only be able to guess certain stretches of the pathway because their starting- and end-points are given by indications of quality.

We may undoubtedly relate this train of thought to that discussed above in Chapter 1, especially in the long note 32, in which Freud had left in abeyance the question of whether the thoughts constructed by the analyst had ever actually existed. But it is clear that the phenomena to which Freud was referring in the passage we have just quoted do not validate the notion that thought unaccompanied by indications of quality must leave some sort of trace. Rather than being a proof of the existence of the traces, one might regard these gaps in the indications of quality as being 'true' gaps in thought. One will necessarily have to fill these in 'subsequently', but having filled them in satisfactorily would not license the conclusion that equivalent traces must have been left before the filling in. Now, it is clear that it is precisely these gaps which are of therapeutic interest, and which are also the metonyms of the unconscious. Where there are gaps in the indications of quality, the question of the unconscious comes to the fore. But these gaps might not tell us anything about the 'original' traces which filled these gaps without our knowing it.

9. One of the assumptions Freud *thought* he could discard was the one discussed above in connection with the problem of remembering thought. 'A discharge from ω which I had to assume in my other account now becomes unnecessary.' (Ibid.)

10. It was because Ferenczi attempted to solve the problem Freud's own early work had posed that Freud took such a great interest in his work on the 'Intellectual Stages', a greater interest than any other analyst has shown, so far as I am aware. The collaboration on the 'Lamarckian hypothesis' we noted above (note 3) was an attempt to work out some of the hypotheses set forth in Ferenczi's 'Stages' paper. Ferenczi eventually shifted the focus from the level of the sense of reality to a more organic developmental sequence in *Thalassa: A Theory of Genitality* (1924). Indeed, the sequence he established in that book was a far more biologically oriented approach than Freud would ever countenance, Freud finally remaining, with his theory of instincts, on the borderline between biology and psychology. Cf. the idea Freud mooted in 1910 in a letter to Ferenczi (Jones, vol. II, 499) attempting to relate the mechanism of the *return* of the repressed (and not that of repression itself) to the development of the ego, whereas the mechanism of repression depends on the phase of the libido.

11. Note the following passage from Freud (1939a) SE XXIII 74:

    All these traumas occur in early childhood up to about the fifth year. Impressions from the time at which a child is beginning to talk stand out as being of particular interest; the periods between the ages of two and four seem to be the most important; it cannot be determined with certainty how long after birth this period of receptivity begins.

12. '. . . *ein Sinnesorgan für die Auffassung psychischer Quälitaten* . . .'. At SE V 615, Freud changed this formula slightly: '. . . *eines Sinnesorgans zur Wahrnehmung psychischer Quälitaten.*'

13. '. . . *dass es das Überwiegen der Wortbeziehung über die Sachbeziehung ist.*'

14. As Jones notes (Jones, vol. II, 365): 'this appears to be another one of Freud's ideas that he forgot and then recaptured more than once.' Also (Jones II 200):

    Freud had adumbrated this interesting theory before and he always adhered to it. Ferenczi asked him how it could be applied to congenital deaf-mutes who have no conception of words. His reply was that we must widen the connotation of 'words' in this context to include any gestures of communication.

15. This statement is not strictly accurate, since the patient also has feelings in his or her consciousness. But, by a strange conceptual inversion, psychoanalysis, which seemed to be so much about the life of the feelings, read out of its therapeutic work the importance of feelings. The period of theoretical speculation that resulted in the metapsychological works written in the Great War and in the culminating paper, 'The Unconscious', which expressed more clearly than anywhere else the dominance of verbal consciousness from the standpoint of psychoanalysis, had been instigated with a paper that Freud started in October 1910, entitled 'In what sense may one speak of unconscious feelings?' (see *The Freud/Jung letters* 218F, p. 368 and n11). This paper eventually became section III of 'The Unconscious' ((1915e) SE XIV 177–9). There, Freud made it clear that it was not strictly admissible to speak of unconscious feelings; 'the possibility of the attribute of unconsciousness would be completely excluded as far as emotions, feelings and affects are concerned.' On the side of consciousness, also, the psychoanalyst always deals in verbal reports of states of consciousness, or, to remain truer to the Freudian dialect, the patient reads off the surface of his consciousness. Thus, as far as the analyst is concerned, he is concerned with the words spoken and the words that have come to consciousness.

16. When Freud did intimate that linkage with verbal residues was not a sufficient, or a necessary, condition for becoming conscious, he could not bring himself to reveal an alternative path towards a deeper understanding of the process. For example, in 'The Unconscious' (1915e) SE XIV 203:

As we can see, being linked with word-presentations is not yet the same thing as becoming conscious, but only makes it possible to become so; it is therefore characteristic of the system *Pcs.* and of that system alone. With these discussions, however, we have evidently departed from our subject proper and find ourselves plunged into problems concerning the preconscious and the conscious, which for good reasons we are reserving for separate treatment.

As I have already mentioned, this separate treatment was never to appear.

17. In *Moses and Monotheism* (1939a) SE XXIII 112–3, Freud wrote:

Among the precepts of the Moses religion there is one that is of greater importance than appears to begin with. This is the prohibition against making an image of God – the compulsion to worship a God whom one cannot see. . . . – an expression of the pride of mankind in the development of speech, which resulted in such an extraordinary advancement of intellectual activities. The new realm of intellectuality was opened up, in which ideas, memories and inferences became decisive in contrast to the lower psychical activity which had direct perceptions by the sense-organs as its content. This was unquestionably one of the most important stages on the path of hominization.

Again, in another passage, this time from (1909d) SE X 233 n1: 'As Lichtenberg says, "An astronomer knows whether the moon is inhabited or not with about as much certainty as he knows who was his father, but not with so much certainty as he knows who was his mother". A great advance was made in civilization when men decided to put their inferences upon a level with the testimony of their senses and to make the step from matriarchy to patriarchy.'

18. And even the acquisition of, or perhaps acquiescence under, belief is bound up with the speech function, since, as outlined in the *Project*, judgement is dependent upon the unity conferred upon an object and its variable attributes by the verbal images, such an object – an alien, incomprehensible 'thing', as Freud described it – being first characterized by the scream. In (1930a) SE XXI 67, Freud argued that the scream characterizes the first object in its absence, thus marking off what is phenomenologically discontinuous, temporary and unpredictable – and therefore 'outside' – as continuous and permanent on the level of thought-reality.

19. A phrase that occurred often in Schreber's *Memoirs*, which both Freud and Jung used in their correspondence to remind each other that thinking, even thinking psychoanalytically, is never enough.

20. The allusion is to a noteworthy account of the inalienable character of the fundamental rule, found in Freud (1909d) SE X 166:

> Here the patient broke off, got up from the sofa, and begged me to spare him the recital of the details. I assured him that I myself had no taste whatever for cruelty, and certainly had no desire to torment him, but that naturally I could not grant him something which was beyond my power. He might just as well ask me to give him the moon. (*Ebensogut könne er mich bitten, ihm zwei Kometen zu schrenken.*)

The passage is noteworthy not only for the clarity with which Freud revealed to his patient that the fundamental rule is not a subject for legislation, but also as an indication of how the analyst, as the representative of this law, can very easily encourage the formation of an identification of the analyst with the tormentors, the torturers, so commonly found, in obsessional neurosis, as delegates of the father. When the analyst assured the patient that he had no taste for cruelty, that he had no desire to torment him, he encouraged both the conversion of this disclaimer into a phantasy of its opposite, and the identification of all torture or cruelty with the inflexibility of the fundamental rule, that is, in the final analysis, with the inflexibility of symbolic reality, or, broadly speaking, with language. We might venture the hypothesis that those analysts who identify the 'Law' with the laws of language have managed to purify the transference to a point where the Master is identified with the legislator of language; the question of the dissolution of such a transference remains in abeyance.

CHAPTER 3

1. A number of authors have noted this feature of the additions to the dream-

book, of whom Wilden (1968, 1973) has drawn most attention to the fundamental change in the conception of symbolism that this involved.

2. On the short story style of 'Katherina' see Schönau (1968) and Rohner (1966).

3. Leclaire (1966) also emphasized the *instantaneous* appearance of the feeling of certainty, and the accompanying feeling of liberation that Freud (and James, 1890, vol. I, pp. 679ff; Rosenzweig (1968)) described when analysis restores to consciousness a name that has been forgotten. See Freud (1901b) Chapter I.

4. For an account of the concept of symbolism as it has been understood in various schools of analysis, see the article on *Symbolism* in Laplanche and Pontalis (1973). It is worthwhile noting that certain works on the psychoanalytic concept of the symbol do not bear on what either Laplanche and Pontalis or I mean by 'symbol', but cover a much broader field, which would more profitably be called that of the sign. See, for instance, Axelrod (1977) and Mitchell (1973). Such uses of the term symbol have affinities with the discussion in Ricoeur (1970). But the *psychoanalytic* concept of the symbol would seem to correspond more nearly with Pierce's concept of the 'icon'. See Pierce (1897, 1932) and Dewey (1946).

5. Laplanche and Pontalis (1973, p. 443) wish to draw out a further distinction: moral literal, in addition to figurative/literal.

We should also note that Breuer's emphasis on *sound* association was not taken up by Freud in the *Studies* to the extent that he was to emphasize it in, for example, *The Interpretation of Dreams*.

6. Ferenczi summed up the theory of hysteria as follows ((1919) pp. 102–3): '. . . every hysterical symptom, considered from whatever aspect, is always to be recognized as a heterotype genital function. The ancients were, therefore, right when they said of hysteria: Uterus loquitur!'

7. The most detailed account of this theory is to be found in Ferenczi (1924), but a less speculative version was expressed in Ferenczi (1919). Cf. also Ferenczi, 1926, p. 48:

Passing or 'transitory' symptoms which I have observed in my patients during their analyses have sometimes revealed a sudden displacement of genital sensations of sexual excitations to the whole surface of the body. . . . In a whole series of cases of repressed male homosexuality I found that in moments of sexual excitement the whole surface of the skin became burning hot. It is not unlikely that the German slang expression used of homosexuals 'hot brothers' has its origin in this symptom.

Another argument of note, this time from Ferenczi (1924), p. 22, occurs during Ferenczi's discussion of the hypothesis that the cannibalistic phantasies of babies are derived from attempts to return to the womb:

The sole argument – at all events the argument of moment to the psychoanalyst which emboldens us to offer this daring hypothesis is the uniformity and unmistakeableness with which the symbolic identity of penis and tooth recurs, both in dreams and in neurotic symptoms. According to our conception the tooth is therefore really a primal penis

(*Urpenis*), whose libidinal role, however, the child who has been weaned must learn to renounce.

Obviously this notion of the *Urpenis* touches, as we have been keen to point out, on the theory of symbolism. Ferenczi continued:

> It is not that the tooth is therefore the symbol of the penis but rather, to speak paradoxically, that the later maturing penis is the symbol of the more primitive boring implement, the tooth. The paradoxical character of this supposition is perhaps moderated, however, by the consideration that every symbolic association is preceded by a stage in which two things are treated as one and so can represent each other.

Clearly this latter consideration does not *resolve* the 'paradox'; but we may well ask: what *is* the paradox?

8. Cf. Freud (1901a) SE V 659:

> The dream-thoughts which we first come across as we proceed with our analysis often strike us by the unusual form in which they are expressed; they are not clothed in the prosaic language usually employed by our thought, but are on the contrary represented symbolically by means of similes and metaphors, in images resembling those of poetic speech. There is no difficulty in accounting for the constraint imposed upon the form in which the dream-thoughts are expressed. . . . If we imagine ourselves faced by the problem of representing the arguments in a political leading article or the speeches of counsel before a court of law in a series of pictures, we shall easily understand the modifications which must necessarily be carried out by the dream-work owing to *considerations of representability in the content of the dream.*

The reference to the three traditional forms of discourse upon which the art of rhetoric is founded – poetry, demagogy and the law – indicates clearly what sort of language we must expect to hear on the royal road to the unconscious. Cf. Mahony (1974) who would relate Freud's therapy of rhetoric with a pre-Aristotelian conception of the curative word, a mixture of *epôdê* and *thelktêrion*; alternatively, one could view Freud's conception as grafting the *Rhetoric* on to the *Poetics*.

9. Ferenczi, the first psychoanalyst to 'test' the more general validity for another language of interpretations originally derived from German linguistic usage, was extremely wary in his early writings of giving symbolic interpretations not based upon verbal plays. For example, in Ferenczi (1908), p. 19 n7, he wrote:

> A synonym of cohabitation that is commonly used in vulgar Hungarian ('to shoot') is probably the reason why in dreams of impotent patients under my treatment situations so often recur in which the chief part is played by the (mostly clumsy) use of weapons (e.g. rusting of the rifle, missing the target, missing fire in shooting, etc.)

Ferenczi did not think to base his argument upon the 'similarity', seemingly so obvious to the 'post-Freudian' eye, of shape of a gun and a penis.

10. The clearest and sharpest statement of this position was added in 1925 as a footnote to (1900a) SE V 506:

> But now that analysts at least have become reconciled to replacing the manifest dream by the meaning revealed by its interpretation, many of them have become guilty of falling into another confusion which they cling to with equal obstinacy. They seek to find the essence of dreams in their latent content and in so doing they overlook the distinction between the latent dream-thoughts and the dream-work. At bottom, dreams are nothing other than a particular *form* of thinking, made possible by the conditions of the state of sleep. It is the *dream-work* which creates that form, and it alone is the essence of dreaming – the explanation of its peculiar nature.

11. Although the debate in the Society over the meaning of examination dreams, and the footnotes that Freud added and deleted in his discussion of these dreams in *The Interpretation of Dreams*, indicate that Stekel was as likely as Freud to use linguistic usage. See (1900a) SE IV 274; Minutes III pp. 76ff, and p. 81, and the sentence that Freud added to *The Interpretation of Dreams* in 1911, only to remove it in 1914: 'Stekel, basing himself on a very common idiomatic usage, has suggested that the "little one" is a symbol of the male or female genitals.' (SE V 363). What Freud would certainly not have found in Stekel's work, though, was a concern with the esoteric history of language upon which Jung was embarking, and of which Freud gave evidence in his paper on Abel's 'The antithetical meaning of primal words'. Finding common ground with Stekel in the sphere of linguistic usage was no longer a sufficient guarantee of the wellfoundedness of a symbol.

12. Freud had given a similar interpretation of the play in a letter to Fliess, Freud *Origins* (190a) SE I 265–6, dated 15 October 1897.

13. Freud sent an offprint of the paper on sexual theories to Jung in December 1908, mentioning his obsession with the 'nuclear complex' of little Hans (Herbert) (*The Freud/Jung Letters*, 118F, p. 186). 'Family Romances' (1909c) was written as a part of Rank's book *Der Mythus von der Geburt des Helden*, whose preface bore the date December 1908 (see editorial note, SE IX 236).

14. This theme of concealment of the truth is the heir to the dissolution of the seduction hypothesis; as so often, Ferenczi's work clarifies this relation: see Ferenczi (1927b, 1933)

15. It is interesting to compare this attempt to escape from the 'dreary' maternal aetiology with Jung's later typology of the manifestations of the mother archetype, the plurality of *types* doing the work of the variety of mother–father–child *relations* in generating diversity; see Jung 1938/1954.

16. The theme of the rescue had a personal importance for Freud, as we see from his account of the incident of Monsieur Joyeuse in Freud (1901b) SE VI 148–9. See Raboul (1959) and the exchange in the *Freud–Abraham Correspondence*, in which Abraham, involved in a detailed philological

enquiry into the text of Oedipus Rex, questioned Freud as to the detailed meaning of the rescue fantasy, since he read the meeting of Laius and Oedipus at the 'crossroads' as a homologue of such a phantasy (Freud, 1965a, pp. 324–6).

17. The account given here might lend support to a particular theory of 'impulse' or 'desire', one which denies that desire is prior to its own prohibition, one which would inscribe the desire for the mother in a schema 'already laid down', whereby such a desire already evokes its own repudiation by a 'third term' (the father). On this particular theory of desire, see Lacan (1956–57); Deleuze and Guattari (1975) esp. pp. 60ff; Foucault (1976) pp. 50–67; and Forrester (1980). Deleuze and Guattari make certain claims about the history of the Oedipus complex that have a close affinity with those I am making here.

18. Following Freud, we will leave enigmatic the 'something else besides'.

19. My argument in this section puts into question the assertion of Laplanche and Pontalis (1973) p. 283, that 'the history of these researches [into the Oedipus complex] is in reality coextensive with that of psychoanalysis itself', their implication being that the Oedipus complex was, in a sense, 'there', 'from the beginning'. I have tried to show that Freud did *not* discover the Oedipus complex *as such* during his self-analysis, as is maintained by Strachey, Jones, Laplanche and Pontalis and many others. Rather, he discovered Oedipal impulses. If we mean by the Oedipus complex the nucleus or core of a neurosis, then it seems clear that Freud did not establish this until the period 1908–10. Deleuze and Guattari (1975, pp. 60–6) have some illuminating comments to make on the development and the function of the Oedipus complex in the early years of psychoanalysis.

20. The first full-scale argument concerning the Oedipus complex is to be found in *Totem and Taboo* (1912–13). Volume XII of the *Standard Edition* (1911–13) is completely lacking in any reference to the Oedipus complex or the nuclear neurosis, and it includes the paper on 'The Disposition to Obsessional Neurosis' (1913i), where one might have expected some discussion of the topic.

21. E.g. Ibid., 199F, p. 332. It is subtle indications of this sort that warrant the conclusion already stated in Chapter II: Jung was acting as the stimulus for reviving themes and topics that Freud had dealt with in detail long before, in the *Project* and *The Interpretation of Dreams*, but which had been 'forgotten'. Freud was right when he claimed that he was not plagiarizing; but he certainly owed Jung something. For an alternative reading of passages such as this, emphasizing the sense in which their intellectual collaboration was an attempt to co-opt the other into each's own brand of psychosis, see Roustang (1976) Chapter III 'A chacun sa folie' pp. 72ff.

22. *Wandlungen und Symbole der Libido* was translated into English in 1915, under the title *The Psychology of the Unconscious*. The work in Jung's *Collected Works* that corresponds to it is vol. V, *Symbols of Transformation*, which is a heavily revised and de-Freudianized version of the original.

23. Even before Freud had turned his attention to symbolism and its relation to myth, his pupils had published on the subject: Abraham's *Traum und Mythus: eine Studie zur Völkerpsychologie* (1909) and Rank's *Der Mythus von der Geburt des Helden* (1908). Both these works drew heavily upon an

assumption that the dream symbols provided the key to mythological symbolism, deriving their dream symbols from the section on typical dreams in *The Interpretation of Dreams*, and from the symbols that, although not published as yet in psychoanalytical works, were gradually being accepted in psychoanalytical circles in this period. We approach here a rather peculiar paradox: Abraham in particular emphasized the shocking character of the Freudian dream-symbols ('. . . none of Freud's teachings, however much they diverge from current schools of thought, has been so violently attacked as that on the interpretation of symbols.' – Abraham (1909) p. 162). Yet none of these symbols had as yet been published under Freud's signature, and, as Abraham's work amply demonstrated and recognized – despite itself –, most of these symbols were not derived from psychoanalysis, but rather from the work of comparative mythologists, who had been happily making known the scandalous meaning of ancient myths for decades, without the wrath of shocked public opinion disturbing the peace of the universities. As Freud wrote to Stanley Hall on November 23, 1913 (Freud, 1960a, p. 310):

> That it is just the question of sexual symbolism to which you take exception does not worry me. You will surely have observed that psychoanalysis creates few new concepts in this field, rather it takes up long-established ideas, makes use of them, and supports them with a great deal of evidence.

For a fuller discussion of this episode, see Chapter 5, pp. 193–4.

24. His early criticisms of Jung's work (in 1911) centred around this methodological point. See *The Freud/Jung Letters* 288F, p. 473.

25. Jung never attempted to bring his toxin theory into line with the chemical hypotheses concerning the aetiology of the neuroses and the psychoses that Freud proposed in the *Three Essays on Sexuality*. Rather, for Jung, the hypothetical toxin determined an abnormality of brain function, rather than of sexual function.

26. See *Totem and Taboo* (1912–13) SE XIII 125, where Freud first examined and then rejected the various 'sociological, biological and psychological explanations (in which connection the psychological motives should be regarded as representing biological forces)' of the incest taboo, and then turned to Darwin's hypothesis of the primal horde as being more satisfying than any other. 'It is of a kind quite different from any that we have so far considered, and might be described as "historical"'.

27. Why an area of research, which had been one of the most active in the decade up to the war, suddenly lost its interest may find an answer in the issues raised in Chapter 5. Whatever the explanation, the turn away from history and language towards sociological modes in the 1920s and later is striking.

28. What could be more probable than that the figure of speech 'swallowing something' which we use in talking of an insult to which no rejoinder has been made, did in fact originate from the innervatory sensations which arise in the pharynx when we refrain from speaking and prevent ourselves from reacting to the insult? All these sensations and innervations belong

to the field of 'The Expression of the Emotions', which, as Darwin has taught us, consists of actions which originally had a meaning and served a purpose. These may now for the most part have become so much weakened that the expression of them in words seems to us only to be a figurative picture of them, whereas in all probability the description was once meant literally; and hysteria is right in restoring the original meaning of the words in depicting its unusually strong innervations. Indeed, it is perhaps wrong to say that hysteria creates these sensations by symbolization. It may be that it does not take linguistic usage as its model at all, but that both hysteria and linguistic usage alike draw their material from a common source. (Breuer and Freud (1895d) SE II 181).

29. Freud (1916–17) SE XVI 312.
30. Freud (1926d) SE XX 133–4.
31. Freud (1912–13) SE XIII 122–3.
32. Freud (1923b) SE XIX 35.
33. Bakan (1958) points out a certain ambivalence of Freud's towards the Hebrew language. In the Hebrew Preface to *Totem and Taboo* SE XIII xv, Freud proclaimed himself 'ignorant of the language of holy writ'. Bakan adduces internal evidence, such as the long Hebrew dedication in the Bible that Jakob Freud gave to his son in 1891 (Jones, vol., I 22–3), and the intimate friendship between Freud and the Hammerschlag family (Jones, vol. I, p. 179 states that Freud was taught Hebrew by Professor Hammerschlag at school), to indicate that Freud did have some knowledge of Hebrew. If Freud did know Hebrew the connection of the two separate determinations of the word 'geseres' is less 'strained'. If he didn't know Hebrew we are left with the form of argument he employed, indicating that unknown languages can provide links in the chain of associations.
34. Cf. (1940a) SE XXIII 166: 'Dreams make an unrestricted use of *linguistic symbols*, the meaning of which is for the most part unknown to the dreamer. Our experience, however, enables us to confirm their sense. They probably originate from earlier phases in the development of speech.' (My emphasis).
35. Leclaire (1968) argues quite cogently that this interpretation of Freud's concerning the piece of yellow clothing is a good example of the manner in which an analyst's 'key signifiers' impose themselves unconsciously: the piece of yellow dress worn by Gisella Fluss, for which the memory of the yellow flowers, analysed in (1899a) SE III 311–313, was a cover.
36. The one major source on the development of psychoanalytic theory that also locates the break between the Freudians and the Jungians in the debates around the concept of symbol is Dalbiez ((1941), vol., I pp. 105ff). Dalbiez characterizes the two different conceptions of the symbol as being the difference between 'dramatization' and 'symbolization'. Dramatization involves the movement from abstract to concrete, from concept to image, and is individually determined. Symbolization moves from one concrete element to another, from one perceptual image to another, and is universal, the same relations between image A and image B being found in all human beings. Dalbiez characterizes symbolization as Freud's concept and dramatization as Silberer's and Jung's. As my discussion will have shown, this is too simple a view and distorts their more complicated positions.

Certainly Jung believed that symbols were universal; indeed, for him, these symbols (archetypes) were the primary universals, the key point of disagreement picked up in Jones' paper discussed below. What Dalbiez is perhaps trying to capture is the idealist strain in Silberer's and Jung's interpretations, whereby an abstract concept 'leads' the visual symbol, thus allowing 'climbing up a staircase' to symbolize a prospective spiritual ascent rather than a wish for sexual intercourse. Again, the 'radical empiricism' with which Dalbiez characterizes the Freudians (Jones and Flournoy) is opposed to this idealism. But I would prefer to call the extreme Freudian position 'biologically reductionist', involving as it does a reduction of perceptual elements to biologically determined primary concerns, which are received onto the level of representation by means of a transparent projection of biologically determined 'units'. Jung's symbols certainly do not reduce in the same manner; rather, they stay on the level of representation, but receive hidden support from traditionally accepted human themes, such as 'Wisdom', 'innocence' and 'rebirth'. Dalbiez implies that 'penis' is somehow more concrete than 'wisdom', without articulating the additional argument that is necessary to make this so: the 'locking' of representation on to the body in some manner, whether this is done by invoking the universal affective significance of the penis, or by making a claim about the genesis of representation out of a primary, 'pre-representational' attention to the body. Both these arguments can be found in psychoanalysis. The development of Lacan's theory clearly demonstrates how the penis or the phallus can become as abstract as any Jungian might have wished.

37. Lacan (1959, E704) remarks that this is the crucial passage in Jones' refutation of Silberer, quibbling with Jones over the misinterpretation of the word 'ephemeral'. He then turns the refutation on its head in the following manner: "Toutes 'idées' dont le plus concret est le réseau du signifiant où il faut que le sujet soit déjà pris pour qu'il puisse s'y constituer: comme soi, comme à sa place dans une parenté, comme existant, comme représentant d'un sexe, voire comme mort, car ces idées ne peuvent passer pour primaires qu'à abandonner tout parallélisme au développement des besoins." Hence Jones' argument based on the biologically determined primary ideas is converted into an argument – and a very good one at that – against the equation of biological need with human desire.

38. Cf. Derrida (1967), pp. 409–10, quoted in Wilden (1968), p. 259:

It would be easy enough to show that the concept of structure and the word "structure" itself are as old as the episteme – that is to say, as old as western science and western philosophy. . . . Nevertheless, up until the "event" which I wish to define [that is, the change in the use of the concept of structure], the structure – or rather the structurality of the structure – . . . has always been neutralized or reduced, and this by a process of giving it a centre or referring it to a point of presence, a fixed origin. The function of this centre was not only to orient, balance, and organize the structure – but above all to make sure that the organizing principle of the structure would limit what we might call the *freeplay* of the structure. . . . The centre also closes off the freeplay it opens up and makes possible. *Qua* centre, it is the point at which the substitution of contents, elements, or terms is no longer possible.

CHAPTER 4

1. Nietzsche (1889), 'Reason' in Philosophy, section 5.
2. Freud (1966a), March 23 1923, p. 122.
3. Buttmann (1824), p. 103.
4. From the Anglo-American tradition, there are a number of articles that have employed a notion of propositional transformation similar to that which I will expound: Colby (1963, 1975), Boden (1974), Moser et al (1969), Suppes and Warren (1975). All of these tie the notion of transformation in with transforms performed by a computer programmed to employ the mechanisms of defence, usually as outlined by Anna Freud (1936), on a given input. For example, Suppes and Warren (1975), p. 405: '. . . propositions represent thoughts or impulses in the unconscious. . . . it becomes natural to define the defence mechanisms as transformations of propositions. By a transformation we mean a function that maps unconscious propositions into conscious propositions.' They also note: We use "actor–action–object" rather than Freud's 'subject–verb–object' . . . in order to emphasize the non-linguistic character of propositions. (Ibid. p. 407 nl). One might well ask the question: why did Freud employ the terms 'subject–verb–object', if it wasn't to emphasize the linguistic character of the propositions? That he did conceive of them in linguistic terms indicates, I would argue, that he wished to connect them directly to propositions uttered in analysis, a point I will refer to more than once in this chapter. On this point, Suppes and Warren are also clear: '. . . it is fair to say that what we have in mind is something that corresponds more to the production of conscious dispositions that endure across time, and not to the production of momentary propositions arising on a given occasion.' (Ibid., 408.)

  It is also appropriate to note that none of these authors takes account of the distinction between the subject of the enunciation and the subject of the statement, as did Freud in the Schreber case, when he noted that it is possible for the subject to deny a proposition as a whole, as well as denying individual parts within it ((1911c) SE XII 64–5). This oversight on the part of these later writers allows certain mechanisms of defence, which were regarded as fully distinguishable from one another by Freud and Anna Freud, to lose their distinctive character, e.g. Suppes and Warren find that 'reversal' and 'reaction formation' do not appear as distinct to the computer, thus indicating the fact that they do not distinguish transforms within a proposition from transforms acting on the proposition as a whole. Boden, on the other hand, treats the material to be transformed as linguistic, noting that the 'unfamiliarity' of computers with natural languages is one of the major difficulties they encounter in simulating the twists and turns of propositional transformation: '. . . it would hardly occur to anyone to remark that Freud's theoretical insights were crucially dependent on his background understanding of natural language; but computer programs employing oversimple models of language-use sometimes make "absurd" errors in psychological interpretation which are directly attributable to this linguistic crudity.' (243–4). As we shall see in this chapter, but especially in the discussion of the sentence derived from the analysis of Freud's dream '*Non Vixit*', it would seem worthwhile to try and integrate the formal aspect of the propositional transforms that the above-cited authors concentrate upon, which also is our concern, with that feature of the practice of psychoanalysis that so often seems to defy a discussion above the level of anecdotal: namely, the 'intuitive' manner in which interpretations and constructions are made in practice, the aptitude that Reik attributed to 'the third ear', which is in essence the searching for syntactical isomorphisms which, when writ large on the level of theory, approximate to the method of propositional transformation.

5. Cf. Freud (1905e) SE VII 40–41: '. . . it [the symptom] cannot occur more than once – and the capacity for repeating itself is one of the characteristics of a hysterical symptom – unless it has a psychical significance, a *meaning*. The hysterical symptom does not carry this meaning with it, but the meaning is lent to it, soldered to it, as it were, . . .'

6. Freud (1950a), SE I 352: '*Es ist also die* Symbolbildung *so fester Art jene Leistung, welche über die normale Abwehr hinausgeht.*' The translation in SE, 'symbol-formation of this stable kind', does not seem quite to capture the notion of 'fixity' to which Freud attributed so much importance.

7. The concern with synthesis, rife in early analytical circles, and reminiscent of the debates in Renaissance philosophy of science which Galileo brought to a close, could perhaps be replaced with a contrast between analysis and dialectics, rather than analysis and synthesis. In such a light, Freud was obviously both an analyst and a dialectician: one has only to think of the dialectical form of argument he employed so often, or the fact that many of his works were couched in the form of a debate with an opponent or a neutral 'third party', e.g. large sections of *The Interpretation of Dreams*, *The Question of Lay Analysis*, 'Screen Memories', the discussion of the primal scene in 'From the History of an Infantile Neurosis', *Introductory Lectures*, *Inhibitions, Symptoms and Anxiety* (dialogue with Rank), etc.

8. We might formulate the aim of psychoanalysis as follows: the end of analysis is a dialogue between analyst and analysand that is no longer interrupted either by symptomatic formations or by transference phenomena. That such an aim conflicts with the 'analytic attitude' of the analyst points up on the one hand the purely theoretical character of this goal, and, on the other hand, the difficulties that psychoanalytical theorists have always experienced in determining both practical and theoretical criteria for the end of analysis. Cf. Freud (1937c); Balint (1952) and the discussion of the latter in Lacan (1975a) esp. pp. 242ff, and the interesting comments in Leclaire (1971) pp. 26ff, on the practice which has arisen in certain analytical circles of introducing a second analyst simply in order to terminate the analysis.

9. Freud (1950a) SE I 234. The Editors of the Standard Edition note, on SE I 234 n2, that this idea is due to Breuer. (See Breuer and Freud (1895d) SE II 188–9 n, where he reflects that 'the mirror of a reflecting telescope cannot at the same time be a photographic plate.')

10. In 1925 Freud added a note to *The Interpretation of Dreams* (1900a) SE V 540 'I have since suggested that consciousness actually arises *instead of* the memory-trace. (. . . *das Bewusstsein enstehe geradezu* an Stelle *der Erinnerungsspur*.)'

11. Cf. also a comment made at the Vienna Society in 1909, *Minutes* II, p. 216: '. . . the distinction between conscious and unconscious cannot be applied to memory. Remembering something has nothing to do with consciousness.'

12. Cf. Freud (1911c) SE XII 71. The metaphor of 'silence' is a striking one in Freud's work, attaching particularly to Thanatos, in contrast to the 'noise' of Eros (cf. (1930a) SE XXI 119; (1940a) SE XXIII 165).

13. In the *Project*, Freud headed one of the sections of Part II Psychopathology 'The Hysterical *Proton Pseudos*' (the first lie of hysteria). What this lie amounted to was a 'peculiar kind of symbol-formation'. See note 6 above.

14. I use the term 'transitional object' in a sense similar to that introduced by Winnicott, though I have extended it to cover those symbolic objects which are the bridge to symbolic reality (that is, lies), which are necessary if stable symbolic reality is to be constructed, but which, in the course of a 'normal' development, are exchanged for other items. Cf. Winnicott (1953).

15. Hobbes (1839), vol. III, p. 23.

16. Obviously this paragraph relates closely to the more familiar psychoanalytical concept of 'acting out'. Of the early psychoanalysts, Ferenczi (1927a, p. 72) was the one who was most concerned with the problem of lying: "Human beings are a part of the environment [for the infant], differing greatly in importance from all other objects in the world, particularly in one significant respect: all other objects are equally equable, always constant. The only part of the environment which is not reliable is other persons, particularly the parents. . . . Even animals do not vary greatly, they do not lie against their natures; once known, they can be depended upon. The human being is the only animal which lies." Ferenczi's most detailed discussion of the relation of the lie to the progress of the cure is to be found in (1927b). In his very last papers, he revived the 'seduction theory' by combining the notion of a trauma with this deception practised on children by adults. Cf. also an early paper, Ferenczi (1909/39), pp. 170–1.

17. On the notion of 'iterability' and its relation to the mark and language, see Derrida (1971, 1977), Searle (1977).

18. By 'association technique' Freud meant the methods employed by Bleuler, Jung and the Zurich group, in which the patient was meant to give a one- or two-word answer to a standard list of 100 words, which the experimenter would read out to him one at a time. Cf. Freud's comments on a similar technique that a *patient* employed in the early 1890s, during the period of the pressure technique, in (1895d) SE II 276.

19. Cf. the same importance attached to the 'simplest expression', or 'original expression', in (1931b) SE XXI 237:

> It is difficult to give a detailed account of these [trends] because they are often obscure instinctual impulses which it was impossible for the child to grasp psychically at the time of their occurrence, which were therefore only interpreted by her later [*erst eine nachträgliche Interpretation fahren*

haben], and which then appear in the analysis in forms of expression [*Ausdrucksweisen*] that were certainly not the original ones.

20. Amongst whom one can include Stekel and Tausk (1914), who gave papers employing the method to the Vienna Psychoanalytical Society, and Abraham (1911, pp. 144–5), (1920, pp. 350, 358), who employed it in his series of papers on cyclothymia (manic-depressive psychosis).

21. The middle voice is introduced to take account of this stage between active and passive, corresponding to '*Wendung gegen die eigene Person*'. 'That it is not superfluous to assume the existence of stage (2) is to be seen from the behaviour of the sadistic instinct in obsessional neurosis. There is a turning round upon the subject's self *without* an attitude of passivity towards another person. . . . The active voice is changed, not into the passive, but into the reflexive, middle voice.' (Ibid. SE XIV 128).

22. The verbs that might characterize the sadistic side of the anal-sadistic phase include: 'master', 'destroy', 'dismember'. One of the themes that Lacan weaves into his theory of the mirror-stage is that of the dismemberment of the body, in dreams or in phantasy, as a derivative of the fundamental disunity of the body as experienced, its unity only being secured through an identification with the other seen in the mirror. Now this dyadic relation that gives rise to the unity of the ego also threatens to destroy it, so that 'aggressivity' arises on the foundation of this relation of unification and otherness, itself founded upon the 'body in pieces'. When we put this alongside of Lacan's use of the Hegelian dialectic of master and slave with which he characterizes a certain relation of ego and other found in obsessional neurosis, which involves the 'waiting-for-death' of that neurosis, the Freudian notion of 'mastery', gaining its status as a component-instinct from its *source* in the musculature, and often equated with the active mode of a verb, seems to disappear, being replaced by an aggressivity that arises out of the necessary structure of the relation between the ego and its object, retroactively bringing into being a phenomenology of the 'body in pieces' and tending towards the dialectic between thought as inner negation and death as outer negation. (Cf. Taylor (1975) pp. 148ff.) Such a reading will also displace the symbol from its function in 'mastering' unpleasure, in favour of the dialectic of presence and absence, or Eros and Thanatos, as in Lacan's many and varied disquisitions upon the '*fortida*' game of *Beyond the Pleasure Principle*. But such a reading will also be in concert with a *primary* aggressivity, found in the work of Klein, and plausibly founded upon the later Freudian notion of the death instinct. Using such a later version of the theory of sado-masochism, Laplanche built a reading of the 'grammar of fantasy' ((1970), p. 166) upon a non-sexual 'hetero-aggressivity', prior to the splitting off of the sadistic and masochistic components of a *sexual* component-instinct. Insofar as I am following the basic outline of 'Instincts and their Vicissitudes', in which Freud had not recognized as primary the profound problems of masochism, such issues will not be discussed in detail. Suffice it to be said that I see no difficulty in adapting the notion of a propositional structure to the later theoretical position, if we can find a means to make acceptable the notion of a conditional primal sentence.

23. We can only note in footnote the important consequences of this reformulation of the mechanism of projection. It puts in a secondary position a conception of projection as marking an 'expulsion' from an 'inside' to an 'outside', thus bringing into conflict the 'grammatical' mode of psychoanalysis with what we might call the 'topological' mode, employed in an informal manner by Klein and with an attempt at mathematical formalization in the more recent work of Lacan. The simple equation of 'projection' with 'expulsion' would amount to an elision of the distinction between the subject of an enunciation and the subject of a statement; it thus corresponds to a basic feature of Kleinian theory whereby the infant 'makes' the world through his own fantasmatic activity of projection and introjection. The subjectivism of the epistemological foundation of this theory leads to great difficulties in introducing 'others' into the world. The advantage of the grammatical mode is that 'others' are there from the start, insofar as one will allow that all propositions are subject to a more general version of the 'paranoid principle' we have outlined above. The general version will read as follows: the subject of an enunciation never coincides with the subject of a statement. This now general principle, which we might call the principle of the duplicity of the subject, highlights the similarity between the mechanism of projection (first person is excluded from being subject of the statement) and the necessary condition for a language (as opposed to a code) – hence the rather strange characterization by Lacan (1948, E111/17) of all knowledge as paranoid in character.

24. Freud later formulated more clearly his conviction that basic transformations of 'verbs' or 'instincts' do not involve a transformation of content. (This might not apply to the transformation known as 'sublimation' – perhaps a method of defining sublimation). See (1915c) SE XIV 127 and (1918b) SE XVII 26.

25. Freud (1911c) SE XII 63. One notes that this proposition, 'I hate him', seems to disobey the principle of the exclusion of the first person subject. But, as Laplanche and Pontalis (1973, p. 353) point out, the proposition, 'He hates me', is treated as the *excuse* for the cause of the hatred felt for the other, which is the primary symptom of paranoia. One might have to add a sub-clause to the principle, permitting a return of the subject to the first person in cases where there is a 'good enough reason'.

26. Anzieu (1959, p. 33) notes that the three women in the dream of Irma's injection correspond to three widows of men who Freud had regarded as rivals, so that 'ces veuves sont pour Freud des avertissements du destin'.

27. Safouan (1974, p. 34) notes the repetition of structure found in Freud's analysis of this dream, and gives it as a reason for the correctness of his own technique, of asking the analysand to give associations starting from a recurrent phrase; in the case Safouan discusses, the recurrent phrase used for the purpose of 'free association' was 'You behave . . .'

28. Cf. Freud (1899a) SE III 311, which describes a scene in which Sigismund and John, 'as though by mutual agreement', 'fall on the little girl' and deprive her of her flowers.

29. The passage is placed in brackets in SE, but not in the original German text.

30. In the case-history of the Ratman, Freud implied that reported speech can find no place in the unconscious – a notion that is closely related to the

reasons which had earlier led him to separate speeches in dreams off as a special category of the manifest content, derived entirely from speeches actually heard in real life. Freud compared the Ratman's attitude to his own ideas to the *lèse majesté* that is involved both in insulting the Emperor and in reporting such insults. See (1909d) SE X 178–9.

31. Whether the unconscious has a means of representing 'if' and 'but' is a debatable point. In *The Interpretation of Dreams*, the ingenuity of the means of representation adopted by the dream-work is quite clear, e.g. the representation of dependent clauses by means of 'prologues' etc. But certainly the 'pressure' of the unconscious often forces the protasis into the indicative, in order to represent it as a fulfilled wish, as in (1899a) SE III 316–17.

32. Cf. the incident recounted by Freud in the third person in (1901b) SE VI 215–6:

> In the course of some theoretical discussions I heard someone at a particular time repeatedly using the expression: 'If something suddenly shoots through one's head'. I happened to know that he had recently received news that a Russian bullet had passed right through the cap hat his son was wearing on his head.

The soldier in question was undoubtedly Freud's own son. The 'impersonal' reference of the '*es*' used in this phrase allows one to maintain a tension between the 'I' and the 'it'. This tension is capable of discovery in ordinary language: 'The impersonal 'it' is immediately connected with certain forms of expression used by normal people, "It shot through me," people say . . .' ((1926e) SE XX 195) Or, from the *New Introductory Lectures* (1933a) SE XXII 72: 'This impersonal pronoun seems particularly well suited for expressing the main characteristic of the province of the mind – the fact of its being alien to the "I".' The proximity of *das Ich* to its function in sentences is also indicated by a sentence added in 1925 to *The Interpretation of Dreams* (1900a) SE IV 323: 'The fact that the dreamer's own 'I' appears several times, or in several forms, in a dream is at bottom no more remarkable than that the "I" should be contained in a conscious thought several times or in different places or connections – e.g. in the sentence "When *I* think what a healthy child *I* was".'

33. Timpanaro (1974/6, p. 131 n8) cites this passage as allowing one to set the limit the other side of the divide between predisposing causes and linguistic determinations, so that the *Begünstigungen* could become the *vera causa* of the slip. His argument appeals to Occam's razor in order to eliminate precisely those factors that were of interest to Freud: the determining causes that lie *within* the boundaries determined by the 'compliance of the linguistic material'.

34. The fixation process can take place at all levels of language: phonemic (e.g. the 'fort/da' example, (1920g) SE XVIII 17); morphemic (e.g. the '*Glanz auf der Nase*' (1927e) SE XXI 152); sentential (e.g. 'It was like a slap in the face!' (1895d) SE II 178); supra-sentential (e.g. Jensen's *Gradiva* (1907a)).

35. Cf. Freud (1939a) SE XXIII 114:

> At some point between [the development of speech and the end of the matriarchy] there was another event which shows the most affinity to what we are investigating in the history of religion. Human beings found themselves obliged in general to recognize 'intellectual' [*geistige*] forces – forces, that is, which cannot be grasped by the senses (particularly by the sight) but which none the less produce undoubted and indeed extremely powerful effects. If we may rely upon the evidence of language, it was movement of the air that provided the prototype of intellectuality [*Geistigkeit*]. . . . Now, however, the world of spirits [*Geisterreich*] lay open to men. They were prepared to attribute the soul [*Seele*] which they had discovered in themselves to everything in Nature.

36. A phrase that runs through the system of delusions that Schreber recorded in his *Memoirs*, and which Freud and Jung took up in their correspondence as a sharper version of the analytic rule, citing it whenever the other might have forgotten to conduct a necessary piece of analysis. For example, *The Freud/Jung Letters*, 213J, September 29, 1910, p. 356: 'I use the winged word "Why don't you say it (*scil.* aloud)?" every day in analysis, where it proves its efficacy.'

CHAPTER 5

1. Dr Johnson (1818), p. xi.
2. There are many works on this subject, written by historians of ideas and by historians of science. I will mention just the following: Burrow (1966); Young (1973); Foucault (1966/70); Mandelbaum (1971) pp. 163–269.
3. Why the recognition of the importance of philology has been overshadowed by discussion of the relations between biology and social thought is a complex matter. Suffice it to mention two possible factors.

   (i) An effect of fascination by what one might call the Great Chain of Knowing that positivism engendered, whereby a chain of sciences – running: mathematics, physics, chemistry, biology, psychology, sociology – became scientific by a process of diffusion of models along the chain. The undoubted importance of biological models in the nineteenth century could thus plausibly be read as corresponding to the stage at which the development of the sciences focused on the link between biology (just-become-a-science) and psychology/sociology (desperately-wanting-to- or almost-about-to-be-sciences).

   (ii) The creation of the concept of literature and its subsequent study as literary criticism has sometimes obscured the importance of an earlier study of linguistic texts that dispensed entirely with the combination of commonsense moralism and aesthetics that has come to be associated with 'languages'. Such a clouding has been facilitated by the attempt of philosophy both to base itself upon language while conceiving of language in as formal a manner as possible. A representative work in this little history is Ogden and Richard's *The Meaning of Meaning*, which, in attempting to supply the foundations for the study of literature, finds itself irresistibly attracted by the routine apparatus of logical positivism – the verificationist theory of meaning, etc. – while being first and foremost an attack upon philology. The conjunction of their approach, involving a divorce from the more ambitious intellectual programme that philology represented, with Malinowski's equally vitriolic attack upon philology and the establishment of a new research programme for anthropology, is an indication of the nineteenth century configuration that existed previously: the fusion of the sciences of ethnology and of literature on the basis of a philological methodology.

4. Some of the general histories of linguistics drawn on for this section are: Blumenthal (1970), Jankowsky (1972), King (1969), Koerner (1973), Lehmann (1967), Pedersen (1931), Robins (1967), Trim (unpublished lectures, 1974–5). Works by Cassirer (1953–7) have also been invaluable.
5. See Humboldt (1882, 1836); Miller (1968).
6.   Grimm, for example, drew up a table of correspondences for labials, dentals, and gutturals between Greek, 'Gothic', and High German: the *p*, *b*, and *f* of the Greeks become respectively *f*, *p*, and *b* in Gothic and *b* or *v*, *f*, and *p* in High German; *t*, *d*, *th* in Greek become *th*, *t*, d in Gothic, and *d*, *z*, *t* in High German. The totality of these relationships determines the courses of history; and instead of languages being subject to that external yardstick, to those things in human history that should, according to Classical thought, explain the changes in them, they themselves contain a principle of evolution. Here, as elsewhere, it is 'anatomy' that determines destiny. (Foucault, 1966/70, p. 287)

And on p. 294, Foucault writes:

By separating the characters of the living being or the rules of grammar from the laws of a self-analysing representation, the historicity of life and language was made possible. . . . But whereas nineteenth-century biology was to advance more and more towards the exterior of the living being, towards what lay beyond it, rendering progressively more permeable that surface of the body at which the naturalist's gaze had once halted, philology was to untie the relations that the grammarian had established between language and external history in order to define an internal history. And the latter, once secure in its objectivity, could serve as a guiding-thread, making it possible to reconstitute – for the benefit of History proper – events long since forgotten.

7. And the peculiar consequence of Saussure's theory is the denial of the lawlike character of these evolutionary laws of phonetic transformation. See Saussure (1916/59), pp. 91ff.
8. On language seen through Darwinian spectacles, see Schleicher (1863) and Bateman (1877). It has been frequently pointed out that the 'tree' and 'branch' model of the history of languages antedated the Darwinian theory, and that linguistic science's notion of development was independent of that

of biology, although the Darwinian metaphors received a special welcome in philological circles.

9. The 'nationalism' associated with the collation of these heritages, found most prominently in the German language works of this period, can obviously be related to the pressures towards unification and homogenization of State institutions; but we should not mistake these pressures for the 'causes' of the appearance of these nationalistic themes. Rather, we must not forget to take into account the change in the position of language itself, from the eighteenth century on: by becoming an object of study, a proliferation of languages and cultures based upon these languages preempted the unification of civilization that the seventeenth and eighteenth centuries had assumed, whether it be via the medium of Latin or French. The international language movement is salutary in this respect, its significance being of the same order for us as the drive towards the construction of formalized languages that began to make itself felt in the mid century, and to which the history of philosophy in the twentieth century bears witness. No living language achieves the utopic transparency of expression that the linguistic idealists wished for. The recognition of this truth, that language and the world are always necessarily 'out of step' one with the other, became possible, and then constitutive of the study of language, when spoken languages revealed their opacity, their necessarily mythic and irrational dimension, and their seemingly irreducible plurality, amounting to the thousand or so languages that philologists now saw as equivalent one with another.

To put it another way, our hypothesis is that the new function of language revealed by philology gave rise to two 'reaction formations': the program for the construction of a formal language and the program for constructing a language that could be spoken without necessarily producing the ambiguity and mythic dimension that all other spoken languages produced. Perhaps the only successful fruit of the latter program was the construction of modern Hebrew. See Sprague (1888), Guérard (1922), Flügel (1925).

10. On historicism, the classic work is Friedrich Meinecke's *Historismus*, (1957/72). Other basic texts are Antoni (1940), Burke (1937), Collingwood (1946), Iggers (1968), Lee and Beck (1953–4), Mandelbaum (1938), Mandelbaum (1971).

11. We should not mistake this comparative method for an import from the 'dominant' model of comparative anatomy, as some writers have assumed (Ackerknecht (1954); Putschke (1969)). This argument is put in a different perspective by Foucault (1966/70), and there is a more theoretical discussion of the methodological points at issue in Foucault (1969/72), pp. 149ff. Nor would it seem viable to claim that the comparative method was 'invented', perhaps in the same way that that warhorse of the historiography of ideas, the Cartesian method, was invented, and *then* applied to a diverse range of sciences: biology, history, linguistics, etc., since this would imply a divorce of method and object that is a very rare phenomenon in the history of science.

12. Bunsen (1868) p. 294, cited in Burrows (1967) pp. 195–6.

13. Ibid., p. 395, cited in Burrow (1967) p. 196.

14. Cf. Foucault (1966/70), pp. 297–8:

Having become a dense and consistent historical reality, language forms the locus of tradition, of the unspoken habits of thought, of what lies hidden in a people's mind; it accumulates an ineluctable memory which does not even know itself as memory. . . . The truth of discourse is caught in the trap of philology. Hence the need to work one's way back from opinions, philosophies, and perhaps even from sciences, to the words that made them possible, and, beyond that, to a thought whose essential life has not yet been caught in the network of any grammar. This is how we must understand the revival, so marked in the nineteenth century, of all the techniques of exegesis. This reappearance is due to the fact that language has resumed the enigmatic density it possessed at the time of the Renaissance.

15. Inman (1868). See also the review in *Anthrop. Rev.*, vol. VI, 1868, pp. 378–386. Another book of Inman (1869) *Ancient pagan and modern Christian symbolism exposed and explained*, London, 1869, was read with pleasure by Jung when he started his labours on the question of mythology in 1909, though he was to criticize it quite firmly after a while; see *The Freud/Jung Letters*, 157J, 159J, 162J, pp. 251–64. Perhaps it was this experience that persuaded Jung that he would have to become "his own philologist", as he admitted a little while later.

16. Bopp (1816). See Pedersen, (1931) pp. 254ff, and Verburg (1949–50); Schleicher (1861–2); Pedersen (1931) pp. 265ff, esp. pp. 270–2, and Marx (1967b).

17. On this strain in the history of linguistics, see Brücke (1856) and the paper which made great use of Brücke's physiological work, Raumer (1856). Brücke, following Du Bois-Reymond (father), Chladi *et al.*, wished to show how the three basic vowels were determined by the physiology of the vocal organs. But another aspect of his programme intersected here: the wish to produce a universal and objective phonetic script. Objectivity was thus searched for from 'both sides': the objectivity of the symbol (the written *vs.* the spoken) and the objectivity of the natural *vs.* the cultural. As Rothschuh (1973) p. 235 notes, 'during his years at Vienna, Brücke returned to one of his favourite ideas: the so-called '*Pasigraphie*'. He wrote a book in which he attempted to represent with specific signs the sounds used in various languages. In this fashion, Brücke hoped to establish a unified phonetic writing method and be able to read every foreign language without prior preparation.' Whether Brücke's pupil Freud shared this enthusiasm, we do not know.

18. Bunsen (1854), vol. II, p. 78 cited in Burrows (1967) p. 197.

19. An interesting discussion of Müller's theory and the more general topic of the root in the nineteenth century philological tradition can be found in Porset (1977).

20. See Müller (1873), (1875), vol. IV pp. 433–72. Cf. Critchley (1958, 1960).

21. The most important articles on *Völkerpsychologie* written by Lazarus and Steinthal are to be found in their journal, *Zeitschrift für Völkerpsychologie und Sprachwissenschaft*, founded in 1860, and which ran until 1890, when it was changed into the *Zeitschrift des Vereins für Völkskunde*. Thurnwald self-consciously revived the journal in 1925, with the significantly changed

title, *Zeitschrift für Völkerpsychologie und Soziologie*, i.e. sociology replaced linguistics as the means by which to establish the science of
Völkerpsychologie. The main articles of programmatic import in the
original journal are: Band I: *Einleitung*; Band II: *Verhältnisse der Einzelnen
zur Gesammtheit*; Band III: *Einige synthetische Gedanken zur
Völkerpsychologie*. Steinthal's general work, *Einleitung in die Psychologie
und Sprachwissenschaft*, (Berlin, 1871), indicates the manner in which the
general science of linguistics was meant to stand on a more general
psychology, but that this psychology could never be established without the
foundation of a theory of language.

Secondary works on this school are few and far between. Some remarks
are to be found in Karpf (1932) pp. 41–51; Ribot (1885) pp. 50ff.; de Vries,
(1961).

22. Müller renounced such an ideal, despite his conception of a limited number
of linguistic roots functioning as the source of all thought. See Müller
(1888a) and the perspicacious review by Regnard (1888), who states that the
key question for the discipline of etymology is: are there laws for the evolution of the *sense* of a word? A valuable and cautious review of the
question, with some tentative attempts to establish such laws, is to be found
in Meyer (1910).

23. Burrows (1966) pp. 109–10, discusses this work and concludes: ' . . . the
overall impression one receives is that the subjects which are combined to
form modern anthropology owed more, methodologically, to geology and
comparative philology than to evolutionary biology.'

24. All of these writers were studied by one or a number of the early
'philological' psychoanalysts. Frazer's work seemed to be the most
significant of the anthropological works that Freud made use of in writing
Totem and Taboo, and continually supplied him with facts illustrating
psychoanalytic theory. Kuhn's work was used extensively by Abraham and
by Jung in their works on myth. Winckler was cited in a passage added to
The Interpretation of Dreams in 1909. Stucken's work was criticized in
Freud (1913f), and Silberer (1914) made extensive use of his work. When
Abraham was writing his *Traum und Mythus* Freud wrote to him *a propos*
of the work that he and Rank were doing on hero myths and then said:

> But I think you ought to tackle the astral significance of myths, which
> now, since the discoveries of Winckler (Jeremias, Stucken) about the
> ancient oriental world system can no longer be ignored . . . I believe
> there is also room for a psychological explanation, because in the last
> resort the ancients only projected their phantasies on to the sky. (Freud,
> 1965a, p. 29)

25. It was such a conception of the passivity of the language-speaker in the face
of a system of signs already laid down that informed Steinthal's work and
elicited W. D. Whitney's critical essay (Whitney, 1873). Whitney could not
understand how any one could deny that mankind in the past, and children
in the present, learnt language by a process of trial and error directed
towards the practical purpose of communication. Steinthal, in a mixture of
Herbartian and Hegelian languages, emphasized the sense in which no

human being could ever be said to be outside the unity conferred by language. Cf. the comment of Foucault (1966/70) p. 323:

> How can man be the subject of a language that for thousands of years has been formed without him, a language whose organization escapes him, whose meaning sleeps an almost invincible sleep in the words he momentarily activates by means of discourse, and within which he is obliged, from the very outset, to lodge his speech and thought, as though they were doing no more than animate, for a brief period, one segment of that web of innumerable possibilities?

26. We may thus contrast the Humboldtian emphasis on 'force' and 'energy' with the Saussurian emphasis on 'system' and 'law'. Freud's conception falls between these two, since he obviously conceived of a system of signification proper to the determination of the subject, while conceiving of the dynamics of meaning as a force, or, perhaps, a 'charge', that accompanies the word. We might even conceive of the Q of the *Project* as an attempt to give more precision to the Humboldtian notion of creative force, so that we can finally read Q as signifying 'quantity of meaning'.

27. See in particular, Jones I 405–12; Dorer (1932). The discussions by Amacher, Ellenberger, Macintyre, who mention the Herbart connection, add little to Jones' account. Andersson (1962), pp. 10–14, includes a good discussion of the affinities of Freudian and Herbartian psychology.

28. We should note in passing that Jones attempted to distance Freud's theory of unconscious conflict and repression from Herbart's by remarking that Herbart's theory accorded a primacy to the conflict of *ideas*, whereas Freud's turned around a conflict of *affects*. By now, it should be clear that this opposition, one that has bedevilled much of the discussion of the exact nature of Freudian theory, is misleading, if not completely wrong. More important, I believe, is the statement we have quoted a number of times, where Freud emphasized that repression acts *only* on memories, so that the contrast with Herbart should be in terms of idea/memory, not idea/affect. And it is precisely this dimension of the past, lacking to Herbart's psychology, that the *Völkerpsychologischen* introduced, when they felt themselves sent to the history of language in their search for the foundations of psychology.

29. Such a use of a notion of the 'battle of ideas', themselves in an unconscious condition, can be found in Steinthal (1862b), pp. 168–171.

30. (1910c) SE XI 82 gives the passage as follows: 'while I was in my cradle a vulture came down to me, and opened my mouth with its tail, and struck me many times with its tail against my lips.'

31. When we compare the argument concerning the 'vulture' with that concerning the 'tail', it is less clear that Freud ignored the seemingly obvious equation of the bird with the mother, 'deducible', one would have thought, from the fact that it is doing something which is very similar to what a mother does to a child. In fact this is one of the points where the two accounts which Freud gave differ markedly: in the paper read to the Society, he noted the equation 'tail = penis' and thus concluded that Leonardo's 'phantasy' (assuming that it was such, because he gave no

credence whatsoever to the hypothesis that this memory of Leonardo's was an actual memory, even one that was partially distorted) was homosexual in character: 'to take the penis ('tail'; in Italian, it means precisely that) into the mouth and suck on it.' (*Minutes* II p. 340). In the published paper, Freud expanded on this homosexual phantasy, indicating its origin in the 'organic impression . . . indelibly printed on us' (SE XI 87) of sucking at the mother's breast. Freud felt secure in giving this meaning to the phantasy, since Leonardo had attributed the event to a period 'while I was in my cradle' (quoted by Freud in Italian: '*essendo io in culla*' – Ibid.) Despite the fact that Freud assigned a deep-lying meaning of the phantasy to the experience of suckling at the breast – which he had done by close textual reading rather than by mythological reference – it is clear from the rest of the paper, as well as from the fact that this item is lacking from the earlier version of the paper, that the actual weight of explanation falls on the Egyptian elucidation of the 'vulture' element. What was also of greater importance for Freud than the simple 'vulture = mother' is the homosexual aspect of the phantasy: the tail is first and foremost a penis, not a nipple, and we are dealing here with the 'mother-with-a-penis'. The element 'penis', as we have seen, finds 'linguistic' rather than 'natural analogic' evidential support.

32. Freud's account is slightly ambiguous on this point. But Horapollo's text is quite clear; see Horapollo (1840) pp. 23ff.
33. Indeed, Freud recognized this at one point in his account: 'it appears that the sources to which [Leonardo] had access contained no information about this remarkable feature [i.e. Mut's combination of maternal and masculine characteristics].' (1910c) SE XI 94.
34. Jones' account of the argument that Freud used is strictly misleading in this respect:

> In the book Freud had made a good deal of the mythological associations of this bird, which in Egypt was regarded as a Mother-Goddess (Mut) though equipped with a male organ, and since it was often cited in Catholic theology he thought it likely that Leonardo was aware of the maternal symbolism. (Jones, vol. II, 390)

In this description, what exactly the Catholic theologians cited is left unambiguously vague; one might call Jones' account a systematic and symptomatic (mis)reading.
35. Boas (1950) doubts whether Leonardo knew of the Horapollo text, thus casting doubt on the last link with the Egyptians that we have left intact.
36. Spector (1972) pp. 58ff, constructs an argument to show how the Egyptian material does have significant psycho-biographical relevance to Freud, rather than to Leonardo. See also Rosenfeld (1956) and Anzieu (1959) pp. 44ff. A more broad-ranging discussion of what Freud's 'Leonardo' reveals about Freud can be found in Barande (1977).
37. As it is easy to do when we read Freud's further speculations concerning '*Instinkt*', Ibid., SE XXIII 100ff.
38. The distance between the methodology and conceptual support-system of Freud and that of twentieth century historians of ideas is best brought out

when we focus on the concept of 'tradition'. The conflict between the two approaches lies behind the debate over Leonardo, as can be seen in Shapiro's criticism of Freud's argument concerning the 'influence' on Leonardo of Egyptian and Classical sources. Simply put, the concept of 'influence' bears the brunt of a historian's argument, and much of such history will consist in 'influence-chains': the classic example of this genre is Lovejoy's *The Great Chain of Being*. Theoretical work on the methodology of such an historian then revolves around refining the concept of 'influence', cf. Skinner (1969). What such a methodology does not confront is the implicit continuity that is assumed between a 'tradition' as it impinges on the individual, under the cloak of 'influence', and the 'intention' of the historical actor, taken to be transparent to the actor in question, but also invisibly permeated with tradition – a veritable 'historical influencing-machine'. The historical subject thus forms the nodal point of opacity in such an account, while the account itself depends on the manner in which such a subject 'knits' the web of influences together. The problems in Freud's methodology are totally other.

39. The phrase 'Specimen Dream' (*Traummuster*) is Freud's, but the dream itself has received a great deal of attention in psychoanalytic literature since Freud, as an object upon which one can suitably practise a new theory or a new reading of Freud's self-analysis. Certainly there are two major re-readings of this dream: Erikson (1954), Anzieu (1959), pp. 24–40, which followed and greatly expanded upon the discussion of the dream that Lacan gave in his *séminaire* of 1954–5, recently published as Lacan (1978), pp. 177–204. It will be the reading of Anzieu and Lacan that I will follow in large part here, since they have given a plausible further analysis of the dream, drawing upon the diligent and remarkably accurate attempts at assigning the real-life identities of the figures in this and other of Freud's dreams that Anzieu's book makes. One should note that the second edition of Anzieu's book, although larger in overall scope, omits some of the more interesting comments on the dream of Irma's injection that he had made, probably when under the influence of Lacan, in the earlier edition. It is the latter that I have used. (See also, on this dream, Grinstein (1968) pp. 21–46; Schur (1966); Schur (1972) pp. 79ff.)

40. The SE translation of this title is 'The Theme of the Three Caskets' which, although mellifluous, is strictly inaccurate, in a manner which is of some importance in the light of the reading of the paper that I will give. Despite its heavy-handedness, for the purposes of my discussion I have translated the title as 'The Motive for the Choice of a Casket'. Insofar as 'choice' and 'decision' are crucial concepts in the theory and practice of analysis, this paper may be said to throw considerable light upon them. See the most interesting discussion in Granoff (1975) pp. 518–49, and in Granoff (1976) pp. 140–63.

41. Whether the fact that trimethylamin is one of the decomposition products of semen, remarked by Lacan (1978), p. 190, is of significance for any further re-interpretation of the dream, I will leave for consideration on some future occasion.

42. Anzieu (Anzieu, 1959, p. 39), following Lacan, remarks:

Freud dreamt that dreams have a symbolic meaning and he dreamt it in symbols as rigorous as they are transparent. To the question he had been asking for some months, namely, whether dreams have a meaning, the dream of Irma's injection replied, saying, not only do dreams contain the meaning of our desire, but also that this meaning stems from their symbolic structure.

Or perhaps, to put it more simply (see Lacan (1978) p. 190), Freud's question was: 'What is the meaning of the dream?' And he dreamt the following 'reply': 'Meaning'.

43. Some notes upon the people who figure in the dream may be of interest:

(i) Mathilde Breuer figures as a widow in the structure of the dream, indicating the murderous character that Freud's relation to the three authorities had.

(ii) Anzieu had deduced that Irma was Anna Hammerschlag solely on the basis of the footnote to Freud's text in which he mentions that 'the sound of the word "ananas" bears a remarkable resemblance to that of my patient Irma's family name' (SE IV 115), an inspired piece of detective work that Freud's letter to Abraham confirms.

(iii) Sophie Schwab-Paneth was the niece of Professor Hammerschlag, and thus the cousin of 'Irma'. She had married Josef Paneth, a friend of Freud's who had made possible his visits to Hamburg to see Martha when they were only engaged, and who is the 'friend Josef' of the *Non Vixit* dream; he died in 1890. He was a most suitable candidate for the position of rival, since he had written a history of the subconscious in 1884, which he had sent to Nietzsche for his comments.

44. Lacan touched upon the connection between the theme of three women found in both the dream of Irma's injection and the theme of the three caskets, Lacan (1978) p. 189:

Quand nous analysons ce texte, il faut tenir compte du texte tout entier, y compris des notes. A cette occasion, Freud évoque ce point des associations où le rêve prend son insertion dans l'inconnu, ce qu'il appelle son ombilic.

Nous arrivons à ce qu'il y a derrière le trio mystique. Je dis *mystique* parce que nous en connaissons maintenant le sens. Les trois femmes, les trois sœurs, les trois coffrets, Freud nous en a depuis démontré le sens. Le dernier terme est la mort, tout simplement.

45. Jones (vol. II, p. 404) called it 'one of the two most charming things he ever wrote' and confessed that he had 'a personal fondness' for this paper, such that it was his favourite. He continued:

It would be interesting to know what had stirred the theme in Freud. He was occupied with the dull work of correcting proofs in the spring of 1912 when the idea suddenly occurred to him that there must be a connection between the two Shakespeare scenes just mentioned and the judgement of Paris. . . . There was the approaching engagement of his second daughter Sophie, which was formally announced in the following month . . . a year later he mentioned to Ferenczi that his interest in the theme must have been connected with thoughts of his three daughters, particularly of the youngest, Anna; . . . (Jones, vol. II, p. 405)

46. We may peremptorily list them: an Estonian folk-epic drawn from Stucken's *Astralmythologie*, Grimm's *Märchen*, Roscher's *Ausführliches Lexicon der griechischen und römischen Mythologie*.

47. Freud (1950a), SE I 264–5:

A scene then occurred to me which, for the last 29 years, has occasionally emerged in my conscious memory without my understanding it. My mother was nowhere to be found: I was screaming my head off. My brother Philipp . . . was holding open a cupboard [*Kasten*] for me, and, when I found that my mother was not inside it either, I began crying still more, till, looking slim and beautiful, she came in by the door . . .

48. This point is, in fact, the crux of the paper; it also marks the point of transition in Freud's own self-analysis: from the 'sexual megalomania' of the dream of Irma's injection – 'I have them all', that is, he did not choose – to the recognition of the ineluctable necessity (*Verhängnis*) of death, which must be chosen, under pain of the tragic outcome to which a refusal to choose would lead. It is also the point at which Freud shifts from an identification with his father – 'I have them all', – that is, all of his father's three wives – to a refusal of such an identification, perhaps, as Granoff has argued, via a pardoning of the father's sexual profligacy, such a pardon opening up the possibility of a choice. On the question of the three wives of Freud's father, see Granoff (1975), pp. 318ff, Schur (1972, pp. 20ff).

49. Ibid., SE XII 301: ' . . . *eine flächenhafte, allegorische Deutung*' . . .

50. The whole passage runs:

Freud attaches great significance to verbal expression – one of the most important components of thinking – because the double meaning of words is a favourite channel for the displacement and improper expression of affects. . . . Judging by my own experience, it is impossible to understand the meaning of the *Three Essays* and of the 'Fragment . . .' without a thorough knowledge of *The Interpretation of Dreams*. By 'thorough knowledge' I naturally do not mean the cheap philological criticisms which many writers have levelled at this book, but a patient application of Freud's principles to psychic processes.

I have not been able to establish the identity of these many philological critics, and it would be of great interest to be able to do so.

51. E.g. Freud (1900a) SE V 407:

. . . the course of linguistic evolution has made things very easy for dreams. For language has a whole number of words at its command which originally had a pictorial and concrete significance, but are used today in a colourless and abstract sense. All that the dream need do is to give these words their former, full meaning or to go back a little way to an earlier phase in their development (*in dem Bedeutungswandel des Wortes ein Stück weit herabzusteigen*). (added 1909)

52. See, for instance, Ferenczi (1909a) pp. 49ff; Ferenczi (1909b), p. 176; Ferenczi (1911) p. 151; Ferenczi (1913) *passim.*; Abraham (1909) pp. 161–9; Stekel, who referred off the cuff to Kleinpaul for support for one of his symbolic equations in the *Minutes* III, p. 67; Reik similarly drew on Kleinpaul to prove that belief in vampires owes its origin to wet dreams, *Minutes* III, p. 312. Kleinpaul was one of the philologists whose recurrent and insistent reference to the centrality of sexuality in primitive thought and forgotten languages was a source of continual comfort and support for the 'embattled' psychoanalysts.

53. This work took as its themes ghosts, souls and immortality, 'the fauna of hell', 'angels of death', 'the cult of the soul, its seat and its fetishes', mostly drawn from Classical and Old Germanic sources.

54. A fear that was realized in 1901, when Fliess told Freud that 'the thought-reader reads in others only his own thoughts (*Der Gedankenleser liest bei den Anderen nur seine eigenen Gedanken*).' (Note that the translation given in Freud (1950a) *Origins*, 7 Aug. 1901, p. 334 – 'the thought-reader merely reads his own thoughts into other people' – involves a subtle shift that changes the entire balance of this remark of Fliess'.) The relation of this theme with Freud's later rapprochement to telepathy is clear, and we may find occasion to specify the philological context of Freud's stubborn openmindedness to telepathic phenomena.

55. Cf. Freud (1950a) SE I 245: 'All sorts of things lie behind the wording of the telegram in the dream: the memory of the etymological delicacies that you lay out before me . . . (*Die Erinnerung an die etymologischen Genüsse, die Du mir vorzusetzen pflegst . . .*)' (translation modified).

56. It is certainly significant that the book on *Bisexuality in Man* was Freud's attempt to restore an intimacy with Fliess that had already suffered irreparable damage: he mentioned the project directly after he had cited Fliess' accusations of 'thought-reading'. (Freud (1950a) *Origins*, 7 Aug 1901, p. 334) The idea itself seemed to impose upon him a collaboration with the true author of the idea, the author who could not but feel insulted by the prospect of the thought-reader also passing off as his own thoughts those that had been *freely* 'read' to him, as the acrimonious dispute over priority of 1904 witnessed. See Freud (1960a), pp. 259–60; Jones, vol. I, 345–7; Abrahamsen (1946) pp. 1–44.

57. Abraham had originally wanted to follow philology as a career, but found that the need for a remunerative profession preempted him. His acquaintance with English, Spanish, Italian, Rhaeto-Romanic, Danish, Dutch, French, Greek and Latin, the result of his early love, prepared him well for his essays into comparative mythology. In his correspondence with Freud, he often remarked on the pleasure that the prospect of doing philological work afforded him.

58. We should note the primacy of the philological method, whatever the final 'causes' assigned to the myth, since the methods by which primitive man

made fire and love were themselves deduced from the meaning of words in the primitive languages, a philological triumph that had very little recourse to the alternative mode of prehistoric detective-work supplied by archaeology.

59. Much of little Hans' analysis revolved around the question of the origin of babies. But it is clear that, despite the emphasis that Freud and Hans' father placed on the fact that the baby was a 'lumpf' that came out of Mummy, the question of the role of the father was just as important as that of the mother, especially insofar as an answer to that question might throw light on the 'premonitory sensations' he experienced in his widdler 'whenever he thought of these things' (SE X 134). On the one hand, this problem had originally proved too much for little Hans: 'his attempt at discovering what it was that had to be done with his mother in order that she might have children sank down into his unconscious,' (SE X 135), the result being his phobia. On the other hand, Hans' parents never communicated to him the exact nature of the father's role in procreation; Freud, halfway through the analysis, had noted their 'hesitation to give him information which was already long overdue'. But Hans groped his way towards some resolution of the problem, so that his final phantasy included a representation of the process by which a penis turned into a baby: some sort of disappearance and replacement that involved Hans becoming 'like Daddy'. It is clear that it is not only the passive homosexual trend that is at issue here, but also those issues connected with the development of the concept of the Oedipus complex that we discussed in Chapter 3, pp. 84ff.

60. Abraham (1909, p. 200) noted that the Prometheus myth asserts the primacy of the masculine function in procreation, a parallel achievement to little Hans' disappearing and reappearing penis-child.

61. On the first page of the same work, Freud wrote: 'The first thing that attracts our attention about the figure of Moses is his name, which is "Mosheh" in Hebrew. "What is its origin?" we may ask, "and what does it mean?"' (SE XXIII 7). Having then argued that the name is Egyptian in origin, Freud asked: if his name was Egyptian, then surely the bearer of this name was Egyptian? 'In relation to ancient and primitive times, one would have thought that a conclusion such as this as to a person's nationality based on his name would have seemed far more reliable and in fact unimpeachable.' (SE XXIII 9). Behind this argument, we cannot help but see an allusion to that primaeval state of language in which there is an unambiguous relation between word and thing designated, a state akin to that magical power of words ascribed by Freud to the talking-cure in 1890 and analysed in parallel with animism in *Totem and Taboo* (1912–13): there is something about a name that 'sticks' to a thing.

62. And what could be more arbitrary than 'kinship'? – To be born, without any say in the matter, as the child of a mother, to find that mother is linked in some obscure and ineluctable fashion to a 'father' – and yet the force of psychoanalysis is to indicate the unavoidable and unresolvable character of this position. Cf. Granoff (1975), p. 534:

Is it then possible to not become the father of one's father? Isn't it then to escape from the intolerable situation of being born, without having a word to say about it, from the desire that gave a woman to this father? The intolerable character of destiny, it is all to be found rooted therein.

63. The felicitous coinage, 'polyglot unconscious', is Timpanaro's. He notes that many of the slips recorded by Freud in *The Psychopathology of Everyday Life* require an unconscious passage from a word in one language to a related word in another, finding this highly implausible (Timpanaro (1976), pp. 80–1). But Freud's argument seems to go one step further and demands a knowledge of *etymologies* of words, both in foreign and native tongues. Cf. Timpanaro (1976), pp. 91–2:

> . . . Freud introduces an antithetical distinction between the 'typical' symptom and the 'historical' symptom . . . which has an undoubted affinity with similar problems that were an issue of debate for other human sciences during the same period. . . . These were problems which all arose from the schism between science and history which became manifest in European culture towards the end of the nineteenth and the outset of the twentieth century. The solution . . . was to be contained in the notion of the collective unconscious. It was, as we know, a solution that posed more problems than it resolved. But it would nonetheless have been interesting, even if to my mind unconvincing, had an attempt been made to apply it to the theory of 'slips' whereas neither Freud nor the Freudians have ever done so.

Timpanaro is pointing, quite correctly, to the *necessity* for such a theory in psychoanalysis. I have tried to show that there were elements for this theory present in the practice and expectations of analysts, even if the fully articulated theory is not to be found expounded.

64. Marx (1966) recognized the peculiarly fertile possibilities of a concatenation of aphasia and philology, and attempted to find a pathway of influence between the two disciplines, concluding that there was a definite mutual lack of interest between them. My argument is that Freud and the early psychoanalysts represented the meeting-point of the two disciplines, although I accept – and endorse from my own research – Marx's conclusion that modes of direct influence are difficult to demonstrate (in the sense of 'demonstrate' and 'influence' normally accepted by those historians of ideas who pay attention to the level of rigour of such an argument). One telegraphic way of expressing the thesis I have put forward is: Jackson + Kleinpaul = Freud.

65. Cf. Jung's account of psychoanalysis, ((1912) CW IV 146):

> Every psychological element has its special history. Every sentence I utter has, besides the meaning consciously intended by me, its historical meaning, which may turn out to be quite different from its conscious meaning. . . . The analysis which the literary historian makes of the poet's material is exactly comparable with the method of psychoanalysis, not excluding the mistakes that may creep in. . . . The psychoanalytic method can be compared with historical analysis and synthesis in general.

He continued his account by conducting a 'comparative study' of rites of baptism, in order to find 'its original meaning'. And he notes that it was this close relation of psychoanalysis to the historic-literary method – to philology – that made it difficult for medical men to understand it and to accept it.

66. Freud ((1901b) SE VI 257):

> I believe in external (real) chance, it is true, but not in internal (psychical) accidental events. With the superstitious person it is the other way round. . . . But what is hidden from him corresponds to what is unconscious for me, and the compulsion not to let chance count as chance but to interpret it is common to both of us.

The 'personal' tone of these very interesting comments allows us to conclude, I believe, that the 'superstitious person' of whom Freud was thinking was Fliess. When Fliess called Freud a thought-reader, just before he was to receive his complimentary copy of the *Psychopathology*, Freud replied:

> If I am such a one, throw my Every-day Life unread into the waste-paper basket. It is full of references to you: obvious ones, where you supplied the material, and concealed ones, where the motivation derives from you. . . . Having said this, I can send it to you without a word as soon as it comes in . . . (Freud, 1950a), *Origins*, 7 Aug. 1901, p. 334; (translation modified.)

67. As Granoff points out, the 'occult' dimension of Freud's thought runs from the numerological concerns he shared with Fliess, via the occult significance of names that Freud and Ferenczi discussed in their correspondence, to the papers that he finally allowed himself to publish, due account having been taken of the 'considerations of external policy' (Jones, vol. III, p. 423). Granoff himself disavows a detailed consideration of this issue, but does point up its connection with the primary concern of the psychoanalyst: 'the travels of words' (Granoff (1975), pp. 290ff), noting that for the contemporary French psychoanalyst such phenomena are more covered than illuminated by their possibly quite correct characterization as 'effects of the signifier'.

CONCLUSION

1. Freud's report of part of what the Ratman said during the first hour of his treatment, in Freud (1909d) SE X 162.
2. For example, the special place that Freud accorded to speeches heard in dreams was a problem that perplexed me for a long time. The fruit of that perplexity is large parts of the chapter on grammar and of the chapter on the metapsychology of speech. Very little reference to the initial problem will be found in those chapters.
3. Jones I 351. See the discussion in Granoff (1975), pp. 264ff.

Bibliography

Instead of puns, give us proofs!

Kurt Mendel (1910)

The bibliography includes all those works cited in the text and, in addition, a number of works that I have found provided great assistance and stimulation, although I did not find a specific occasion on which to mention them in the text or notes.

A *Works by Freud cited in the text*

I have not given the paginations of the two German texts employed (the *Gesammelte Werke*, and the *Studienausgabe*); these can be easily located by referring to the *Sigmund Freud Konkordanz*.

Gesammelte Werke, Bände 1–17 (London, 1940–52); Band 18 (Frankfurt am Main: 1968).

Studienausgabe, 10 vols with unnumbered *Ergänzungsband*, (Frankfurt am Main: S. Fischer Verlag, 1969–75).

Sigmund Freud Konkordanz und Gesamtbibliographie, zusammengestellt von Ingeborg Meyer-Palmedo (Frankfurt am Main: S. Fischer Verlag, 1975).

The Standard Edition of the Complete Psychological Works of Sigmund Freud, 24 vols, trans. from German under the general editorship of James Strachey, in collaboration with Anna Freud, assisted by Alix Strachey and Alan Tyson (London: The Hogarth Press and the Institute of Psychoanalysis, 1953–74).

Cocaine papers, ed. Robert Byck (Stonehill, 1974).

(1886f) Translation with preface and footnotes of J.-M. Charcot's *Leçons sur les maladies du système nerveux*, vol. III (Paris: 1887) under the title *Neue Vorlesungen über die Krankheiten des Nervensystems insbesondere über Hysterie*, Vienna.

(1888b) 'Aphasie', 'Gehirn' in Villaret's *Handwörterbuch der gesamten Medizin*, I (Stuttgart) esp. pp. 88–9.

(1888–89) Translation with preface and notes of H. Bernheim's *De la suggestion et de ses applications à la thérapeutique* (Paris: 1886) English translation of 'Preface to the Translation of Bernheim's *Suggestion*' SE I 73–85.

(1890a) 'Psychical (or mental) treatment' SE VII 283–302.

(1819b) *On Aphasia* (London: 1953).

(1893a) With Breuer, J., 'On the psychical mechanism of hysterical phenomena' SE II 3–17.

(1893c) 'Some points for a comparative study of organic and hysterical motor paralyses' SE I 159–72.

(1893h) Lecture 'On the psychical mechanism of hysterical phenomena' SE III 27–39.

(1894a) 'The neuro-psychoses of defence' SE III 45–61.

(1895b) 'On the grounds for detaching a particular syndrome from neurasthenia under the description "anxiety neurosis"' SE III 90–115.

(1895d) With Breuer, J., *Studies on hysteria* SE II.

(1896a) 'Heredity and the aetiology of the neuroses' SE III 143–56.

(1896b) 'Further remarks on the neuro-psychoses of defence' SE III 162–85.

(1896c) 'The aetiology of hysteria' SE III 191–221.

(1899a) 'Screen memories' SE III 303–22.

(1900a) *The Interpretation of Dreams* SE IV–V.

(1901a) *On Dreams* SE V 633–86.

(1901b) *The Psychopathology of Everyday Life* SE VI.

(1905c) *Jokes and their relation to the unconscious* SE VIII.

(1905d) *Three Essays on the Theory of Sexuality* SE VII 130–243.

(1905e) 'Fragment of an analysis of a case of hysteria' SE VII 7–122.

(1906a) 'My views on the part played by sexuality in the aetiology of the neuroses' SE VII 271–9.

(1907a) *Delusions and dreams in Jensen's 'Gradiva'* SE IX 7–95.

(1908b) 'Character and anal erotism' SE IX 169–75.

(1908c) 'On the sexual theories of children' SE IX 209–26.

(1909a) 'Some general remarks on hysterical attacks' SE IX 229–34.

(1909b) 'Analysis of a phobia in a five-year-old boy' SE X 5–149.

(1909c) 'Family romances' SE IX 237–41.

(1909d) 'Notes upon a case of obsessional neurosis' SE X 155–249.

(1910a) 'Five lectures on psychoanalysis' SE XI 9–55.

(1910c) *Leonardo da Vinci and a Memory of his Childhood* SE XI 63–137.

(1910e) ' "The antithetical meaning of primal words" ' SE XI 155–61.

(1911b) 'Formulations on the two principles of mental functioning' SE XII 218–26.

(1911c) 'Psychoanalytic notes on an autobiographical account of a case of paranoia (Dementia paranoides)' SE XII 9–82.

(1912b) 'The dynamics of transference' SE XII 99–108.

(1912–13) *Totem and Taboo* SE XIII 1–161.

(1913f) 'The motive for the choice of a casket (The theme of the three caskets)' SE XII 291–301.

(1913i) 'The disposition to obsessional neurosis' SE XII 317–26.

(1913j) 'The claims of psychoanalysis to scientific interest' SE XIII 165–90.

(1914c) 'On narcissism: an introduction' SE XIV 73–102.

(1914d) 'On the history of the psychoanalytic movement' SE XIV 7–66.

(1915c) 'Instincts and their vicissitudes' SE XIV 117–40.

(1915e) 'The unconscious' SE XIV 166–204.

(1916–17) *Introductory Lectures on Psychoanalysis* SE XV–XVI.

(1918b) 'From the history of an infantile neurosis' SE XVII 7–122.

(1919e) ' "A child is being beaten" ' SE XVII 179–204.

(1920g) *Beyond the Pleasure Principle* SE XVIII 7–64.

(1923a) 'Two encyclopaedia articles' SE VIII 235–59.

(1923b) *The Ego and the Id* SE XIX 12–66.

(1924c) 'The economic problem of masochism' SE XIX 159–70.

(1924d) 'The dissolution of the Oedipus complex' SE XIX 173–9.

(1924f) 'A short account of psychoanalysis' SE XIX 191–209.

(1925a) 'A note upon the "Mystic Writing-Pad" ' SE XIX 227–32.

(1925d) *An Autobiographical Study* SE XX 7–74.

(1926d) *Inhibitions, Symptoms and Anxiety* SE XX 87–172.

(1926e) *The Question of Lay Analysis* SE XX 183–258.

(1927e) 'Fetishism' SE XXI 152–7.

(1930a) *Civilization and its Discontents* SE XXI 64–145.

(1933a) *New Introductory Lectures on Psychoanalysis* SE XXII 5–182.

(1937c) 'Analysis terminable and interminable' SE XXIII 216–53.

(1937d) 'Constructions in analysis' SE XXIII 257–69.

(1939a) *Moses and Monotheism* SE XXIII 6–137.

(1940a) *An Outline of Psychoanalysis* SE XXIII 144–207.

(1940b) 'Some elementary lessons in psychoanalysis' SE XXIII 281–6.

(1950a) *The Origins of Psychoanalysis. Letters to Wilhelm Fliess, Drafts and Notes: 1887–1902* (London: Imago, 1954); partly, including 'A Project for a Scientific Psychology', in SE I.

(1960a) *Letters 1873–1939,* ed. E. L. Freud, trans. T and J. Stern (London: 1961).

(1963a) *Psychoanalysis and Faith. The Letters of Sigmund Freud and Oskar Pfister* (London: 1963).

(1965a) *A Psychoanalytic Dialogue. The Letters of Sigmund Freud and Karl Abraham,* ed. H. C. Abraham and E. L. Freud (London: 1965).

(1966a) *Sigmund Freud and Lou Andreas-Salome: Letters,* ed. E. L. Pfeiffer (London: 1972).

(1974) *Briefe über das Es* (Correspondence with Georg Groddeck) (München: Kindler, 1974).

(1974) *The Freud/Jung Letters,* ed. William McGuire, trans. R. Manheim and R. F. C. Hull (London: 1974).

B *Other works*

Abraham, Karl, *Selected papers on psychoanalysis* (SP), with an introductory memoir by Ernest Jones, trans. by Douglas Bryan and Alix Strachey (London: Hogarth Press and the Institute of Psychoanalysis, 1927).

——, *Clinical papers and essays on psychoanalysis* (CP), edited by Hilda Abraham, translated by Hilda Abraham and D. R. Ellison (New York: Basic Books, 1955).

(1908a) 'The psychosexual differences between hysteria and dementia praecox' SP, pp. 64–79.

(1908b) 'The psychological relations between sexuality and alcoholism' SP, pp. 80–9.

(1909) *Dreams and myths. A study in folk-psychology* CP, pp. 151–209.

(1911) 'Notes on the psychoanalytical investigation and treatment of manic-depressive insanity and allied conditions' SP, pp. 137–56.

(1920) 'Manifestations of the female castration complex' SP, pp. 338–69.

Abrahamsen, David (1946), *The mind and death of a genius* (New York).

Abricossoff, Glafira (1897–8), *L'Hystérie aux XVIIe et XVIIIe siècles,* no. 31 (Paris: Thèse méd.).

Ackerknecht, E. M. (1954), 'On the comparative method in anthropology' in: R. F. Spencer (ed.), *Method and Perspective in Anthropology,* Minneapolis.

Adler, Alfred (1912/17), *Über den Nervösen Charakter* (Wiesbaden: Bergmann, 1912) translated as *The Neurotic Constitution* (New York: Moffat, Yard, 1917).

Alajouanine, T. A. (1968), *L'aphasie et le langage pathologique* (Paris: Baillière).

Amacher, Peter (1965), 'Freud's neurological education and its influence on psychoanalytic theory' *Psychological Issues* vol. IV, no. 4, monograph 16.

—— (1972), 'Freud, Sigmund' *Dictionary of Scientific Biography*, vol. 5, pp. 171–81.

Andersson, Ola (1962), *Studies in the prehistory of psychoanalysis. The aetiology of psychoneuroses and some related themes in Sigmund Freud's scientific writings and letters 1886–96* (Svenska Bokförlaget/Norstedts, Scandinavian Univ. Book).

Antoni, Carlo (1940), *From history to sociology: the transition in German historical thinking*, foreword by B. Croce, transl. Hayden V. White (London: Merlin Press, 1962)

Anzieu, Didier (1959), *L'autoanalyse* (Paris: P.U.F).

Ardener, Edwin (1971), 'Social anthropology and the historicity of historical linguistics' in: Ardener, E., (ed.) *Social anthropology and language* (London: Tavistock) pp. 209–41.

Axelrod, Charles D. (1977), 'Freud and science' *Theory and Society 4*, pp. 273–294.

Babinski, J.-F. (1886), 'Le transfert' *Revue de l'hypnotisme I*.

Bachelard, Gaston (1938), *The psychoanalysis of fire*, translated by Alan C. M. Ross (London: Routledge & Kegan Paul, 1964).

—— (1940), *The Philosophy of no. A philosophy of the new scientific method*, trans. G. C. Waterston (New York: The Onion Press, 1968).

Bakan, David (1958), *Sigmund Freud and the Jewish mystical tradition* (New York: Schocken Books, 1965).

Balint, M. (1952), *Primary love and psychoanalytic technique* (London: The Hogarth Press).

Barande, Ilse (1977), *Le maternal singulier* (Paris: Aubier-Montaigne).

Barrucand, Dominique (1967), *Histoire de l'hypnose en France* (Paris: P.U.F).

Bastian, Charlton (1887), 'On different kinds of aphasia, with special reference to their classification and ultimate pathology' *British Medical Journal 2*, pp. 931–7, 985–90.

Bateman, Frederic (1877), *Darwinism tested by language* (London: Rivingtons).

Benveniste, E. (1971), 'Remarks on the function of language in Freudian theory' in: *Problems in General Linguistics*, trans. Mary Elizabeth Meck (University of Miami Press) pp. 65–75.

Bérillon and Farez, P. (1902), *Comptes rendus du deuxième congrès international de l'hypnotisme expérimental et thérapeutique, tenu à Paris du 12 au 18 Août 1902* (Paris: Vigot Frères).

Bergson, Henri (1896), *Matter and memory*, translated by Nancy Margaret Paul and W. Scott Palmer (London: George Allen & Co. Ltd., 1912).

Bernfeld, Siegfried (1944), 'Freud's earliest theories and the school of Helmholtz' *Psychoanalytic Quarterly 13*, pp. 341–62.

—— (1949), 'Freud's scientific beginnings' *American Imago 6*, pp. 165–96.

—— (1951), 'Sigmund Freud, M. D., 1882–1885' *Int. J. Psa 32*, pp. 204–17.

Bernfeld, Suzanne (1951), 'Freud and archaeology' *American Imago 8*, pp. 107–28.

Bion, W. R. (1967), *Second thoughts; selected papers on psychoanalysis* (London).

Bloom, Leon (1975), 'Ellenberger on Freud's *Aphasia*: Fact and method in the history of science' *Psychoanalytic Review 62*, pp. 615–637.

Blumenthal, Arthur L. (1970), *Language and Psychology. Historical Aspects of Psycho-linguistics* (New York: John Wiley).

Boas, George (1950), *The Hieroglyphics of Horapollo* (New York).

Boden, Margaret A. (1974), 'Freudian mechanisms of defence: a programming perspective' in: Wollheim, Richard (ed.), *Freud. A Collection of Critical Essays* (New York: Doubleday Anchor) pp. 242–70.

Bopp, Franz (1816), *Über das Conjugationssystem der Sanskritsprache*, Hrsg. von K. J. Windischmann, Frankfurt a. M.

Bouchard, M. C. (1865), [On the case of Adèle Anselin] *Gazette medicale de Paris*, no. 31, 5 August p. 489.

Bourneville and Regnard (1876–7), *Iconographie photographique de la Salpêtrière* (Paris: Delahaye).

Brautigam, Walter (1960), 'L'importance des concepts neurologiques de Freud pour la théorie psychanalytique' *L'Evolution psychiatrique 25*, pp. 63–76.

Broca, Paul (1861), 'Perte de la parole. Ramollissement chronique et destruction partielle du lobe antérieur gauche du cerveau' *Bulletin de la Société d'Anthropologie 2* pp. 235–8, trans. by Robert H. Wilkins in 'Neuro-surgical Classic XIX' *Journal of Neurosurgery 21* (1964) pp. 424–31.

Brücke, Ernst (1856), *Grundzüge der Physiologie und Systematik der Sprachleute für Linguisten und Taubstummenlehrer* (Vienna).

Brun, Rudolf (1936), 'Sigmund Freud's Leistungen auf dem Gebiet der organischen Neurologie' *Schweizer Archiv für Neurologie und Psychiatrie 37*, pp. 191–210.

Bunsen, Baron (1854), *Outline of the Philosophy of Universal History applied to Language and Religion*, 2 vols (London).

—— (1868), *God in History*, 3 vols (London: 1868).

Burke, Kenneth (1937), *Attitudes towards history* (New York: The New Republic).

—— (1939–40), 'Freud and the analysis of poetry' *American Journal of Sociology 45*, pp. 391–417.

Burrow, John (1966), *Evolution and society, a study in Victorian social theory* (Cambridge: C.U.P.).

—— (1967), 'The uses of philology in Victorian England' in: R. Robson (ed.), *Ideas and institutions of Victorian Britain* (London) pp. 180–204.

Buttmann, Philip (1824), *Greek Grammar*, trans. from the German (London: Richard Priestley).

Cassirer, Ernst (1950), *The problem of knowledge. Philosophy, science and history since Hegel* (New Haven: Yale University Press).

—— (1953–7), *The philosophy of symbolic forms*, 3 vols, trans. Ralph Manheim (New Haven: Yale University Press).

Castel, Robert (1973), *Le psychanalysme. L'ordre psychanalytique et le pouvoir* (Paris: François Maspero).

—— (1976) *L'ordre psychiatrique* (Paris: Les Editions de Minuit).

Charcot, Jean-Martin (1886–90), *Oeuvres complètes*, 9 vols, (Paris).

—— (1882), 'Sur les divers états nerveux déterminés par l'hypnotisation chez les hystériques' *Comptes rendus hebd. Acad. Sc. 44*, pp. 403–5.

—— (1885a), 'De l'isolement dans le traitment de l'hystérie' *Progrès médical 13*, pp. 161–4.

—— (1885b), 'Sur deux cas de monoplegie brachiale hystérique, de cause traumatique, chez l'homme' *Progrés mèdical, 13*, pp. 227–9.

Chaudhuri, Nirad C. (1974), *Scholar extraordinary: The Life of Professor, the Rt. Hon. Friedrich Max Müller, P. C.* (London: Chatto & Windus).

Cohen, H. (1865/69), 'Mythologische Vorstellungen von Gott und Seele' *Zeitschrift für Völkerpsychologie und Sprachwissenschaft 5* pp. 394–434; *6* (1869) pp. 113–31.

Colby, K. M. (1955), *Energy and structure in psychoanalysis* (New York: Ronald Press).

—— (1963) 'Computer simulation of a neurotic process' in: S. Tomkins and Samuel Messick (eds.), *Computer simulation of personality: frontier of psychological theory* (New York: John Wiley) pp. 165–80.

—— (1975) *Artificial paranoia: a computer simulation of paranoid processes*, General Psychology Series, 49 (New York: Pergamon Press).

Collingwood, R. G. (1946), *The idea of history* (London).

Corraze, J. (1973) (ed.), *Schéma corporel et image du corps* (Toulouse: Edouard Privat).

Cranefield, Paul (1957), 'The organic physics of 1847 and the biophysics of today' *J. Hist. Med. 12*, pp. 407–23.

—— (1958) 'Joseph Breuer's evaluation of his contribution to psychoanalysis' *Int. J. Psa. 39*, pp. 319–22.

—— (1972) 'Breuer, Josef' *Dictionary of Scientific Biography*, vol. II, pp. 445–50.

Critchley, Macdonald (1958), 'A critical survey as to our conceptions of the origins of language' in: Poynter, F. N. L. (ed.), *The history and philosophy of knowledge of the brain and its functions* (Oxford: Blackwell) pp. 45–72.

—— (1960), 'The evolution of man's capacity for language' in: Tax, Sol (ed.), *Evolution After Darwin*, vol. II, pp. 289–308.

Curtius, Georg (1886), *Principles of Greek etymology*, 5th edition trans. Augustus S. Wilkins and Edwin B. England, 2 vols, (London).

H. D. (1971), *Tribute to Freud* (Oxford: Carcanet Press).

Dalbiez, Roland (1936), *Psychoanalytic method and the doctrine of Freud*, 2 vols (London: Longmans, 1941).

Darwin, Charles (1872), *The expression of the emotions in man and animals* (London).

Decker, Hannah, S. (1971), 'The medical reception of psychoanalysis in Germany' *Bull. Hist. Med. 45* pp. 461–81.

—— (1975) 'The Interpretation of Dreams: Early reception by the educated German public' *Journal for the History of the Behavioral Sciences 11*, pp. 129–41.

Dejerine, J. (1906), 'L'aphasie sensorielle et l'aphasie motrice' *Presse médicale 14*, pp. 437–9, 453–7.

Deleuze, Gilles and Guattari, Félix (1975), *L'anti-oedipe*, nouvelle édition augmentée (Paris: Les Editions de Minuit).

Derrida, Jacques (1966), 'Freud et la scène de l'écriture' in: Derrida's *L'écriture et la différence* (Paris: Seuil 1967) pp. 293–340, trans. in *Yale French Studies 48* (1972) pp. 74–117.

—— (1967), 'La structure, le signe et le jeu dans le discours des sciences humaines' in: *L'écriture et la différence* (Paris: Seuil) pp. 409–28.

—— (1971) 'Signature Event Context' *Glyph 1* (1977) pp. 172–97.

—— (1977) 'Limited Inc abc . . .' *Glyph 2*, pp. 162–254.

Descombes, Vincent (1977), *L'inconscient malgré lui* (Paris: Editions de Minuit).

Dewey, John (1946), 'Pierce's theory of linguistic signs, thought, and meaning' *J. Phil. 43*, pp. 85–95.

Dorer, M. (1932), *Die Historische Grundlagen der Psychoanalyse* (Leipzig).

Edelson, Marshall (1975), *Language and interpretation in psychoanalysis* (New Haven and London: Yale University Press).

Ellenberger, Henri F. (1970), *The discovery of the unconscious. The history and evolution of dynamic psychiatry* (London: Allen Lane, Penguin Books).

Engelhardt, H. Tristram Jr. (1975), 'John Hughlings Jackson and the mind–body relation' *Bull. Hist. Med. 49*, pp. 137–51.

Entralgo, Pedro Laín (1969), *The doctor and patient*, trans. by F. Partridge (London: World University Library).

Erikson, Erik H. (1954), 'The dream specimen of psychoanalysis' *J. Am. Psa. Assoc. 2*, pp. 5–56.

Ferenczi, Sandor, *First contributions to psychoanalysis* (1916), trans. Ernest Jones (London: Hogarth Press, 1952). (Abbreviated as *C*.)

——, *Further contributions to psychoanalysis* (1926) (London: Hogarth Press, 1950). (Abbreviated as *FC*.)

——, *Final contributions to psychoanalysis*, edited by Michael Balint, trans. by E. Mosbacher and others (London: Hogarth Press, 1955). (Abbreviated as *Fin*.)

——, (1949), 'Ten letters to Freud' *Int. J. Psa., 30*, pp. 243–50.

(1908) 'Analytical interpretation and treatment of psychosexual impotence in men', *C.*, pp. 11–34.

(1909a) 'Introjection and transference', *C.*, pp. 35–94.

(1909b) 'On the interpretation of tunes that come into one's head', *Fin.*, pp. 175–6.

(1909/39) 'More about homosexuality', *Fin.*, pp. 168–74.

(1911a) 'On obscene words', *C.*, pp. 132–53.

(1911b) 'The psychoanalysis of wit and the comical', *FC.*, pp. 332–44.

(1913) 'Stages in the development of the sense of reality' *C.*, pp. 213–39.

(1919) 'The phenomena of hysterical materialization. Thoughts on the conception of hysterical conversion and symbolism' *FC.*, pp. 89–104.

(1924) *Thalassa: towards a theory of genitality*, trans. Henry Alden Bunker, (New York Psychoanalytic Quarterly: 1938).

(1926a) 'To Sigmund Freud on his seventieth birthday', *Fin.*, pp. 11–17.

(1926b) 'Gulliver phantasies' *Fin.*, pp. 41–60.

(1927a) 'The adaptation of the family to the child', *Fin.*, pp. 61–76.

(1927b) 'The problem of termination of the analysis', *Fin.*, pp. 77–86.

(1933) 'Confusion of tongues between adults and the child', *Fin.*, pp. 156–67.

Flourens, Pierre (1824), *Recherches expérimentales sur les propriétés et les fonctions du système nerveux dans les animaux vertébrés* (Paris).

Flügel, J. C. (1925), 'Some unconscious factors in the international language movement with special reference to Esperanto' *Int. J. Psa. 6*, pp. 171–208.

(1980), 'Philology and the phallus' Forrester, John, in: MacCabe, Colin (ed.), *The talking cure* (London: Macmillan).

——, 'Michael Foucault and the history of psychoanalysis' *History of Science*, in the press.

Foucault, Michel (1954), 'Introduction' to Binswanger, Ludwig, *Le rêve et l'existence*, translated by Jacqueline Verdeaux (Paris: Desclée de Brouwer).

(1961), *Madness and civilization. A history of insanity in the Age of Reason*, trans. by Richard Howard (London: Tavistock, 1967).

(1963/73), *The birth of the clinic*, trans. A. M. Sheridan Smith (London: Tavistock, 1973).

(1966/70), *The order of things* (London: Tavistock, 1970).

(1969/72), *The archaeology of knowledge*, trans. A. M. Sheridan Smith (London: Tavistock, 1972).

(1975/77), *Discipline and punish*, trans. Alan Sheridan (London: Allen Lane, Penguin Books, 1977).

(1976a), *La volonté de savoir* (Paris: Editions Gallimard).

(1976b), *et al.*, 'Le jeu de Michel Foucault', *Ornicar? 10*, pp. 62–93.

Frazer, James (1911–14), *The Golden Bough*, 3rd ed. (London: Macmillan).

Freud, Anna (1936), *The ego and the mechanisms of defence* (London: Hogarth Press, 1968).

Galdston, Iago (1956), 'Freud and romantic medicine', *Bull. Hist. Med. 30*, pp. 499–507.

Gall, François Joseph (1835), *On the functions of the Brain and of Each of Its Parts: with Observations on the Possibility of Determining the Instincts, Propensities, and Talents, or the Moral and Intellectual Dispositions of Man and Animals, by the Configuration of the Brain and Head*, 6 vols., trans. Winslow Lewis, Jr. (Boston: Marsh, Capen and Lyon).

Gardiner, Muriel (1973) (ed.), *The Wolf-Man and Sigmund Freud* (Harmondsworth: Penguin Books).

Gasman, Daniel (1971), *The scientific origins of National Socialism; social Darwinism in Ernst Haeckel and the German Monist League* (London).

Girard, Claude (1972), *Ernest Jones, sa vie, son œuvre* (Paris: Payot).

Glymour, Clark (1974), 'Freud, Kepler and the clinical evidence' in: Wollheim, Richard (ed.) *Freud. A Collection of critical essays* (New York: Doubleday Anchor) pp. 285–304.

Goeppert, Sebastian and Goeppert, Herma C. (1973), *Sprache und Psychoanalyse* (Reinbek bei Hamburg: Rowohlt Taschenbuch Verlag).

Goldstein, Kurt (1910), 'Über Aphasie' *Med. Klin. Beih. 6*, pp. 1–32.

Gomme, George Lawrence (1892), *Ethnology in folklore* (London).

(1908), *Folklore as an historical science* (London).

Gowers, Sir W. R. (1903), *Diseases of the nervous system*, 2 vols, 2nd ed., (Philadelphia: Blakiston's).

Granoff, Wladimir (1975), *Filiations. L'avenir du complexe d'Oedipe* (Paris: Les Editions de Minuit).

—— (1976), *La pensée et le féminin* (Paris: Les Editions de Minuit).

Granville, J. Mortimer (1878–9), 'Re-education of the adult brain', *Brain 2* pp. 317–22.

Green, André (1967), 'La diachronie et le Freudisme', *Critique 238* (March) pp. 359–85.

(1963), 'La psychanalyse devant l'opposition de l'histoire et de la structure', *Critique 194* (July) pp. 649–662.

(1973), *Le discours vivant. La conception psychanalytique de l'affect* (Paris: P.U.F.).

Greenblatt, Samuel H. (1965), 'The major influences on the early life and work of John Hughlings Jackson' *Bull. Hist. Med. 39*, pp. 346–76.

(1970), 'Hughlings Jackson's first encounter with the work of Paul Broca' *Bull. Hist. Med. 44*, p. 558.

Grinstein, Alexander (1968), *On Sigmund Freud's dreams* (Detroit).

Guérard, Albert Léon (1922), *A short history of the international language movement* (London).

Guillain, Georges (1959), *J -M. Charcot, 1825–1893. His life, his work*, ed. and trans. by Pearce Bailey (London: Pitman Medical Publishing Co).

Habermas, Jürgen (1968), *Knowledge and human interests*, trans. Jeremy J. Shapiro (London: Heinemann, 1972).

Head, Henry (1926), *Aphasia and kindred disorders of speech*, 2 vols (Cambridge University Press).

Hegel, G. W. F. (1910), *The phenomenology of mind*, trans. J. J. B. Baillie, 2 vols (London).

Henson, Hilary (1971), 'Early British anthropologists and language' in: Ardener, E. (ed.), *Social anthropology and language* (London: Tavistock, 1971) pp. 3–32.

—— (1974), *British social anthropologists and language: a history of separate development* (Oxford: Clarendon Press).

Herbart, J. F. (1891), *A textbook of psychology*, trans. M. Smith (New York: Appleton).

Herder, J. C. (1972), *Abhandlung über den Ürsprung der Sprache* (Stuttgart: Reclam (Universal-Bibliothek Nr. 8729/30), 1966).

Hettleman, Howard (1974), *Freud: the Project for a Scientific Psychology*, unpublished manuscript, Brandeis.

Hobbes, Thomas (1839), *The English Works of Thomas Hobbes*, ed. Sir William Molesworth, 11 vols.

Hoff, H. and Seitelberger, F. (1952), 'The history of the neurological school of Vienna', *J. Nerv. Ment. Dis. 116*, pp. 495–505.

Horapollo Nilous (1840), *The Hieroglyphics*, ed. and trans. Alexander Turner Cory (London: William Pickering).

Humboldt, C. W. von (1882), *Introduction to the study of language*, Bibliothek Indogermanischer Grammatiker, Bd. iv.

—— (1836), *Über die Verschiedenheit des menschlichen Sprachbaues und ihren Einfluss auf die geistige Entwicklung des Menschengeschlècts* (Berlin: F. Dümmler).

Huxley, T. H. (1874), 'On the hypothesis that animals are automata and its history', Address to the British Association at Belfast, 1874, reprinted in: *Collected essays*, vol. II, ch. 5 (London, 1893).

Iggers, George (1968), *The German conception of history*, (Middletown, Conn.).

Inman, Thomas (1868), *Ancient faiths embodied in ancient names, or an attempt to trace the religious beliefs, sacred rites, and holy emblems of certain nations, by an interpretation of the names given to children by priestly authority, or assumed by prophets, kings, and hierarchs*, London.

—— (1869), *Ancient pagan and modern Christian symbolism exposed and explained* (London).

Isakower, Otto (1939), 'On the exceptional position of the auditory sphere' *Int. J. Psa. 20*, pp. 340–8.

Jackson, J. H. (1931), *Selected writings of John Hughlings Jackson*, 2 vols, (London). (SW)

—— (1925) *Neurological fragments* (Oxford Medical Publications).

—— (1878–80) 'On affections of speech from disease of the brain', SW II pp. 155–83, 184–204.

Jakobson, Roman (1941), *Child language, aphasia and phonological universals* (The Hague, Paris: Mouton, 1968).

——(1971), *Studies on child language and aphasia*, Janua Linguarum, Ser. minor 114 (The Hague: Mouton).

——(1956), and Halle, M., *Fundamentals of language*, Janua Linguarum I ('s-Gravenage: Mouton).

James, William (1890), *The Principles of Psychology* (New York: Dover, 1950).

Janet, Pierre (1885), 'J.-M. Charcot. Son œuvre psychologique' *Revue philosophique 29*, pp. 569–604.

—— (1889), *L'automatisme psychologique* (Paris: Alcan).

Janik, A. and Toulmin, S., (1973), *Wittgenstein's Vienna* (London).

Jankowsky, Kurt Robert (1972), *The neogrammarians; a re-evaluation of their place in the development of linguistic science*, Janua Linguarum. Ser. minor, 116 (The Hague: Mouton).

Johnson, Dr Samuel (1818), *Dictionary of the English Language, with additions by H. J. Todd* (London).

Johnson, William Murray (1972), *The Austrian mind; an intellectual and social history, 1848–1938* (Berkeley, California).

Jolly, Frederick (1878), 'Hysteria', *Ziemssen's Cyclopaedia of the Practice of Medicine*, vol. 14, pp. 473–577.

Jones, Ernest, *Papers on psychoanalysis*, 2nd ed. (London: Baillière, Tindall and Cox, 1918).

——, *Papers on psychoanalysis*, 5th ed. (London: Baillière, Tindall and Cox, 1948).

(1907) 'La vraie aphasie tactile' *Revue Neurologique 15*, pp. 3–7.

(1908) 'Rationalisation in everyday life', in *Papers*, 2nd ed., pp. 8–15.

(1909) 'The difference between the sexes in the development of speech', *Brit. J. Children's Diseases 6*, pp. 413–6.

(1913) 'The Mare and the Mara: a psychoanalytical contribution to etymology', in *On the nightmare* (London: Hogarth Press, 1931) pp. 241–340.

(1916) 'The theory of symbolism' in *Papers*, 2nd ed., pp. 129–86.

(1920) 'A linguistic factor in English characterology', *Int. J. Psa. 1*, pp. 256–61.

(1923) 'Review of Jespersen's *Language*', *Int. J. Psa. 4*, pp. 354–5.

(1927) 'Early development of female sexuality', in *Papers*, 5th ed., pp. 438–51.

(1929) 'Fear, guilt and hate', in *Papers*, 5th ed., pp. 304–19.

Jones I/II/III, *Sigmund Freud, Life and Work* (London: Hogarth Press, 1953–7).

(1959) *Free associations: memories of a psycho-analyst* (London: Hogarth Press).

Jung, Carl Gustav, *The collected works of C. G. Jung* (19 vols), ed. Sir Herbert Read, Michael Fordham, Gerhard Adler, trans. R. F. C. Hull, (London: Routledge & Kegan Paul, 1944–78).

(1907) *The psychology of dementia praecox* CW III 1–151.

(1908) 'The Freudian theory of hysteria' CW IV 10–24.

(1909) 'The significance of the father in the destiny of the individual' CW IV 301–23.

(1911/12/15) *Psychology of the unconscious. A study of the transformations and symbols of the libido. A contribution to the history of the evolution of thought* (London: Kegan Paul, Trench, Trubner & Co., n.d. [1915]. (Also in CW V.)

(1912) 'The theory of psychoanalysis' CW IV 85–226.

(1931) 'Basic postulates of analytic psychology, CW VIII 338–57.

(1934/54) 'Archetypes of the collective unconscious' CW IX Part I 3–41.

(1938/54) 'Psychological aspects of the mother archetype' CW IX Part I 75–110.

(1956) 'Recent thoughts on schizophrenia' CW II 250–5.

(1958) 'Schizophrenia' CW III 258–63.

Kant, Immanuel (1781/87), *Critique of pure reason*, translated by Norman Kemp Smith (London: Macmillan, 1968).

Karpf, F. B. (1932), *American social psychology: its origins, development and European background* (New York).

King, R. D. (1969), *Historical linguistics and generative grammar* (Englewood Cliffs, New Jersey: Prentice Hall).

Klein, Melanie (1975), *The Writings of Melanie Klein*, under the general editorship of Roger Money-Kyrle in collaboration with Betty Joseph, Edna O'Shaughnessy and Hanna Segal, 4 vols (London: Hogarth Press).

Kleinpaul, Rudolph (1885), *Menschen und Völkernamen. Etymologische Streifzüge auf dem Gebiete der Eigennamen* (Leipzig: Reissner).

—— (1888), *Sprache ohne Worte; Idee einer allgemein Wissenschaft der Sprache*, Leipzig, 1888; reproduced with preface by T. A. Sebeok, Approaches to semiotics, *19* (The Hague: 1972).

—— (1893), *Das Leben der Sprache und ihre Weltstellung* (Leipzig: Friedrich).

—— (1898), *Die Lebendigen und die Toten in Volksglauben, Religion und Sage* (Leipzig: Göschen).

—— (1916), *Die deutschen Personennamen. Ihre Entstehung und Bedeutung* (Berlin: Neudruck).

Koerner, E. F. K. (1973), *Ferdinand de Saussure. Origin and development of his thought in Western studies of language. A contribution to the history of linguistics*, Schriften zur Linguistik, Band 7, (Vieweg).

König, Karl (1962), *Die Schicksale Sigmund Freuds und Josef Breuers*, (Stuttgart: Verl. Freies Geistesleben, Studien und Versuche, Band 3).

Kuhn, Adalbert (1859/86), *Die Herabkunft des Feuers und des Göttertranks. Ein Beitrag zur vergleichenden Mythologie* (Berlin: Dümmler, 1859) augmented and reprinted in Kuhn's *Mythologische Studien*, Band I (Gütarsloh: C. Bertelsmann, 1886).

Kussmaul, A. (1878), 'Disturbances of speech' *Ziemssen's Cyclopaedia of the Practice of Medicine*, vol. 14., (1878) pp. 581–875.

Lacan, Jacques (1966), *Écrits* (Paris: Seuil).

—— (1977), *Écrits, a selection*, trans. Alan Sheridan (London: Tavistock).

(1948) 'Aggressivity in psychoanalysis' E101–24/8–29.

(1956–7) 'Séminaire. La relation d'objet et les structures freudiennes' *Bulletin de Psychologie 10*, pp. 851–4. (Comptes rendus by J.-B. Pontalis).

(1957) 'The agency of the letter in the unconscious or reason since Freud' E 493–528/146–78.

(1959) 'A la mémoire d'Ernest Jones: Sur sa théorie du symbolisme' E697–717.

(1973) *Les quatre concepts fondamentaux de la psychanalyse. Séminaire XI* (Paris: Seuil).

(1975a) *Les écrits techniques de Freud. Séminaire I* (Paris: Seuil).

(1975b) *Encore. Séminaire XX* (Paris: Seuil).

(1978) *Le moi dans la théorie de Freud et dans la technique de la psychanalyse. Séminaire II* (Paris: Seuil).

Ladame, P. (1900), 'Aphasie motrice pure sans agraphie, aphémie pure' *XIIIe Congres Int. de méd., Paris, 1900*, section 7: Neurologie (Paris: Masson, s.d.,) pp. 29–53.

Laffal, Julius (1964), 'Freud's theory of language' *Psychoanalytic Quarterly 33*, pp. 157–75.

Lamoulen, Jacques (1966), *La médecine française et la psychanalyse de 1895 à 1926*, Thèse méd., Paris no. 309.

Lange, Frederick Albert (1865), *The history of materialism and criticism of its present importance*, translated by Ernest Chester Thomas, 3rd edition, with introduction by Bertrand Russell (London: Routledge & Kegan Paul, 1925).

Langer, Suzanne (1948), *Philosophy in a new key* (1942) (New York: Mentor, 1948).

Laplanche, Jean (1970), *Vie et mort en psychanalyse* (Paris: Flammarion).

Laplanche, Jean and Leclaire, Serge (1961), 'L'inconscient. Une étude psychanalytique' *Les temps modernes 183* Juillet 1961 pp. 81–129; translated by Patrick Coleman in *Yale French Studies 48*, 1972, pp. 118–75.

—— (1968), 'Fantasme originaire, fantasmes des origines, origine du fantasme' *Les temps modernes 19*, no. 215, 1964, trans. as 'Fantasy and the origins of sexuality' *Int. J. Psa. 49* (1968) pp. 1–18.

Laplanche, Jean and Pontalis, J.-B. (1973), *The language of psychoanalysis* (London: Hogarth Press).

Lebzeltern, Gustav (1973), 'Sigmund Freud und Theodor Meynert', *Wien. klin. Wschr. Jg. 85 H. 23*, pp. 417–22.

Leclaire, Serge (1966), 'Compter avec la psychanalyse' *Cahiers pour l'analyse 1* pp. 55–70.

—— (1967), 'A propos d'un fantasme de Freud: note sur la trangression' *L'inconscient 1*.

—— (1968), *Psychanalyser* (Paris: Seuil).

—— (1971), *Démasquer le reel*, (Paris: Seuil).

Lee, Dwight E. and Beck, Robert N. (1953–4), 'The meaning of historicism', *American Historical Review 59*, pp. 568–77.

Lehmann, Winfred P. (1967) (ed. and trans.), *A reader in nineteenth-century historical Indo-european linguistics* (Bloomington: Indiana University Press).

Lesky, Erna (1965), *Die Wiener Medizinische Schule im 19. Jahrhundert* (Graz-Köln: Verlag Hermann Böhlaus Nachf.).

Levin, Kenneth (1974), *Sigmund Freud's early studies of the neuroses, 1886–1905*, unpublished dissertation, Princeton University.

Litowitz, Bonnie E. and Litowitz, Norman S. (1977), 'The influence of linguistic theory on psychoanalysis: a critical, historical survey', *Int. Rev. Psa. 4*, pp. 419–48.

Lichtheim, L. (1885), 'On aphasia' *Brain 7*, pp. 433–484.

Lovejoy, Arthur O. (1936), *The great chain of being* (Cambridge, Mass.: Harvard University Press).

Macintyre, Alasdair C. (1958), *The unconscious. A conceptual analysis* (London: Routledge & Kegan Paul).

Maclagen, Eric (1923), 'Leonardo in the consulting room' *Burlington Magazine 42*, pp. 54–7.

Magnan, V. (1878–9), 'On simple aphasia, and aphasia with incoherence', *Brain 2*, pp. 112–23.

—— (1885), 'Des anomalies, des aberrations et des perversions sexuelles' *Progrès médical 13*, pp. 84–6.

Mahony, Patrick J. (1974), 'Freud in the light of classical rhetoric' *Journal for the History of the Behavioral Sciences 10*, pp. 413–25.

Major, René (1974), 'The revolution of hysteria' *Int. J. Psa. 55*, pp. 385–95.

(1977) *Rêver l'autre* (Paris: Aubier Montaigne).

Malinowski, B. (1930), 'The problem of meaning in primitive languages', Supplement I to Ogden C. K. and Richards. I. A., *The meaning of meaning*, 3rd rev. ed. (New York: Harcourt, Brace, 1930).

Mandelbaum, Maurice (1938), *The problem of historical knowledge; an answer to relativism* (New York).

(1971), *History, man and reason. A study in nineteenth century thought* (Baltimore: The Johns Hopkins Press).

Mannoni, Octave (1968), *Freud: the theory of the unconscious*, trans. Renauld Bruce (London: Pantheon, 1971).

Marcus, S. (1974), 'Freud und Dora. Roman, Geschichte, Krankengeschichte', *Psyche 28* pp. 32–79.

Marshall, John C. (1974), 'Freud's psychology of language', in: Wollheim, Richard (ed.), *Freud. A collection of critical essays* (New York: Doubleday Anchor, 1974) pp. 349–65.

Marx, Otto M. (1966), 'Aphasia studies and language theory in the nineteenth century', *Bull. Hist. Med. 40* pp. 328–49.

—— (1967a), 'Freud and Aphasia', *Am. J. Psychiatry 124*, pp. 815–25.

—— (1967b), 'The history of the biological base of language', in Lenneberg, Eric H., *Biological foundations of language* (New York: John Wiley) pp. 443–69.

—— (1970), 'Nineteenth century medical psychology: theoretical problems in the work of Griesinger, Meynert, and Wernicke', *Isis 61* pp. 355–70.

McGrath, William J. (1967), 'Student radicalism in Vienna' *J. contemp. history 2* pp. 183–201.

—— (1974), 'Freud as Hannibal: the politics of the brother band' *Cent. Europ. Hist. 7*, pp. 31–57.

Mead, George Herbert (1904), 'The relations of psychology and philology' *Psychological Bulletin 1* pp. 375–91.

Meige, Henry (1925), *Charcot artiste* (Paris: Masson).

Meinecke, Friedrich (1957/72), *Historismus*, trans. by J. E. Anderson as *Historism: the rise of a new historical outlook* (London: 1972).

Mendel, Kurt (1910), 'Review of the Freudian standpoint' *Neurologisches Centralblatt 29*, trans. and reprinted in Jung, CW, IV 76–7.

Merz, John Theodor (1904–12), *A history of European thought in the nineteenth century*, 4 vols (New York: Dover, 1965).

Meyer, Adolf (1904), 'A few trends in modern psychiatry' *Psychological Bulletin 1* pp. 217–40.

Meyer, Richard M. (1910), 'Bedeutungssysteme' *Zeitschrift für Vergleichende Sprachforschung auf dem Gebiete der indogermanischen Sprachen 43*, pp. 352–68.

Meynert, T. (1871), 'Vom Gehirne d. Saügeth.' in: Stricker's *Handbuch der Lehre von den Geweben* (Leipzig) pp. 694ff.

—— (1885), *Psychiatrie*, trans. by B. Sachs as *Psychiatry. A clinical treatise on diseases of the fore-brain based upon a study of its structure, function and nutrition* (New York and London: Putnam's, 1885), facsimile with new introduction by Stanley W. Jackson (New York: Hafner, 1968).

Miller, Robert Lee (1968), *The linguistic relativity principle and Humboldtian ethno-linguistics: a history and appraisal* (The Hague: Mouton).

Miraillé (1896), *L'aphasie sensorielle*, Thèse méd., (Paris).

Mitchell, Juliet (1974), *Psychoanalysis and feminism* (London: Allen Lane).

Mitchell, William H. (1973), *The implicit prospective dimension of the symbol in the early works of Freud, 1893–1900*, unpublished dissertation, Duquesne University (1973); *Diss. Abs.*, vol. 34, no. 9, (March 1974) pp. 6045–6–A.

Mortimer, J. (1878–9), 'Re-education and the adult brain' *Brain 2*, p. 319.

Moser, U., Zeppelin, I. von and Schneider, W. (1969), 'Computer simulation of a model of neurotic defence processes' *Int. J. Psa. 50*, pp. 53–64.

Moutier, François (1908), *L'aphasie de Broca* (Paris: G. Steinheil).

Müller, F. Max (1856) 'Comparative mythology' in: *Selected essays*, vol. I (London: Longman, 1881) pp. 299–424.

—— (1864), *Lectures on the science of language* (London).

—— (1871), 'On the philosophy of mythology' in: *Selected essays*, vol. I (London: Longman, 1881) pp. 577–623.

—— (1873), 'Mr. Darwin's philosophy of language' *Fraser's Magazine* (May, June, July).

—— (1875), *Chips from a German workshop*, 4 vols (London: Longman, Green & Co.).

—— (1888a), *Biographies of words and the home of the Aryas* (London: Longman).

—— (1888b), *Three introductory lectures on the science of thought* (London: Longman).

—— (1901), *My autobiography. A fragment* (London).

—— (1902), *Life and letters of Friedrich Max Müller*, Müller (ed.), 2 vols (London).

Nietzsche, Friedrich (1889), *Götzendammerung, oder wie man mit dem Hammer philosophiert*.

Nunberg, H. and Federn, E. (1962–76) (eds.), *Minutes of the Vienna Psychoanalytic Society*, 4 vols (New York: International Universities Press).

Ogden, C. K. and Richards, I. A. (1923), *The meaning of meaning*, 3rd rev. edn. (New York: Harcourt, Brace, 1930).

Ombredane, André-Georges-Lucien (1951), *L'aphasie et l'elaboration de la pensée explicite* (Paris: P.U.F.).

Oswald, J. H. (1866), *Das grammatische Geschlect und seine sprachliche Deutung. Eine akademische Gelegenheitsschrift* (Berlin: Baderborn).

Owen, A. R. G. (1971), *Hysteria, hypnosis and healing. The work of J.-M. Charcot* (London: Dennis Dobson).

Pedersen, Holgar (1931), *Linguistic science in the nineteenth century, methods and results*, authorized translation from the Danish by J. W. Spargo (Cambridge, Mass.).

Pick, Arnold (1894), 'Zur Symptomatologie der functionnellen Aphasien nebs Bemerkungen zur Migraine opthalmique' *Berlin klin. Wft. 31*, (19 March).

—— (1900), 'De l'importance du centre auditif du langage comme organ d'arrêt du langage' *XIIIᵉ Congrès Int. de Médecine, Paris, 1900*, section 7: Neurologie (Paris: Masson, s.d.) pp. 16–29.

(1913) *Die agrammatischen Sprachstörungen* (Berlin).

Pierce, C. S. (1932), 'The icon, index and symbol' in: *Collected papers*, vol. II (Cambridge, Mass.).

—— (1897), 'Logic as semiotic: the theory of signs' in: *Philosophical Writings*, ed. by J. Buchler (New York: Dover, 1955).

Pontalis, J.-B. (1965), *Après Freud* (Paris: René Julliard).

—— (1974), 'Freud in Paris' *Int. J. Psa. 55*, pp. 455–8.

Porset, Charles (1977), 'L'idée et la racine' *Revue des sciences humaines* (*Lille III*) *166*, pp. 185–204.

Pribram, Karl H. (1962), 'The neuropsychology of Sigmund Freud' in: Bachrach, Arthur J. (ed.) *Experimental foundations of clinical psychology* (New York: Basic) pp. 442–468.

—— (1969), 'The foundation of psychoanalytic theory: Freud's neuropsychological model' in Pribram, K. H. (ed.), *Adaptation*, (Harmondsworth: Penguin) pp. 395–432.

Pribram Karl, H. and Gill, Merton (1976), *Freud's Project reassessed* (London: Hutchinson).

Prichard, J. C. (1833), *Remarks on the application of philological and physical researches to the history of the human species*, Report of the British Association, p. 530ff.

Putschke, Wolfgang (1969), 'Zur forschungsgeschichtlichen Stellung der junggrammatischen Schule' *Zeitschrift für Dialektologie und Linguistik 1*, 1969, pp. 19–48.

Quine, Willard Van Orman (1953), *From a logical point of view* (New York: Harper & Row, 1963).

Raboul, J. (1959), 'Une illusion mnémique de Freud' *La Psychanalyse 5* pp. 217–24.

Rank, Otto (1909/64), *The myth of the birth of the hero and other writings*, Philip Freund (ed.) (New York: Vintage).

Rank, Otto and Sachs, Hans (1913), 'Die Bedeutung der Psychoanalyse für die Geisteswissenschaften', trans. in *Psychoanalysis as an art and a science, a symposium*, by Rank, Sachs *et al.* (Detroit: Wayne University Press, 1968).

Rapaport, David (1951), *Organization and pathology of thought* (New York: Columbia University Press).

Rapaport, David and Gill, Merton M. (1959), 'The points of view and assumptions of metapsychology' *Int. J. Psa. 40*, pp. 153–62.

Raumer, Rudolf von (1856), 'Die sprachgeschichtliche Umwandlung und die naturgeschichtliche Bestimmung der Laute' *Zeitschrift für die Österreichischen Gymnasien 5*, pp. 353–73, partially translated in Lehmann, *op. cit.*

Regnard, Paul (1888), 'Review of Müller's *Biographies of words . . .*' *Revue philosophique 26*, pp. 76–9.

Reynolds, Russell (1869), 'Remarks on paralysis and other disorders of motion and sensation dependent on Idea', read to the medical section at the annual meeting of the British Medical Association (Leeds, July 1869) *Brit. Med. J. 2* pp. 483–5.

Ribot, Theodule (1881), *Les maladies de la mémoire* (Paris: Baillière).
—— (1885), *La psychologie allemande contemporaine*, 2nd edn. (Paris).

Ricoeur, Paul (1970), *Freud and Philosophy: an essay on interpretation*, trans. by Denis Savage (New Haven and London: Yale University Press).

Rieff, Philip, *Freud, the mind of the moralist* (London: Victor Gollancz, 1960).

Riese, Walter (1947), 'The early history of aphasia' *Bull. Hist. Med. 21* pp. 322–34.

—— (1954), 'Hughlings Jackson's doctrine of consciousness' *Journal of Nervous and Mental Disease 120*, pp. 330ff.

—— (1958a), 'The pre-Freudian origins of psychoanalysis' in: Masserman, J. H. (ed.), *Science and Psychoanalysis 1* (New York, 1958) pp. 145ff.

—— (1958b), 'Freudian concepts of brain function and brain disease' *J. Nerv. and Ment. Disease 127*, pp. 287–307.

—— and Gooddy, W. (1955), 'An original clinical record of Hughlings Jackson. With an interpretation' *Bull. Hist. Med. 29* pp. 230–8.

—— and Hoff, Ebbel C. (1951), 'A history of the doctrine of cerebral localization' *Journal of the History of Medicine and Allied Sciences 5* (1950) pp. 50–71; 6 (1951) pp. 439–70.

Riley, Denise, *Marxism for infants* (Cambridge: Street Editions, 1977).

Ringer, Fritz (1969), *The decline of the German mandarins: the German academic community from 1890 to 1933* (Cambridge, Mass.: Harvard University Press).

Rivière, Jacques (1924), 'The three main theses of psychoanalysis' in: Cioffi, F. (ed.), *Freud* (London, 1973) pp. 25–41.

Roazen, Paul (1973), *Brother animal. The story of Freud and Tausk* (Harmondsworth: Penguin).

—— (1976), *Freud and his followers* (London: Allen Lane).

Robins, R. H. (1967), *A short history of linguistics* (London: Longman).

Rohner, Ludwig (1966), *Der deutsche Essay: Materialen zur Geschichte und Ästhetik einer literarischen Gattung* (Neuwied).

Rosen, George (1972), 'Freud and medicine in Vienna. Some scientific and medical sources of his thought' *Psychological medicine 2*, pp. 332–44.

Rosenfeld, E. M. (1956), 'Dreams and vision. Some remarks on Freud's Egyptian bird dream' *Int. J. Psa. 37*, pp. 97–105.

Rosenzweig, Saul (1968), 'William James and the stream of thought' in:

Wolman, Benjamin B. (ed.), *Historical roots of contemporary psychology* (New York: Harper & Row) pp. 163–76.

Ross, James (1887), *On aphasia* (London: J & A Churchill).

Rothschuh, K. E. (1973), *Geschichte der Physiologie* (Berlin: Springer-Verlag), 1953, trans. and ed. Guenter B. Risse (Huntington, New York: Robert E. Krieger).

Roustang, François (1976), *Un destin si funeste* (Paris: Editions de Minuit).

Safouan, Moustapha (1968), 'De la structure en psychanalyse. Contribution à une théorie de manque' in: Ducrot, Oswald, *et al.*, *Qu'est-ce que le structuralisme?* (Paris: Seuil) pp. 239–98.

—— (1974), *Etudes sur l'Oedipe* (Paris: Seuil).

Saussure, Ferdinand de (1916/59), *Cours de linguistique générale* (1916), edited by Charles Bally and Albert Sechehaye in collaboration with Albert Reidlinger, translated by Wade Baskin as *Course in General Linguistics* (1959) (London: Fontana/Collins, 1974).

Schafer, Roy (1976), *A new language for psychoanalysis* (New Haven and London: Yale U.P.).

Schapiro, Meyer (1956), 'Leonardo and Freud: an art-historical study' *Journal for the History of Ideas 17*, pp. 147–78.

Schilder, Paul Ferdinand (1935), *The image and appearance of the human body: studies in the constructive energies of the psyche* (Psyche Monographs, 4) (London, 1935).

Schleicher, August (1861–2), *Compendium der vergleichenden Grammatik der Indogermanischen Sprachen* (Weimar) trans. Herbert Bendall (London, 1877).

—— (1863), *Die Darwinische Theorie und die Sprachwissenschaft*, (Weimar) trans. A. V. W. Bikkers, as *Darwinism tested by the science of language* (London: John Camden Hatten, 1869).

Schönau, Walter (1968), *Sigmund Freuds Prosa* (Stuttgart: Metzlersche Verlagsbuchhandlung).

Schoenwald, Richard L. (1954), 'A turning point in Freud's life: "Zur Auffassung der Aphasien"' *Osiris 11*, pp. 119–26.

—— (1955), 'Recent studies of the younger Freud' *Bull. Hist. Med. 29*, pp. 261–8.

Schorske, Carl (1960–1), 'Politics and psyche in *fin de siècle* Vienna' *Am. Hist. Rev. 66* pp. 930–46.

—— (1966–7), 'The transformation of the garden: Ideal and society in Austrian literature' *Am. Hist. Rev. 72* pp. 1283–1320.

—— (1967), 'Politics in a new key: an Austrian triptych' *J. Mod. Hist. 39* pp. 343–86.

278   *Language and the Origins of Psychoanalysis*

—— (1973), 'Politics and patricide in Freud's *Interpretation of Dreams*' *Am. Hist. Rev. 78*, pp. 328–47.

Schreber, Daniel Paul (1903), *Memoirs of my nervous illness*, trans., ed., with an introduction, notes and discussion by Ida Macalpine and Richard A. Hunter (London: Dawson, 1955).

Schrenk-Notzing, Albert Freiherr von (1889), 'Un cas d'inversion sexuelle amélioré par la suggestion hypnotique' *1ᵉ Congrès Int. de Hyp. exp. et thérap.* (Paris: Doin) pp. 319–22.

Schur, Max (1966), 'Some additional "day residues" of the "specimen dream of psychoanalysis"' in: Loewenstein, R. M., Newman, L. M., Schur, M. and Solnit, A. J. (eds), *Psychoanalysis – A general psychology* (New York: International Universities Press) pp. 45–85.

—— (1972), *Freud living and dying* (London: Hogarth Press).

Searle, John R. (1977), 'Reiterating the differences: a reply to Derrida' *Glyph 1*, pp. 198–208.

Séglas, J. (1892), *Les troubles du langage chez les aliénés* (Paris: Rueff).

—— (1894), 'Des obsessions. Conférences sur les maladies mentales à l'hospice de la Salpêtrière (28 Jan. 1894)' *Journal de médecine et de chirurgie pratiques* (25 Fév.) pp. 3–23.

Silberer, Herbert (1909), 'Bericht über eine Methode, gewisse symbolische Halluzinations-Erscheinungen hervorzurufen und zu beobachten' *Jb. psychoan. psychopath. Forsch. 1* pp. 513–25, trans. in Rapaport (1951) pp. 195–207.

—— (1910), 'Phantasie und Mythos' *Jb. psychoan. psychopath. Forsch. 2* pp. 541–622.

—— (1912), 'Über die Symbolbildung' *Jb. psychoan. psychopath. Forsch. 3* pp. 661–723, translated in Rapaport (1951), pp. 208–233.

—— (1914/17), *Probleme der Mystik und ihrer Symbolik* (Leipzig and Vienna, 1914) translated by S. E. Jelliffe (1917) (New York: Dover, 1971) under the title *Problems of mysticism and its symbolism*.

Skinner, Q. R. D. (1969), 'Meaning and understanding in the history of ideas' *History and theory 8*, pp. 1–56.

Solomon, Robert C. (1974), 'Freud's neurological theory of mind' in: Wollheim, Richard (ed.) *Freud. A collection of critical essays* (New York: Doubleday Anchor) pp. 25–52.

Spector, Jack Jerome (1972), *The aesthetics of Freud; a study in psychoanalysis and art* (London: Allen Lane).

Sprague, C. E. (1888), *Handbook of Volapük* (London).

Steinbach, M. (1953), 'Die Übertragung, Geschichte und Entwicklung einer Theorie' *Psyche 7*, pp. 6–25.

Steiner, Andreas (1964), '"Das nervöse Zeitalter". Der Begriff der

Nervosität bei Laien und Ärzten in Deutschland und Österreich um 1900' *Zürcher med. geschichtliche Abhandlungen*, N.R. 21.

Steinthal, H. (1855), *Grammatik, Logik und Psychologie, Ihre Principien und ihr Verhältnisse zu einander* (Berlin: Fer. Dümmler).

—— (1862a), 'Die Prometheussage in ihrer ursprünglichen Gestalt' *Zeitschrift für Völkerpsychologie und Sprachwissenschaft 2* pp. 1–29.

—— (1862b), 'Die Sage von Simson' *Zeitschrift . . . 2*, pp. 129–79.

—— (1864), *Philologie, Geschichte und Psychologie*, 1.

—— (1868), 'Beurteilung' *Zeitschrift . . . 5*, p. 103.

—— (1871), *Einleitung in die Psychologie und Sprachwissenschaft* (Berlin).

Steinthal, H. and Lazarus, M. (1861), 'Einleitende Gedanken über Völkerpsychologie, als Einladung zu einer *Zeitschrift für . . .*', *Zeitschrift. . . . 1*, pp. 1–73.

Stekel, Wilhelm (1910), 'Vorschläge zur Sammelforschung auf dem Gebiete der Symbolik und der typischen Träume' *Jb. psychoan. psychopath. Forsch. 2*, pp. 740–1.

—— (1911/43), *Die Sprache des Träumes* (Wiesbaden) the second edition of which was translated by Eden and Ceder Paul, as *The interpretation of dreams* (New York: 1943).

—— (1923), 'The meaning of the dream symbolism' in: van Teslaar, J. S. (ed.), *An outline of psychoanalysis* (New York: Boni and Liveright).

—— (1922), *Twelve essays on sex and psychoanalysis* (New York: Critic and Guide).

—— (1956), *Autobiography*, ed. Emil A. Gutheil (New York: Liveright).

Stengel, E. A. (1954), 'A reevaluation of Freud's book *On aphasia*; its significance for psychoanalysis' *Int. J. Psa. 35*, pp. 85–9.

—— (1963), 'Hughlings Jackson's influence on psychiatry' *Brit. J. of Psychiatry 109*, pp. 348–55.

Stewart, Walter A., (1969), *Psychoanalysis: the first ten years, 1888–1898* (London: George Allen & Unwin).

Stocking, George (1968), 'From physics to ethnology' in: *Race, culture and evolution. Essays in the history of anthropology* (London: Collier-Macmillan) pp. 133–68.

Stucken, Eduard (1907), *Astralmythen. Religionsgeschichtliche Untersuchungen* (Leipzig).

Suppes, Patrick, and Warren, Hermine (1975), 'On the generation and classification of defence mechanisms' *Int. J. Psa. 56*, pp. 405–414.

Szasz, Thomas (1962), *The myth of mental illness* (St. Albans: Paladin, 1972).

Tausk, Victor (1914), 'Contributions to a psychoanalytic exposition of melancholia' *Minutes* IV 30 Dec. 1914, pp. 272ff.
—— (1918/19), 'On the origin of the "influencing machine" in schizophrenia' *Psychoanalytic Quarterly 2* (1933) pp. 519–56.
Taylor, Charles (1975), *Hegel* (Cambridge University Press).
Temkin, Owsei (1947), 'Gall and the phrenological movement', *Bull. Hist. Med. 21*, pp. 275–321.
Timpanaro, Sebastiano (1976), *The Freudian slip, Psychoanalysis and textual criticism*, trans. Kate Soper (London: NLB).
Tort, Michel (1966), 'De l'interprétation ou la machine herméneutique' *Les temps modernes 237*, (Feb. 1966) pp. 1461–93; *238* (Mar. 1966) pp. 1629–52.
Trim, J. L. M. (1974–5), *History of Linguistics,* unpublished lectures (Cambridge).
Trousseau, Armand (1868–72), *Lectures on clinical medicine*, and translated by Bazire and Cormack, 5 vols (London: New Sydenham Society).
Veith, Ilza (1965), *Hysteria. The history of a disease* (Chicago and London: University of Chicago Press).
Velikovsky, Immanuel (1934), 'Can a newly acquired language become the speech of the unconscious? Word-plays in the dreams of Hebrew-thinking persons' *Psychoanalytic Review 21* pp. 329–35.
Verburg, P. A. (1949–50), 'The background to the linguistic conceptions of Franz Bopp' *Lingua 2*, pp. 438–68.
de Vries, Jan (1961), *Forschungsgeschichte der Mythologie* (Fribürg-München: Karl Alber Verlag).
Walshe, F. M. R. (1961), 'Contributions of John Hughlings Jackson to neurology' *Archives of neurology 5*, pp. 119–31.
Walton, G. L. (1882/3), 'Deafness in hysterical hemianaesthesia' *Brain 5*, pp. 458–72.
Wernicke, C. (1874), *Der aphasische Symptomencomplex* (Breslau).
Whitney, William Dwight (1873), 'Steinthal and the psychological theory of language' in: *Oriental and linguistic studies* (New York).
Whorf, Benjamin Lee (1956), *Language, thought and reality. Selected writings*, foreword by Stuart Chase, edited and introduced by John B. Carroll (Cambridge, Mass.: MIT Press).
Wilden, Anthony (1968), *The language of the self: the function of language in psychoanalysis*, translation of Lacan's 'Fonction et champ de la parole et du langage en psychanalyse', with notes and commentary (Baltimore: The Johns Hopkins Press).

—— (1972), *System and structure, Essays in communication and exchange* (London: Tavistock).

Winckler, Hugo (1901), *Himmels- und Weltenbild der Babylonier als Grundlage der Weltanschauung und Mythologie aller Völker* (Leipzig: J. C. Hinrichs).

Winnicott, D. W. (1953), 'Transitional objects and transitional phenomena' *Int. J. Psa. 34*; partially reprinted in *Playing and reality* (Harmondsworth: Penguin, 1974) pp. 1–30.

Wittgenstein, Ludwig (1967), *Lectures and conversations on aesthetics, psychology and religious belief* (Berkeley: University of California Press).

Wollheim, Richard (1971), *Freud* (London: Fontana/Collins).

—— (1974), (ed.), *Freud. A collection of critical essays* (New York: Doubleday Anchor, 1974).

Wundt, Wilhelm (1900/09), *Völkerpsychologie. Eine Unterschung der Entwicklungsgesetze von Sprache, Mythos und Sitte*, Leipzig: Wilhelm Engelmann, 1900 (part I, vols 1 & 2), 1909 (part II); authorized trans. by E. L. Schaub (London: 1916).

Young, Robert M. (1970), *Mind, brain and adaptation in the nineteenth century* (Oxford: Clarendon Press).

—— (1971), 'Darwin's metaphor: Does Nature select?' *The Monist 55*, pp. 442–503.

—— (1973), 'The historiographic and ideological contexts of the nineteenth century debate on man's place in nature' in: Teich, M. and Young, R. M. (eds.), *Changing perspectives in the history of science* (London: Heinemann).

Zilboorg, Gregory (1952), 'Some sidelights on free association' *Int. J. Psa. 33*, pp. 489–95.

Index

I have not thought it useful to give some such entry as 'Freud, *passim*' in the index, nor are there detailed listings for 'language', 'symbolism', 'grammar'.

282